HUMAN RIGHTS IN OUR
OWN BACKYARD

PENNSYLVANIA STUDIES
IN HUMAN RIGHTS

Bert B. Lockwood, Jr., Series Editor

A complete list of books in the series
is available from the publisher.

HUMAN RIGHTS IN OUR OWN BACKYARD

Injustice and Resistance in the United States

Edited by

William T. Armaline,
Davita Silfen Glasberg,
and Bandana Purkayastha

PENN

UNIVERSITY OF PENNSYLVANIA PRESS

PHILADELPHIA

Published by
University of Pennsylvania Press
Philadelphia, Pennsylvania 19104-4112
www.upenn.edu/pennpress

Printed in the United States of America on acid-free paper
10 9 8 7 6 5 4 3 2 1

Library of Congress Cataloging-in-Publication Data
Human Rights in our own backyard: injustice and resistance in the
United States / edited by William T. Armaline, Davita Silfen Glasberg,
and Bandana Purkayastha.—1st ed.
    p.   cm. — (Pennsylvania studies in human rights)
ISBN 978-0-8122-4360-4 (hardcover : alk. paper)
  Includes bibliographical references and index.
  1. Human rights—United States. 2. Human rights—Government pol-
icy—United States. I. Armaline, William T. II. Glasberg, Davita Silfen.
III. Purkayastha, Bandana, 1956–. IV. Series
JC599.U6 H85   2011
323.0973—   2011024455

CONTENTS

Dictionaries define "enterprise" as "adventure," "undertaking," "resourceful," "energy," "pluck," "boldness," and "audacity." It is in this spirit that the editors and authors of *Human Rights In Our Own Backyard* propose to advance our deep understanding of human rights. Even better—they also advance the sort of understanding that will encourage their readers to take action—to lobby, organize, and redirect the path of our communities and the nation. One of the strengths of this reader is that the editors and authors have subsumed the stalwarts of sociology—social problems, racism, sexism, homophobia, classism, xenophobia, and class dominance—under the more generic term, human rights. This is a stunning achievement. It clarifies how parsimonious human rights principles—notably equality, self-determination, and human dignity—can help us to organize our thinking, collaborate with others, and take action. Human rights principles are so simple a five-year-old can intuitively understand them, while they befuddle most adults. This wonderful book helps to clarify human rights for us.

None would say that human rights are simple, but the international human rights community has emphasized their universality. They apply as much to the peoples living in the United States as they apply to the peoples of Papua New Guinea. *The problem is that Americans have become obsessed with human rights violations elsewhere and fail to recognize the human rights violations in our own country (that is, in our own backyard).* I would like to address a few preliminary questions, most of which are touched on by chapter authors but which merit emphasizing.

First, since human rights laws, treaties, and constitutional issues lie within the domain of the legal profession, why are we social scientists qualified to engage this enterprise? Second, why have human rights made such a dramatic appearance in the American academy in the past few years? A related question is why has human rights become a global movement and why has the movement accelerated during the past decade? Third, if human rights are universal, why do we say that they are multilayered, embedded, and contingent? Fourth, why is it important to be self-critical as Americans? And finally, I would like to briefly discuss what I believe is one of the greatest obstacles to the realization of human rights in America, and that is the tenacious hold that corporations have on communities.

Let's take them in that order. First, what distinctive qualifications do social scientists bring to the table to analyze and advance human rights? As this reader makes clear, human rights are embedded in neighborhoods, communities, culture, communication, and society. None are better trained in studying and understanding these dimensions than social scientists. Yes, of course, many human rights must be codified, making the distinctive skills of lawyers important, but we are increasingly aware that human rights are relational and depend on processes that are embedded in institutions, communities, and depend not only on peoples' relations with one another, but their relations to the land, natural resources, and the environment, and yes, the arts and sports. There is room for everyone under the human rights tent. But, let me be clear: it will not be easy since people of privilege and wealthy corporations want to have no part in sharing their human rights with others. Discrimination advantages those who discriminate, and extending food rights to the poor is not in the interest of corporations and banks. Except of course, as the saying goes, "what comes around goes around." Therefore, we try to be ethical.

Second, why are human rights catching hold in *the American academy*? To address that question we need to initially ask why human rights have become a *global movement,* especially during the past decade. After all, the Universal Declaration of Human Rights (UDHR) was approved by the United Nations General Assembly over sixty years ago, in 1948. These questions are complicated, but I will be brief. The consensus is that new communications technologies fueled economic globalization that in turn created immense economic inequalities, ecological disasters, and population displacement (e.g., Kurasawa 2007). Yet the same communications technology that drove economic globalization also opened up opportunities for global civil society, which is to say, nongovernmental organizations (NGOs), such as the World Social Forum, La Campesina, Shackpeople International, Centre on Housing Rights and Evictions, Center for Economic, Social and Cultural Rights, and, quite literally, many thousands of others. These NGOs, often affiliated with the United Nations, are dedicated to advancing human rights, locally, nationally, and internationally.

But why have human rights made such a dramatic appearance in the American academy in the last few years? As mentioned above, rapid and intensive economic globalization has had an adverse impact on communities and sometimes on the peoples of entire countries, such as Nigeria, where foreign oil companies ruined the environment and caused intense intergroup rivalries, Bolivia, which contended with the privatization of water by Bechtel Corporation, and many poor countries in which the United States dumped subsidized agricultural products, driving peasant-farmers off their lands.

It can be speculatively concluded that people in the American academy were sufficiently alarmed by these developments that we turned to human rights as an alternative to positivism (by which I mean the view that the discovery of truth relies strictly on the understanding that facts are objective). We have made something of a U-turn. We are discovering ethics. The American Association for the Advancement of Science now has a section devoted to human rights, and the American Sociological Association (2009) has adopted a comprehensive resolution on human rights. One suspects that we academics are making this U-turn because of what is happening in our own country, that is, our own backyard—joblessness, homelessness, food insecurity, racism, sexism—and elsewhere. We may be willing to abandon positivism to embrace equality, human dignity, and human security. Yes, we are discovering ethics.

This brings me to the third point. We can think of human rights as universal (that is, the American has identical rights as a tribesman from Papua New Guinea). *To illustrate, everyone is entitled to food, health care, housing, a decent job, education, and has the right to voice their opinions. Then we can go from there and contend that those that are especially vulnerable need special protections* (Turner 2006). Yet there is variation from one society to another. Language rights are more important in Papua New Guinea than in, say, Puerto Rico. Human rights are also complexly and inexplicably layered, since individual rights are embedded in families and small groups, in tribes, religious faiths, communities, villages, cities, and entire societies. An important lesson that the human rights tradition teaches us is that we must affirm the human rights of others and provide a defensive shield to protect them, just as they affirm our human rights and provide the same shield to protect us. It is a collective project. Another lesson that human rights teach us is that we enact and affirm others' (and our own) human rights interpersonally through recognition of others—sometimes as individuals and sometimes as groups. The American who travels to Papua New Guinea may wish to take seashells as a sign of respect, but would also want to be especially admiring of a people who can sustain 830 different languages. That same American may lobby Congress when returning home to increase the wages multinationals pay in Papua New Guinea because they are now paying sweatshop rates.

Americans are beginning to realize that the scope of human rights extends beyond civil and political rights, which are, of course, recognized in the U.S. Constitution. We can be proud of our forefathers and foremothers who championed these rights, including, among others, freedom of speech, freedom of the press, freedom of religion, and right to a trial by jury. Along with France, and later, Spain, the United States led the way in defining these rights, and bolstering them with institutions, laws, and judiciary processes. These rights form the basis of the 1966 International Covenant on Civil and Political Rights (ICCPR) and are incorporated into most state constitutions. The rest of the world, including France and Spain, but also Argentina, Bolivia, India, Mali, and Portugal and most other countries, has absorbed these rights into their constitutions, and gone forward, developing provisions for economic, social, cultural, and environmental rights. Where is the United States? Left behind in the dust, I am sorry to say. This volume provides a roadmap for students to understand why this is the case and how to change it. A main reason why human rights are multilayered and contingent is that they are embedded in everything that is social or cultural. If, as positivists, we take what people say in social surveys as hard, indisputable facts about human rights, we will end up empty-handed.

Fourth, it is exceedingly important to be *self-critical* as Americans. The rest of the world has advanced Human Rights Treaties, including those under the umbrella of the UN Human Rights Council, but also those of the United Nations Educational, Scientific, and Cultural Organization (UNESCO), the International Labour Organization (ILO), and ones protecting environmental rights that are under the umbrella of the UN Environment Programme (UNEP). (I tell my students that while other countries ratify human rights treaties, the United States instead ratifies trade treaties!) Technically the United States is party to no human rights treaty (for a summary of UN treaties, see American Civil Liberties Union-North Carolina 2010). Nor has the United States revised its Constitution to include fundamental human rights as most other countries have done. Brazil, for example, has detailed provisions for labor rights and also includes the right to food. All European countries have elaborated social rights in their constitutions. The Republic of South Korea has especially detailed provisions guaranteeing education; South Africa incorporates language and cultural rights; and some countries, including Rwanda, have explicit language guaranteeing women's rights. And many countries have constitutional provisions for environmental protection and peoples' rights to a safe environment (Blau and Moncada 2006). It is quite true that constitutions are not very specific, but they are more important than laws because constitutional provisions are harder to change than are laws, and, besides, constitutions provide the framework for laws, and are fundamental in public discussion and debate.

All the chapters in this fine book are reflectively self-critical. They suggest in various ways that criticality is important if we as a nation and people can overcome American exceptionalism, with its overtones of arrogance and inflated sense of self-importance. Yet criticality is not the central goal of these chapters, but rather how the United States can grapple with advancing and securing human rights: working toward economic justice, enforcing labor rights, guaranteeing food and housing as human rights; providing universal quality education; upholding the rights of indigenous Americans; advancing civil and political rights; adopting a more humane immigration policy and a more rational refugee policy; recognizing sexual citizenship; eliminating racial discrimination and discrimination against women; stopping sex trafficking; and ending violence. The authors clearly stake out the position that human rights violations are prevalent in the United States— indeed *Human Rights in Our Own Backyard*. It is important to remember that the dominant view has been that human rights violations occur elsewhere, but this view not only decontextualizes human rights but also sustains a discourse in America of the "good guys" (us) vs. "the bad guys." We know from the historical record that change comes from within, and the contributors to this volume fully endorse the view that Americans themselves will transform the United States.

I wish to conclude with my own "backyard" experiences. I have learned quite a bit over the past few years about how corporations exploit poor people in American communities. I am not referring to wage theft (which is a crime committed by small businesses primarily), nor am I referring to sweatshops, which still exist in the United States. Instead, I am referring to the power of corporations that is derived from their rights as persons under Supreme Court interpretations. I should provide a background.

The Human Rights Center of Chapel Hill and Carrboro is located in one of the North Carolina's poorest communities, Abbey Court. Founded as a laboratory for students to understand and advance human rights, it is a home base for them to learn firsthand how immigrants and refugees struggle and, hopefully, develop a deep sense of empathy with them. It is more successful than any could have imagined, with collaborations with student groups, and two elementary schools. Occasionally the day laborers come to my classes to discuss their experiences, including those of crossing the border to work in the United States. We celebrate their festivals (Las Posadas and Thingyan) with our neighbors. We also petition the towns to pass resolutions: to adopt the UDHR, a bill to criminalize wage theft, and petitions to adopt fair trade.

The biggest challenges we face are property owners who perceive non-profits as threats to their moneyed interests. Specialized charity organizations may be relatively safe (since towns need them to carry out programs they cannot afford), but a human rights center that advocates labor, housing, and immigrants' rights is at risk. Americans are aware of the inordinate power of lobbyists in Washington, D.C., as upheld in a 2010 case, *Citizens United v. Federal Election Commission*, but may not be fully aware that lobbyists are exercising their personhood rights. They may not be aware of the extent to which all corporations exercise "personhood rights," including in our own backyards. These were defined in an 1886 Supreme Court decision (*Santa Clara County v. Southern Pacific Railroad*) and upheld in subsequent decisions. For the most part, attention has focused on national or state cases such as the 2002 *Kasky v. Nike, Inc.* case in which Nike claimed California cannot require factual accuracy of the corporation in its public relations campaigns. Yet, under the cloak of personhood rights, corporations run slipshod over the rights of people at the local level, through development and land grabs, befouling and polluting streams and lakes, and evading local ordinances and building codes. Corporations of course are careful to stay clear of wealthy and middle-class neighborhoods, but have no qualms when it comes to poor, working class, African American and immigrant neighborhoods. Because municipal revenues depend on the taxes that corporations pay, cities rarely protest.

The reason I have explored this here is that we social scientists often attribute human rights violations to the attitudes that people have—whether it be racism or sexism—or structural impediments, such as those associated with the evolution of indigenous policies in the United States, or the macro dynamics of capitalism. I think that we are less likely to consider how local, powerful corporations are harming the welfare of the poor in our own communities. A dynamic and effective human rights movement in the United States would need to start in small towns, big towns, and suburbs. We have a long haul ahead of us, but the movement is underway. As the editors and authors of this volume advocate, *let's bring human rights to our own backyards.*

Introduction

Human Rights in the United States

Most people in the United States assume that this country provides the gold standard for rights-bearing democracies. Indeed, a 2007 national survey of U.S. adults by the Opportunity Agenda found that 80 percent of respondents believed "the U.S. does a better job than most countries when it comes to protecting human rights." This perception is echoed in dominant U.S. scholarship and politics as well. Often discussions among scholars and public officials in the United States frame human rights issues as concerning people, policies, or practices "over there": hunger and war on the African continent, political repression in "communist" China or Cuba, or public health disasters in Haiti, Burma, or elsewhere in the "third world." However, as will be evident in this book, many of the greatest immediate and structural threats to human rights, and some of the most significant efforts to realize human rights practice, can be found "in our own backyard."

The historical relationship between the U.S. government and formal human rights as articulated in international human rights instruments (international law) is a contentious one. Particularly in the inter-world-war years and in the period immediately following World War II, U.S. government representatives and several well-known scholars and activists such as Eleanor Roosevelt and W. E. B. Du Bois were central in shaping the birth and development of formal human rights instruments, the United Nations, and modern international law. At the same time, the United States joined many Western European and colonial powers in simultaneously curbing formal human rights when their political and economic interests were threatened by the reach of emergent international law. As many scholars have pointed out (e.g., Lauren 2003), the United States often joined England, South Africa, and others in claiming that state sovereignty outweighed any international concern over the rights of, for example, African Americans in the segregated United States, indigenous Africans under South African apartheid, or Indians under English colonial rule. In short, the United States has the dubious distinction of talking the human rights talk—especially when it comes to the actions of others—but failing to walk the human rights walk when international law and standards conflict with the power or interests of the United States as a "sovereign nation-state."

We might find little change in this distinction today between championing human rights in theory and having them guide practice. Though the United States clearly supported the famous Nuremburg trials of Nazi war criminals, we witness the complete disregard for the Geneva Conventions, the UN Convention Against Torture (CAT), and the constitutional right to due process under the law (also a well-established human right) in the recent wars in Iraq, Afghanistan, and the Pakistani border regions. As documentation of torture at Guantanamo Bay and Abu Ghraib is released, we have yet to see the closing of Guantanamo and otherwise secret prisons for "enemy combatants," as we have also yet to see a full investigation of those behind their design or employment. Domestically, the United States has been cited repeatedly by human rights organizations such as Human Rights Watch and Amnesty International for egregious violations of civil and human rights. Such claims include the questionable and racially disparate use of capital punishment, the aggressive caging of the poor and people of color in the largest and most aggressive carceral system in the world, and the broad failure to curb rising rates of rape and violence against women in the self-proclaimed center of freedom and democracy. The obvious tension between the historical and contemporary discourse of the U.S. government—as a supposed beacon of democracy and civil rights (especially following the election of Barak Obama as president) whose actions (or failures to act) have often resulted in massive insults to the human dignity and rights of populations foreign and domestic, is a central theme of this reader. As a result, this book is organized around a uniquely sociological approach that critically approaches the role and significance of the U.S. government—"the state"—in the broader struggle to realize universal human rights practice.

This body of work has been organized to focus on the struggle to formally recognize concepts of human rights and realize human rights practice in the United States, drawing primarily upon sociological literature and perspectives. Thus, it is important to define what is meant by the *human rights enterprise* (Armaline and Glasberg 2010) as a central concept moving forward. As a uniquely sociological concept, the human rights enterprise refers to any and all efforts to define or realize fundamental dignity and "right" for all human beings. More typically, under the dominance of law and political science, human rights are primarily defined and discussed in relation to human rights instruments, or human rights as they have manifested as international law. Human rights instruments include the Universal Declaration of Human Rights (UDHR), the two covenants (International Covenant on

Civil and Political Human Rights, International Covenant on Economic and Social Rights), various international conventions (such as the Convention on the Rights of the Child and Convention on the Elimination of Racism), regional human rights treaties, and the regulatory bodies assigned to each treaty, meant for implementation, information dissemination, and enforcement. Where sociology does not presuppose the relevance or inevitability of the state, human rights instruments and the formal human rights regime comprise only one small piece of the larger whole. The human rights enterprise represents this whole, where grassroots struggles outside of and potentially against the formal state arena are seen as equally relevant to interpreting, critiquing, and realizing human rights in practice. The human rights enterprise should, again, be seen as the sum total of *all* struggles to define and realize universal human dignity and "right."

Sociological lenses also shift the focus of human rights analyses from states and the decisions and behaviors of their leaders to institutional structures and practices: how are societies organized that institutionalize human rights issues and problems? For example, how is it possible for the United States to have civil rights legislation, and to have signed and ratified the International Convention on the Elimination of All Forms of Racial Discrimination (CERD or ICERD), and yet still suffer tremendous racial disparities and unequal treatment of underrepresented racialized populations? A sociological analysis of these questions would seek to examine institutionalized discrimination and systemic racism as the focus, rather than an emphasis on the potentially intentional, overt denials of human rights by individual state elites. Further, it is not enough to simply talk about law and the manifest intentions or responsibilities of states in theory. The actual implementation, consistent enforcement, and affirmative, deliberate protection of human rights are critical to analyzing the role of states in the human rights enterprise as seen through a sociological lens.

Moreover, a sociological analysis of human rights expands beyond the role of states to include private organizational actors, such as multinational corporations, as potential threats to human rights practice. Large and often global corporations, whose formal standard operating procedures, rules, cultures, and informal practices in the pursuit of profit create and reproduce human rights violations, now rival the power and reach of many states. For example, when corporate producers rely on sweatshops to manufacture consumer goods, or when private banks engage in predatory lending, they violate the human rights of stakeholders, often regardless of whether or not their hosting state(s) ratified human rights instruments designed to prevent such violations. Thus, the role and relative power of corporations and other significant private actors are crucial to an analysis of the contemporary human rights enterprise.

Also critical to a sociological lens is a focus on people's struggles—often grassroots struggles—to define and claim human rights. Drawing upon their notion of what constitutes fundamental human dignity, various groups continue their struggles to shape the meaning of human rights while creating or changing the mechanisms for realizing them. Often, as this volume shows, such grassroots understandings of human rights do not neatly fit within the formal discourse of human rights instruments. Nonetheless, such struggles, against the grain of formal definitions and enforcement mechanisms of human rights, invest in this enterprise with dynamism and nuance, as projects to be claimed and shaped within situated contexts, rather than a set of conditions that can be otherwise taken for granted. Such struggles may be focused against states or private institutions, on local conditions or transitional economic and political relations. In the end, they must be seen as significant in the larger human rights enterprise, engaged in the work of illuminating and resisting human rights violations, defining and interpreting concepts of human rights, and building toward their realization.

Contributions to this volume reflect our unique approach to the broader human rights enterprise through: (1) looking at human rights as the contested terrain of all peoples, (2) offering perspectives on realizing human rights that go beyond state and state-policy centered approaches to defining or pursuing human rights practice, (3) offering analysis and critique of formal human rights instruments, (4) interrogating the very structure of institutions as the arena and framework affecting human rights, and (5) locating the United States as a significant site and state player in the larger struggle for universal human rights practice. As one implication of our consciously sociological approach to the study and realization of human rights, we should highlight another unique feature of this book. Where we do not accept the state as unquestionable and inevitable in its role(s) or existence, we do not believe that fundamental human dignity is limited to the "rights" somehow bestowed upon people by rulers. This is, first, a fundamental contradiction. If we have fundamental "rights" as human beings, why do they need to be legitimated or granted by state authorities? Second, a purely "rights" discourse assumes that states are required to reach such conclusions or practices that would seek to prioritize or protect the fundamental dignity of people within a society or community. The editors and contributors to this volume do no accept the assigned and assumed roles of states in realizing human rights practice at face value. Instead, readers will find a diverse range of critiques and perspectives on the real and potential relationships between state and society with regard to defining or practicing human rights.

Organization of the Book

Substantively, the body of this reader is organized into types of rights, some of which are defined by formal human rights instruments to which the United States is party. Readings grouped under the heading "Economic Rights" take up the issues of economic justice and the notion of extreme poverty as a combination of deprivation of adequate wages and isolation, discrimination, and marginalization that lead to deprivation of access to critical resources for survival, as outlined by Arjun Sengupta's 2007 report to the UN. These include the right to decent work conditions in sweatshops; the right to fair and reliable wages and jobs by contingency workers (the fastest growing category of workers); and the right to equal treatment in access to mortgage loans.

The readings in the section headed "Social Rights" explore the human rights symptoms of a society structured around the notion of private property, individual rights, and personal responsibilities under contemporary American capitalism. What happens when the right to food and shelter, the right to equal access to equal quality education, and the right to health care are institutionally privatized and presumed to be the problems of individuals? How have groups organized to claim these rights?

The readings in the section headed "Cultural Rights" extend the exploration of citizenship in their examination of the rights of Native Americans and the rights of immigrants to open religious and cultural practice in the United States. Similarly, the readings grouped together as "Political and Civil Rights" explore the "tension" between security and human rights as well as the ramifications of this for immigrants and migrants. This section also examines the notion of citizenship as a criterion for eligibility for human rights, particularly for immigrants and LGBT (gays, lesbians, bisexual and transgendered) persons.

The section on the Convention on the Elimination of All Forms of Racial Discrimination (CERD or ICERD) contains readings that largely emphasize racial inequality in the criminal and legal systems of the world, consequently focusing on the U.S. track record of racial oppression via the criminal justice system—particularly for children. This section also considers the U.S. refusal to attend international conferences against racism, questioning the rationale for such a contradictory position.

The Convention on the Elimination of All Forms of Discrimination against Women (CEDAW) raises concerns about the unequal and often abusive treatment of women around the world. The readings in this section highlight the foundations of women's rights in the United States, as well as the cultural underpinnings of violence against women and sex trafficking in the United States.

Finally, although the question of resistance to human rights violations in the United States occurs throughout these readings, the concluding section on "Human Rights and Resistance in the United States" describes efforts to move the nation forward toward a greater embrace of human rights in everyday practice and political discourse. This final section addresses an important question for human rights activists and advocates in the United States: how do we translate the global language of human rights into local policies and practices?

The closing chapter examines and questions the United States as the "gold standard" of human rights discourse and practice. Despite the poor track record of human rights in the United States, two of the important factors that contribute to great potential for progress are the rights to free speech and free assembly. These freedoms enable resistance groups to flourish and challenge government and political leaders in the United States, and pave the way for human rights activists to change one of the strongest and influential powers in world history from within. We encourage both formal and creative extralegal (informal) alternatives to embrace and realize human rights now, through organized campaigns, direct action, and civil disobedience rather than assuming "change will come" somehow through top-down governance. Our stance reflects both a nuanced understanding of the human rights enterprise (as beyond the formal state arena and legal discourse), and an understanding of the history and future of human rights not so much defined by the pluralistic efforts of state governments and actors, rather by the struggle between the more or less powerful, the haves and have nots, the rulers and the ruled.

While we treat various human rights issues separately by sections, we recognize the interdependency of these rights. For example, without economic rights it becomes difficult to take advantage of political and social rights. What good is the right to vote or marry if one lacks the fundamentals of survival—such as food or shelter? Conversely, how might one fight for rights to food and shelter without rights to speech and political organization? Thus, political, social, cultural, and economic rights are intertwined in a mutually reinforcing fashion. Although the readings in this book are grouped by type of right, they are also meant to indicate how these rights are interrelated and interdependent.

PART I

ECONOMIC RIGHTS

A ll human beings have the right to the economic, social, and cultural rights that are the prerequisites for human dignity and survival. In the United States, economic, social, and cultural rights are particularly contested. Among the many necessary and inalienable rights identified in the Universal Declaration of Human Rights (UDHR) are several that address the notion of economic rights. These include housing, the right to work, the freedom to choose where to work, fair and humane work conditions, protection from unemployment, equal pay for equal work, fair living wages for work done, reasonable limitations to the hours of work demanded, and the right to create and join unions to protect their interests as workers.

Economic rights are key to human dignity and survival, as well as the ability to secure social rights such as housing, education, health care, and food. Economic justice is strongly related to issues of racialized and gendered inequality. But what happens when the rights of employers to make business decisions concerning their private capital and employment practices clash with individuals' rights to jobs, fair wages, and the like? What happens when the rights of workers in one country are at odds with the rights of workers elsewhere? What effect have the changes in the global economy had on workers' rights?

Moreover, although the UDHR focuses on the rights of workers, economic rights extend to consumers as well. What is the relationship between the rights of workers and those of consumers? Are their rights necessarily contradictory? Additionally, people consume more than manufactured, tangible goods; they also consume credit to access important necessities of life like housing. What role do institutions providing credit to purchase homes play in the realm of human rights, equality, and economic justice? How do individuals resist the power of major institutions like multinational corporations and large national/international banks to gain economic justice?

Chapters in this section explore these questions, exploring the rise of sweatshops and the resistance of colleges to licensing garments made in sweatshops; the rise of contingency workers to replace full-time permanent workers; and the specter of predatory mortgage lending and its role in reproducing racialized economic inequality.

CHAPTER ONE

Sweatshirts and Sweatshops: Labor Rights, Student Activism, and the Challenges of Collegiate Apparel Manufacturing

Julie Elkins and Shareen Hertel

On a sleepy December weekend in 2004, just twelve days before Christmas, the *Hartford Courant*, the hometown newspaper for the University of Connecticut, delivered a startling gift. Splashed across the front page, above the fold, with a huge accompanying color photograph, was the headline: "As Colleges Profit, Sweatshops Worsen" (Kaufman and Chedekel 2004: 1). The face of a tired, middle-aged Mexican woman—a factory worker in a textile plant that manufactures sportswear bearing the university's friendly Husky dog mascot and classic navy and white UConn logo—dominated the front page. The photograph was taken in a small town a few miles from the U.S. border and a lifetime away from the leafy campus of a university known nationally and internationally for its academic human rights programs.

The news story was indeed a paradoxical gift—because it revived a spirited debate on campus over the ethics of university procurement of athletic wear. It propelled a move by UConn to revisit its position on corporate social responsibility. And it opened the way for collaboration between UConn and other universities and colleges nationwide in efforts to raise the living and working conditions of the people who manufacture logo-bearing apparel and other products in factories around the world.

But cynics might ask: why bother trying to remedy poor working conditions a continent away? Is it beyond the mandate of a public university to improve the social welfare of people only tangentially connected to it through a long and complicated business supply chain? Even if it were the responsibility of a university to protect workers' rights, aren't the means for doing so woefully inadequate to the task (or overly complex)?

The responses to the cynics are multidimensional. This chapter explores the normative foundations for the university's responsibility to protect and promote workers' rights. It analyzes the role student activists have played as a catalyst for change in related university policies over time. And it explores the changing institutional landscape that UConn and other colleges and universities now navigate on a daily basis in the course of doing business in the global marketplace.

Normative Background and Literature Review

The University of Connecticut is a public institution. Under national labor law, all public institutions are required to uphold worker rights and labor standards covering everything from working hours and wages to health and safety, nondiscrimination, and protections from forced labor, hazardous child labor, and other forms of abuse. The United States has ratified a number of binding international treaties on human rights which obligate the country to ensure that state institutions (such as UConn) along with private sector actors (such as private universities, colleges, and companies) are regulated by national labor law.

For example, the United States has ratified the International Covenant on Civil and Political Rights (ICCPR), which prohibits slavery and forced labor (Article 8) and protects workers' right to freedom of association (Article 22). The United States has also ratified several of the core labor rights treaties developed over the past century by the International Labour Organization (ILO), including ILO Convention 105 on forced labor and ILO Convention 182 on the worst forms of child labor. Labor rights are also included in the labor side accord to the North American Free Trade Agreement (NAFTA), so the Mexican woman staring out from the front page of the *Hartford Courant* is also protected (at least in theory) by regional trade law covering workers' rights in the United States, Mexico, and Canada.

In addition, there are a number of examples of "soft law" (i.e., nonbinding norms) that influence U.S. government action on labor rights enforcement, albeit less directly than "hard law" such as the treaties discussed above. The ILO Declaration on Fundamental Principles and Rights at Work of 1998, for example, outlines the fundamental or "core" set of labor rights that includes nondiscrimination, protection against forced and child labor, and the rights to freedom of association and collective bargaining.[1] The Limburg Principles (1986) and Maastricht Guidelines (1997) spell out the manner in which states should implement economic rights (including labor rights). The Organization for Economic Cooperation and Development (OECD) *Guidelines for Multinational Enterprises* and the UN *Norms on the HR Responsibilities of Transnational Corporations and Other Business Enterprises* further outline the respective responsibilities of states and corporate actors in relation to human rights.

But in practice, how far does the law extend beyond the borders of the United States? How aware is an institution like the University of Connecticut of what goes on beyond its campus, behind the walls of factories that its licensing or bookstore staff may never visit in the course of procuring goods for sale with its logo?

The normative obligations for international human rights are complex. States are the entities responsible for enforcing international human rights law, companies aren't. Corporations are only legally responsible for upholding the national laws of the countries in which they operate, and in which they are chartered. But states have a three-fold responsibility to respect, protect, and fulfill rights (Dine 2005).[2] The responsibility to respect rights means that neither the state nor its agents can violate rights directly. The responsibility to protect means the state is obligated to prevent non-state actors (like companies) from violating rights through effective enforcement of the law. States must prevent, investigate, and punish abuse by non-state actors—including companies—and provide access to redress for victims of abuse (UNHRC 2007b, 9; 2008, 7-8). The responsibility to fulfill means that the state is responsible for creating an "enabling environment" in which rights can be enjoyed, by establishing government institutions and policies.

UConn is a state institution (a public university) and is thus responsible for *protecting* the rights of people in its supply chain by ensuring that the companies that produce its logo-bearing products are observing national law. Companies, in turn, have a responsibility not to be complicit in human rights abuse. They should not contribute to or profit from abuse (Khan 2005: 4). But the standards that bind companies to avoid complicity in abuse are largely voluntary. They range from company-specific "codes of conduct" to industry-wide or sector-based standards that commit companies voluntarily to respect workers' rights and the rights of people in communities affected by corporate operations, over and above what national law would require. There are literally thousands of corporate codes—ranging from the UN Global Compact to the code that UConn affixes to every licensing agreement with a supplier—covering multiple aspects of corporate social responsibility (Leipziger 2010; National Research Council 2004).

Public universities, like UConn, and private sector companies have adopted "codes of conduct" largely in response to public pressure from consumers, investors, and students, in the case of colleges and universities.[3] Such voluntary standards are not legally binding unless affixed to contracts with suppliers, a form of "hybrid" law (UNHR 2006: 13). But regardless of the legal status of companies' human rights obligations, activists on the ground have asserted that "workers rights are human rights" and have left academics and policymakers to sort out the nature of legal obligations and translate those obligations into practice through regulation and enforcement (Hertel 2009).

The creative strategy of framing workers rights as human rights undergirded by international law became integral to new union and grassroots organizing of the late 1990s and has only intensified over the past decade into the early twenty-first century (Compa 2008; Seidman 2007). And the tactic of involving consumers directly in transnational advocacy—through "social movement unionism," as Margaret Levi has termed it (Levi 2003)—is the hallmark of the kind of organizing central to UConn's story of student activism on sweatshops.[4]

Case Study

Corporate Social Responsibility (CSR) is a broad term that covers a range of actions by companies that make business decisions that go beyond the bottom line to create safe and fair working conditions for their employees and subcontractors. While CSR efforts are not new, there has been a recent focus on the world of sewn apparel that has created a new stakeholder: the university. Specifically, colleges and universities have begun to recognize the institutional power they have through the licensing contract of their logo-bearing goods. Instead of perpetuating the institutional oppression of workers (who are most often women), universities have been insisting that licensees that are granted permission to use institutional logos must adhere to basic standards in the treatment of their workers.

This new stakeholder interest in CSR began in the early 1990s, sparked by the child labor scandal involving the logo wear of talk show host Kathy Lee Gifford. In response to a national outcry, President Bill Clinton asked his administration to initiate formal actions to address sweatshop labor in sewn apparel, which inspired the creation of the Fair Labor Association (FLA). The FLA is an NGO that has three major constituencies in its board structure: industry representatives, university representatives, and representatives of NGOs.[5] This was the first formal national association that had a particular focus on college logo apparel. While some stakeholders welcomed the efforts of the FLA, others (particularly university student groups) openly criticized the FLA for its strong ties to licensees. This growing concern inspired the formation of the national student NGO called United Students Against Sweatshops (USAS) in 1998.[6] Shortly following the emergence of USAS, another NGO called the Workers Rights Consortium (WRC) was founded.

Both the FLA and WRC have similar missions; however, their board structures and methods of achieving their missions can at times conflict. The FLA works directly with licensees and plant owners. If a possible labor violation is brought to the attention of the FLA by a licensee, the licensee may hire a nonbiased third party to investigate the alleged violations, issue a report, and work with the licensee to remediate any issues. The WRC works directly with the workers. Most reports are filed by workers directly to the WRC and a field investigator of the WRC staff meets with workers inside and outside the plant to investigate the situation. The WRC does contact management and the licensee but often receives less cooperation than the FLA experiences based on the method of reporting, and types of investigations. Since the FLA and WRC have very different procedures to investigate an alleged issue, the two organizations have historically issued reports that may have conflicting findings.

The WRC was created in the late nineties and was intentionally structured on a shared governance principle with one-third of its board from USAS, one-third from universities, and one-third from among independent labor rights experts. While some universities were already invested in providing leadership against sweatshop labor issues, many institutions of higher education were pressed by student activists to begin or increase their involvement. USAS is probably one of the most powerful student activist movements since the 1960s. The movement quickly aligned itself with WRC and lobbied against universities to curtail their participation in the FLA. Over time, universities have made individual choices to be solely part of the FLA or the WRC, part of both NGOs, or none at all.

Understanding the Evolution of Student Protest Politics

This new student activist movement looks quite different from the movements of the late 1960s. Like the campaigns of the past, the contemporary movement continues to work against issues of inequity in power, discriminatory practices, and oppression; however, the grassroots efforts of the late twentieth and early twenty-first century have had greater scope owing to the movement's use of the Internet as a mobilizing tool. Individual university student groups can have instant access to information on one another's activities as well as updates on manufacturing conditions literally across the world via text, Facebook, Twitter, email, and other technological advances. They can use the same technology to share information, coordinate protests, and refine a consistent organized national effort. This social movement has also benefitted from the creation and presence of paid USAS staff in Washington, D.C., who are in close contact with other NGOs (for example, by sitting on the board of the WRC). This technological edge was instrumental in the coordinated launch of the Designated Supplier Program (DSP) proposed by USAS in the fall of 2005, to be discussed shortly.

Recently there has been a resurgence of student activism and these movements have grown quickly, fueled by technology.[7] In addition to formal modes of communication, social networking groups such as Facebook are constructed so that individuals can join easily, connecting them to thousands of other members instantly. This casual interconnectedness with international politics has become a powerful force in the student movement. In 2007, Facebook reported over 21 million registered users (Needham and Company 2010: 4) and by 2010 over 500 million users[8] (Facebook 2010). It is no mystery why student activism has taken to optimizing these technological freeways to gain support, foster new movements, and coordinate action. Despite these strides and budding student organizations for change such as USAS, there has also been significant resistance and "old-school" style protests.

The typical college student is at a university for four years and often views the world through the prism of eight consecutive sixteen-week semesters. Time moves quickly for students and they commonly want transformational change to happen instantly. While first-order change may be achievable in the course of a sixteen-week semester, actual transformational change (such as that called for in the DSP) is typically not possible. Transforming relationships with licensees, and implementing a complex program such as the DSP, is not possible in an academic year. Students frequently view this as a block to transformational change or as a consequence of resistance on the part of the administration to make any real changes to "business as usual."

Navigating the Organizational Landscape

The alphabet soup of newly formed NGOs discussed above has reached out specifically to the universities with the most power. Power in the college logo-apparel world translates into schools that have the most successful Division I football and men's basketball teams. Logo wear translates into significant financial royalties for top athletic teams. Major licensees (such as Nike, and Adidas) pursue championship-level athletic teams for exclusive contracts that bring in millions of dollars in revenue every year. These licensees assist in outfitting sports teams as well as paying the growing salary demands of hall-of-fame caliber coaches. This power dynamic, coupled with student activism, has created opportunities for universities to disrupt the institutionally supported cycle of oppression and to demand that licensees improve the wages, treatment, and working conditions of apparel workers.

One of the first significant accomplishments of the contemporary antisweatshop movement was working with major licensees to encourage them to reveal their lists of subcontractors. There was a great deal of opposition by major licensees to making their supplier lists public. Companies argued that they could not reveal their subcontractors for fear of compromising their business interests. But intense pressure from USAS as well as from universities and leading labor rights NGOs ultimately led licensees to begin sharing the lists of their subcontractors publicly.

This was an important first step toward encouraging licensees to work more directly with the manufacturing plants that were sewing the logo wear. Currently, it is rare that a licensee owns the plant (or plants) that sew its goods. This subcontracting structure provides licensees the ability to contract with plants for the lowest price margin in an effort to increase their profits. Unfortunately, it frequently creates an environment in which licensees drive down payments, as small subcontractors compete against each other for orders in a field that is saturated with more plants than the current market can support. This often results in what is known as "cut and run" business practices (e.g., licensees making and breaking contracts at the expense of manufacturers that are left holding excess inventory). Revealing the source—the subcontractor—increases the accessibility of information for universities, which can also increase accountability and transparency.

The other significant accomplishment of the late 1990s student antisweatshop movement was the adoption of codes of conduct for collegiate apparel manufacturing. The Collegiate Licensing Company (CLC), the FLA, and the WRC all have slightly different codes. But the goals are the same. Universities can mandate that their licensees sign on to a code of conduct in order to become or remain a licensee entitled to use the university logo. Tying human rights practices to business interests was an important step because it was the first clear communication from universities that they expected licensees to follow a specific manner of conducting business—and extended these expectations to their subcontractors. Some of the most significant articles of the various codes of conduct focus on child labor, working hours, pay, safety, pregnancy provisions, sexual harassment, physical coercion, and health care. While universities have experienced considerable support from licensees willing to sign on to codes of conduct, there is little evidence that doing so has actually changed corporate behavior to comply with these codes (Wells 2007). Nevertheless, it does appear that tying human rights to business practices was a critical first step in clarifying expectations. It is important to note that, to date, there is not a clear plan on how to guarantee compliance with the codes. Currently the code comes into play after significant violations have occurred. In the future, in order to effectively create change in the supply chain, new plans will need to specifically address compliance within the codes of conduct. In the next section, issues such as supply chain, policy, and student activism will be examined under the lens of the evolution of corporate social responsibility at UConn.

Identifying Key Steps in UConn's Experience with Corporate Social Responsibility

UConn became fully engaged in the antisweatshop labor movement in 2000, when a group of students formed a chapter of USAS on the Storrs campus. They participated in a well-coordinated activist action aimed at focusing the attention of the university president's office on sweatshop labor issues related to logo apparel. The students conducted a sit-in and presented a list of demands that urged UConn's president Philip Austin to take a national leadership role on the complex issue of sweatshop labor and university logo wear. President Austin responded by appointing a task force made up of faculty and staff to examine this issue and draft a set of recommendations for his consideration.

The task force urged the president to take a number of actions, including (1) pressing licensees to release a list of their subcontractors, (2) signing onto a code of conduct, and (3) joining the newly formed WRC along with the FLA. UConn not only joined the WRC but became one of the first schools to join the its board and participated on the search committee that hired the first WRC director, Scott Nova. The task force delivered a set of recommendations to President Austin, who in turn met with USAS students and then accepted all recommendations but one: to join the (FLA). USAS students were adamant that the FLA board structure and close ties to major licensees were problematic and would compromise the goals set forth by UConn and USAS. Given the strong student opposition to the FLA, President Austin decided not to have UConn join the association but instead committed to reexamine this issue annually. UConn eventually joined the FLA, but not until 2008, reasoning that it was critical to be an active participant at all appropriate venues in the national dialogue on corporate social responsibility.

The next few years were formative but critical ones for the antisweatshop labor movement. In 2005, following extensive media coverage of problems in UConn's logo apparel supply chain (including the *Hartford Courant* article discussed in the opening of this chapter), there was another significant push by USAS at UConn. A second task force was created to assess what had been accomplished over the past five years and to examine several pivotal issues in detail. It delivered another set of recommendations, which included adding child labor and wage issues to the CLC code of conduct used by UConn with its licensees. The most significant recommendation was to institute permanent communication strategies internally to campus constituents and externally to the WRC and other universities on sweatshop labor issues.

Specifically, the task force recommended that the president create a permanent committee on sweatshop labor issues and appoint a staff member as a spokesperson. The president accepted all of the recommendations made by the task force and instituted the President's Committee on Sweatshop Labor (subsequently renamed the President's Committee on Corporate Responsibility). Thereafter, UConn quickly established a national profile on corporate social responsibility issues, designating a half-time staff member out of the Division of Student Affairs to oversee related complex issues. President Austin wanted to have this person not only be able to work with the press but also directly with student activists. In the fall of 2005, USAS launched a nationwide campaign to urge universities to "sign on" to USAS's newly unveiled Designated Supplier Program. The next section will examine the key elements of the DSP and the complex nuances of the national campaign.

Explaining the Designated Supplier Program

The DSP was authored by USAS with significant collaboration on the part of the WRC in the fall of 2005. Student chapters of USAS sent copies of this complex plan to university presidents nationwide, urging that they sign on to the DSP. The major premise underlying the DSP was that past efforts had resulted in little concrete change in the university logo apparel sector—despite the disclosure of subcontractors and the formulation of codes of conduct by multiple monitoring organizations.

On the surface, the DSP seemed very straightforward: simply have universities agree to do business *only* with licensees that were doing the right thing, and designate these companies as their suppliers. But the reality of the DSP was much more complex, including provisions such as:

1. Right to freedom of association and to engage in collective bargaining
2. Right for workers to be paid a living wage

3. Require that licensees be in compliance with codes of conduct and international labor standards
4. Commitment of licensees to maintain a long-term relationship with suppliers
5. Require that collegiate apparel must constitute the majority of production in a DSP factory.

This ten-page document quickly became a catalyst for national discussion and university engagement on the complex issues surrounding sweatshop labor and logo apparel. Universities could not actually sign on to it—but eight colleges or universities came forward individually and issued similar statements that spoke to signing on "in principle" to the concepts of the DSP.[9]

Soon after, a DSP Working Group was formed from among these original eight schools to begin to look at the DSP with USAS and offer suggestions on how to adapt the program, preserve the spirit of the proposal, but create changes aimed at increasing the number of universities that would support the DSP. Several major universities urged the WRC to hire an expert attorney on antitrust issues to draft a request for a business review letter from the United States Department of Justice (DOJ). Some schools had serious concerns that the DSP would create antitrust concerns and leave individual universities vulnerable to legal suits by licensees. One central concern was that the DOJ would view schools as competitors in apparel wear and thus create antitrust issues.

A business review letter was submitted to the DOJ but withdrawn several months later when it appeared that it might not receive a favorable ruling. Anticipating personnel changes in the wake of the 2008 presidential election, USAS and the WRC intended to resubmit the DSP to the DOJ—but have yet to do so. Many schools will not go forward without a business review letter. For the DSP to be effective, however, schools with large royalties from football and men's basketball would have to participate in the program to generate the financial leverage to encourage other licensees to participate in the DSP.

For a time, USAS continued to offer the DSP as the only way to address the complex issues of sweatshop labor in university logo apparel sector, while officials at leading universities continued to dialogue on other possible ways to bring about change. Some labor experts, licensees, antitrust attorneys, and universities remain strongly opposed to the DSP. But even if the DSP as originally proposed does not come to fruition in the future, it is abundantly clear that the DSP has created change. Now there is ongoing dialogue about sweatshop labor issues on university campuses involving students, faculty, and staff—dialogue that may never have occurred so pervasively without the DSP. Many universities have designated staff to keep up with the volume of changes, and the complexities and turns involving the DSP. Some schools have appointed staff within their president's office to work on labor rights issues. This commitment of resources has been necessary to meet the broader array of corporate social responsibility issues (including sustainability goals) that have begun to transform the landscape among colleges and universities.

Yet the impact on the shop floor, where university apparel is actually produced, is often difficult to measure. The final section of this chapter briefly explores emerging trends in the area of labor rights measurement and enforcement.

Challenges on the Horizon

The emergence of the DSP has heightened attention to labor rights in campuses across the United States, and has put the manufacturers which produce apparel and other logo-bearing goods for colleges and universities on notice that these issues matter to an important constituency—namely, students and the universities and colleges they attend throughout the United States, Canada, and elsewhere. Although collegiate apparel represents only a fraction of the world textile market, it is a high-profile segment and one that some of the top sportswear manufacturers, in particular, are eager to court.

But what are the chances for real transformation of labor conditions through voluntary initiatives such as the DSP? Can universities and colleges truly be the catalyst for industry-wide reform? Or are countertrends in an increasingly competitive global marketplace so strong that they will undercut even the best-intentioned manufacturers and universities? During a global economic downturn unparalleled in recent history, will workers' rights be a casualty of consumers' own concern for their wallets and futures?

The contours of the global marketplace are certainly sobering. Even before the recent market downturn, scholars of labor rights such as Canadian political scientist Donald Wells predicted the difficulty of making meaningful change in labor rights through purely voluntary CSR initiatives. In 2007, Wells pointed to the "formidable structural constraints" that bind the hands of NGOs which advocate for improved labor rights (Wells 2007: 63-65). Given these constraints, Wells has argued that "the 'soft power' of the 'NGO-industrial complex' is too weak to regulate international labour standards effectively" (65). Similarly, voices as diverse as those of business ethics scholar David Vogel of the University of California-Berkeley and sociologist Gay Seidman of the University of Wisconsin-Madison have argued force-fully for a move beyond corporate social responsibility as purely a voluntary effort, and toward citizen involvement in holding governments accountable for effective labor rights enforcement through enhanced regulation (Vogel 2005; Seidman 2007).

We view this as a significant turn in the academic discourse on labor rights—and foresee students as critical to holding the U.S. government accountable for labor and economic rights fulfillment at home and beyond. Students were integral to the electoral victory of U.S. president Barack Obama.[10] Yet the challenge is to engage students not only during their college years but afterward, as citizens, in continued support of labor rights. "Sweat-free" product purchasing is only one vehicle. The much harder sell will be convincing the general public to support reform of corporate regulation, taxation, trade policy formulation, overseas development assistance, and other policies that could alter the macroeconomic and geopolitical context in which labor rights are embedded.

As former U.S. secretary of labor Robert Reich has argued, change won't happen and won't be sustained unless individual consumers see themselves as citizens with a responsibility for improving the shared fate of themselves and people at the other end of the global supply chain (Reich 2007).[11] This seems far from likely in the current political climate, in which the post-Obama glow has given way to increasing partisanship amidst the deepening recession.

Yet opportunities for change exist, even in an economic downturn. Joe Bozich, CEO of Knight's Apparel (the leading supplier of logo-bearing apparel for U.S. universities), has pioneered a new choice called "Alta Gra-cia," a brand of collegiate apparel marketed explicitly as environmentally and socially responsible. The brand takes its name from the factory based in the Dominican Republic, where the clothing is made. In this factory, workers are paid a living wage three and a half times the Dominican mini-mum wage. They are fully unionized. And the factory collaborates directly with the WRC on monitoring. While the DSP aimed at achieving trans-formational change of the global market over time, Alta Gracia clothing offers consumers the ability to "take pride in clothes that make a difference" today, as stated on its own website.[12] As much as social movements rely on the changes in individual attitudes, beliefs, and actions, innovations such as Alta Gracia may ultimately be the way change happens among apparel licensees—one licensee at a time.

Student activism helped move labor rights from the margins to the cen-ter of university policy action in the 1990s. This chapter has taken stock of resulting changes in normative discourse, the institutional landscape, and corresponding university policies, along with the ongoing challenges of labor rights implementation. Students are poised to play a vigorous role in transforming public policy on human rights and economic development; the question is whether or not they will, and how the political system and society will respond.

CHAPTER 2

Labor Rights After the Flexible Turn: The Rise of Contingent Employment and the Implications for Worker Rights in the United States

Andrew S. Fullerton and Dwanna L. Robertson

If many scholars and journalists are correct, long-term job security may be a thing of the past in the United States—a trend that may not bode well for the economic human rights of the U.S. workforce. Some say there has been a fundamental shift in the way employers view the notion of "jobs" and that long-term, secure employment is simply incompatible with this new twenty-first-century vision of the employment relationship in a free market society (Bridges 1994; DiTomaso 2001). In contrast to the traditional, secure full-time job, many jobs created today are "contingent" in nature—temporary, short-term work with no guarantee of benefits or stability.[1] Some even argue that all workers are really contingent workers "in that employers increasingly want their employees to act as if they are subcontractors" (DiTomaso 2001: 250). For example, subcontractors generally bid for jobs—with the lowest bidder getting the work—and receive *only* wages for their work (no benefits). Along the same vein, contingent workers tend to make less money, perform menial or repetitive tasks, receive few (if any) benefits, and experience little opportunity for occupational advancement, all while contending with minimal protection against intimidating workplace conduct, such as harassment or discrimination (Parker 1994; Rogers 2000). Their inability to make decisions that substantively affect their work or even use existing advanced skills demonstrates to the contingent worker that they are easily replaced, leading to an ever present instability concerning their work lives. Consequently, unlike mid-twentieth-century workers, today's worker steps out into a very uncertain employment environment. Contingent employment represents a challenge to international human rights instruments articulating one's rights to work, join a labor union, and receive protection from unemployment. In this chapter, we build on the earlier discussion by Julie Elkins and Shareen Hertel that focused on workers' rights in the context of sweatshop labor at textile plants outside the United States that import collegiate apparel to the United States, and examine the evolution of insecure or contingent employment and the threat it poses to basic economic and political human rights for workers in the United States.

While reports on the death of job security may be exaggerated, the rise of contingent labor in recent decades is an important phenomenon with its roots in the postwar period of economic prosperity and the corporate responses to subsequent economic crises. Jobs in the period immediately following World War II (1945-1970) in the United States were governed by a social contract between capital and labor, which built upon the gains made in earlier periods of the labor movement, including the establishment of an eight-hour work-day in the 1930s (Kimeldorf and Stepan-Norris 1992).

Labor movement gains in the first half of the twentieth century culminated in the federal policies and discourse of the Franklin Delano Roosevelt administrations. Where the New Deal is relatively well known and often discussed, as is Eleanor Roosevelt's critical role in the establishment of the UDHR, FDR's efforts to establish an "Economic Bill of Rights" toward the end of his life is also worth noting here. Often in discussions of the history of human rights instruments, the United States is appropriately characterized as having resisted the notion of economic rights, those giving all people the right to subsistence to provide for (at least) survival or (at best) an enjoyable quality of life. The United States did this generally because such rights were characterized as anticapitalist (threatening the ability of capitalists to exploit labor for profit), and thus "anti-American," as such rhetoric expanded during the cold war. However, as a closer look at FDR's policy initiative shows, there is a historical precedent for establishing economic human rights in the United States. Neubeck (2006: 5-6) recalls in his recent work on economic rights and welfare policy:

President Roosevelt's Economic Bill of Rights included the right to employment and to wages high enough to provide adequate food, clothing, and recreation; the right to a decent home, education, and health care; and protection from economic fears due to problems over which people had no control. President Roosevelt died in 1945, but his economic human rights concerns, shared by others worldwide, were directly reflected in the drafting of the Universal Declaration of Human Rights adopted by the UN General Assembly in 1948.

Where we will discuss the relevance of contingent work with regard to international law shortly, we mean to make two points here. First, readers might immediately recognize the contrast between FDR's vision of the economic rights necessary for a stable, peaceful democracy, and the current condition of labor in the United States, particularly in the context of a persisting economic recession and mortgage crisis—indeed, the deepest economic crisis since the Great Depression, ended in part through FDR's New Deal and the economic boom during and following World War II. As an illustration of this contrast, even during periods of "economic growth" between 2001 and 2008, one in five U.S. children lived in poverty—the highest child poverty rate in the industrialized world (Neubeck 2006). Second, the ever-decreasing socioeconomic position of the U.S. working class and an expanding un-/underemployed segment, who live a vastly different reality from that envisioned by FDR, is in part due to the rise of contingent employment since the 1970s, a marked departure from dominant practices of the New Deal and economic prosperity following World War II. This departure would accompany the rise of global neoliberal capitalism as we now know it, and fundamentally change the already exploitive relationship between capital and labor toward what might be currently observed.

This previous social contract between capital and labor (pre-1970), manifested in part as the "capital-labor accord," guaranteed workers long-term job security and rising wages in exchange for worker commitment, employer loyalty, and labor peace (Bluestone and Harrison 1982; Harrison and Bluestone 1988; Harrison 1994; Gordon 1996; Rubin 1996). The capital-labor accord created a work environment in which secure employment was the norm and insecure forms of employment were less prevalent and due largely to worker preferences. Theoretically, if they proved themselves loyal and productive, workers could expect to spend the majority of their careers with a single employer.

The capital-labor accord was made possible by the economic prosperity of the 1950s and 1960s. When profits were continually rising, e U.S. employers could afford increasingly larger payrolls and were able to treat labor as a fixed cost of production. However, in response to the economic crises and declining corporate profits of the 1970s, employers began to seek ways to reduce labor costs and increase flexibility in their relations with employees (Harrison and Bluestone 1988). This desire for greater flexibility among employers manifested itself in dramatic changes to both production systems and labor relations. Bureaucratic rigidities associated with mass production led U.S. companies to adopt "lean production" strategies used by Japanese producers (Womack, Jones, and Roos 1990; Graham 1995) in the transition to a system of "flexible specialization" (Piore and Sabel 1984; Capelli et al. 1997). Flexible specialization, or mass customization, allows employers to produce goods on a large scale while maintaining the ability to quickly shift product lines in response to changes in consumer demands (Piore and Sabel 1984; Capelli et al. 1997; Rubin 1996; Wallace and Brady 2001). However, U.S. firms combined flexibility in the production process with flexible (i.e., insecure) employment, which is a significant departure from the Japanese model that combined flexible production with a guarantee of lifetime employment.

This "flexible turn" (Fullerton and Wallace 2007) in production systems affected the nature of the relationship between workers and employers in the United States beginning in the early 1970s and led to increasing employer reliance on contingent employment. In the mid-1980s, economist Audrey Freeman coined the phrase "contingent work" to describe work arrangements that were conditional on an employer's need for labor and those that lacked the traditional attachment between employer and worker (Kalleberg 2000; Parker 1994). To fully understand contingent work, we must contrast it to standard work (as it has been known since the New Deal era). Standard work relationships are defined as traditional full-time wage and salary employment that lasts for an indefinite and continuous period of time, and is performed at the employer's place of business and under the employer's direction (Polivka and Nardone 1989; Kalleberg 2000; Connelly and Gallagher 2004). In contrast, Freeman describes contingent work relationships as those driven by the market's demand for a specific product or service; thus, employers establish conditional and transitory relationships with workers to reflect the market's demand (Polivka and Nardone 1989). This is important because when contrasting contingent work with standard work, we see the interconnection between the security of work and the security of other social rights, such as basic health care and education (Sen 1999). Promoting a contingent workforce, in essence, promotes an insecure society.

Scholars and labor activists remain interested in the reasons for growth in contingent employment, especially since the 1970s. Scholars seek to identify the common social forces that induced this trend. The motivation for employing contingent workers is more than just paying low wages and denying benefits in order to cut employment costs; contingent work affords businesses flexibility in the retention of workers only when their labor is needed, without the burden of legal liability. By replacing permanent employees with contingent workers, chronic job insecurity and episodes of unemployment have become common for working populations. No matter which sector of employment is examined, the majority of contingent workers (with the exception of professionals and technical workers) share demographic similarities as well—they are disproportionately composed of the young, the elderly, minorities, and women (Barker and Christensen 1998; duRivage 1992; Parker 1994; Rogers 2000; Sweet and Meiksins 2008).

Even though income instability is a major component of poverty, other factors contribute heavily—a lack of basic security and the inability to gain access to better lives through economic and social development (Sengupta 2007). And while the United States has adopted the flexible business model that advances insecure employment, the United Nations (2006) recognizes the harm perpetuated by insecure employment on the contingent worker through stigmatization, discrimination, and isolation, calling these effects a violation of human rights. In other words, because of the social exclusion to gain secure employment, a worker is incapable of meeting basic human needs, such as food, shelter, clothing, education, and health care. Collectively, the chapters by Deric Shannon, Barret Katuna, Abraham P. DeLeon, and Kathryn Strother Ratcliff focus in detail on these basic human needs. Contingent work creates a turbulent, exclusionary world that the powerless workers must navigate.

Temporary Agency Employment

Contingent work is often thought of in terms of temporary agency employment, and indeed, temporary workers are a key element in the contingent labor market. While workers often believe that temp work provides an avenue to permanent employment (e.g., "temp to perm" positions), companies actually use temporary help to avoid offering long-term, secure employment (Henson 1996; Parker 1994; Polivka 1996; Rogers 2000; Van Arsdale 2008). Overall, temp work offers little more than compensation for the worker— generally quite a bit less than what the traditional worker earns. Temp workers are often alienated from the meaningful ability to organize with little or no access to unions or even other coworkers (Kalleberg 2000; Parker 1994; Peck and Theodore 2007; Sengupta 2007). Temp workers are routinely stigmatized as unskilled or unemployable (Barker and Christensen 1998; Henson 1996; Parker 1994; Rogers 2000). On the other hand, the business enjoys a diminished legal obligation to the worker, avoiding costs for benefits such as health care, pension plans, vacation time, worker's compensation plans, and unemployment insurance benefits. Additionally, employers are able to cut costs associated with recruiting, screening, interviewing, or training new employees. The temp agencies provide all the human resource services and charge fees to their corporate clients for doing so (Gonos 1997, 2001). Consequently, scholars contend it is not a coincidence that temporary work and temporary staffing agencies are more common in poor and industrial areas (Theodore and Peck 2002; Van Arsdale 2008).

The growth of the modern temporary employment agency in the United States is quite remarkable, especially since the 1970s. Some scholarly literature promotes the idea that such growth is the result of the increasing demand for flexibility in the employment relationship (Gonos 1997; Ofstead 1999). This argument assumes that the growth was organic; temp agencies merely facilitated the needs of the worker to find work and the needs of the employer to find workers to perform work. Other scholars take issue with the suggestion that the growth of temporary employment agencies is primarily the result of changing market behavior and other structural forces (Barker and Christensen 1998; Gonos 1997; Hatton 2007; Sweet and Meiksins 2008). They argue, instead, that temporary employment is by nature exploitive, resulting in a devalued workforce and greater labor discrimination and inequality (Gordon 1996; Theodore and Peck 2002). This argument assumes foreknowledge of the negative effects to the employees and the benefits to the companies and the temp agencies. In fact, some scholars contend that temp agencies played an active role to intervene in traditional employment relations, acting as *change agents* in the functioning of labor markets (Barker and Christensen 1998; Gonos 1997; Hatton 2007, 2008; Ofstead 1999; Pfeffer and Baron 1988; Sweet and Meiksins 2008).

Even though "temp agencies" are commonplace in the current American labor market, they are a recent product of the twentieth century. They existed as early as the 1920s, but did not become firmly established until after World War II (Henson 1996; Van Arsdale 2008). Two of the most prominent temp agencies today, Kelly Services, Inc. (formerly Kelly Girls), and Manpower, Inc., were founded in 1946 and 1948, respectively. Once considered only for marginal employment, they have now gained entry into primary labor markets. Although clerical work is still considered a mainstay, nearly all occupational sectors use a temporary workforce (Alonzo and Simon 2008). Temporary industrial workers typically perform unskilled labor assignments, such as construction, light assembly, physical maintenance, and inventory work. Most workers find temporary work through a temporary staffing agency (Henson 1996; Rogers 2000).

The concept of "temp work" is a bit of a misnomer (Gonos 1997). It is not defined by the temporary nature of the work, per se, because some provisional jobs last for years, but rather by its temporary "triangular employment relationship" (Gottfried 1992; Gonos 1997). As the actual employer of the worker, the agency pays the wages agreed upon and owed to the worker. The business client then pays the agency a predetermined fee for the labor of the worker—depending on the type of job and skill required. In other words, workers receive their paychecks from the agency and are, in fact, employed by the temp agency. And *unlike* the standard work model, the temp worker works at the *client's* place of business (not at the temp agency) and takes direction from the client, *not* the agency (this may sound suspiciously like a subcontractor).

The rise of the modern temporary staffing agency forever altered the employer-employee relationship. By the mid-1960s, employees became defined in terms of costs to the companies—objectified in the same language as inventory—and no longer as investments. Temp agencies advanced into the industrial sector by marketing a labor flexibility model as the means to maintain economic equilibrium. Exploiting the macroeconomic uncertainty of the 1970s, temp agencies capitalized on a prevalent managerial reluctance to commit to long-term employment and growing legal obligations, promoting a "wider strategy to control employment costs and to extend hire-at-will/fire-at-will contract conditions, rather than simply as fill-ins" (Theodore and Peck 2002: 469). By 1974, temp agencies employed nearly a quarter million workers, selling the service of the "disposable" worker to businesses (Peck and Theodore 2007). Temp agencies marketed the ease of which to "use" and "dispose" of the temp worker for the specific job or task, rather than make a long-term commitment of secure employment.

The temporary staffing industry also used the law as a political process to socially construct their legitimacy as employers and businesses. Both state and federal governments assumed predisposed positions of favor toward the "business and entrepreneurialism" of the temp agencies, leading to major self-serving deregulation and "yield[ing] big payoffs for business" (Gonos 1997: 97). By restructuring the employment relationship, the temporary staffing industry was able to circumvent important legislation allowing for the right to organize: the National Labor Relations Act of 1935, which established the legal basis for union representation in the United States, and Article 22 of the ICCPR, which the United States ratified in 1992 and states, "Everyone shall have the right to freedom of association with others, including the right to form and join trade unions." Temporary employment serves as an unfortunate legal barrier to union organizing, because temporary workers are not considered employees of the firms where the work takes place and it is generally harder to organize workers who face the constant threat of job loss. Because of the "supportive framework ultimately provided by government institutions" and the "relative quiet of organized labor" temp agencies gained exponential organizational strength through the 1970s (Gonos 1997: 83, 98). Thus, almost in a reciprocal shift, as union bargaining power declined, businesses expanded their use of temporary and contingent workers (Carré 1992; Gonos 1997). The government's legitimization of the triangular employment relationship enabled the temporary employment industry to restructure the employment relations of the New Deal era, plainly relocating labor from the core of permanent workers to the periphery of temporary workers (Gonos 1997: 105). The temp agency was framed as the employer, not the business using the worker. The business utilizing the temp worker became the customer. The work performed was no longer *work*, but merely a *service*. And, finally, the temp worker was an employee of the agency, not the business at which s/he performed the work. Temp work became institutionalized and the temporary employment industry was recognized as valid by both state and federal legislation, all while American workers received reduced protection, reduced training, and slow wage growth. Throughout the 1980s and 1990s, companies transitioned to flexible forms of production, often ridding themselves of permanent (union) workers in order to use a flexible labor strategy (Van Arsdale 2008).

What might be most telling is that both state and federal governments began using temp workers in the 1980s, further legitimizing temporary employment (Gonos 1997). By 1989, practically every federal department authorized the use of temp workers. Amazingly, just as temp workers had been objectified in the mid-1960s as little more than inventory, this tactic was reused when the U.S. government justified its use of temp workers by stating, "it was not hiring workers but purchasing services, and hence the practice would be treated according to *guidelines covering purchases, not employment*" (Gonos 1997: 102; emphasis added). The objectification of temporary workers by both private employers and the U.S. government is completely at odds with the notion of a fundamental human right to "life, liberty and security of person" and "just and favourable remuneration ensuring for himself and his family an existence worthy of human dignity" (UDHR, Art. 3, 23).

The 1980s saw an exponential growth in the use of temp agencies and workers: more than 1,500 temp agencies were launched between 1978 and 1988, "employing" nearly a million workers (Henson 1996; Van Arsdale 2008). The groups most heavily concentrated in temporary employment include younger workers, women, African Americans, and Latinos (Morris and Vekker 2001: 378). From 1982 to1992 temp work increased by approximately 250 percent (Henson 1996). Even in the turbulent times of the early 1990s, companies increasingly turned to temp agencies to attain flexibility within their labor forces (Kalleberg 2000, 2003; Osterman 2000). "Labor flexibility" became known as the hallmark of the New Economy, creating competitive advantages for the United States in a global economy, further cementing the position of the temp agency within the economic structure (Mehta and Theodore 2001). Approximately 10 percent of the net employment growth in the 1990s was through temporary employment. The number of temp workers expanded from approximately a quarter million in the 1970s to 3.6 million in 2000. Unfortunately, temp workers are also among those hardest hit during economic recessions—temporary employees were 23 percent of net U.S. job losses in the early 2000s recession (McGrath and Keister 2008; Peck and Theodore 2007). A recent survey reveals that the demand for temporary and contract employees from October through December in 2008 decreased by 19.5 percent from the same quarter of the previous year (American Staffing Association 2008). Not only do temp workers lack the benefits, protections, and security of standard employment, they, as this demonstrates, are the first to experience job losses during an economic downturn.

The American Staffing Association—a professional organization for the temporary staffing industry—promotes its member agencies as "the jobs people" who provide "flexibility" and "choice" to their employees. There are reports that examine these claims. In 2001, 48 percent of temp workers were covered by health insurance, 11 percent by their employer (the temp agency); in 2005, only 40 percent were covered, 8 percent by their employer. While many agencies claim that temp workers actually *prefer* temporary arrangements so that they can have flexibility (for family, college, etc.), the trend shows a weakening in this argument. In 2001, 45 percent of temp workers reported that they preferred the alternate work arrangement to traditional ones, but in 2005 this percentage decreased to 35 percent, and in 2008 only 23 percent of temp workers reported that they preferred alternate work arrangements to traditional ones (American Staffing Association 2008; Bureau of Labor Statistics 2005, 2008). Additionally, there has been a sharp decline in the number of temp workers who report attending school—from 28 percent in 2001 to just 5 percent in 2005.

The Economic Consequences of Contingent Work

Temporary employment plays a central role in the new flexible workplace, but many contingent workers are not employed through temporary staffing agencies. Definitions of contingent work are typically based on a measure of perceived job insecurity. The Bureau of Labor Statistics (BLS) estimates the size of the contingent workforce to be between 2 and 4 percent of the total workforce, depending on the restrictiveness of the definition (e.g., excluding self-employed workers and wage/salary workers with less than one year of job tenure). In this chapter, we adopt a less restrictive definition: workers, regardless of their employment status and job tenure, who expect to lose their jobs within the next twelve months, are contingent. Based on responses to a question on perceived job security from the General Social Survey, 10.1 percent of workers were contingent in 2006.[2]

Contingent workers by definition do not have secure jobs, but this does not automatically translate into lower wages. While there is some evidence that bad job characteristics tend to cluster together (Kalleberg, Reskin, and Hudson 2000), not all contingent workers are in low-paying jobs. Some professionals work as independent contractors for an employer on a project-by-project basis, and might consider their jobs insecure but rewarding in terms of pay while the job lasts. Tilly (1996) offers one structural explanation for the disadvantage of contingent workers. They are often located in secondary labor markets where employers rely more on the use of "bad" contingent labor such as involuntary part-time work. If the reliance on contingent labor is primarily a secondary-labor market employer strategy, then one plausible hypothesis is that contingent workers earn less than noncontingent workers due primarily to occupational segregation and lack of union support.

We investigate the relationship between contingent employment and economic rewards using data from the 2006 General Social Survey and the 2005 Current Population Survey (CPS) Contingent Worker Supplement (U.S. Department of Commerce 2005). We present descriptive statistics in Table 1 and the results of a cross-tabulation of contingent work and union membership in Table 2. Contrary to expectations from previous research, contingent workers are slightly more likely to be union members than noncontingent workers. Nearly 15 percent of union workers are contingent, compared to 10 percent of nonunion workers. These differences are not statistically significant (results available upon request), which suggests that rates of contingent work are very similar for union and nonunion workers. However, there may be different economic consequences of contingent work for union and non-union workers.

Based on a regression analysis of earnings, we find that being a contingent worker leads to a predicted 36 percent decrease in earnings relative to secure workers. However, given the economic benefits and job security that union membership provides, it is possible that the relationship between contingent work and earnings is different for union and nonunion workers. We examined the relationship between contingent work and earnings separately for union and nonunion workers. We found that for union members, being a contingent worker only leads to a predicted 11 percent decrease in earnings, which is not statistically significant. Contingent union workers make predicted annual earnings of $41,834, whereas noncontingent union workers are predicted to make only slightly less ($37,017). However, for nonunion members, being a contingent worker leads to a predicted 40 percent decrease in earnings, which is statistically significant. This translates into a substantial difference in predicted annual earnings ($27,919 versus $16,858). Analyses based on data from the 2005 CPS Contingent Work Supplement provide further evidence that the contingent work wage gap is only statistically significant and substantively important for nonunion workers. On balance, these results suggest that contingent employment is found in both the union and nonunion sectors, but union workers are protected from the negative economic consequences of insecure employment that most nonunion workers must face.

Table 1. Descriptive Statistics for Contingent Work and Earnings in the U.S., 2006

Variable	Mean	SD	Range	Description
Log earnings	42.42	39.96	0.5–225	Annual earnings ($000)
Union Member	0.13	0.31	0–1	1 = labor union member, else = 0
Contingent Work	0.11	0.31	0–1	1 = very/fairly likely to lose one's job in next 12 months, else = 0

Source: 2006 General Social Survey; $N = 488$.

Table 2. Cross-Tabulation of Contingent Work and Union Membership

Contingent work	Union membership		Total
	0 (Nonmember)	1 (Member)	
0 (Noncontingent)	383	53	436
	(89.91%)	(85.48%)	(89.34%)
1 (Contingent)	43	9	52
	(10.09%)	(14.52%)	(10.66%)
Total	426	62	488
	(100%)	(100%)	(100%)

Source: 2006 General Social Survey; $N = 488$. Based on a chi-square test, the association between union membership and contingent work is not statistically significant ($^2 = 1.11$, $p = 0.29$).

Conclusion: A Right to Secure Employment?

The rise of contingent forms of employment such as temporary work since the "flexible turn" in employment relations in the early 1970s has had important consequences for the economic and social well-being of workers in the

United States. The results presented in this chapter suggest that contingent work is associated with low wages, particularly for nonunion workers. Contingent workers, such as temporary agency employees, are in a weak bargaining position in the labor market. As a result, they experience negative economic and social consequences, including low pay, few or no benefits, and an increased likelihood of health problems associated with subjective job insecurity. These findings raise the question of whether or not long-term job security is possible for most workers in a flexible economy. If not, this is of particular concern to the provision of "just and favourable conditions of work and to protection against unemployment" (UDHR, Art. 23). "Just" work conditions must include a work environment that is free of the constant threat of unemployment. Additionally, the triangular employment relationship found in temporary jobs effectively denies many workers the right to organize, which in turn limits their rights to security and dignity at work. Corporate and government policies that treat contingent employment as a cost-saving device and means of creating flexibility at work do so at the expense of the security and dignity of U.S. workers.

Although the results from this chapter do not paint an overly optimistic economic picture for contingent workers in today's workplace, they do suggest one possibility for closing the wage gap between contingent and secure workers. The finding of virtually no wage gap between contingent and noncontingent workers in the union sector suggests that a resurgence in labor organizing and related efforts (e.g., living wage campaigns) can help mute the negative economic consequences of insecure employment. If the size of the unionized workforce continues to rebound from its low of 12 percent in 2006 (Hirsch and MacPherson 2010) in the next few years, we may see a weakening of the link between contingent employment and low wages. Insecure jobs are found in every occupation and sector of the economy, but union representation limits the ability of employers to translate job insecurity into lower wages. A revitalized labor movement is essential to the fight for human rights, including the right to organize, earn a living wage, and feel secure in one's job.

CHAPTER THREE

Preying on the American Dream: Predatory Lending, Institutionalized Racism, and Resistance to Economic Injustice

Davita Silfen Glasberg, Angie Beeman, and Colleen Casey

Since the 1990s, Cleveland, Ohio, had developed a reputation for the terrific effect nonprofit activist organizations had on redevelopment in the city, so much so that Cleveland became known as "the Comeback City." But the foreclosure crisis at the end of the 1990s burst the city's bubble: real estate speculators were buying cheap, distressed property, making minimal repairs, and then quickly "flipping" the houses for highly inflated prices. In order to make that happen, the "flippers" needed the help of appraisers and, more important, out-of-state mortgage companies that were more than happy to provide mortgage loans with little or no documentation. Even worse, mortgage banks were exploiting the unsuspecting home buyers who suddenly found themselves paying inflated mortgages for substandard housing that needed expensive repairs. The banks began aggressively calling homeowners to offer them refinancing deals that would help them get out of debt and pay for the much-needed repairs. Other times the bankers would drive around the neighborhood looking for homes that clearly needed repairs and offer the homeowners financing deals to fix their homes (Kotlowitz 2009). Can't afford a standard mortgage? No problem: the banks offered "adjustable rate mortgages" that seemed truly affordable now, and would not increase until years later. These arrangements seemed too good to turn down, even though they also seemed too good to be true. The problem is they were. And they didn't just hurt the individual homeowners; they destroyed whole communities in foreclosures with vacant houses subject to severe vandalism. And they tended to target people by race too. Entire neighborhoods and groups identified by their racial categories were plunged into the isolation and deprivation of extreme poverty that Arjun Sengupta (2007) reported to the UN.[1] One community organizer complained that the city "was at the mercy of the lenders and real estate brokers" (Kotlowitz 2009: 34). These banking practices, that ultimately cause homeowners to lose their property to foreclosure and thus deprive them of their equity and accumulated assets, are referred to as "predatory lending." As the term suggests, the practices prey on the unwary and unsuspecting homeowners for the short-term gain of the lender and the long-term, often permanent detriment of the homeowner.

Predatory lending as such violates people's human rights in several ways. The United States has ratified the UDHR that would appear to prohibit the practice and consequences of predatory lending. For example, Article 17 asserts the right to own property and the protection from arbitrary deprivation of one's property. Article 25 provides for the right to adequate shelter, among other elements of a decent standard of living, and the right to security should one lose one's job, become ill or disabled, widowed, or too old to work, all of which are beyond an individual's control. The United States has also ratified the ICERD, which specifically asserts the right to freedom from racialized discrimination in all its forms. In particular, Article 5 lists the rights outlined in the UDHR, including a right to own property and a right to housing regardless of one's racialized categorization. The patterns of the practice of predatory lending targeting people and communities of color violate the United States' presumed commitment to enforce nondiscriminatory policies and practices. In her chapter that looks at food and housing insecurity in the aftermath of Hurricane Katrina, Barret Katuna takes note of further instances of discrimination targeting people of color in the United States.

Civil Rights legislation in the United States has sought to secure the civil, social, and political rights of groups as outlined in the UDHR and ICERD, particularly for racialized minorities: everyone has the right to vote, to equal education, to job opportunities, and to decent housing. Denial of these, because of one's membership in a racially defined group, is illegal and a clear violation of human rights. However, civil rights legislation does not speak to the question of economic rights that would enable one to access these civil, social, and political rights in a meaningful way. If one cannot afford to purchase adequate housing in an economically viable neighborhood, one is de facto denied equal access to quality education, job opportunities, and so forth. This is why examining access to housing is so fundamentally crucial to understanding civil rights. Economic justice and civil rights are inextricably bound together as human rights.

As this paper goes to print, you can't pick up a newspaper or listen to news broadcasts without hearing about a growing crisis in "subprime lending" and the consequent crisis of foreclosures. Congress and state legislatures have held hearings to examine the problem and define strategies for managing the crisis, and presidential candidates on the stump gave at least nodding acknowledgement that a problem exists. However, the language used to describe the subprime mortgage "crisis" presents the problem as an unfortunate symptom of an economy in flux, affecting people seemingly randomly, regardless of their racialized category. At least some of the press accounts of the mortgage crisis (as well as former president George W. Bush) suggest that it may be the result of individuals making very poor financial decisions. Such discourse obscures the question of economic justice and civil rights that give broader meaning and context to the right to housing. Moreover, to speak in the bland, neutral terms of "subprime lending" masks the actual practice—*predatory* lending as a more explicit form of economic injustice through institutionalized practices that perpetuates racialized inequality. We argue that economic justice and institutional racism are serious human rights issues in the United States, and as such, predatory lending is an important practice to be examined.[2] What is predatory lending, and how is it distinct from subprime lending? How do the patterns of predatory lending reproduce and institutionalize racialized inequality?

The Meaning of Economic Inequality: Personal Problem or Economic Injustice?

Some researchers have explored the factors that affect racialized economic inequality, but they often remain focused on job opportunities and income (Kmec 2003; Dodoo and Takyi 2002; O'Connor, Tilly, and Bobo 2001; McCall 2001; Browne et al. 2001; Darity and Myers 2001; Grodsky and Pager 2001). For example, Wilson (1987) found that employers tended to use racial stereotypes to help determine whom they would hire for a variety of jobs. While the study focuses on racialized inequality, it still emphasizes access to jobs as the source of income inequality and tends to return to questions of individual investments in things like education as a strategy for change. It also presents racialized economic inequality as reducible to the actions of "racist" individual employers, rather than a broad patterned array of institutional practices. Further, there is a problem in focusing on the effect of simple income inequality rather than that of wealth.

Income is the amount of money (usually in wages or salaries) that an individual receives for work performed. Wealth, on the other hand, is *accu-*

mulated over time, and includes such things as property (including one's home), stocks and bonds, and capital gains. Each generation does not begin from the same place with a "clean economic slate," since each generation's opportunities for personal investments in education and the like are based on the abilities of the previous generations to accumulate wealth to pay for such opportunities (see, e.g., Avery and Rendall 2002). That accumulation of material resources can translate into greater life chances because of the owner's ability to transfer equity into opportunity such as tuition for higher education and training for oneself as well as for others (for example, offspring). This case of class-based inequality is also racialized, given that African Americans and other people of color have had less of a chance to generate wealth and accumulate resources to enhance their opportunities. Sengupta (2007) calls this "extreme poverty" in which inadequate income as well as discrimination, isolation, and marginalization deprive people of access to vital resources needed for survival. What has historically affected wealth distribution? More specifically, what is the role of institutions in the reproduction of racialized inequality of wealth, and thus of racialized economic injustice?

Historical Legacy of Race and Property

Economists, historians, and sociologists have documented how slavery as an institution created persisting wealth inequality, which is reproduced with each generation (America 1990; Feagin 2000). Ransom and Sutch (1990) demonstrated that white Americans gained a significant portion of their wealth from the ownership of slaves. They calculated that prior to the onset of the Civil War, slave property made up almost 15 percent of total private assets in the United States. They estimated that by 1860, the wealth of southern planters by way of slave property amounted to more than $3 billion. These calculations offer evidence of what Feagin (2000) calls "undeserved impoverishment and enrichment." By this Feagin means that the lives of white Americans have been unjustly enriched while people of color have continued to suffer unjust impoverishment due to centuries of slavery, legalized and de facto segregation, as well as persisting institutionalized racism.

Undeserved enrichment and impoverishment is part of a historical legacy of racial and economic injustice that has concentrated wealth and power into white controlled institutions. Those defined as white have been able to reap the benefits of systemic racism, past and present, by accumulating and passing on property and wealth. Therefore, whiteness has taken on a certain value of its own. As Harris (1993) argues, whiteness itself is a form of property that is closely guarded and protected by government institutions. The Supreme

Court case of Johnson and Graham's *Lessee v. M'Intosh* (1823) directly established whiteness as property by ruling that whiteness was a prerequisite for ownership of property (Harris 1993). This set the stage for the numerous court cases that would follow in which immigrants petitioned the courts for the right to be defined as white (Lopez 1996). As such, Harris argues,

> whiteness became an exclusive club whose membership was closely and grudgingly guarded. The courts played an active role in enforcing this right to exclude—determining who was or was not white enough to enjoy the privileges accompanying whiteness. In that sense, the courts protected whiteness as any other form of property. (1993: 1736)

Essential to protecting *whiteness* as property was the denial of property to anyone defined as nonwhite. Historically, government policies and laws have directly and indirectly prevented people of color from gaining property. Native American land was taken through legal definitions of property based on white cultural practices. During slavery, laws were written to ensure the property of white slave masters while stripping people of color of theirs.

For the most part, poor white people did not own slaves, yet still they were granted access to some form of property that placed them above their African American counterparts. Unlike freed slaves, white indentured servants were offered freedom dues. For men, these dues included 10 bushels of corn, 30 shillings, and a gun. Women received 15 bushels of corn and 40 shillings, and some newly freed servants were guaranteed 40 acres of land. Hence, there has clearly been a historical legacy that has ensured that being white will grant one greater access to wealth, opportunities, and better life chances.

Wealth Inequality and Race:
Mortgage Lending and Asset Acquisition

The historical legacy of establishing and protecting whiteness as property carries with it enormous economic consequences for whites and people of color and the reproduction of institutionalized and racialized economic injustice. We see these consequences in the persisting racialized wealth gap discussed above. Mortgage and lending practices play an important role in reinforcing and intensifying this gap by institutionalizing whiteness as property, which ensures undeserved enrichment for white people and impoverishment for people of color. Lending institutions, policies, and practices have maintained white control of property.

A brief historical look at mortgage lending in the United States provides some insight into patterns of racialized wealth inequality between the end of World War II and the late 1970s. Following the war, part of the federal effort to provide economic aid to returning soldiers included a program to give them access to affordable mortgage loans, administered through the Federal Housing Act (FHA). Research has shown that not all returning soldiers had equal access to the opportunity offered by the FHA program: people of color were routinely denied such loans (Feagin and Sikes 1994; Lipsitz 2006; Brown et al. 2003). The FHA program also strongly favored white suburban neighborhoods to the exclusion of granting mortgages for homes in the inner cities. Eventually the low-interest mortgages whites accessed through the FHA were paid off, leaving the homeowners with accumulated equity in their property, an element of wealth denied people of color. That equity could then be translated into material resources to invest in upward mobility opportunities for the homeowners as well as their children. Moreover, the homeowners' properties had appreciated considerably in value over the years, so that the amount of equity they accumulated was substantially greater than the *initial* price of the property (Hirsch 2000; Goering and Wienk 1996).

Knowing that access to mortgage lending and property acquisition was systematically denied to people of color and that neighborhoods with high concentrations of such populations were routinely redlined, Congress was somehow motivated in 1977 to pass the Community Reinvestment Act (CRA), forcing banks to provide mortgages to severely underserved communities).[3] Twenty-five years later, investment capital does appear to have made its way into underserved communities to some extent, but it has increasingly done so in a form never intended by the legislation: economically poor communities and communities of color are increasingly targets of clients of "predatory lending." Predatory lending practices ensure a loss of wealth for individual people of color, and translate into cumulative losses for entire communities of color. This continues the legacy of unearned enrichment for whites and undeserved impoverishment for people of color, which further solidifies whiteness as a form of property protected by racist policies and practices. In this way, predatory lending reinforces and reproduces racialized economic inequality and injustice, compounded over time. The social construction of the contemporary foreclosure crisis as one of a broad "subprime" problem in a softening economy masks the real issue: *predatory* lending is at play, exacerbating institutionalized, racialized economic inequality and violating the human rights of those systematically victimized by the practice.

One important element of wealth is access to mortgage lending and the acquisition of property (see Denton 2001; Shapiro 2001; Wolff 2001; Flippen 2001). The question, then, is how whites and people of color compare in their ability to secure mortgage loans and purchase homes as key elements of wealth acquisition. In order to explore this question, it's useful to understand the distinction between subprime lending and predatory lending.

Subprime Lending Versus Predatory Lending

While observers often use the term "predatory lending," the concept has not been clearly defined or distinguished from the more general "subprime" lending. As indicated earlier, predatory lending involves practices of extending credit that injures the borrower, usually by depleting equity the borrower has previously amassed in home ownership and ultimately forcing the loss of the homes in foreclosures (Goldstein 1999; Bradley 2000). These practices may involve one or more of several techniques of subprime lending. Prime-rate lending is credit extended only to the lowest-risk borrowers, typically individuals with excellent credit and some asset accumulation. Subprime lending is credit extended at interest rates higher than the prime or best rate to people who appear to be a higher risk for a loan (people with no or bad credit, with high credit card balances, and no assets). In truth, almost everyone who borrows money pays interest rates above the prime rate, or subprime loans. The point of subprime lending is to help the borrower gain a loan in order to build a good credit record by repaying the loan.

The key here is that not all subprime lending is predatory. Predatory lending is a subcategory of subprime lending, in that it harms rather than helps the borrower with interest rates well beyond the risk posed, carries terms far more punitive than those applied to prime lending, and in general attacks and erodes the equity position of the borrower rather than helps to build it.

Subprime lending has increased dramatically over the last quarter-century. For example, refinancing mortgage loans rose from 80,000 in 1973 to 790,000 in 1999; the number of financial institutions specializing in such lending rose during this time period from 104,000 to 997,000 (U.S. Department of Housing and Urban Development-U.S. Treasury National Predatory Lending Task Force 2000). Furthermore, between 1994 and 2003, the total dollar value of subprime loans rose from $35 billion to $332 billion (Lord 2005), an increase of 948 percent.

Mortgage refinancing has been the leading use of subprime lending, constituting 80 percent of the massive increase since the 1970s (U.S. Department of Housing and Urban Development 2000). Of greatest concern is that this increase in subprime mortgage refinancing occurred when refinancing loans were aggressively marketed to consumers as a way to bundle accumulated credit card debts, home improvements, and other outstanding liabilities into the mortgage, increasing the possibility that the homeowners could lose their homes (Mansfield 2000). By the end of 2008, foreclosures had risen by more than 129 percent in a single year; subprime adjustable rate mortgages were at the root of more than a third of all new foreclosures (Mortgage Bankers Association 2008).

Not all predatory lending is illegal. Lenders are legally allowed to aggressively encourage borrowers to shift consumer debt (such as credit card debt) into mortgages. We interviewed several people identified by Connecticut Fair Housing as in danger of foreclosure in our research to understand the meaning of predatory lending. One person indicated that the bank called her (a practice called "cold-calling") and said "'you know you can make your payments right at the bank.' . . . They [the banks] were selling . . . credit cards and they dumped everything in [the mortgage]." Sometimes lenders also aggressively encourage repeated refinancing. Another person said that the lender came to his house to talk him into rolling his credit cards into a refinanced mortgage: "He [the banker] said, 'see, it's gonna be this much less because you won't be paying this for your credit cards . . . 'cause that's all being paid off [with the mortgage] and you'll have the monies. . . .' He made it look like I'd be stupid if I didn't get the loan."

Lenders may also apply extraordinarily high annual interest rates, well beyond that justified by the risk. One person we spoke to indicated that he paid 15 percent for a loan at a time when the going mortgage rates were close to 7 percent. Or banks will push the use of adjustable rate mortgages (ARMs), which are significant factors in foreclosures. The idea behind ARMs is that the monthly payments during the first year or two of the loan are much lower than the total monthly payments the borrower has been struggling to pay. After two years, the monthly costs substantially rise, often well beyond the borrower's ability to pay. Lenders frequently lured borrowers with the lower monthly costs initially, telling them not to worry about the increase later because "of course" the borrower's financial situation will be much better by then. Or the interest rates will be so much lower by then that the borrower can simply refinance the mortgage at the lower rate.

One man noted that he asked repeatedly for assurances that the loan he was getting was a fixed rate loan (the monthly charges for which would not change from one year to the next) and received reassurances that it was. It was not until he faced foreclosure that he found out he had in fact received an ARM, and the rate had ballooned to a height he could not afford. The ARM is a legal instrument, the dishonest sales tactic used to get this borrower to sign for one is not.

Other predatory practices are not legal, but are still common. For example, predatory lenders often fail to disclose loan terms, provide a good faith estimate, inform the borrowers that they have a specific number of days to change their minds, or itemize all charges on the loan before or during the closing. One man we spoke with was asked if he was shown any of these documents before or during the closing (when all documents are signed and the loan finalized). He said, "No, I don't know. I know that there was a ton of stuff sent after the closing." Other lenders illegally change loan terms at closing. Another man said that the bank kept coming to his house pressuring him to refinance his home. The lender first briefly reviewed some of the documents, but then shrugged, telling the borrower, "Well, just sign it, don't worry about a thing, just sign it." The man said the lender "kept talking to me about anything. . . .and kept my mind totally off the loan. . . .I didn't even know I was signing loan papers. I mean he was really good. . . .I kept asking him, well what's this paper for. And he . . . shrugged everything off." Worse yet is the practice of falsifying loan applications, including forging signatures on loan documents. One man said, "he [the banker] kept saying 'well, just in case, why don't you fill out a couple of those [documents] in case I mix up this one, I can at least fill out, you know without me having to come back to you.'"

These are just a few examples of the illegal practices that are rampant in predatory lending that dramatically increase the likelihood that borrowers will default on a mortgage and lose their homes in foreclosure. But beyond the fact that banks have routinely engaged in predatory practices, both legal and illegal, is the pattern of the targets of such practices. Subprime lending appears to be related at least in part to the ascribed or assumed race of the borrower (Gruenstein and Herbert 2000; NCRC 2007; Bradley 2000; Williams, Nesiba, and McConnell 2005). This relationship is important because in addition to the large number of subprime refinancings, first-time homeownership gains for many borrowers who have historically been excluded from mortgage markets have been fueled by higher-priced, subprime innovations.

In Connecticut, subprime lending increased by over 42 percent in the 1990s; notably, the increase was by more than 85 percent in neighborhoods where more than half the population were people of color (Collins 2000). Case studies in major metropolitan areas around the country indicate similar patterns (ACORN 2000; Cincotta 2000; Bunce et al. 2001). Ross and Yinger (2002) found compelling evidence of a link between subprime lending and race. More recently, our own research using data for low-income communities in Chicago, Indianapolis, St. Louis, Cleveland, and Hartford echoes these results. We found a strong link between the racial categorization of the borrower or the borrower's neighborhood and the likelihood of becoming a target of predatory lending: in essence, as the borrower becomes "less white" the odds of an equitable loan decreases, and that is the case not only for low-income but for moderate-income African American borrowers alike. In stark terms, for example, African American borrowers in Hartford are almost three times more likely than white borrowers to receive high-cost mortgages, *regardless of their income*. Similarly, the higher the proportion of people of color in a community as a whole, the lower the odds of an equitable loan. As the National Community Reinvestment Coalition (2007) noted, "income is no shield against racial differences in lending." One activist we interviewed who worked to help victims of predatory lending keep their homes estimated that "90 percent of our clients are minorities."

Taken together, this body of research suggests that banking practices are promoting and reinforcing racialized economic injustice, robbing people of color of an equal opportunity to build equity and wealth. Furthermore, we argue, this is significant because it's a nuanced continuation of historical practices and policies that together *institutionalize* racialized injustice insofar as individual prejudice is no longer necessary for the continuation of racialized inequality. Further, such economic injustice eats away at the bases for meaningful civil, social, and political rights.

What Is to Be Done?

Clearly, a great deal must be done to achieve economic and racial justice, an increasingly heeded call to action. Many NGOs and legal activists have filled the breach left by the state's inactivism and failure to enforce and secure the human rights identified in ratified conventions like UDHR and ICERD. Community activism and the rise in watchdog organizations in local communities and states challenge the obstacle to equality posed by predatory lending. For example, in 2008 in Nashville, Tennessee, the Nashville Homeless Power Project organized a modern squatters' rights march of poor and homeless families to reclaim vacant HUD homes on property that had been rezoned for development of luxury housing. They asserted that they were not going to leave the reclaimed homes voluntarily. Organizers noted that the group had already "covertly taken over more than a dozen other vacant houses in the city," and would continue to do so until all the homeless had homes (www.riseup.net).

In Chicago that same year, a sheriff refused to evict tenants from rental properties whose owners had defaulted on mortgages. Sheriff Tom Dart noted that many of these tenants had in fact paid their rents regularly and on time, and had no idea that the buildings in which they lived were foreclosed on by the banks because the landlords collecting their rents had stopped using that money to pay the mortgages. "Where mortgage firms see pieces of paper, my deputies see people. . . .[E]victions are part of our job. What isn't part of our job, however, is to carry out work on behalf of the multi-billion-dollar banks and mortgages industries," he told reporters (www.suntimes.com/news/otherviews/1211633,cst-nws-evict09.article).

In addition to local resistance, lawyers are developing effective and aggressive strategies to challenge foreclosures, and they are increasingly successful. Judges who hear the individual cases of highly aggressive predatory lending practices that set the stage for mortgage defaults are becoming less inclined to automatically side with the banks if even a small anomaly occurs in the mortgaging paperwork or procedures. Such anomalies are increasingly viewed by courts as violations of statutes such as the Truth in Lending Act, Fair Debt Collection Practices Act, and Real Estate Settlement Procedures Act. Courts that determine that a violation of statutes has occurred may allow the borrower to cancel the loan, which in and of itself stops the foreclosure. In such cases, any payments the borrower has made must be credited entirely toward the principal of the mortgage (the bank does not get any interest), and the borrower can refinance the balance of the principal at better terms than the original, predatory loan. So far, 36 states have passed legislation against predatory and subprime lending (Seidenberg 2008). Cities have also passed local ordinances limiting the rates lenders can charge and creating watchdog lists of predatory lenders. Some of the local ordinances have been enforced (Chicago); others (such as Cleveland) have been met with high resistance from lenders and overturned by the feds, suggesting that in some cases local and state efforts can be limited by the decisions made/actions taken at the federal level.

On the national level, the Association of Community Organizations for Reform Now (ACORN), an economic justice social movement organization that organizes, trains, and provides information and resources to local communities nationwide, has taken up predatory lending as a key issue on their agenda in a concerted effort to get national legislation addressing this crisis. Amanda Ploch's chapter underscores the way in which the Hartford chapter of ACORN initiates economic and social human rights changes through the mechanism of stories. Congress is increasingly paying attention to predatory lending, a first step in gaining legal and legislative protections. Local activist organizations, such as Connecticut Fair Housing, offer help to people in danger of foreclosure and organize challenges to the legislature to address the problem of predatory lending. These are but a beginning in a growing protest against predatory lending. The challenge will be to unmask the social construction of subprime lending as an unfortunate and unanticipated symptom of a temporary but deep economic downturn, and to highlight the *preda-*

tory nature of these practices. Moreover, organizations such as the National Community Reinvestment Coalition are beginning to socially reconstruct predatory lending as an issue of racialized economic injustice. This reconceptualization is all the more significant in its power to continually affect other human rights issues, such as educational opportunity, access to adequate housing, and improvement of one's standard of living. Economic justice is the key to making civil, social, and political rights real and meaningful. And the security of the roof over one's head, without predators cynically engineering the eventual loss of that roof, is an important part of economic justice.

And what happened to Cleveland, the city that was "at the mercy of the banks" in its isolation and deprivation? Community organizers brought the worst offender of the house "flippers" to the attention of the judge in Cleveland's housing court. He helped the Building and Housing Department cite the flipper for code violations on a house he was too slow in repairing before resale. When the flipper didn't show up in court for the citation, the judge located him at a local donut shop and placed him under house arrest for 30 days in one of his own "dilapidated structures." It wasn't long after his sentence was up that the flipper left town to relocate and continue his flipping business in Columbus, Ohio. But word gets around among community organizations: he was convicted of fraud in Columbus (Kotlowitz 2009). Clearly, the long march toward human rights and away from the isolation and deprivation of extreme poverty and racial discrimination happens not just through the courts and the UN, but also more locally, through communities' refusal to wait for federal policy and UN agreements to catch up to their plight.

PART II

_____

SOCIAL RIGHTS

A ll human beings have a right to the basic necessities of survival, including adequate food, clothing, shelter, potable water, health care, and education without discrimination. In the U.S. capitalist political economy and culture of competitive individualism and individual rights and responsibilities, the presumption is that each individual must be economically self-sufficient to provide to his or her own life chances. In this scenario, jobs are the antidote to poverty and compromised survival.

These rights raise important questions. Clearly not everyone can provide for his or her own life chances: children must rely on adults to provide for them, as do the elderly and the infirm. The economy has never been one typified by full employment, even in its most prosperous periods, and so what happens to those individuals who are unemployed? In the previous section we were introduced to the notion of underemployment, a situation where people have highly insecure contingency work; how are these workers to provide for themselves? And what happens when a major storm wipes out the tenuous existence of those who have managed to scrape together a meager living and housing? How are the rights of these individuals to be secured?

Moreover, the Universal Declaration of Human Rights stipulates that human rights education itself is a human right. That is, the goal of education must go beyond the technical basics of reading, math, and even critical thinking skills; the goal must be the full development of human potential and an understanding and respect for the human rights of everyone. How well do schools do that? Is human rights education an integral aspect of the basic curriculum, or is it an afterthought (if included at all)? What implications does this have for education, and for human rights implementation? Whose responsibility is it to ensure that human rights education become an indispensible goal of the educational process?

The chapters in this section take a pointed look at these questions by examining questions of providing food for the hungry and housing for the homeless; human rights education; economic justice and community activism; and health care inequalities in the U.S.

CHAPTER FOUR

Food Not Bombs: The Right to Eat

Deric Shannon

> Capitalism cannot guarantee human rights for all, only real human
> freedom can guarantee and protect our rights, rights which are
> safeguarded by our belonging to an international community of free
> workers, not by writing them onto paper.
> —Zabalaza Anarchist Communist Front, Human Rights Day Statement

Since the terrorist attacks in the United States on September 11, 2001, the U.S. government has ostensibly been preoccupied with protecting its citizens from violence. But where 25,000 people died from terrorist attacks between 2001 and 2005, an estimated 25,000 die *every day* from another form of violence—hunger and preventable diseases (Robinson 2005). It would seem that food security is a more pressing and immediate human rights issue than security from terrorism, and yet food security remains a largely ignored problem.

In 2007, 36.2 million people in the United States lived in food-insecure households—12.4 million of them were children.[1] Furthermore, "households with children had nearly twice the rate of food insecurity (15.8 percent) as those without children (8.7 percent)" (USDA 2009). Single parent households headed by women, African American households, and Latino households were disproportionately affected by food insecurity (2009). In a society espousing positive ideals like "equality," "freedom," and "liberty," in the wealthiest nation on the planet, hunger remains an issue all too familiar with a significant portion of its population—particularly those marginalized due to race or gender. Barret Katuna's chapter (6) underscores problems of food insecurity—that in the context of inadequate relief responses in Hurricane Katrina-ravaged New Orleans, they disproportionately impacted the African American population of this region. Furthermore, in our capitalist society, which produces for profit rather than human need, "Food leftovers are the single-largest component of the waste stream by weight in the United

States. Americans throw away more than 25 percent of the food we prepare, about 96 billion pounds of food waste each year" (EPA 2009).

Against this backdrop of significant hunger and deprivation, the U.S. government, in 2002 alone, spent an estimated $348.6 billion (or 17 percent) of the federal government's annual expenditures on defense (U.S. Department of Commerce, Bureau of the Census 2004). Furthermore, the War Resisters League (2009) suggests that government reporting on military spending, particularly when it is juxtaposed with social spending, is deceptive and leaves out current expenditures on the military due to past commitments. This spending is deemed "necessary" by a nation that outspends the next ten nations combined on its military (Global Security 2009).

It is within this context that Food Not Bombs (FNB), a decentralized network of collectives that recovers food that would otherwise go to waste and serves it to anyone who wants to eat, operates. Over the course of four years, I worked with the Sea Board FNB collective,[2] doing participant observation for more than two years. Most of the activists I worked alongside explicitly referred to the hunger and waste statistics, while highlighting the contradiction of the amount of resources the state puts toward military might (to presumably reinforce security from terrorism) as one of the reasons they were involved in FNB.

Introducing Food Not Bombs

FNB began in 1980 in Cambridge, Massachusetts. It was conceived and created by anarchist, Quaker, and Marxist antinuclear activists in the Clamshell Alliance (for a more complete history of FNB, see Butler and McHenry, 2000). It has been identified as a "decentralized network of autonomous chapters which function internally on a consensus basis" that "has spread to every continent, with affiliated groups in Turkey, South Africa, Australia, Argentina and India, to name just a few" (Day 2005: 40).

Again, the activity of FNB is fairly uncomplicated. They recover food that is wasted and serve vegetarian meals to anyone who is hungry. Most FNB collectives gather this wasted food through "dumpster diving" (reclaiming wasted food from the trash) and through donations from participating individuals and businesses. They then take this recovered food, prepare a meal, and serve it either in community spaces (typically in public parks where they can gather populations experiencing poverty) or activist gatherings (such as protests, book fairs, and conferences). But FNB activists see their work as much more than just serving food to hungry people.

A Cultural Approach to Social Change

Members of FNB take pains to make it clear that what they do is not charity. Rather, they are freely sharing a meal with anyone who wants to eat. Furthermore, rather than registering with state agencies and working in conjunction with them, members of FNB prefer to "generally ignore the authorities" and "allow them as little contact" with their FNB activism as possible (Butler and McHenry 2000: xi). FNB collectives also attempt to "operate outside of the dominant economic paradigm," recovering wasted food and serving it for free (xi). This attempt to escape cooptation by institutions such as the state and capitalism also lends itself to a politics focused on prefiguring the society that members wish to create—a society free of structured hierarchical constraints and organized domination and coercion.

As Peter Gelderloos (2006: 64-65) writes, FNB has modified itself in four major ways from soup kitchens and other charitable groups that distribute food:

> Meals are vegan, to draw attention to the violence of industrial meat production and its role in exacerbating global poverty and hunger. . . . Meals are served in the open, to resist the shame and obscurity with which poverty is made invisible, to make a visible, political act out of serving free food, and oftentimes to meet homeless people on their own turf, in the urban parks where they congregate. Thirdly, Food Not Bombs sets itself in opposition to charity, ideally avoiding the paternalism of traditional soup kitchens and striving for the ideal of cooking and eating meals together, to blur the distinction between the giver and receiver of charity. Finally, Food Not Bombs is anti-militarist. This orientation manifests itself in the name, in the distribution of literature by many chapters portraying militarism as a drain on social resources and a cause of poverty, and in the location of Food Not Bombs within anti-war, anti-globalization, and other leftwing opposition movements (either through the other affiliations of Food Not Bombs activists or the collaboration between Food Not Bombs and other protest groups, whereby a Food Not Bombs chapter might cook meals for a protest or conference).

Thus, FNB activists are attempting to create a template for a coming society without the need for organizations like FNB. They are a social movement, dedicated to radical social change that reflects the anarchist currents in a variety of the newest social movements (Day 2005). Interestingly, and largely because of these anarchist tendencies, the FNB collective that I worked with created a "street definition" of "rights"—one that stressed the direct action of the people to guarantee those "rights" rather than relying on the state to do so.

Rights and Direct Action

This excerpt from my field notes illustrates an interesting tension in the practice of FNB:

> The flier on the wall (that's been there the entire time I've worked with FNB and I just thought to really analyze now) reads: "Because food is a right, not a privilege" just below a picture of a purple fist clutching a carrot. . . . Most of the group define their politics as anarchist and being organized around "anarchist principles" is a source of pride for nearly every FNB activist I've talked to—in this particular collective and others. If food is a "right" and these folks are opposed to the state, who is to be the guarantor of that "right"? Who is to provide people with this food as a right if not the state?

Indeed, Donnelly (2003: 13) writes that "Human rights ground moral claims to strengthen or add to existing legal entitlements." Likewise, Merry (2006a: 228) notes that "legal frameworks govern the practice of human rights." What possible use could an anarchist group have for legalism and the states that practice it?

This question is partially rhetorical. Anarchists have historically fought in short-term struggles for reforms (like the one for the eight-hour workday, for example) in a revolutionary *process*. Chomsky (2009: 73) writes that, while his vision of a future "good" society is anarchist, his short-term goals include defending and strengthening "elements of state authority which, though illegitimate in fundamental ways, are critically necessary right now to impede the dedicated efforts to 'roll back' the progress that has been achieved in extending democracy and *human rights*" (emphasis added).

In many ways, my fellow activists in FNB would be inclined to agree. In the time I worked with them, participants in Sea Board FNB could be seen in protests targeting state involvement in queer politics (the passage of antidiscrimination laws), campaigns demanding the state to try President George W. Bush for war crimes, and participating in groups who were pressuring the state to hold people accountable for a particularly vicious, racist beating that took place close to our locale. However, through conversations during cooking, eating, and cleaning, it became clear that these activists saw the means and ends of FNB in quite a different way—one that articulated a vision of a future society without the need for centralized and coercive authority (i.e., the state) to "grant" the rest of us anything, much less the food we need to survive.

It should be stressed that for the participants of FNB, the means *are* the ends. That is, attempts are constantly being made and revisited in a self-reflective practice to see that the methods to organize the group reflect the kind of society desired. This focus leads to a practice of direct action, as most members of the group oppose state power. After all, direct action is the exact opposite of relying on the state to meet our needs and desires.

Perhaps, anarchist Voltairine de Cleyre explained the concept of direct action best (2004: 47-48):

> Every person who ever thought he had a right to assert, and went boldly and asserted it, himself, or jointly with others that shared his convictions, was a direct actionist. Some thirty years ago I recall that the Salvation Army was vigorously practicing direct action in the maintenance of the freedom of its members to speak, assemble, and pray. Over and over they were arrested, fined, and imprisoned; but they kept right on singing, praying, and marching, till they finally compelled their persecutors to let them alone. The Industrial Workers are now conducting the same fight, and have, in a number of cases, compelled the officials to let them alone by the same direct tactics.
> Every person who ever had a plan to do anything, and went and did it, or who laid his plan before others, and won their co-operation to do it with him, without going to external authorities to please do the thing for them, was a direct actionist. All co-operative experiments are essentially direct action.

Thus, direct action is the strategy we use to see to our own needs without having to rely on external authorities. But direct action is also used because it teaches us lessons in self-organization, self-sufficiency, and self-government. To work for a stateless future means practicing in the here and now these things and providing a challenge to the hegemonic ("common-sense") notions that naturalize fundamentally coercive and dominating institutions such as the state (and this can—and is—extended to other oppressive institutions and practices like capitalism, patriarchy, white supremacy, heteronormativity, etc.). FNB, and other groups like it, then, assert human rights as inalienable, and challenge the state's authority to enforce human rights when the state itself is often a source of human rights denials.

FNB activists use a process similar to that of the Salvation Army as described by de Cleyre. Members tend to ignore the state and pursue meeting a need they recognize as disregarded by the state rather than petitioning the state to do it for them (Gelderloos 2006; Butler and McHenry 2000). They also often suffer police repression, continue going about their work despite arrests, and, surprisingly, sometimes win the right to feed hungry people—all the while pointing out the fundamental absurdity that the state "governs" the right to feed the hungry and will put people in cages for meeting a human need that it has no interest in addressing in a meaningful way itself (see, e.g., Political Base 2009, for one example of an FNB collective raided by riot police and being arrested hundreds of times before winning the right to feed people).

This ambivalence was spelled out clearly when a neighboring FNB was targeted by local law enforcement. This group was told they could not serve food publicly without the proper permits. It wasn't going to cost them much and members of that group decided that they might pay the fee. Sea Board FNB met to discuss how we could help them in the situation and as the conversation ensued, a number of members expressed their disagreement:

> Chris shakes his head as he tells the group that our friends might actually pay for the permit and submit to state bureaucracy. "Look," he says, "I understand what they're going through. They want to feed people. No one wants them to stop doing that. But if they're gonna get a permit from the state, they should stop calling themselves Food Not Bombs. That's just not what we do."
> Amanda adds, "I agree. This is something we should be doing on our own. Period. It waters down our activism to allow the state to manage it."
> At this point, I say, "Yeah. I really understand what they're getting at here, but so many FNB activists have been arrested to avoid doing this. We shouldn't change that history. Hell, if they need volunteers who can risk arrest, I'd do it. I've been arrested for a lot sillier reasons. Anyone else feel that way?"

Nearly everyone at the meeting raised their hands. This willingness to risk arrest in another locale demonstrates the importance of sidelining the state to these activists, as well as shows just how ridiculous it is that we cannot simply feed our fellow human beings without a centralized and coercive bureaucracy interfering. Perhaps this is the larger lesson to be learned here—that state bureaucracy leads to the management and defanging of radical challenges to the capitalist economic context within which it operates (and one need only give a cursory glance at the "worker's paradises" of the former USSR, China,

North Korea, etc., to see that this state of affairs does not differ significantly in so-called "socialist" states).

By Way of Conclusion—Human Rights Without the State

Human rights as a strategy for change and the discourse that surrounds it has been accused of being a liberal and reformist approach to meeting human needs rather than a comprehensive radical approach to changing social relations (for an interesting discussion, see Zizek 2004). Interestingly, members of Sea Board FNB never got into the details of rights discourse like scholars do, despite its prominent place on their literature, flyers, and so on. Never once did I hear anyone talk about where rights "come from." Never once was there a conversation among the group about what foundations upon we might lay this idea of "rights." Indeed, there was no talk of "natural rights," of whether we should ground them in human nature, or perhaps in some socially constructed morality. Neither did we discuss the liberal assumptions that underlie things like the social contract. Some have suggested, and I believe rightfully so, that such discourse alienates people from implementing the ideas behind "human rights" (Blattberg 2007).

The definition of "rights" employed by FNB activists is, I argue, a "street" definition—one that is grounded in a belief that we can create a new world free of coercive institutions like the state. Indeed, the state is often the *violator* of human rights, not their benevolent guarantor. Sometimes this is directly the case, as in state-sponsored terror or genocide. Sometimes this is the case indirectly, when the state is seen to belong to the "public" sector that relegates "private" sector tyrannies, such as the epidemic levels of men's violence against women in many societies, to individual rather than collective legal issues that need to be addressed socially (see, e.g., Mackinnon 2006 passim). Issues such as these are precisely why international conventions and covenants are established and signed by states: they cannot be trusted to ensure human rights without them. And yet those states are endowed by these same conventions and covenants with enforcing the rights established by them!

FNB activists implicitly ask the question: What if we took seriously this idea of organizing for change in ways that mirror the kind of society we wish to create? Could we really expect an institution based on authoritarian control and bureaucratic management to kindly "grant" us access to basic human necessities like food and water, as well as a chance at living a dignified life? Wouldn't an institution organized like that guarantee bureaucratic and managerial outcomes? If the power of the state rests on its ability to use socially "legitimated" violence, can we really expect nonviolent outcomes? These questions might seem leading, simplistic, and lacking nuance at face value. But for those who have experienced state management in the welfare system; or for those who have experienced state violence, being caged for fighting for human dignity; or for those who have experienced the endless bureaucratic mess that accompanies state management of poverty and hunger, questions such as these have an immediate salience.

Thus, the direct actionists of FNB not only provide a challenge to rampant hunger, they also demonstrate that, should we make that leap, perhaps it is possible to organize ourselves in such a way that meets human needs and challenges hierarchical management, rather than repeating and reinforcing it. Indeed, we can demonstrate the possibilities for creating such a society by the work we do in the here and now. To many, the prospect might seem alien and scary, but perhaps it's not just hunger that is unnecessary and demeaning. Perhaps it is the hegemonic ruling practices that go unchallenged that guarantee things like hunger and violence remain rather than be challenged and dismantled. Perhaps we can organize our world around positive ideals like freedom, equality, and democracy and come to live in a world free of institutionalized hierarchies like the state, capitalism, white supremacy, patriarchy, and so on. And the "way forward" toward those positive ideals is through our own efforts, unlearning the reliance we have on centralized authority to see our needs for us.

CHAPTER FIVE

The Long Road to Economic and Social Justice

Amanda Ploch

I mean, okay, so when you first meet someone on a door, who's never been really involved in their community before but understands that like there's something about their neighborhood or their community that could be better and should be better if only politicians paid attention, and the only way we're going to get politicians to pay attention is if people start becoming involved, like that's how those conversations kinda start. So there're people that I've been working with since a year ago who became involved in ACORN because the city of Hartford was not cutting a tree that was in a park that was destroying a roof, but they're still involved because once you get people to understand how you can get the city to be accountable to you because it's your right as a resident of Hartford just as much as it's the right for anybody else who lives anywhere else in the city, then that's when you start talking about power. And you can talk about bigger issues.

—ACORN staff member

The interconnected economic and social human rights are a challenging cause to mobilize around in the United States, especially given the lack of attention to economic rights domestically. In the United States, a tradition of individualistic responsibility means that we are each presumed to be personally responsible for our own economic well-being rather than that society must be organized to facilitate individuals' ability to provide for themselves and their families. A human rights perspective emphasizes, however, that the ability to provide for oneself and one's family is rooted in how we are organized as a society. At their most basic level, economic human rights are those rights that "require that each and every person [has the ability to] secure(s) the resources necessary for a minimally decent life" (Hertel and Minkler 2007: 3). These can include workers' rights and the right to an adequate standard of living, as explained in Articles 23 and 25 of the Universal Declaration of Human Rights. In the UDHR, economic and social rights occur together, and there is recognized overlap between economic human rights and their role in individuals' social rights (Sen 1999). Rights that focus on adequate earnings, for example, are taken in conjunction with rights to adequate shelter. Therefore, if we really consider social human rights, we also need to consider rights that are dependent on economic achievement.

Some countries, such as South Africa, have significantly embraced economic rights, such as by codifying them in national law. In the United States, however, the government and other dominant institutions often fail to recognize systematic structures that prevent individuals from attaining a decent life; human rights standards therefore receive little attention in domestic legislation. Earlier chapters by Andrew Fullerton and Dwanna L. Robertson and Davita Silfen Glasberg, Colleen Casey, and Angie Beeman call attention to domestic economic rights injustices. With these difficulties in mind, many organizations have risen to the challenge of fighting on behalf of economic rights issues. In Deric Shannon's chapter, he underscores how through rights and direct action, Food Not Bombs (FNB) brings about culturally mindful social changes through its radical social movement organizing. Here, I focus on the Hartford chapter of ACORN, and their tactic of using stories to initiate change.[1] The use of stories in not unique to ACORN. National organizations such as the American Civil Liberties Union (ACLU) and Human Rights Watch routinely use stories to gain supporters for their causes. In this chapter, I highlight this tactic, and I look at what these stories might illustrate about economic and social human rights work in the United States.

Founded in Arkansas in 1970 (Delgado 1986: 39), ACORN has had more than1,200 neighborhood chapters (ACORN 2009). Though there are paid staff, the heart of each chapter is the group of community members who decide what issues to tackle, plan the course of action, and lead the chapter. The handling of local and municipal problems is essential to ACORN chapters, especially when these are starting out. Issues can include anything from trash pickup problems and property deterioration due to absentee landlords, to fixing streetlights and preventing unsafe food from being sold at local grocery stores, all of which were pursued in Connecticut. Another significant focus for ACORN has been home foreclosures. Since many Hartford residents are unaware of their rights, unsure of whom to turn to, and simply scared of losing their homes, ACORN has reached out to educate individuals and push public officials to protect their citizens in the midst of foreclosures.

ACORN additionally organizes to address labor rights issues. For example, it has pursued the passage of legislation meant to improve paid sick day coverage. Also, many ACORN chapters, including Hartford's, have advocated for a living wage, as the minimum wage in many areas is too low to sustain an individual or family.

Keeping this context in mind, I interviewed two ACORN staff members and three local ACORN community members. These interviews reveal how stories can serve a variety of purposes, such as eliciting responses from politicians, increasing community awareness of issues, and symbolizing a topic. Additionally, these stories show how ACORN views its role within the current sociopolitical environment and the challenges of utilizing the language of economic rights and human rights within the United States.

Stories and Activism

In looking at stories, it is crucial to understand how a given social movement "frames" the problems. A frame can be thought of as the combination of concepts, ideas, and interpretations of events that are used to view the problem. "Shared meanings and definitions that people bring to their situation" (McAdam, McCarthy, and Zald 1996: 5) can be essential in allowing activism to occur on the part of individuals. Indeed, "framing processes," as social movement scholars have pointed out, show how a given concern is turned from an abstract problem into a specific issue that can be addressed and acted upon by a group of individuals (1996). Part of this process can include bringing to light the ways in which a problem, such as lack of affordable housing or overpriced food, can be due to larger societal forces that the individual did not create, yet has the ability to address and fix (McAdam 1982).

Stories can be indicative of how organizations frame issues and an important device for carrying out a movement's goals. Though the use of stories in institutional settings is sometimes seen as taboo and against norms of professionalism and order, their careful use can encourage action (Polletta 2006). Of course, the danger exists that telling a story of one's victimhood can cause the storytellers to be seen as "passive" agents and thus impede activism; yet, Polletta argues, "to claim oneself a victim is not necessarily to trade agency for passivity" (111). Additionally, the way stories are told can reveal much about the environmental constraints working to affect the organization's actions and how the organization itself views its work. These different facets of storytelling seem to be evident in the case of ACORN, as it strives for economic and social human rights for its members.

Unification, Action, and Exemplars: The Functions of Stories

Within ACORN, the personal stories of individuals in the organization have been used to achieve several purposes. While some stories are targeted for making politicians listen to the organization's concerns, others are meant to capture the interest of the public. Others can even come to create cohesion among members, even when this is not the intended effect. Indeed, some stories can serve several purposes at once.

As many Hartford residents have been affected by the foreclosure crisis, personal stories have been used by ACORN to illustrate to politicians the human face of foreclosures and encourage them to better protect homeowners in Hartford. Using personal stories to highlight how the foreclosure crisis comes to affect residents can create a sense of empathy and urgency on the part of politicians.

As the comments of one member suggest, however, a powerful part of these stories is not just the effect that they can have on politicians, but on other community members as well:

> The foreclosure, it's by listening I get more motivated, listening to all the people testimony, and when you see people sits there and they cry, and they lose their house and you see them walk out of their house without getting no answer, this when we had to take it up to the city council and said this is a problem. . . . We had a newspaper ad, where we had one woman from East Hartford, we had one woman from here, a couple usually here in Hartford . . . because we usually put the people in general to give they testimony. Let people hear what you have to say. It's not gonna be our testimony; you have to speak it from your heart.

For this member, the emotion of the stories themselves was crucial. Individuals had shared their personal stories in order to show politicians, many of whom might not have been affected personally by the foreclosure crisis, how foreclosure was impacting residents in very real ways. Additionally, for this member, a significant element of the stories seems to be that these narratives increased her own desire to take action. Though this may not have been an expected result of the stories, this effect is notable nonetheless.

The use of stories and narratives seems prominent for ACORN. For example, one member's story became the heart of the paid sick days campaign, and came to represent it for many of those involved in the organization. Additionally, stories were presented at city council hearings, and dispersed to the public in newspapers.

The importance of stories within ACORN is of little surprise given the role of personal stories within many social justice organizations, whether they are fighting on behalf of individuals in economic need, such as the Poor People's Economic Human Rights Campaign (PPEHRC), or helping abused women (Ford Foundation 2004: 26, 28, 61-63). The use of personal experiences and emotion not only affects politicians and organization members, but can be used to reach out to the larger community in which this activism takes place. ACORN has sought to have a wide reach within the Hartford area, yet many residents are still unaware of the organization; the advertisement mentioned by the member can thus serve as a valuable way for the community to become more aware of ACORN's work.

In some instances, the creation of stories based around ACORN's work may be beyond the control of the organization, yet at other times the group may have a significant role in the shape that stories can take. For example, the organization began a "homesteading campaign," where they looked for home-owners facing eviction who were willing nonetheless to remain in their houses and refuse to leave. In searching for "homesteaders," ACORN was in particular looking for individuals and families whose eviction would be deemed especially troubling, such as those with young children or the elderly. The stories of such individuals might be particularly likely to generate media attention, allowing ACORN's message to be spread even more within the Hartford area. Though the media might shape the final version of these stories, ACORN's role is con-siderable given its ability to organize community members within a campaign.

Furthermore, some stories have come to epitomize a given campaign. In discussing ACORN's efforts to pass legislation that would grant more favor-able paid sick day coverage to workers, one story seemed to take on sym-bolic status. Three of the five people I interviewed specifically mentioned one member in connection with paid sick days coverage. One interviewee explained a bit of this individual's circumstances:

we have a member, she works in school system, and she has to work two part-time jobs, and she work as a bus monitor, she works in the school system and between that two part time jobs it's not giving her enough hours to get the paid sick day off. So we had to use her as a testimony to talk in front of the city council, what her experience like. And she was very sick with her foot, say she out of work, and she was out of work she wasn't getting paid to be out of work. She had to be home and her boss would threaten, said well if you don't come to work, you're going to have to lose your job, because she's not getting paid with the paid sick day. So we had to push that to make certain paid sick days gets passed.

Once again, a person's story illustrated to politicians the need to take relevant measures, which in this case entailed supporting more extensive paid sick day coverage. Additionally, the fact that this person was mentioned several times relating to a particular issue indicates that her personal story has become representative of what that campaign is about. Given the various ways in which stories are used within ACORN, it is informative to consider what the stories of individuals reveal about the struggle to attain economic rights.

Aggression, Language, and Power: ACORN's Work for Economic and Social Rights

These narratives are not useful just as possible tools; the use of language also shows how ACORN envisions its role in furthering economic and social human rights. Additionally, even without using "human rights" language or concepts, ACORN is expanding the attainment of these rights in American society.

Quite significantly for ACORN, its work is not limited to lobbying and other similar "behind the scenes" political work; the organization also engages in marches and other "actions" meant to generate attention and force the targets of its activities to listen to what ACORN has to say. Tactics that may upset the authorities, instigate arrests, or cause some sort of disturbance seem to be the hallmark of ACORN's actions. The organization has gained a reputation among many as being "aggressive" in its activities. Examples of these "aggressive" events include demonstrations near government and business offices, and large amounts of members congregating within a building at once. One member explained how some in power have sought to disrupt the organization's planned actions, and how an official even intentionally avoided ACORN members:

> I got locked in a building and I'm not too happy with that . . . . We went into this building and they shut down the elevators with us on it to keep us from moving.... It is illegal, but they say they can do it. So I'm not too thrilled with that. But we do do it. . . . In Detroit, we took over Washington Mutual, and the tellers in the bank they sit there, they didn't know what to do. There was nothing but red shirts all over. . . . They called the police, and then the people on the outside were walking around.

This story indicates that members may meet with resistance from powerful opponents that may frustrate their efforts. But, as the following quote suggests, such resistance does not dampen their resolve to mobilize in support of human rights:

> so we get . . . on the bus to go to the high sheriff's office to do action on him, because what he was doing he was taking foreclosed properties lists, the lists, and he was selling them to lawyers.... So when we got on the bus, I heard something in the back of the bus, but I didn't pay any attention to it. And our bus driver happened to be a member of ACORN, and he had his ACORN hat on, and so we were, we had two buses, two busloads. We were driving, on our way, and all the sudden motorcycle cops came and we said, "We're important—we get a police escort." What they were doing was directing the driver in the first bus to follow them, and then they took us behind these abandoned factories near train tracks. So of course some of the members said, "Oh my gosh, they're going to kill us." [note: she says this in a tone as if to show that there wasn't really a danger of that]. Then they told us, first they said that our buses were overloaded and they counted everybody on the bus, and neither bus was overloaded. Then they mysteriously said okay, they found that the bus that I was on had a broken taillight, which the police broke . . . They broke it—that's the noise I heard . . . .They told us that we had to get on the first bus. And we said no, we're not getting on that bus, because you already accused us of being overloaded, then it will be overloaded. We were back there I think for two hours, and finally they said well you can go. But that gave the sheriff time to close his office and he left. So we couldn't do an action against him.

This sequence of events captures several key aspects of ACORN's strategies. First, ACORN directly confronts those who have the power to change policies and business practices. Second, the use of high numbers of people is key. Third, those in power sometimes actively seek to prevent ACORN from carrying out its activities. Fourth, ACORN intentionally chooses such tactics in order to gain a reaction and attention from officials, businesses, and the public.

Perhaps most important, the relaying of these stories indicates that members value the reputation that the organization has for challenging those in power. Tales of how politicians, police, and other officials have been leery of ACORN's actions illustrate the challenges of conducting work that relates to economic rights issues within the United States. Given the ways in which the government is often unwilling to expand economic protections for citizens, these tactics may be a fruitful way to encourage political change.

In the midst of these narratives and explanations of ACORN's strategies, "economic rights" and the related concept of "human rights" are largely absent. When asked if human rights connected to ACORN's work, or if human rights were used in the work of the organization, one staff member replied:

> We use economic rights language. Um, and I mean to expect that, the things that we fight for we just fundamentally believe are basic, we believe that they're basic human rights. We believe that people have a right to a decent living, and a right to a decedent education, and a right to good schools, and a right to health care. So we don't really use the term human rights, but the way that we describe things, we definitely describe them as, it is right that people should have paid sick days. And we get into, you know, all kinds of economic arguments and rationales, and all those things, but from a basic starting point, our members move on an issue because they care deeply about that issue.

The other staff member echoed this idea that although ACORN may in a sense focus on economic and social human rights, the specific terms might not be employed. One explanation for this omission of human rights language, as explained by a staff member, was that ACORN's work was sometimes best achieved by using other language:

> It depends on who you're talking to. You don't need to . . . I mean, okay, so when you first meet someone on a door, who's never been really involved in their community before but understands that like there's something about their neighborhood or their community that could be better and should be better if only politicians paid attention, and the only way we're going to get politicians to pay attention is if people start becoming involved, like that's how those conversations kinda start. So there're people that I've been working with since a year ago who became involved in ACORN because the city of Hartford was not cutting a tree that was in a park that was destroying a roof, but they're still involved because once you get people to understand how you can get the city to be accountable to you because it's your right as a resident of Hartford just as much as it's the right for anybody else who lives anywhere else in the city, then that's when you start talking about power. And you can talk about bigger issues . . . The more people become involved,

the bigger the vision gets. So that would be the perspective from the membership I think. . . . Because there's so many people involved, and because you're linked up with neighborhoods across the state, and you're linked up with neighborhoods across the state, and you're linked up with people all around the country, then you can have realistic discussions about what steps you can actually take to bring about economic justice and social justice and racial justice and every other justice that exists in the world. So I think that is a conversation about rights. That is a conversation about. . . .You may not use that language necessarily, but getting involved in ACORN to me is about the practical application of . . . of doing something about that.

Later comments further explained the staff member's thoughts on the importance of language in looking at human rights issues:

I guess the other thing too is like the language that you learn in school is one thing but you end up, it's the membership who makes the decisions about what they fight for, and so it's their language that becomes all the more important. . . . But it's not necessarily scholastic, or from a . . . policy, policy language.

These comments illustrate a characteristic of economic and social human rights discourse: Although the language of rights—and the classification of rights into categories such as economic rights or social rights—may be more familiar to academics, politicians, and those in power, the people on whose behalf organizations work in attaining these rights may not always give these concepts the name of human rights. In some instances "human rights" or related concepts may not be the framework in which community members view their struggles. Though individuals may point out the injustices around them and the inability of government to protect their needs, the idea of human rights was not readily used within the stories and discourse of those I interviewed.

This particular situation—where human rights received little explicit use—comes at a time when, on the whole, "In the United States there is a growing movement to view poverty and welfare reform in human rights terms" (Neubeck 2006: 16). Organizations such as the Poor People's Economic Human Rights Campaign, the Kensington Welfare Rights Union (Philadelphia), and others have used human rights language as part of their human rights enterprise (Ford Foundation 2004). Perhaps, in the future, groups like ACORN will be more likely to use human rights language, due to an increasing appreciation for the human rights framework domestically as suggested above.

The lack of human rights language in my interviews with those at ACORN may reflect that human rights in general, and economic and social human rights specifically, though present in some organizing work, is not fully utilized across many organizations and in mainstream society generally. Some politicians might be hesitant to support issues based on a human rights perspective, and such an angle may not engage community members. Looking at issues in terms of local problems or failures of business or government may be a more successful vantage point for certain groups than looking at a given situation as an economic human rights issue or connecting it to human rights concepts.

Significantly, even without more clearly utilizing concepts and language from economic human rights and the human rights discipline, ACORN can nonetheless be said to further the cause of economic and social human rights, in both government and community. In making community members aware of how the status quo is unfair and awakening in them a sense that they can take action to improve their personal situations, ACORN is changing America's view of issues at the core of human rights. Addressing housing rights and pushing for measures to protect the economic well-being of community members are activities that align with economic human rights concerns. Through its efforts to promote justice and a better life for community members, ACORN is increasing acceptance of human rights values and economic rights within the United States.

Conclusion

Stories have the powerful potential to be used in many ways to promote the goals of ACORN, as they do for many organizations working on behalf of justice issues. Politicians can be moved to action, group members can be driven to keep working, and community members can be drawn to the stories of particular individuals. Additionally, some stories reflect the challenges of economic and social rights activism in the United States, and sometimes even indicate how ACORN values its reputation as an "aggressive" organization that courageously works to help communities. The stories also show the lack of explicit use of economic and social rights language for many activists. It thus seems that while some groups may have found success in using human rights language, its utilization and acceptance has not yet been adopted within organizing work and in American society as a whole. Using activism to build awareness of justice issues may serve to combat reticence toward human rights that still exists; because of this, without more clearly using "human rights" language or concepts, ACORN may still increase acceptance of human rights values in American society. Also, as more groups adopt human rights in their work, opportunities for ACORN and other organizations to use such concepts will likely grow as well.

It may indeed be a long time before economic and social justice is realized to the full extent that ACORN and other activist groups hope. The work of changing the opinions of politicians and the general public concerning economic rights may be slow going and challenging. Despite this, activists will continue the work of improving their communities, not only walking down the long road to economic justice, but also protesting, marching, and refusing to let their voices go unnoticed.

CHAPTER SIX

Hurricane Katrina
and the Right to Food and Shelter

Barret Katuna

In 2005, Arjun Sengupta, UN independent expert on the question of human rights and extreme poverty for the Human Rights Commission in Geneva, called on the international community to "recognize the existence of conditions of extreme poverty ... as indications of the worst form of indignity inflicted upon human beings, which should be regarded as a denial of human rights" (Sengupta 2007: 45). Sengupta was not talking about a Third World country; he was addressing conditions he witnessed in the United States in New Orleans, Louisiana, in the aftermath of Hurricane Katrina that made landfall on August 29, 2005. In June 2008, I spent a week volunteering for Habitat for Humanity, one of many NGOs assisting in the rebuilding effort of the Gulf Coast. Before my housing construction responsibilities began, I joined volunteers to prepare lunch for a group of homeless people who resided under a bridge in a community known as "Tent City" and learned of residents' heightened anxiety in post-Katrina New Orleans.

Chances to make major inroads in rebuilding have largely failed with the destruction of public housing, lack of access to food stamps, increased housing costs, and unequal attention to the needs of the African American population. The treatment of New Orleans residents following Hurricane Katrina has not only prompted national outcry, but has increasingly garnered international attention from the UN as a human rights violation of the right to life that encompasses an individual's right to food, shelter, and security. One natural disaster brought international attention to a problem largely overlooked in the United States: persistent hunger and homelessness. As Deric Shannon points out in his chapter, organizations such as

Food Not Bombs have organized in response to food insecurity in a nation with bountiful resources. This chapter calls attention to latent human rights violations that persist at a heightened level in the aftermath of Hurricane Katrina, and analyzes the inattention, denial, and obstacles that have prevented Katrina victims from acquiring basic resources. This analysis builds on human rights literature pertaining to development as an economic and social human right and offers a theoretical assessment of the human rights enterprise in the United States.

Defining the Problem:
Hunger and Homelessness in New Orleans

Hunger and homelessness in the city of New Orleans existed at exceptionally high levels before Hurricane Katrina. A U.S. Census Bureau report, based on data from 2000, ranked New Orleans second among large American cities in poverty concentration. The local African American population, representing 67 percent of New Orleans inhabitants, accounted for 84 percent of residents living in poverty, while urban neighborhoods accounted for the largest pockets of poverty. Thirty-eight percent of the poor people of Orleans Parish lived in regions of extreme poverty including the Lower Ninth Ward and Mid-City. Many of these regions were further disabled after the storm because they are in low-lying areas (Katz 2006).

Anticipating that many poor people would be unable to leave the city in a Category 5 storm, Mayor Ray Nagin urged those without transportation from the city to take shelter in the New Orleans Superdome. Dyson (2005) reports that the Louisiana National Guard stocked the Superdome with 90,000 liters of water and 43,776 "meals ready to eat." This amount of food and water would suffice for 15,000 people over a three-day period. However, a BBC report (2006) notes that more than 30,000 people lived in this structure for four days. Katrina challenged city officials to supply and distribute food to an unanticipated number of individuals.

Not only was there an inadequate food supply for the remaining citizens of New Orleans, there were also harsh living conditions. Dyson (2005) notes that the intensity of the hurricane fractured the roof of the Superdome in two areas, exposing inhabitants to rainfall. On September 3, 2005, at least 5,000 people still waited for buses to transport them to higher ground. The inefficient evacuation plan did not account for the vast number of individuals, primarily African Americans, who lacked the means to leave the city (Dyson 2005; Carmalt 2006). It took almost a week for the Federal Emergency Management Agency (FEMA) and the National Guard to evacuate the last inhabitants by bus. Humanitarian relief efforts addressed urgent concerns and left many systemic problems behind.

Dyson (2005) reports that, while federal funds came to the city, they were not addressing the public needs of those who were impoverished before the hurricane. Reconstruction efforts benefited predominately white suburban neighborhoods. Mohr and Powell (2007) and Cohen (2006) point out the nation's inability to deal with the natural disaster and take note of the blatantly racist policies in the rebuilding effort given the scarcity of resources for the large impoverished and displaced African American population.

FEMA assisted displaced persons by issuing temporary trailers to residents whose houses were uninhabitable. Sutherland (2008) reports that as of July 2008, more than 3,000 FEMA trailers remained in New Orleans as many residents continued to reside in these trailers due to a lack of running water and electricity in their houses. FEMA issued a mandate for all trailer dwellers to vacate their trailers before March 2009 with noncompliance resulting in fines.[1] The city has agreed to issue extensions enabling residents to continue to dwell in the trailers under dire circumstances. Insurance difficulties, corrupt agreements with housing contractors, and the difficulty of securing governmental aid prevent individuals from returning to their homes (Sutherland 2008). Housing costs also challenge individuals wishing to purchase or rent homes.

Boulard (2008) and Gardner (2008) note an escalation in housing costs in post-Katrina New Orleans. Apartment rents have increased with rent costs that have tripled (Henry J. Kaiser Family Foundation, 2008). Dewan (2008) reports that homelessness doubled in the aftermath of the hurricane; 60 percent of the homeless people of New Orleans reported that they became homeless as a result of Katrina. City officials are aware of the eyesore of homeless people occupying public spaces in makeshift communities such as "Tent City" and are working to eliminate this housing option.

Food accessibility is an ongoing impediment according to Neubeck (2006) who notes that, following Hurricane Katrina, the U.S. government took measures to reduce federal spending, which negatively affected needy families. While food stamp benefits were ultimately not reduced, Congress reauthorized Temporary Assistance for Needy Families (TANF) and incorporated further work guidelines without federal assistance for states to initiate these changes. Emergency aid to the region addressed (but did not completely satisfy) the needs of the citizens of New Orleans in the storm's wreckage. This persistent poverty and hunger contradicts the United States' commitment to the human rights enterprise.

Development as a Human Right:
International Conventions and Implementation

The human right to development encompasses the human right to food and shelter. This section traces the acknowledgement of this right through UN human rights conventions that define the right to development, which includes economic and social rights. The United States played a key role in drafting the 1948 UDHR. Additionally, the United States signed and ratified the ICERD of 1969 and the 1976 ICCPR. While the United States has shown support for the International Covenant on Economic, Social and Cultural Rights (ICESCR), the government has failed to ratify this document.

Article 22 of the UDHR grants the human right to social security needs. In particular, the article provides for this right "through national effort and international cooperation and in accordance with the organization and resources of each State, of the economic, social, and cultural rights indispensable for [the individual's] dignity and the free development of [the individual's] personality." In addition, Article 25 makes specific claims to the right to food and shelter. The article reads, "Everyone has the right to a standard of living adequate for the health and well-being of himself [or herself] and of his [or her] family," demonstrating the intended universality of this right. Specifically, the article guarantees this right in all circumstances and guarantees "the right to security in the event of unemployment, sickness, disability, widowhood, old age, or other lack of livelihood in circumstances beyond [the individual's] control." Signatories of the UDHR reaffirmed human rights claims with the 1993 Vienna Declaration and Programme of Action. Sengupta (2007) notes that the United States reaffirmed its commitment to social development goals through its affirmation of the 1995 Copenhagen Declaration on Social Development, and the 2000 Millennium Development Goals (MDGs) that collectively address global poverty and development issues and set a deadline at 2015.

UN officials and scholars expand on the meaning of the MDGs to draw support for their implementation. Robinson (2006) notes the relationship between the right to housing and a sustainable standard of living. The premises of the UDHR regarding housing encompass governmental responsibilities to provide security and livability measures. Sanitation, electric temperature control, and running water are vital components of the right to housing to apply to individuals of all social classes. Hansen (2002) elaborates further by addressing cultural norms of the ICESCR. He acknowledges initial recognition by the Committee on Economic, Social, and Cultural Rights in 1991 to guarantee culturally specific housing with the technological conveniences fitting of a nation's conventional way of life. This statement warrants acknowledgement of the disparity in the United States between the elite and the poor.

Sengupta (2007) argues that violations in relation to shelter and security in the wake of the flooding clearly violated Article 6 of the ICCPR that guarantees the right to life, a "non-derogable right" that is nonnegotiable even in times of national emergencies or natural disasters. He identifies the problematic nature of the evacuation plan that subsequently failed to meet nondiscrimination standards of the ICCPR through its disregard of the weaknesses of an immobilized population. Further, Carmalt (2006) identifies the U.S. violation of Article 26 of the ICCPR, which ensures freedom from discrimination and equal legal protection for all persons. Citing United States Census Bureau statistics from 2000, she states, "In Orleans Parish, discriminating on the basis of ownership of private vehicles equated to discrimination on the basis of race, since African Americans were over twice as likely to be without a personal vehicle than whites" (Carmalt 2006: 4). The state of Louisiana's insufficient response to aiding this burdened population accounted for concentrated despair for the African American community.

The right to life encompasses food rights; Article 11 of the ICESCR calls attention to the human right to food. Künnemann (2002) notes that the right to food is the only right that is listed as "fundamental" in the entire text of the ICESCR. Access to food should be ongoing; individuals must not live with the uncertainty of adequate nutrition. Künnemann also introduces the "normative content of the right to adequate food" in his analysis of Article 11. Human dignity must not be called into question in the attainment of food. General Comment No. 12 of Article 11 notes that available food must meet cultural standards and nutritional value and that progressive measures are to be taken to restore access to food. If, for example, circumstances arise (such as natural disasters preventing food circulation), states are obligated under the ICESCR to work toward the full realization of food access in an expedient manner. Article 11 acknowledges that there are two situations that preclude states from not adequately addressing the individual's right to food, namely obstacles pertaining to distribution, and an inadequate national food supply. Hurricane Katrina created problems in food circulation days after the storm; however, today the country certainly has the capacity to enable food availability. Further, Hansen (2002) states that, in 1991, the Committee on Economic, Social, and Cultural Rights clarified that food distribution should take place in a manner that encourages future self-reliance for food acquisition. International conventions outline expectations of signatory nations and necessitate a discussion of accountability and legal grounds for the full realization of these rights.

A rights-based approach to development is a common method of examining national shortcomings (Robinson 2005; Sengupta 2002; Wolfensohn 2005). Robinson (2005) states that this approach takes citizen participation into account through individual empowerment to address policy shortcomings, accessibility of information regarding national policies, and commitments based on international conventions. Accountability is the key component to the rights-based approach to development. The recognition of the interconnected nature between basic human rights (such as food and shelter) and the realization of other rights (including political participation, for example), are paramount to said approach. In sum, these scholars present a framework in which civil society members assert human rights. Sengupta (2002) defines the right to development as an ongoing process: "to be carried out in a manner known as rights-based, in accordance with the international human rights standards, as a participatory, non-discriminatory, accountable and transparent process with equity in decision-making and sharing of the fruits of the process" (Sengupta 2002). Former UN High Commissioner for Human Rights Louise Arbour (2006) acknowledges the individual responsibility of each UN Member State to nationally secure development rights and recognizes the need for special efforts to provide development relief in times of environmental crises. Numerous international conventions outline a nation's responsibility to its citizens in meeting development rights. Yet, as it is seen in the United States, the government does not hold itself accountable.

UN Acknowledgment of Human Rights Violations in Post-Katrina New Orleans

The recent demolition of a public housing community in St. Bernard Parish and further scheduled destructions lacking community approval incited a response from the UN In February 2008, Miloon Kothari, UN special rapporteur on adequate housing as a component of the right to an adequate standard of living, and on the right to non-discrimination in this context and Gay McDougall, UN independent expert on minority issues, issued a joint statement condemning the demolition of public housing after bringing concerns to the U.S. government in December 2007. They underscored the discriminatory nature of these demolitions given the fact that 12,000 homeless people, many of whom are African American, lack housing opportunities in a context of high rental fees and elevated housing prices. They cited long waiting periods before the public housing complexes are available for habitation and the failure of the local government to consult with community residents before the demolitions (UN News Centre 2009). In October 2008, special rapporteur on adequate housing as a component of the right to an adequate standard of living, and on the right to non-discrimination in this context, Raquel Rolnik (UN 2008) called attention to the prevalence of discriminatory practices that prevent Americans from gaining access to housing due to racism and intolerance of diverse beliefs and backgrounds. She suggested that nations make the right to adequate housing a constitutional priority enforceable under a nation's judicial system.

The issue of access to housing warrants a discussion of the numerous internally displaced persons (IDPs) in the region. Sekaran (2006) and Gardner (2008) note the refusal of the United States to recognize hurricane victims as IDPs with vital humanitarian needs, in accordance with the UN Guiding Principles. Cohen (2006) acknowledges the expectation of nondiscrimination and a timely response that is inherent in the guiding principles. In his 2005 report, *In Larger Freedom*, former UN secretary general Kofi A. Annan encouraged Member States to incorporate the UN Guiding Principles on Internal Displacement regarding the protection of IDPs "as the basic international norm for protection of such persons, and to commit themselves to promote the adoption of these principles through national legislation" (Annan 2005, 70). The United States has taken a firm stance regarding assistance to IDPs; Cohen (2006) notes that in 2005, as the people of New Orleans dealt with the hurricane, U.S. officials were reaffirming the government's commitment to protecting IDPs by voting for the World Summit Document at the UN. She argues that the United States avoided using the term IDP to refer to the displaced victims in an effort to live up to its international status and to avoid compliance with the Guiding Principles. High homelessness rates in New Orleans attest to the United States' noncompliance. In its significant role in foreign policy, the United States is failing to address domestic development rights that encompass the human rights enterprise.

U.S. Resistance to Identifying Human Rights Abuses

Ignatieff (2005) defines "American exceptionalism" as the U.S. government's assertion that it acknowledges human rights, while simultaneously resisting their full realization within its borders. Civil society actors and NGOs enhance the human rights effort both at home and abroad while the government fails to recognize its internal shortcomings. Neubeck (2006, 162) notes that the U.S. State Department excludes the country from its annual report on the status of human rights in over 190 nations and regions. Sunstein (2005) points to the fact that the U.S. Constitution does not have a specific section pertaining to economic and social rights. Judicial review of the Constitution denotes that the courts can enforce the rights as defined. Civil society and socially minded U.S. representatives are quick to point out human rights abuses that the government seems to have overlooked.

Hafner-Burton and Tsutsui (2005) explain the reasons for state ratification of international treaties and subsequent noncompliance. They argue that, while governments are encouraged to ratify international conventions, they are not given the proper means to ensure compliance: "these international agreements may at times provide governments with a shield for increasingly repressive behaviors after ratification" (2005: 1378). Without institutional checks and balances of compliance, NGOs carry the burden of enforcement. On a similar note, Gilmore (2007) states that nonprofit organizations end up providing public resources for which the government is responsible. Inefficient governmental bureaucracies rely on privately funded organizations such as FNB, as Deric Shannon discusses in his chapter, and the Association of Community Organizations for Reform Now (ACORN) that Amanda Ploch examines in her chapter, that see it as a moral duty to uphold human dignity. Gilmore speaks of the "non-profit industrial complex" and notes that governmental abandonment and market failure propound the creation of NGOs that meet the (unmet) needs of the public.

Emerging Trends: The Future of the Human Right to Food and Shelter in New Orleans

In June 2007, Senator Christopher J. Dodd (D-Conn.) introduced Senate Bill 1668 (the Gulf Coast Housing Recovery Act of 2007) in the 110th Congress, to provide affordable housing to victims of the 2005 hurricanes. Among the 11 co-sponsors was Barack Obama, at the time representing Illinois. Key components of the bill include a requirement for the FEMA administrator to allow Louisiana to use funds under the Road Home Program and a directive for the Secretary of Housing and Urban Development (HUD) to channel funds to specific communities. Other key factors of the bill include the provision of funds to HUD through FEMA to subsidize rent, an extension of the HUD Disaster Voucher Program, deadlines for the Housing Authority of New Orleans to attain a specified occupancy level, the prevention of the demolition of public housing units and encouragement of their repair in some instances, as well as the instatement of a right of return for individuals who had previously lived in public housing. While Senate Bill 1668 did not pass and no further action will be taken on it given that the 110th Congress has since ended, the passage of the American Recovery and Reinvestment Act of 2009 demonstrates the federal government's ongoing attention to the rebuilding effort of New Orleans. In particular, Section 601 of this act directs that President Obama establish an arbitration panel under FEMA direction to intervene in requests for recovery assistance from damages associated with Hurricanes Katrina and Rita, which followed a month later. Furthermore, Section 602 specifies the rights of individuals to access funds from the hazard mitigation grant program associated with these two hurricanes.

Additional local governmental efforts indicate progress; Boling and Adler (2008) cite a New Orleans Food Policy Advisory Committee report that acknowledges healthful food access problems confronting New Orleans that gained acceptance from the New Orleans City Council. For example, the number of supermarkets in New Orleans has diminished since Katrina. Before August 2005, 38 supermarkets each served 12,000 residents. The 2008 report identified 18 functioning supermarkets each serving 18,000 residents. The national average for residents per supermarket stands at 8,800 customers. Clearly, there are obstacles to grocery shopping for residents without vehicles. While a shuttle service is part of the accepted plan to enable access to healthful food, difficulties persist. Another viable long-term solution involves a state financed program to provide loans and grants to supermarkets in areas with scarce grocery resources (Boling and Adler 2008). Those who cannot afford to purchase food face considerable obstacles in food bank distribution programs. Citing the uncertainty of the United States Farm Bill, the Food Bank of Central Louisiana and the Louisiana Food Bank Association asked for state funding in April 2008. The approved $5 million in funding, however, was not sufficient to meet the food insecurity crisis of Louisiana (Millhollon 2008).

The inadequacy of the governmental response to Hurricanes Katrina and Rita have led the way for civil society's response. The PPEHRC and U.S. Human Rights Network challenge the government to end domestic poverty and underscore the United States' disregard for the UDHR and refusal to ratify the ICESCR (Neubeck 2006). Grassroots volunteer efforts help through fundraising and physical rebuilding efforts. As of December 2006, the Bush-Clinton Katrina Fund had raised $130 million to assist the people of the Gulf Coast (Bush-Clinton Katrina Fund, 2009. New Orleans Area Habitat for Humanity (NOAHH) reported that in 2008, with the help of 24,000 individuals, it had built 84 homes in Orleans, Jefferson, and St. Bernard Parishes (New Orleans Area Habitat for Humanity 2009). An official count from September 20, 2010, notes that since the establishment of NOAHH in 1983, its volunteers have built 418 homes in New Orleans and were in the process of building 13 more homes (New Orleans Area Habitat for Humanity 2011).

Final Thoughts

An examination of the history of poverty in New Orleans, as well as of human rights conventions that the United States has signed and ratified, demonstrates the gravity of ongoing human rights violations pertaining to food and shelter in our country. Public accounts of extant poverty demonstrate that the specter of human rights violations will persist in the absence of concentrated governmental and NGO attention to rebuild the ailing infrastructure. Fundraising and voluntary efforts have been widely successful in assisting in the region's restoration. However, attention for the afflicted region will wane, as Hurricane Katrina becomes a distant memory for those who live out of range from the wreckage. Anniversaries of Hurricane Katrina and threats of impending storms draw attention to the ongoing needs of the region.[2] When Hurricanes Gustav and Ike threatened the Gulf Coast region in late summer 2008, I recognized some of the residents from "Tent City" in a television news report. And I wondered, how much longer will we allow Americans to endure such poverty? Both international and U.S. attention hint at an expectation and a hope for future alleviation of the poverty that limits citizens' access to housing, food, and human dignity.

CHAPTER SEVEN

Education, Human Rights, and the State: Toward New Visions

Abraham P. DeLeon

> Human rights education is not a passing teaching fad. It is not a
> whimsical invention from designer seminars mulling over dreams for
> the twenty-first century. Human rights education is an international
> obligation with a half-century history.
> —Andreopoulos and Claude 1997: 3

Education is rife with issues of equity and social justice. From the opportunity to attend quality schools, to receiving a healthy and nutritious lunchtime meal, to how special education services are meted out, public schooling is entrenched in the fight for a better and more just world. In this tradition, a central problem for education should be to engage and respond to concepts of "rights," perhaps most important to figure out what the international establishment of human rights (denoted below as HR) would, could, or should mean in the context of educational theory, philosophy, and practice in the United States. As the quote that opened this chapter demonstrates, HR education now has a considerable history on which to build, and should be a fundamental component when we envision an educational experience rooted in social justice.

Unfortunately, however, much traditional HR theory, advocacy, and scholarship are rooted in a liberal paradigm that relies on the state as main arbiter and agent for realizing human rights in practice. Interestingly, there have been rigorous critiques against the state from critical scholarship that sees the bureaucratic and hierarchical nature of traditional nation-states as unable or unfit to respond to the needs and rights of historically oppressed people. As a scholar who is rooted in a critical educational paradigm, I share the view that the discussion of HR is paramount to discussions of civic duty, responsibility, and working toward a more equally just society. This stems from a theoretical and professional position (also with significant history) that suggests the role of the educator and scholar as potentially transformative figures—where one's contribution to society is to help in changing it "for the better."

Though still emergent, there has been some scholarship on public education and HR in the United States (Andreopoulos and Claude 1997; Banks 2009; Cole 2006; Davies 2000; Flowers 2003; Osler 2002; Print et al. 2008; Robeyns 2006; Wronka 1994). I would like to explore some of this literature on HR and education, and although Joel Spring (2000) has done some of this initial work, I will build upon this literature in what follows through a critical pedagogical lens. My particular theoretical approach or lens draws upon both critical pedagogy and anarchist theory (Amster et al. 2009; Darder, Torres, and Baltodano 2009; DeLeon 2008). Second, I offer a critique of formal human rights discourse through deconstructing some of its underlying ideological assumptions about the relationship between HR and the state. Specifically, I will critique the assumption that states can ultimately provide HR in the way that it has been discursively constructed (Armaline and Glasberg 2010; Nozick 1974; Turner 2010), just as there is some problem with assuming that states provide public education absent of ideologies and practices of domination.

According to formal HR instruments, states are constructed as the key agents and international players involved in defining (representation by state) and (in part through their obligations to "respect, protect, and fulfill" the rights/components of treaties to which they are party) realizing HR. That said, there is arguably a contradiction in relying on the same hegemonic structures (states) whose actions (in World War II, for example) inspired the very creation of HR in the first place. As Armaline and Glasberg (2009) argue,

> The irony is that HR instruments' content are intended to protect individuals and groups from abuses by (for instance) the state, yet require states to both implement these instruments and monitor their own compliance. That is, HR instruments formally expect and depend on states to choose the protection and provision of human rights over all other interests in the face of their conflict. Though this is not a new revelation, little has been done to address it . . . [it is a] persistent flaw in the ability of HR instruments to operate as ultimately effective mechanisms in their present form.

This critique will helpfully expose one of the glaring contradictions in the literature on HR, while illustrating how deconstructing formal HR discourse might be informative for both HR and critical educational/pedagogical agendas. In fact, I argue that education should be a central locus in how new political struggles are formulated, while also thinking about the roles that education can play in supporting new forms of resistance and social movements. The concept of HR is paramount to developing healthy, productive, and socially just communities. However, this chapter will also demonstrate that we need to stay vigilant in how such social change plays out through complex and important discursive constructions like that reflected in HR instruments and the more formal HR regime.

Human Rights and Education

It seems apparent that connections exist between HR and the project of public education. Even before the UDHR and the Convention on the Rights of the Child (CRC) were expressed and formalized, public education had a particular tie to the concept of protecting children and providing a healthy, welcoming, and rigorous academic and social environment (Clapham 2007; Spring 2010). "The right to education involves not only obligations to refrain from interfering with the right [to education] by closing schools, or discriminating against certain pupils, but also includes obligations . . . by providing compulsory, free primary education for all" (Clapham 2007: 124). Although this right has not always been described or employed as a solution to social problems like racism, sexism, classism, or the recent neoliberal assault on public education (Darder et al. 2009; Hickey 2006; Hursh 2008), schools have professed a unique mission in educating all students fairly and justly (Spring 2000). In this way, one could easily argue that the manifest goals of public education are closely intertwined with the concept of HR, despite how they have been lived or expressed.

Although there is an implicit assumption that those of us working in education are advocating for some outgrowth or concept of HR, this has not been made explicit in scholarly literature or formal teacher education. In fact, few sources make the link between human rights and education, other than providing educational activities or classroom frameworks for studying HR (Andreopoulos and Claude 1997; Banks 2009; Cole 2006; Davies 2000; Flowers 2003; Osler 2002; Print et al. 2008; Robeyns 2006; Wronka 1994). In this sense, there is much more work needed to explore the discursive and theoretical links between HR and education, how HR frameworks help us to rethink public schooling in the United States, and the role that education can play in advancing HR practice in the United States.

Some literature reflects parallels between critical (education) theory and the stated intentions of rights to education according to formal HR and international legal discourse. Cole (2006: 4) suggests,

> Schools do not have to be places where pupils/students are encouraged to think in one-dimensional ways. They can be and should be arenas for the encouragement of critical thought, where young people are provided with a number of ways of interpreting the world, not just the dominant ones.

Cole's insistence on the centrality of critical thought and postmodern approaches to interpreting truth/knowledge demonstrates a potential link between HR and scholarship in critical education. Though arguably "Western" and universalist in nature (though I don't mean to suggest a position on these debates here), formal HR instruments reflect a significant mixture of cultural interpretations of central concepts (of, for example, "right," humanity, and substantive measures of dignified survival). This alone flies in the face of linear, modern concepts of knowledge and truth. Further, formal HR instruments reflect a relatively critical perspective on power and governance, where concepts of HR by definition potentially limit oppression by setting baseline limits on the extent to which anyone can be exploited or abused by (for example) the powerful.

International HR discourse also seems to suggest the potential for education to play a role in the broader HR enterprise. UNESCO (n.d.) declared that education,

> should encompass values such as peace, non-discrimination, equality, justice, non-violence, tolerance and respect for human dignity. Quality education based on a human rights approach means that rights are implemented throughout the whole education system and in all learning environments. (para. 2)

As most critical educators would suggest, this is not often the reality of public schooling in the United States (Spring 2010). However, schools can, and maybe should, be common terrains for critical educational and HR agendas.

Critical pedagogical theory, for example, calls on educators to rethink practices that are rooted in ideologies of domination, while simultaneously reflecting on our role in resisting or participating in the reproductive functions of mainstream public education (Darder, Torres, and Baltodano 2009). Human rights scholars and educators also call on us to be reflexive and take an active stance toward resisting frameworks and ideologies of domination (Blau and Moncada 2005; Campbell 2006). As Banks (2009: 101) argues,

> for human rights ideals to be implemented in schools and to become meaningful for children and youth, these ideals must speak to and address their own experiences, personal identities, hopes, struggles, dreams, and possibilities. In other words, for students to internalize the concept of human rights, they must have experiences in the school, as well as in the larger society, that validate them as human beings; affirm their ethnic, cultural, racial, and linguistic identities; and empower them as citizens in the school and in the larger society.

Banks highlights common threads (validation, difference, linguistic rights, ethnic identity, etc.) found in formal HR instruments/discourse and educational scholarship on critical and effective pedagogical practices (Print et al. 2008; Robeyns 2006). Here we see, for example, the dual concern for fostering welcoming, diverse, democratic educational spaces (such as classrooms), and for validating the humanity and situated knowledge of all students. Where these are broad, fundamental parallels, they relate to other links worth exploring here.

For example, the Organization for Security and Co-operation in Europe (OSCE) Office for Democratic Institutions and Human Rights (ODIHR) produced a book on how HR should be expressed in a variety of global educational systems. ODIHR (2009: 7) provides us with a vision of how human rights education should be expressed:

> The right to education provides an entry point to the enjoyment of all human rights. It includes human rights education, the right to learn about those rights, and the ways and means to protect and promote them in our societies. Within the education system, human rights education promotes a holistic, rights-based approach that includes both "human rights through education," ensuring that all the components and processes of education—including curricula, materials, methods and training—are conducive to learning about human rights, and "human rights in education," ensuring that the human rights of all members of the school community are respected.

This outline presents educators with a vision of critical pedagogy centered on the notion of HR. There is a rich history of literature in critical education on the importance of building community and its link to empowering educational experiences for students, families, and teachers and administrators who work in schools (Darder et al. 2009; Freire 2000; McLaren 2006). Unfortunately, this has been difficult to create and find in current practice, in great part because the institution of public education often embodies the same racism, classism, sexism, deference to state hierarchy (versus local, democratic community control), and other oppressions that pervade all of society (Anyon 1997). Where schools can be centers of grassroots community building, they are often more so mechanisms for expressing power relationships and maintaining the status quo. Many critical pedagogical theorists have tried to conceptualize how teachers and students might resist these tendencies.

Interestingly, HR educational literature, and its demands on educators seem to invoke the work of Brazilian educator and activist Paulo Freire and his notion of the banking concept of education. As Freire (2000: 72) argued, "education . . . becomes an act of depositing in which the students are the depositories and the teacher is the depositor. Worse yet, it turns them into 'containers,' into 'receptacles' to be 'filled' by the teacher." In this traditional and oppressive model of education, teachers simply "fill" the students with knowledge that is supposedly neutral, objective, and rational. They force students to memorize and recite a form of knowledge that is not given its full social, political, and economic context. This decontextualized knowledge is often alien to and alienating for the student—especially members of non-dominant social groups—and does not help them to understand how complex relationships of power are (re)produced, employed, and potentially resisted. If students and teachers are meant to drive social change, be it for HR practice or other justifiable goals, they must first see themselves as subjective participants in the creation of knowledge and history (as Freire recognized in his scholar-activism in Latin America). As previously suggested by Banks (2009), part of validating the humanity of the student (and teacher) is validating their situated knowledge, culture, and experiences in the educational process. "Banking" education, still dominant in much of the industrialized world, might be seen as contradictory to both HR education and critical pedagogical agendas. It is inherently dehumanizing and alienating to teachers and students, and tends to strengthen and reproduce status quo power relationships through the unquestioned legitimation and dissemination of dominant ideological and epistemological perspectives disguised as "truth," "fact," or "common sense" (indeed, banking education is often hegemonic in form and effect).

As Freire (2000: 72) further notes, "the scope of action allowed to the students extends only as far as receiving, filing and storing the deposits." In this way, the local and situational knowledge forms that students bring to the table are devalued for the largely Eurocentric and Western forms of knowing, reified in most public schools across the United States, and through standardized testing and curriculum, as demonstrated by (still dominant) "No Child Left Behind" legislation. As Meintjes (1997: 66) argues, "human rights education as empowerment requires enabling each target group to begin the process of acquiring the knowledge and critical awareness it needs to understand and question oppressive patterns of social, political, and economic organization." There is an opportunity here for the emergent field of "Human Rights Education" to fulfill such a call as informed by critical pedagogical theory as demonstrated in Freire's work, noted above. Human rights education should resist traditional modes of learning and rethink how domination is reproduced through traditional educational experiences. "This will require the ability to envision, develop and function within new non-dominating patterns of organization in which the human dignity of everyone is protected and promoted" (66).

As scholars such as Spring (2000) have argued convincingly, HR education can be positioned to resist these practices in the United States and elsewhere. As I have tried to illustrate thus far, critical educational/pedagogical scholarship, and public schools might be fertile terrains for the development of HR discourse and practice in the United States, thanks to somewhat obvious parallels in the guiding theories and goals of public schooling and the formal HR regime. Still, just as the agendas of HR and critical education share some common goals and potentially common strategies, they share a common problem in their uncritical reliance on states. I would suggest that some work is needed to first unpack some of the assumptions within the formal discourse and traditional conceptions of HR if one seeks their explicit integration in sound public school curriculum, internal organization, and everyday practice. A central concern here is the notion that HR can be realized through traditional state structures. As I discuss below, a critical pedagogical lens, informed also by anarchist theory, can be useful in deconstructing traditional ways of thinking about the HR enterprise and some limitations of statist ideologies and approaches to realizing HR practice.

Human Rights, Anarchist Theory, and
Discourses of the State

Before I begin to deconstruct the notion of the state in HR scholarship and discourse, it is beneficial to begin with a common understanding of anarchism and its relationship to and growing influence on educational theory and practice. As I have written elsewhere about anarchism (DeLeon 2006, 2008, 2009), it is has been commonly misrepresented and misunderstood.

Often constructed as violent, chaotic, and politically naive, anarchism has been dismissed as utopian, wild, dangerous, and nihilist in that it offers critique with little vision outside of traditional political structures and frameworks (Amster et al. 2009). However, anarchism should be thought of instead as a framework in which to situate praxis that is grounded in direct action, autonomous organization, and a rigorous critique against coercive and hierarchical social structures rooted within notions of social justice. Deric Shannon's chapter that focuses on the right to eat and the work of Food Not Bombs illustrates how FNB operates outside of the state structure to initiate direct action.

Anarchist theory also provides an activist framework that eschews the notion that activists need to defer to larger authoritative and bureaucratic organizations, the same type of problem plaguing our conversations around the concept of HR and its implementation. Human rights is usually situated within legal discourses and not through the lived resistance of communities in different social, political, and economic contexts (Campbell 2006). Instead, anarchism pushes activists to work immediately and autonomously by participating in direct action politics and tactics, rather than waiting for the permission to realize social justice by state (or otherwise constructed) authorities. Although these ideas tend to, predictably, make many traditionalists in academia and other political arenas nervous, anarchism provides the vigilance to make sure that coercive institutions and experiences are monitored and resisted. In this way, anarchist theory shares affinities with educational movements that have sought to transcend narrow definitions of educational experiences.

As some critical scholars have noted, HR is mired in the state and its various discourses of legitimacy (Armaline and Glasberg 2009). For some anarchists, the idea that we should have to petition the state for "rights" and the notion that states can be the only location for this discourse obscures the ways that human beings have historically organized themselves in informal ways, sometimes using direct and autonomous forms of self governance (Lynd and Grubacic 2008). Throughout history, the state (as with other forms of hierarchical rule) has been responsible for untold suffering for human populations, especially those constructed as expendable. The death penalty, unending war, destruction of the environment, cutbacks to vital social services, and other oppressive practices seem to be how states— particularly powerful ones such as the United States—function under a capitalist, hegemonic, and neoliberal social order. This is not to suggest that states—more accurately, collective institutions typically subsumed by the state—provide nothing positive for populations they supposedly represent. In fact, Turner (2010: 141) argues that the tensions between anarchist theory and the state do not "require the abandonment of the state system altogether." However, we are still wise to think about couching social justice movements, be it through HR, public education, or both (HR education), in an inherently hierarchical institution with a markedly bad record when it comes to facilitating equality and shared human dignity. Turner (144) suggests how we might rethink how the formal HR regime is informed by anarchist theory:

> Without erecting a world government that might merit the same criticisms as bureaucratic states, human rights law protects personal rights and promotes a political culture that elevates the rights of individuals above the whims of authoritarian governments. While not exactly the vision of nineteenth century anarchists, anarchism itself should be thought of as a dogma. Its own internal logic should welcome the widest range of revisionism. Thus human rights necessitate a cautious rapprochement between anarchist theory and governing institutions.

Turner is advocating for a HR project grounded in anarchist theory and praxis. However, his welcoming of the tenuous union between the state, HR, and anarchist theory does not, in my humble opinion, push us far enough. States and their various structures have been at the center of historical injustices, as also problematically and most recently linked to capitalist logics and unbridled neoliberal ideologies (Hickey 2006).

Though implementing HR practice has proven difficult given the historical contradictions between the thrust of formal HR instruments and the actual (hierarchical) structure and often times problematic practices of states, we see increasing global acceptance of HR discourse in formal policy and informal grassroots arenas of social struggle. Douzinas (2007: 33) provides some direction on this phenomenon:

> The rhetoric of human rights seems to have triumphed because it can be adopted by left and right, the north and south, the state and the pulpit, the minister and the rebel. This is the characteristic that makes them the only ideology in town, the ideology after the end of ideologies, the ideology at the end of history. After their institutional inauguration, they were hijacked by governments that understood the benefits of a moral-sounding policy. They have become ingrained in the new world order.

Douzinas's critique of HR pushes us to recognize the broad appeal that it has had with states and other traditional structures because of how the concept of "human rights" has been discursively constructed. Formal HR provides a discourse through which preemptive wars can be waged in the name of humanitarian intervention by powerful states and their corporate partners, while simultaneously providing the discourse through which populations might resist such aggressions. Attempts by the George W. Bush administration to justify imperial warfare in the Middle East as somehow an effort to combat the human rights abuses of Saddam Hussein's Baath Party and Afghanistan's Taliban Regime (both previous clients of the United States) against women and ethnic minorities is an obvious example here. Indeed, domestic populations in Iraq and Afghanistan have documented and protested the massive human rights violations resulting from the current "War on Terror," such as the high rate of civilian casualties in drone bombing raids and the mythically accurate tools of modern Western warfare. Those of us interested in realizing HR practice need to find strategies to counter the ability of the powerful to employ HR discourse as an ideological tool to ensure domination, while simultaneously promoting HR discourse and HR instruments as counterhegemonic tools of democratic, grassroots, social justice movements (as arguably intended by many, but not all of its original "founders"). Here we might return to critical education and public schooling as a terrain to develop HR discourse and praxis in the United States.

It needs to be asserted again that hierarchical and coercive institutions, such as the state, may not provide the foundations for HR or any other project that seeks to disrupt oppressive and inherently unequal social relationships on their own. This is where the critical project of education becomes a powerful tool in resisting and seeking alternatives to such oppressive structures, whether at the university or secondary level. Combined with anarchist models of resistance to and critique of the state, students and teachers can begin to see outside of these hegemonic approaches to HR and public education. For example, HR education might encourage students and teachers to think about what HR would look like if the state were not in charge of how rights are defined, distributed, and realized. What are the possibilities and limitations of a formal "rights" discourse for realizing particular social justice goals, or in addressing particular social problems? Such inquiry helps to develop students and teachers as engaged, critical social participants, where authority is subject to reflection and critique, where the real (vast) terrain of possibility for social change (as reflected in the HR enterprise rather than simply the formal HR regime) can be considered and developed in classrooms and other educational environments. If nothing else, this seems to reflect a most democratic pedagogical approach to both HR and state theory, where through the exploration of HR theory and praxis, students and teachers also unpack their relationship to states and other hierarchical structures (often purported to "represent their interests," typically regardless of consent or participation).

At the same time, like the formal HR regime, education (including the emergent area of HR education) is bound within traditional, historically oppressive and coercive state structures. This requires critical reflection. As it has been noted throughout this chapter, the heinous actions of states (typically partnered with corporations and the private sector) inspired the development of formal HR instruments in the first place. At the same time, we can observe the assumption that states can usher in both empowering forms of public education (as a human right) and broader human rights practice. For example, UNESCO (n.d.) advocates how states can ensure, "the right to education for every child and in promoting education for human rights, democratic citizenship, peace and non-violence and intercultural education; including establishment of frameworks and guidelines" (para. 4). Contemporary observers of U.S. domestic and foreign policy would be hard pressed to find evidence of the U.S. government as a champion of "peace," "non-violence," or "intercultural education." Clapham (2007: 125) also mentions the role the state plays in how HR and education converge. "The state must ensure that schools and programmes are accessible to all." He highlights, in particular, that education needs to be "accessible to all, nondiscriminatory and physically and economically accessible" (125). All these goals are worthwhile—ones that we as educators need to continually strive for. However, history does not suggest such an altruistic role for public schooling in the United States in practice. Because schools reflect the larger society in which they are located, they unfortunately tend to manifest— even exacerbate or reproduce—these same social problems, such as structural inequalities along lines of race, class, and (though decreasing) gender (Spring 2010). Schools are inherently unequal and sort students according to social class, race, and other social markers (Darder et al. 2009). Like the formal HR regime, schools are immersed in these complex relationships of power that make resistance to these material and ideological structures very difficult. States, and players in the formal HR regime (including intergovernmental and nongovernmental organizations), exist within the abstract realm of state and legal discursive constructions. Because of this contemporary reality, deconstructing such discourse becomes a paramount activity for *both* the HR enterprise and critical educational agenda in the United States.

Even the notion of "right" might be problematized in this crucial process of deconstruction. Let us consider what Wilson and Mitchell (2003: 5) claim in their critique of "rights" discourse. As they argue,

> the social critique of rights examines how a rights regime creates certain types of subjectivities (victims, perpetrators) and certain types of acts (e.g. common crimes versus crimes against humanity). This framing of the social world often does an injustice to the complex range of subjectivities in a social or historical setting. Human rights reports tend to bifurcate individuals into either victims or perpetrators, but these same individuals might wish to assert another alterative identity (e.g., survivors, freedom fighters).

This also speaks to the critiques of hierarchical and coercive state structures made by critical theorists, particularly anarchists (Sartwell 2008). The concept of "rights" is further complicated by the assumption of legitimacy in state policy and practice, especially when the state is assumed to properly represent their domestic population (most notably in Western forms of "democracy). As Wilson and Mitchell (2003: 6) argue, common contemporary "rights" discourse "requires a distinction be made between human rights violations (which are committed by an agent of the state authorized to carry out the act) and criminal acts (where the state or political organization is not a party to the action). Yet in many scenarios, criminal and political networks are intertwined and perpetrators are both criminals and political agents and their violent acts are both criminal acts and human rights violations." They also note that most HR is grounded within a "legal positivist" framework that does not account for subjectivity, multiple realities, the complexity of social life and the overreliance on traditional standards of counting and measurement (6). All these hide and obfuscate the nature of HR and how to achieve a new form of radical equality in the face of rampant social problems, unbridled militarism, and neoliberal capitalism. For the conversation on HR to move forward in a meaningful way, or for one's right to education and the critical educational agenda to bear fruit, activists and scholars need to rethink traditional conceptions of "rights" to liberate them from the traditional nation-state.

Conclusion

Traditional HR scholarship is grounded in a discourse that reifies the state as one of the few valid forms of human organization. The broader concept of the HR enterprise, furthered in this volume, begs us to question and rethink what HR would look like outside of the dominant statist paradigm. In fact, "if we are looking for foundations for human rights, then one . . . would say that abstracted and universal forms of human solidarity must arise from these everyday forms of compassion and empathy which necessarily involve a recognition of the other" (Wilson and Mitchell 2003: 9). Wilson and Mitchell encourage us to recognize a need for HR to reflect a politics of difference that supports and celebrates the multifaceted nature of contemporary societies. Class, race, gender, (dis)ability, sexuality, and other forms of identity are complex constructions that need to be explored and formulated within a politics of difference that builds recognition, empathy, and praxis. Furthermore, they suggest that this can only emerge from "everyday forms"—that is, the local interactions of people in real lived contexts. This should be seen in contrast to statist approaches that would assume freedoms and human dignities are somehow legislated from above and outside of local contexts.

As I have argued throughout this chapter, the state has been responsible for grievous crimes against historically oppressed populations. By framing HR and critical education as subject to the arbitration and actions of states, it arguably limits their full potentials for counterhegemony and social justice. However, the underlying goals and strategies of the HR enterprise and critical educational/pedagogical agendas do reflect overlapping conceptions of social justice, and share the need to be decoupled from exclusively state-centered approaches and discourse. For these reasons, critical educational scholarship might engage further with developing the HR enterprise in the United States, in part through the further development of HR education as an emergent and important field in curriculum design, teacher education, and so forth. Finally, HR educators might draw from critical pedagogical theory, demonstrated, for example, in the classic works of Paulo Freire to ensure that critical educational and HR movements take shape more fruitfully as reflexive, truly democratic struggles from below.

CHAPTER EIGHT

Health and Human Rights

Kathryn Strother Ratcliff

The health of Americans falls far short of what it might be. Although we have one of the most expensive and technologically sophisticated health care systems, our collective health suffers. Americans usually look at the state of our national health through an individualistic lens (Ratcliff 2002), a tendency that has Americans defining health very narrowly, as consisting of the physical and mental well-being of individuals. They assume that measures of public health are reducible to the extent to which individuals experience diseases, physical and mental maladies, and disabilities; seen as the result of viruses, bacteria, injuries, lifestyle choices, diet, and genetic factors rather than as connected to social structural variables, or (for example) the outcomes of public policy. Thus defined, the maintenance or improvement of health becomes dependent on an individual's own actions, and those of doctors, other health care providers, and the health care system rather than the way society is structured and organized. An analysis of health as a social structural issue becomes a conversation about health as a human right rather than one of health as a personal problem. The purpose of this chapter, then, is to offer human rights analysis as an alternative way to think about health. I will discuss health as a basic human right and show that major improvements in American health depend on the extent to which a human rights approach is implemented.

Health as a Human Right

The World Health Organization (WHO), various human rights instruments and interpretive comments, NGOs, and human rights organizations illustrate the push for a definition of health far beyond the individualistic approach. In 1946 WHO defined health as "a state of complete physical, mental and social well-being and not merely the absence of disease or infirmity" (emphasis added), a radical departure from an individualistic biological disease model (Preamble to WHO Constitution). Formal interpretations of UN covenants, such as the Committee on Economic, Social and Cultural Rights General Comment 14 (passed May 2000), have further defined health rights and have explicitly placed health at the center of human rights. The first sentence of the General Comment states that "Health is a fundamental human right indispensable for the exercise of other human rights." And then it states a bold goal: "Every human being is entitled to the enjoyment of the highest attainable standard of health conducive to living a life in dignity."

The General Comment interprets the right to health as a right to "available," "affordable," and "accessible health facilities, goods, and services" without discrimination (Point 12). It goes beyond access to health care by noting that the right to health is "an inclusive right extending not only to timely and appropriate health care but also to the underlying determinants of health, such as access to safe and potable water and adequate sanitation, an adequate supply of safe food, nutrition and housing, healthy occupational and environmental conditions." These conditions are part of the enlarged definition of health and arguably influence measures of physical and mental health. Clearly this definition of health and the declaration of a right to the "highest attainable standard of health" require a paradigm shift in how we think about the causes of health, prevention of ill-health, and solutions to poor health in the United States.

While the UN and WHO declarations about health may have established a new discursive paradigm, this perspective was not sustained in most discussions of health issues in the decades that followed. As recently as twenty years ago, analyses that linked health to human rights would have been seen as radical (Mann 1997: 7). However, in more recent years the landscape has changed, with international and domestic groups moving toward a broader definition of health, and making the connection of health to human rights. Looking at health within a human rights framework requires us to ask different questions, evaluate situations differently, and pay attention to features of our society that are not now defined as relevant to health. In the sections that follow, health and human rights in the United States will be examined by looking at four elements of the human rights approach to health: "the highest attainable standard of health," the right to health care access, the importance of vulnerable groups, and the relevance of "social well-being."

"Highest Attainable Standard of Health"

The inclusion of the wording "highest attainable standard of health" expresses an important aspect of the human rights paradigm. From the time of the 1946 declaration on health as a human right, advocates saw a need for a pragmatic approach tied to what was possible in different countries. The UN charge on health and human rights is not for every country to achieve a standard goal. Rather, it is for each country to reach the highest attainable health given the overall conditions of the country. More could be expected of wealthy nations than might be feasible in very poor nations. Viewed thus, observers have found much to criticize in the United States. Considering the wealth of the United States, this country should be at the top of most country comparisons on health, but this is not the case.

There are multiple indicators that point to failings of the American health system to reach expected levels. The United States ranked 29th in the world in infant mortality in 2004, the latest year that data were available for all countries (MacDorman and Mathews 2008: 2) and tied with Poland and Slovakia. On measures of life expectancy, the U.S. "life expectancy for men (75.2 years) ranked 25th out of 37 countries and territories and 23rd for women (80.4 years)" (Quickstats 2008).

Right to Available, Affordable, and Accessible Health Care

A human rights framework suggests the right to health includes a health care system that is accessible to all without discrimination. Clearly the United States has failed dramatically here. It is the only industrialized nation in the world that does not have a universal health care system. Instead we have a patched-together mixture of access through insurance (largely private), supplemented by government programs (Medicare or Medicaid) that still fail to cover millions of individuals who, as a result, have limited and uncertain access to health care providers.

Many people in the United States have difficulty getting access to good health care primarily because access depends on a job-based system of private health insurance.[1] Over the years many problems have emerged with this system. In bad economic times, many employers cut back on health care coverage, turning full-time covered jobs into part-time jobs without benefits, and otherwise reduce the number of people with job-based health insurance. (The growing numbers of flexible workers, as discussed in an earlier chapter, further exacerbate this trend.) Since the 1960s Medicare and Medicaid sought to fill some insurance gaps among vulnerable populations, the elderly and selected groups of poor, such as extremely poor families with children. However, many Americans, currently estimated at just under 50 million, still have no health insurance.

Poor people, uninsured people, people on Medicaid, and people who live in low-income communities find access to health care difficult because some health care facilities refuse to accept them. Although people with life-threatening, emergency care needs are protected to some extent since federal laws and regulations require that a hospital provide at least minimal care, other poor people find few convenient, competent providers. One endemic problem is that hospitals want patients who pay full fare, and they work to discourage uninsured and poorly insured people from becoming their patients. To this end, hospitals check a person's health coverage to decide if they want to treat the patient, transfer patients to public facilities ("dumping" patients), discourage patient appointments by having long wait times for appointments or uncomfortable waiting rooms ("demarketing," Abraham 1993: 129), or otherwise create barriers to access. Not only do these actions directly contradict any mandate to treat health care as a human right but they also reinforce patterns of discrimination. One observer of the impact of these realities on disadvantaged minority groups summarizes the situation by saying "our system actively assigns racial minorities to an underfunded, overcrowded, and inferior public health sector" (Randall 2002: 52).

Health care reform is frequently on the table at the national level and most directly addresses issues of access. Many groups have analyzed the current reform based on human rights principles. One, the National Economic and Social Rights Initiative led by Anja Rudiger, has specifically laid out financing principles that meet human rights goals (Ten Health Care Financing Principles to Ensure Universality, Equity, and Accountability, nesri.org) as well as analyzed specific payer plans on the basis of these principles. Although the current Obama health care reform efforts will undoubtedly not fulfill all these principles after all the political compromises are made, it is important to keep a human rights framework in mind as the discussions proceed over the next years and decades.

Vulnerable Groups

The human rights perspective mandates paying special attention to vulnerable populations in society. Rather than being content with looking at overall measures of health, it is important to identify problems in the health conditions and treatment of groups that are at some social or economic disadvantage. Not only are overall statistics in the United States worse than other countries, persistent racial and class disparities in health and health care exist. Simply put, vulnerable populations do not do well on the whole.

The evidence of significant disparities is plentiful. Infant mortality, a key measure of health, shows major disadvantages among people of color in the United States. For instance "non-Hispanic" African Americans have an infant mortality rate of 13.63 per 1,000 compared to 5.76 for whites (Mac-Dorman and Mathews 2008: 3). Compared to white Americans, populations of color—particularly African Americans and indigenous populations—have distressingly higher rates of diabetes, heart disease, AIDS, TB, cervical cancer, obesity, and asthma (Randall 2002; Williams 1999).

Statistics in health care and health outcomes show problems tied to restricted access, as well as documenting how vulnerable groups receive worse treatment even if they are able to get access. These treatment disparities were highlighted in a 2003 Institute of Medicine report entitled *Unequal Treatment: Confronting Racial and Ethnic Disparities in Health Care*. The report documents that vulnerable groups "tend to receive a lower quality of healthcare across a range of disease areas (including cancer, cardiovascular disease, HIV/AIDS, diabetes, mental health, and other chronic and infectious diseases) and clinical services" (Smedley, Stith, and Nelson 2003: 2; Randall 2002: 57). Particularly disturbing is the fact that vulnerable groups are *more* likely to have some *un*desirable services. A tragic example: because their diabetes is not appropriately treated early enough, African Americans are *more* likely to have a limb amputated (McBean and Gornick 1994).

Other challenges face vulnerable groups because of communication barriers in interactions with health providers. Our increasing cultural diversity means more patients only speak English only as a second language, if at all. Thus, health care providers may literally be unable to talk to their patients, and can be unprepared to address diverse cultural beliefs, potentially at odds with standard Western medicine. The catastrophic results that can come from failed communication are documented in Fadiman's (1997) book *The Spirit Catches You and You Fall Down*, where she recounts the clash of Western medicine's view of epilepsy with the Hmong view. Although the lack of cultural understanding is often difficult to overcome (financially and in terms of staffing), the system has been unconscionably slow in even recognizing that competent interpreters are critical in a medical situation. Many clinical encounters are often conducted with little more than physical examinations—gathering data from a human as a veterinarian would gather data from an animal: no questions are asked. In other encounters, interpreters not trained in medical language or interpreters wholly inappropriate (young children, hospital maintenance people) have been used (Flores 2005).

"Social Well-Being," Not Just the Absence of Disease

One of the strengths of seeing health as a human right, or though a human rights framework, is that it expands the definition of health beyond "the absence of disease" and physical and mental well-being by saying that *social* well-being is an important part of the definition of health. By doing so it puts a focus on characteristics of American society such as the quality and availability of food, water, housing, and education that are typically overlooked. Earlier chapters by Deric Shannon, Barret Katuna, and Abraham P. DeLeon addressed human rights concerns pertaining to these basic needs. Differential exposure to social, environmental, occupational, economic, and other conditions that are unhealthy must be examined to fully capture the human rights definition of health. Such factors are also important because they contribute to physical and mental health disparities.

Differential exposure to the conditions of social health arises from institutional policies and practices. American society has long-standing structural barriers to equal access to housing, education, and employment. What is notable is that the enduring problems have not typically been viewed as health issues. Housing discrimination is one example. Racial and ethnic segregation, built on early racism and class-based differences in neighborhoods, became entrenched with neighborhood exclusion covenants, government lending practices, and more recently was furthered by lending institution discrimination (Freund 2007; Ratcliff 1980; NCRC 2008). The denial of mortgage loans to those in poor urban neighborhoods, sometimes through "redlining," has had a range of negative impacts. Redlined neighborhoods typically had fewer home owner-occupied housing and far more multifamily rental properties owned by absentee landlords. When an owner does not live in the housing they are less motivated to take care of the conditions of the housing, and that then leads to a plethora of unhealthy conditions, including dilapidated and crowded housing, exposure to lead paint, and increased potential for the spread of communicable diseases like tuberculosis. Desperately rundown neighborhoods also run a higher probability of unsafe streets, violence, and crime. And poverty-stricken neighborhoods are easier targets for excessive advertising by tobacco and alcohol industries because they are less powerful in their ability to demand resources like police protection or fend off the visual blight and compelling influence of advertising promoting unhealthy consumption (Hood 2005).

A human rights framework draws attention to important issues of environmental justice that are relevant to health. Studies consistently show that poor neighborhoods are more likely to have manufacturing companies, which produce toxic hazards, and to have toxic waste facilities. These connections happen in part because poor people move to, or stay in, communities with educationally appropriate job opportunities—meaning areas with blue collar jobs and often dirty industries. It also happens because an industry proposing to move to a lower-income neighborhood can be seductive for the community residents. There is, after all, the possibility of employment and new revenue coming into the neighborhood, even if there are potential health hazards from working in the industry or living in the surrounding community. Finally, it happens because resistance from poor neighborhoods are typically low because such communities lack the financial resources and connections to mount successful campaigns against businesses determined to move to the neighborhood (this would include, for example, significant costs for legal council and independent testing of environmental hazards). Although class is an obvious reason for differential exposure to toxic substances, research indicates that race is an independent factor associated with the placement of toxic waste facilities (Bullard, Mohai, Saha, and Wright 2007).

People in poor communities also suffer because of the lack of resources that could contribute in a positive way toward health. One glaring example is the lack of healthy food in poor neighborhoods. Although "food insecurity" is not as pronounced in the United States as it is in some countries, families in many poor neighborhoods discover it is very expensive or impossible to secure fresh fruits and vegetables. Poor neighborhoods are less likely to have a store from one of the larger chains and more likely to depend on small corner stores with a limited stock and higher prices (Larson, Story, and Nelson 2009). Poor neighborhoods also lack recreational facilities, open green spaces, and bike paths. Some people argue that these neighborhood characteristics directly affect health, such as the rate of childhood obesity (Kipke et al. 2007).

In addition to the direct impact on health, the socioeconomic inequality and racial segregation of neighborhoods in the United States has had profound structural impacts. It has led to inequality in educational opportunity because funding for school resources and the local tax base largely determines staffing quality. The resulting disparities in educational outcomes for neighborhood students then produce wide differences in occupational opportunities, meaning that a childhood in a poor neighborhood increases the risk one will work in a poorly paid occupation that is more likely to present a health risk (Randall 2002). Thus residential segregation is a foundational cause of inequalities in health when we view health more broadly, as embodied in the WHO definition.

Taking this broader view of health in terms of the impacts of the social and economic systems is a major feature of a human rights perspective. A formal human rights discourse also challenges people, organizations, and the government to change conditions so that we move further toward securing a greater realization of fundamental human rights, such as those related to individual and social/public health. We turn now to changes and struggles illustrative of such actions.

Health Reform Initiatives from a Human Rights Perspective

The federal government has often been inconsistent and weak in recognizing the need to address some of the major issues identified by human rights scholars and activists in the United States, but some actions have been taken. Historically the government established programs such as Medicaid, Medicare, and community health centers to increase access to health care. More recently, two examples of federal government initiatives are noteworthy. The first targets health disparities. In 1998 President Bill Clinton condemned as "unacceptable" the existing racial and ethnic heath disparities and authorized the establishment of a National Center on Minority Health and Health Disparities (NCMHD) within the National Institutes of Health (NIH). The various programs that resulted have encouraged research to understand existing disparities, improvement of screening, education and prevention efforts, and changes in service delivery to better serve vulnerable groups. Primary care associations in all regions of the country and various other provider groups have been mobilized to think and act differently. The primary actions coming from this initiative are disease focused and involve increasing access to care and improving quality of care for vulnerable groups. Thus while the initiative represents a significant investment by the federal government in linking health to human rights, it clearly only partially covers the issues that have been raised (Satcher and Higginbotham 2007).

A second government initiative focused on vulnerable groups began in 2000 with Executive Order 13166 and used the Civil Rights Act of 1964 to mandate that every federally conducted program improve health care access by people with limited English proficiency (LEP). The order officially recognized the inadequacy of "veterinary medicine" necessitated when a patient cannot speak English. Ideally it means that a patient will have easy access to a well-trained bilingual medical interpreter. In many health care facilities the implementation of this mandate has dramatically improved care for patients. Yet two problems exist. First, it is an unfunded mandate, requiring considerable initiative and expense from organizations and people to make it happen. Second, as Fadiman's (1997) work so clearly shows, the need is often for more than linguistically competent medical interpreters. To be truly effective, the role needs to be held by a cultural broker, a person who truly understands the health beliefs of particular cultures. To merely translate for a person whose blood testing will require several vials of blood does not address, for example, commonly diverse cultural beliefs concerning the unique role of one's blood in the care of body and soul. In other words, language is not the only barrier to effective communication between caregivers and patients, where not all cultures accept or interpret Western medicinal practices in the same way.

Similar linguistic and cultural concerns have been addressed by numerous local initiatives. One project among Latino/as found that immigrants did not understand the terms used by providers in treating and educating those suffering from diabetes. When more accessible language was used, and culturally attractive diet suggestions were made available, the patients, who had been labeled as "noncompliant," responded much better to treatment (Robert Wood Johnson Foundation 2009).

Such initiatives for reforms certainly do not transform the health conditions of the affected communities but they illustrate many barriers that need to be addressed if the goal of establishing health as a human right is to be fully realized. They show at least some willingness by the state to assume its responsibility for guaranteeing rights to health. Other efforts depend more on struggles where vulnerable communities and groups directly challenge prevailing powers.

Struggles over Health and Environmental Justice

In recent decades there have been many conflicts and struggles with groups and communities seeking to establish their rights to better health or to oppose conditions that would endanger their health. Groups emerge in local communities to challenge local adversaries. For example, one issue that has arisen in numerous community struggles has been the existence of lead paint in older urban housing. In these campaigns, organized community members attempt to force landlords and city officials to have the lead paint removed, and set policy to prevent further harm. The community health issues involved are serious, where lead ingestion can lead to brain and nervous system damage, learning and behavior problems, and slowed growth.

One notable lead paint campaign occurred in Baltimore, Maryland, where the Coalition to End Childhood Lead Poisoning directed its campaign at the owners of rental properties and at political officials who had previously resisted pressure for change. New legislation was passed and new efforts at tougher enforcement were launched. The effectiveness was impressive. By

2003 the frequency of childhood lead poisoning in Baltimore had decreased by 97 percent (Robert Wood Johnson Foundation 2009).

Other struggles have involved drawing on the techniques of community organizing to establish health resources for an entire community. In Oakland, California, a small primary care clinic that aimed to serve the large local Asian immigrant community was deemed inadequate for the needs of the community. The staff and community members reached out to patients and others in the community to demand their right to health care. Through these efforts what had been a single small clinic grew to become a comprehensive primary care facility that served 8,000 families (Robert Wood Johnson Foundation 2009).

The struggles over environmental justice, introduced above and seen by some as an "especially egregious form of denial of human rights" (Writing Group for the Consortium for Health and Human Rights 1998: 463), provide excellent examples of people struggling for their right to health. What is now an acknowledged environmental justice movement began at the grassroots with people concerned about the health of their neighborhoods. In North Carolina in the late 1970s, residents protested the toxicity of their neighborhood caused by the dumping of polychlorinated biphenyls (PCBs), which had been illegally spread along roads and then moved to a landfill in Warren County. Mass actions led to the arrest of more than 500 protesters. The resulting national publicity led to the 1987 report *Toxic Waste and Race* that became a key document for the environmental justice movement. Although initially unsuccessful in stopping the dumping in the local county, the community received some satisfaction nearly two decades later when in 2003 the state decontaminated the soil in the dump.

A case in Pensacola, Florida, also illustrates the potential of citizen mobilization for the right to health. There a neighborhood had been made toxic by two longstanding industries, a chemical fertilizer plant and a wood treatment plant, which used chemicals causing air and groundwater pollution. Residents complained about the pollution, noting the yellow sulfur caked on window screens and the contamination that had leached into their wells. When first challenged, the government response was to dig up the contaminated soil and stack it up. By 1993, more than 200,000 cubic yards had created a pile so high it came to be called "Mt. Dioxin." Recognizing that the leaching problem remained, the government covered Mt. Dioxin with a tarp that slowly deteriorated. Emboldened by 1994 Executive Order 12898, which places environmental injustice complaints squarely within federal laws, the residents, organized into Citizens Against Toxic Exposure (CATE), demanded that the government design a solution that would promote and improve public health.

CATE rejected the relocation of a subset of the community, and held out for a decision that all residents would be relocated (Lerner 2007).

A rather unique example occurred in Oakland, California, when the regional transit authority, BART, proposed building a major parking facility in a poor community. The residents mobilized around claims that the original design would have had a number of negative impacts such as pollution and increased traffic in their community. As a result of the pressure the local groups exerted, the original plan was scrapped and a new design, drawn after significant community participation, was accepted. It created a minimum of environmental and social costs and added community and social service facilities and high-quality affordable housing to the neighborhood. Thus not only were the negative impacts minimized, but community participation produced a design with positive health features (Unity Council 2009).

Conclusion

Examining health from a human rights perspective challenges us to think about individual and public health more broadly—to include the role of social structural and environmental factors. A human rights framework also suggests that states are on some level accountable for the provision of public health, and can be affected by domestic grassroots activism and resistance—as demonstrated in the several examples above. Indeed, community organizing campaigns and governmental initiatives have begun to express and reflect broader definitions of health and its causes. More fully incorporating such a perspective will be challenging because the questions raised, the inequities uncovered, and the rights demanded will be contested by a variety of vested interests. But the needs and potential benefits are great. A health care system and a societal view of health based firmly on the core principles of health as a human right could go far to improve the public health and quality of life for all in the United States.

PART III

CULTURAL RIGHTS

The Constitution of the United States formally articulates that the state cannot establish an official religion, nor can it prevent the creation of a religious group and its practices. This is consistent with the provisions of the Universal Declaration of Human Rights. However, neither document goes beyond the political and civil rights of individuals to ensure the cultural rights of groups. The Constitution's separation of church and state and its provision of freedom of religion imply but do not articulate cultural rights. Is there an important imperative to protect and promote cultural rights not only between nations but within nations? This notion of a presumed imperative of cultural rights as human rights raises several interesting questions about indigenous populations and other subcultures, particularly about Native Americans and ethnic, cultural, and religious subcultures within the United States.

Do ethnic, cultural, and religious subcultures have the right to speak their own languages other than English, practice religions other than the dominant Christianity, live on and use land as they have historically done and still enjoy the benefits enjoyed by the majority of citizens? If shared cultural practices solidify the members of society, do subcultural traditions and practices undermine that solidarity at the expense of individual rights? Are the rights of individuals more important than the rights of subcultures? Are these mutually exclusive?

The two chapters in this section explore these issues as they pertain to Native Americans and religious subcultures of Sikhs, Muslims, and Hindus in the United States.

CHAPTER NINE

We Are a People in the World: Native Americans and Human Rights

Barbara Gurr

This chapter focuses on Native American land rights, a collective right based on cultural beliefs and long-standing practice as much as legal precedent. I examine the struggles of the Western Shoshone People over conflicting meanings and practices tied to their ancestral homelands and interrogate the ways they have relied on ideologically liberal human rights instruments to claim collective rights and address historical and ongoing grievances. Ultimately it is my hope that this chapter will provide an entry point for further exploration of the ways existing international human rights instruments can be utilized in support of indigenous peoples' rights.

Generally speaking, the language and defining frameworks of international human rights law are not entirely theoretically adequate for Native peoples of the United States; derived largely from a Western, liberal perspective, they simply do not speak clearly enough to the complexities of Native worldviews or of Native-U.S. relations. This is not to say there is no use for a human rights perspective for Native American people. Native people need access to basic resources and freedoms to survive, as do others. However, the inextricably related conversation around cultural rights, which incorporates consideration of a group's ability to preserve its way of life and its identity as a distinct group, may ultimately offer greater potential for understanding the community orientation of many Native nations and the communal nature of the violations against them. Efforts to eradicate or assimilate Native American people have historically been enacted against Native peoples as a whole, and have included direct attacks against cultural practices such as language, religious practices, and family structures. A framework of cultural human rights, with its focus on group identity rather than individual rights, might reflect (more accurately) the needs of Native American populations. This framework would also provide a platform to promote, and hopefully address, historic and contemporary grievances of Native American communities.

For the most part, international human rights discourse has focused largely on the universal and inalienable rights of the individual. For instance, with few exceptions, all rights enumerated in the Universal Declaration of Human Rights are the rights of individuals. While it is important to note that the UDHR conceptualizes individuals as involved with different kinds of groups (for instance, the family, religious organizations, labor unions, and political contexts), the individual is still seen as separate and above the community. Obviously, there is much to be gained from an approach that values and protects individual freedom and dignity. Many Native American cultures, however, ascribe to a worldview that differs from the liberal, individualistic perspective embodied in international human rights instruments. While autonomy may be highly valued in many Native cultures, it is necessarily understood as embedded within community; as Grim points out, "Native American identity has rarely been understood in its cultural and social setting . . . Individualism . . . [has] been emphasized in a way that distorts the actual Native stress on individual identity in the context of cultural community" (1996: 353).

This symbiotic relationship between individual and community is described in Cheyenne philosophy in the context of the tipi, the traditional family home: "The individuals are like the poles of a tipi—each has his own attitude and appearance but all look to the same center . . . and support the same cover" (Straus 1982: 125). In this way, individuality "supports a tribal purpose, a tribal identity. Individual freedom does not consist in distinguishing oneself from the group. Indeed, without the tribe there is no freedom. There is only being lost." This sense of collective identity is produced and reproduced in Native American cultures through a variety of dynamic social structures and behaviors, including language, relationships, and ceremony. Many of these practices have deep historical roots with profound meaning for past and future generations.

It is in this sense that Native American individuals cooperatively construct a sense of themselves as Native Peoples, sovereign and distinct from other groups, including other Native nations. It is as Peoples, collectively rather than individually identified, that Native nations seek protection, and in many cases redress, from the state and from the international arena for historic and ongoing violations. Given the emphasis on community that is prevalent in many Native American worldviews, it becomes clearer why the focus of human rights discourse on the individual's inalienable rights as held against state and society may find only partial relevance in Native America. The related concepts emerging from cultural rights discourse, however, seem to apply more aptly to the needs of Native American populations.

Cultural rights are perhaps a more difficult notion to define and apply than traditional liberal rights, due in part to varying understandings of what constitutes "culture." Although a thorough discussion of culture is beyond the scope of this chapter, it is important to note that culture has been increasingly taken up in international human rights scholarship (see, for instance, Cowan, Dembour, and Wilson 2001; Harjo 1992; Kymlicka 1989, 1999). Additionally, the ways "culture" has historically been bound up with the exercise of power are particularly pertinent when considering Native-U.S. relations. The United States spent centuries attempting to impose a particular set of cultural values and behaviors on Native Americans, through the use of legislation, forced removals, and education, among other methods. In many ways this continues into the twenty-first century. As a result, claims to cultural rights in Native America often develop in response to these impositions and their consequences, as Native Americans seek to practice and protect their cultural lifeways in the face of historic and ongoing threats. However, the two conceptual frames—individual human rights and communally held cultural rights—are not neatly separable in terms of Native land rights in the United States. This is due in part to the inextricable relationship between land and identity in Native cultures.

"The Land Is Our Mother"— The Western Shoshone Land Case

For many people, land carries myriad meanings: it is available for commercial and private use, and it provides a potential source of both life and income, for instance. In the global economy, land takes on additional meaning for multinational corporations as a source of revenue and exploitable natural resources. However, for Native peoples, land often carries profound cultural meanings, as well. For many Native nations, particularly those who still enjoy regular access to their ancestral homelands, land can be imbued with a profound sense of historical identity (Silko 1996; Akers 1999). Homeland can be where the ancestors are buried, where sacred ceremonies are performed, and where relatives abide (Silko 1996; Looking Horse 1992; Scarberry 1982). For the Western Shoshone, for instance, Mt. Tenabo is a site of sacred creation stories and continually practiced rituals, a resource for medicinal plants, and provides a source of food and water for the surrounding communities. Western Shoshone Mary Gibson describes it as "a living being, a living relative" (Earthworks 2007), worthy of the same respect given to other relatives. Western Shoshone Carrie Dann describes this sense of relationship by explaining that "We were taught that we were placed here as caretakers of the lands, the animals, all the living things . . . .We see the four most sacred things as the land, the air, the water and the sun . . . .This is our religion—our spirituality—and defines who we are as a people" (cited in Fishel 2006/7: 624).

Land, to Native peoples, is an essential aspect of cultural identity. The loss of land, therefore, imposes an irreconcilable loss to current and future generations that goes beyond financial investment. Many of the treaties signed between the United States and Native nations include the cession of land to the United States. Unlike other Native nations, however, the Western Shoshone never ceded land to what they considered and still consider a foreign government. In the 1863 Treaty of Ruby Valley they retained all rights to the use and enjoyment of their ancestral homeland, Newe Sogobia ("People's Earth Mother"). The United States is in long-standing violation of Western Shoshone land rights as delineated in the treaty. Currently, the violations take several forms, including forced removal of Western Shoshone livestock, location of several U.S. military bases on Western Shoshone land, and federal support of commercial development within Newe Sogobia. The U.S. assumption of sovereignty and exercise of control over Western Shoshone lands is in direct violation of several internationally recognized human rights. These include several articles in the UDHR, such as Article XII (the right to freedom and protection from arbitrary interference with one's privacy, family, home, or correspondence) and Article XVII (the right to own property alone, as well as in association with others; the right to freedom and protection from being arbitrarily deprived of property).

Importantly, the violation of these human rights has also led to increasing threats against Western Shoshone cultural practices, particularly spiritual practices. The current inability of the Western Shoshone to fully engage in traditional ceremonies due to the incursion of the U.S. government and commercial interests on their land is in direct violation of their cultural rights as outlined in several international instruments, including International Labour Organization Convention 169 (particularly Articles XIII–XVII, which specifically discuss indigenous relationships to land) and the UN Declaration on the Rights of Indigenous Peoples. Though the United States refused to ratify this treaty, along with other nations, such as Australia, who share a history of brutal oppression against indigenous populations, the treaty suggests some level of international consensus on the legitimate rights of Native nations with regard to the U.S. government.

The U.S. disregard for the rights of the Western Shoshone has resulted in a long and complex series of maneuvers by both sides contesting the meaning of land and the right to claim it. The latter half of the twentieth century in particular witnessed an increasingly determined effort by the Western Shoshone to protect their land and their sovereignty. This effort entered the domestic legal arena in 1951, when a small band of Western Shoshone put forth a claim to the Indian Claims Commission (ICC). However, the Western Shoshone Nation was not a part of this claim, and in fact quickly rejected the claim and attempted to have it removed, including formally terminating relations with the attorneys claiming to represent them. The ICC, however, moved ahead with the claim despite the Western Shoshone's formal withdrawal of counsel. The ICC eventually decided in favor of the United States, ruling that the "gradual encroachment" of non-Native people and interests into Newe Sogobia supported the federal government's claim to the territory as public lands (*Shoshone Tribe v. United States*, 1962).[1] The United States was ordered to pay approximately fifteen cents per acre to the Secretary of the Interior in exchange for control over approximately 85 percent of Western Shoshone territory. This money remains in a Treasury Department account, as the Western Shoshone Nation refuses to acknowledge any legal sale of their land (see Fishel 2006/7).

The Western Shoshone responded to the appropriation of their land by filing an appeal with the Ninth Circuit, which found in favor of the Western Shoshone in proceedings that rejected the ICC findings. Soon afterward, the federal government filed an appeal with the Supreme Court to force acceptance of payment for extinguished land title. In 1985, the U.S. Supreme Court found in favor of the federal government and ruled that payment made to the Department of the Interior, as "trustee" for the Western Shoshone, constituted their acceptance, despite prolonged and public protest by the Western Shoshone. This decision from the highest U.S. court triggered a bar to further judicial action in the United States, essentially preventing the Western Shoshone from further domestic legal action. However, the Western Shoshone have turned in recent years (and with better success) to the international community for legal redress.

In 1993, the Indian Law Resource Center filed a petition with the Inter-American Commission on Human Rights (IACHR) on behalf of Western Shoshone sisters Mary and Carrie Dann. In their petition to the IACHR, the Danns specifically challenged the Supreme Court's 1985 ruling, arguing that it prevented them from asserting a defense of Western Shoshone aboriginal title against federal trespass actions, thereby depriving them of adequate judicial protection and impeding their use and enjoyment of their ancestral lands. Based on these circumstances, the Danns (representing the Western Shoshone Nation) alleged that the United States was in violation of several articles of the American Declaration of the Rights and Duties of Man (to which the U.S. is party), namely, Article II (right to equality before the law), Article III (right to religious freedom and worship), Article VI (right to a family and to protection thereof), Article XIV (right to work and to fair remuneration), Article XVIII (right to a fair trial), and Article XXIII (right to property).

In July 2002, the IACHR released its findings to the public, stating unequivocally that the United States was in violation of international human rights in its treatment of Mary and Carrie Dann, and supporting the Danns' argument that the U.S. government's use of the ICC to gain control of Western Shoshone lands was illegitimate (cited in Fishel 2006/7). This was the first time any international body had issued a finding that the United States had violated the rights of Native Americans. Prior to releasing its report publicly, the IACHR released a copy in confidence to the U.S. Department of the Interior, which rejected the Commission's report "in its entirety" (Sansani 2003: 2). In fact, one month later, the U.S. Bureau of Land Management proceeded with an armed seizure of more than 400 Western Shoshone horses in its continuing attempt to remove Western Shoshone people from their land.

In order to access the IACHR, the Western Shoshone petition was based largely on liberal human rights claims against the state, and officially presented by two individuals (the Dann sisters). Shortly after their victory with the IACHR, however, the Western Shoshone adopted a stance that, while inclusive of and reliant on a liberal human rights framework, nonetheless more explicitly incorporated cultural rights discourse. In 1999, the Western Shoshone filed a petition with the Committee to End Racial Discrimination (CERD),[2] detailing a pattern of racially discriminatory behavior on the part of the United States, which included violations of right to property, equality under the law, judicial and administrative processes, cultural integrity, and self-determination. This first petition never received a separate decision, but was instead included in CERD's Concluding Observations, in which the committee urged the United States to "take all appropriate measures . . . to ensure effective protection against any form of racial discrimination and any unjustifiably disparate impact" (cited in Fishel 2006/7: 643).

A renewed filing by the Western Shoshone in 2005 was met with strong support from CERD members. In March of 2006, CERD's official report informed the United States that the longstanding issues with the Western Shoshone "warrant immediate and effective action . . . [and] should be dealt with as a matter of priority" (cited in Fishel 2006/7: 646). Furthermore, the

United States was urged to pay "particular attention to the right to health and cultural rights of the Western Shoshone peoples, which may be infringed upon by activities threatening their environment and/or disregarding the spiritual and cultural significance they give to their ancestral lands" (646). That same year, the UNHRC formally chastised the United States for violation of Article I (the right to self-determination and the right to freely determine political status and pursue economic, social, and cultural development) and Article XXVII (the right to enjoy one's own culture, profess and practice one's own religion, and use one's own language).

The violation of the basic human and cultural rights of indigenous peoples by the United States, a member of the international community and a party to several international treaties and organizations including the UN and the Organization of American States, has been formally recognized on the international stage. It remains now to see how—and whether—the United States will address these violations and work to restore dignity and freedom to Native nations. The ongoing struggles between Native peoples and the U.S. government illustrate the continued inability of international human rights instruments to enforce accountability on individual states— perhaps one of the greatest weaknesses of the international system since the inception of international law. Despite formal international censure and ongoing international protest, the United States continues to treat Western Shoshone territory as federal land, supporting the efforts of multinational mining corporation Barrick Gold in Newe Sogobia. The Barrick project, proposed for development on Mt. Tenabo, directly threatens sacred Shoshone ritual grounds, harms important water sources, and will result in the loss of 817 acres of pinon trees, which provide a traditional Western Shoshone food source (see Norrell 2008a, b; Wolf 2009). The damage to Shoshone ways of life that will result from this project is inestimable, and will impact generations to come. The Western Shoshone continue to protest the presence of both the United States and Barrick Gold on their lands. Their efforts to secure their cultural rights to their sacred land and Shoshone practices continue in both domestic and international arenas, and include not only formal international human rights instruments, but also grassroots protests, community trainings and education, and local and transnational coalitions.

The Western Shoshone insertion of cultural rights discourse into the liberal human rights instruments available to them illustrates how individual-oriented human rights and group-oriented cultural rights might be taken up simultaneously by Native American nations. At the same time, the increasing adoption of cultural rights discourse in the Western Shoshone petitions and in both CERD and UNHRC responses signals a growing international willingness to understand cultural rights as potentially unique and profoundly important to human rights practice with respect to indigenous populations. This synthesis of human rights and cultural rights discourses in the Western Shoshone case also reflects the increasing potential of this emerging legal frame for managing claims to human rights violations on a communal scale. Perhaps most importantly, the bold movement of the Western Shoshone from the failed domestic legal arena to international human rights forums marks a shift in human and cultural rights discourse around indigenous people specifically. As Fishel asserts, "With the IACHR Final Report and the CERD Decision, the claims of Indigenous Peoples to ongoing human rights violations by the United States are no longer allegations; they are facts" (2006/7: 648).

The failure of the United States thus far to significantly alter its Indian policies or change its treatment of the Western Shoshone in response to international censure from CERD and the UN Human Rights Committee reflects U.S. unwillingness to acknowledge and respect the rights and dignity of Native American nations. However, the increasing global recognition of indigenous rights, which arguably needs to incorporate both liberal/individual and cultural concepts of human rights, may yet prove productive in bringing the United States to improve and drastically change its relationships with Native American nations. Ultimately, international pressure may force the United States to contend with its own human rights violations in a more productive manner. It can begin by recognizing the cultural rights and human dignity of all peoples in this world, including the Native nations within its own borders.

CHAPTER TEN

Reflections on Cultural Human Rights

Miho Iwata and Bandana Purkayastha

The presence of "new" immigrants[1] since the latter half of the twentieth century, especially groups who trace their origins to Asia, Latin America, and Africa, has increased the cultural, especially linguistic and religious, diversity in the United States. Their presence has also led to new conflicts over the extent to which their cultures—especially their religions and languages— should be accommodated in the United States. In the aftermath of the 9/11 attacks, Muslim and "Muslim looking" people, such as Sikh men who wear turbans as part of their religious practice, experienced acts of hatred in the United States and Europe. These acts varied from personal insults, vandalizing of "Muslim-run" small businesses and places of worship, to murders of Muslims and Sikhs (Talpur 2009). Muslim and Muslim-looking groups have also experienced the negative effects of being racially profiled as "security risks" by a variety of agencies (Narayan and Purkayastha 2009). Their experiences in twenty-first-century United States remind us that people who participate in "other" cultural practices are not always able to enjoy the cultural rights—such as the right to practice religion—that are guaranteed by the U.S. Constitution. In this chapter, we discuss the experiences of immigrant groups and the conflicts over their religio-cultural practices.[2] We focus on religion to discuss cultural human rights and the difficulties of claiming these rights through states. We begin with a brief discussion of "culture" as it is defined in various formal international and national political documents. Then we draw on recent case studies, newspaper reports, and accounts of activist groups, to describe some of the challenges groups face as they practice their religions in the United States. We conclude by discussing some of the debates over granting cultural human rights within states.

What Are Cultural Human Rights?

In the making of the Universal Declaration of Human Rights, indigenous people and other colonized groups actively pursued, and succeeded, in inserting their claim for cultural human rights into the human rights charter (Lauren 2003). These groups had faced significant threats to their cultures because of the actions of groups in power, including the Nazi plans to exterminate the Jews and attempts by colonial powers to "civilize" people. These groups were interested in making sure that UDHR institutionalized rights of groups to practice and sustain their cultures,[3] especially when powerful groups embarked on projects to stigmatize, control, restrict, and, on occasion, exterminate these groups because of "their culture." Barbara Gurr's chapter in this book provides one example of an indigenous group that continues to struggle to regain their right to live in ways that is culturally appropriate to them.

References to cultural human rights are evident throughout the UDHR and its associated instruments. While no instrument exclusively defines these rights, collectively, they address some of the major structural and interpersonal barriers to realizing cultural human rights in practice. The instruments emphasize that the right to practice one's own culture is based on the ability of people to claim a constellation of political, civil, social, and economic rights in order to live a life of human dignity. The UDHR, ICSECR, ICCPR, and ICERD ensure protection of human rights without discrimination based on race, color, sex, language, religion, political or other opinion, national or social origin, property, or birth origin. The UDHR emphasizes nondiscrimination on the basis of language, religion, and other criteria repeatedly; Article 18 specifically states "Everyone has the right to freedom of thought, conscience and religion; this right includes freedom to change his religion or belief, and freedom, either alone or in community with others and in public or private, to manifest his religion or belief in teaching, practice, worship and observance." The ICESCR further emphasizes cultural rights. Specifically, Article 15(1) states, "The States Parties to the present covenant recognize the right of everyone to take part in cultural life." In addition, the ICCPR asserts the right to freedom of adopting religion or belief of choice, and "freedom, either individually or in community with others, and in public or private, to manifest his [or her] religion or belief in worship, observance, practice and teaching" (Art. 18(1)). Furthermore, Article 27 states that, "In those States in which ethnic, religious or linguistic minorities exist, persons belonging to such minorities shall not be denied the right, in community with the other members of their group, to enjoy their own culture, to profess and practice their own religion, or to use their own language."

Recognizing the structural barriers that negatively affect the practice of minority cultures, and the ways in which cultures are used to construct racial differences, the human rights instruments also address the structural context in which cultural human rights can be claimed. The ICERD adds that it seeks to "promote and encourage universal respect for and observance of universal rights and fundamental freedoms for all without distinctions as to race, sex, language or religion." Article 1 of ICERD adds: "In this Convention, the term 'racial discrimination' shall mean any distinction, exclusion, restriction or preference based on race, colour, descent, or national or ethnic origin which has the purpose or effect of nullifying or impairing the recognition, enjoyment or exercise, on an equal footing, of human rights and fundamental freedoms in the political, economic, social, cultural or any other field of public life" emphasizing the notion of discrimination on the basis of culture. The theme of culture is repeated through many ICERD articles. Chapters by Bandana Purkayastha, Aheli Purkayastha, and Chandra Waring and William T. Armaline examine issues of racism in the United States in further detail in regards to contradiction with the language of the ICERD.

Together, these international instruments, have, over time, attempted to establish principles of cultural human rights and the social and political conditions that are necessary for the exercise of those rights. Two important facets of cultural human rights are worth noting. First, they recognize and attempt to protect diverse ways of composing lives of human dignity (i.e., protection against the will of the powerful to homogenize or civilize cultural minority groups). Second, while the UDHR focuses on human rights of individuals,[4] the later instruments recognize cultural practices "in community with others" and structural barriers that affect people "in cultural or any other field of public life." Since states are supposed to enforce these rights, in practice, these assumptions about human rights to enjoy cultural (in this case religious) life freely, is often in conflict with nationalist projects to assimilate "others."

Unlike the UDHR and its conventions, there is no mention of cultural rights per se in the U.S. Constitution, but there is a certainly a constitutional guarantee of religious freedom. This political freedom to practice religion, along with the individual rights to freedom of speech, association, and so on, are assumed to provide a sufficient guarantee for people to practice all types of religions. However, all religions are not practiced like Christianity and religious traces—such as clothes, religious symbols, ways of expressing religious identities—that appear to "spill" onto other arenas of people's lives, often come up against the laws that demarcate the ways rights to religion ought to be exercised. The struggle over cultural human rights—in this case, the right to freely practice religions—becomes especially difficult when "others'" religious practices are considered unacceptable or even against the laws of the United States. As we illustrate in the next section, the right to *religious* freedom does not *sufficiently* deal with structural barriers to the religio-cultural freedom that is necessary for cultural minority groups whose beliefs and practices do not fit the understanding of "religion" of the American major-ity[5] to claim and practice their cultural human rights in the United States.

Another factor complicates the acceptance of cultural human rights in the United States: our understanding of culture is shaped by an ongoing national-ist discourse on cultural assimilation. As in many other nation-states, there is an expectation in the United States that immigrants—those whose language, religion, and so on are distinctive from the mainstream—will merge into a national culture over time.[6] The classical idea of assimilation, espoused in both scholarly circles and popular discourse, reflects the expectation that immigrants will give up or mold their culture and adopt the ("modern," "superior") ways of the dominant mainstream.[7] The idea of *cultural human rights*, that intend to *sustain* groups with distinctive cultures, is at odds with this popular, often taken for granted idea that cultural minority groups will change and *merge* with the mainstream.

The United States has become more multicultural since the last few decades of the twentieth century, but there is a general expectation that oth-ers' cultures can be accommodated within existing structural contexts. Thus people can celebrate their different cultures periodically in weekend fairs and festivals or in private community spaces (or spaces of worship); but there are rarely any discussions about cultural *rights*. The markets have also embraced multiculturalism, so that "cultural items," that is, merchandise marketed on the basis of association with particular cultural groups, are widely evident of consumption through mainstream outlets.[8] In many people's minds, multi-culturalism is equated with the freedom to consume multicultural merchan-dise. In other words, there is a greater recognition of different cultures in the United States, but there are ongoing conflicts over which cultural practices—including which types of religious practices—are to be accommodated. [9]

Questions about people's access to cultural human rights capture these accommodations and conflicts. Since most members of majority groups are able to take for granted the institutional arrangements, patterned interac-tions, and ideologies that help to produce and sustain their religious, linguis-tic, and other cultural practices, they rarely appreciate the barriers minority cultural groups face if their cultures do not fit the ways of the majority. For instance, religions that have congregation-type organizations can fit easily into the definitions of religions and religious institutions codified in laws; those that do not follow such practice—for example, Native American religions, Hinduism—face significant barriers. As we will discuss in the next section, minority cultural practices—specifically, religio-cultural practices—are often marked socially and politically, and subject to a variety of discriminatory practices, so that minority cultural groups are not always able to freely practice their religions.

Living Cultures, Living Religions in the United States

The events after the September 11, 2001, terrorist attacks on the United States catapulted turban-wearing men and hijab-wearing women into the American public's mind. Turbans and hijabs are excellent examples of the religio-cultural expressions we indicated in the previous section, but there are a number of other constraints that impede people's ability to exercise their cultural human rights.

A significant barrier religious minority groups face is that they do not have the right to formal holidays for celebrating religious events (see Narayan and Purkayastha 2009 for accounts of Hindu and Muslim women). Without formal leave, people are not able to practice their religious rituals at appropriate times; at best, they can sacrifice "personal days," or, if they are in schools or college, they can take a day off for celebrations. Indeed, as the United States becomes more multicultural, many workplaces and universities have begun to recognize and respect people's rights to take time off for religious observances. Nonetheless, there is structural inequality built into this system: unlike the majority group—Christians—who are able to enjoy Christmas freely, practitioners of "other" religions have to *make up the missed work* some other time. If they postpone a test in college, it has to be taken on a different day, if they trade work-time with a colleague, they have to substitute for them some other time, if they take a personal day, then they have one less day for personal needs. Importantly, the ability to take time off often depends on employed people's work structure. People who work in hourly wage jobs or temporary jobs do not have the luxury to make such "personal" arrangements to join their community members for religious or cultural celebrations.

Access to public spaces for religio-cultural celebrations is another problematic issue. Religious celebrations that spill onto public space—for instance, the Hindu festival of Diwali, which includes fireworks—cannot be practiced in the United States (e.g., Purkayastha 2009). Muslim or Hindu prayers that occur outside temples and mosques have often been a source of conflict with local officials.[10] Some women have pointed out that when people die, religious rites that cannot be confined to funeral parlors, such as immersing the ashes in the flowing water of rivers, run afoul of a series of local laws (e.g., Ranjeet 2009).

In some instances institutions have attempted to accommodate minority religious practices; but this has led to significant conflict. For instance, over the last few years, a number of U.S. colleges began to install foot-washing stations in restrooms after they realized that Muslim students were using washbasins to wash their feet before their customary prayers (Lewin 2007). However, this public accommodation of a religious practice had ignited a significant controversy about the separation of religious and public matters (e.g., Fox News 2007). Similarly, a San Diego school that allowed children to take several recesses to accommodate prayers of Muslim students ended up canceling this practice after it was challenged as an accommodation to a religious practice ("San Diego School" 2007). A whole series of struggles are underway over building permits for temples, mosques, gurudwaras (Sikh temples) in different locales.

Another religio-cultural conflict involves people's attire in public spaces. Turbans, for instance, have become the symbol of suspicion and controversy, especially since 9/11. The focus on the turban-wearing Al Qaeda and Taliban males in the media inaccurately equates turbans exclusively with Islam. Male followers of Islam are not *required* to wear turbans, although, depending on local cultural norms, some Muslim men do so. However, turbans are a *required* religious symbol for men who practice Sikhism. Sikh men are supposed to display five signs of their faith as a tangible expression of their religious identity. While most people would not dispute Sikhs' right to pray in their gurudwaras, other aspects of their religion generate conflict. Three of these—keeping long hair and beards, wearing a turban, and carrying a ceremonial "dagger" called a kirpan—have generated significant controversies in the United States (and Canada and many European countries). As Valarie Kaur's documentary—*Divided We Fall: Americans in the Aftermath*—shows, the first person killed after 9/11 because he was thought to be an enemy of the United States, was Balbir Singh Sondhi, a Sikh man who was targeted because of his turban.

As "neutral" security rules are set up in airports and in buildings around the country, several religio-cultural symbols have been marked as "security risks." Sikh men have to contend with constant expectations that they take off their turbans. The web-based instructions "Flying While Sikh" on the Sikh coalition website provides a glimpse of the ways in which this group has to remain conscious of their identity at all times to deal with misunderstandings, prejudices, and attacks.[11] The Sikh Educational and Legal and Defense Fund (SALDEF) and a number of other Sikh groups have launched massive cam-

paigns to educate the public about Sikh turbans, and to address the harassment Sikh men face for wearing a required religious symbol. Sikh groups
have begun to identify places where they are most likely to be targeted. For
example, there are reports that Sikhs began to avoid San Francisco airport
because of perceptions of racial profiling.[12] After a significant lobbying by
SALDEF and other Sikh organizations, the Transportation Security Agency
issued a new set of rules in 2007 about Sikhs, but the enforcement of these
guidelines are not always uniform.

Sikhs have also been targeted for carrying kirpans. For instance, in 2008,
a Sikh truck driver was arrested when he arrived at the Stamford, Connecticut, superior court to challenge a traffic violation; the marshals arrested him
for possession of a "dangerous weapon" (Gabhruji 2008). Sikhs have organized all over the country to claim their religio-cultural right to wear this
symbol of their faith. After prolonged lobbying and negotiation, Homeland
Security agreed in 2006 to post pictures of the types of kirpans Sikhs wear,
ranging from "pendants" on necklaces to three- to six-inch "blades." In California, after successful lobbying by the Sikh community, a bill to educate law
enforcement personnel about Sikh turbans and kirpans passed the Assembly
(77-0) and the Senate (36-0), but it was vetoed by Governor Schwarzeneggar
in October 2009.[13]

The controversies and conflicts over the Sikh religious symbols show how
access to cultural rights intersects with access to civil and political rights.
Recently, two U.S. army personnel were removed from active duty for failing
to cut their hair and remove their turbans, as part of the army's rule (from
1981) to remove all *visible* signs of religious affiliation (Hanifa 2009). In the
case of these (Sikh) physicians, their recruiters had assured them they could
keep their beards and turbans, and they encountered this rule after they com-
pleted their medical training and sought active duty. From the Sikh perspective, being able to wear a turban is an issue of religious freedom. However,
the "neutral" security rules, which lead to targeting Sikh religious symbols or
the hate crimes they have experienced, illustrate the nexus of cultural human
rights and political and civil human rights violations. Since groups like the
Sikhs have to maintain a vigil to safeguard themselves against institutionalized discrimination or interpersonal hate crimes, their lives are diminished
compared to other Americans who do not have to contend with such rights
violations every day.

Such controversies are not only about Sikh religious symbols. Controversies over hijabs demonstrate the religio-cultural practices that are not, as yet,
accommodated in the United States. The Qur'an, the holy book of Islam, asks
people to be modestly dressed and in many Muslim cultures, women wear

hijabs[14] to conform to this standard. Like the conflation of the turban with "Muslim Terrorist," the hijab has become a symbol of Muslim women's subordination and traditionalism among large sections of the American mainstream. Thus, for many Americans, the hijab acts as a symbol of Muslims' nonassimilation into modern ways. It becomes a marker of "foreignness," despite the fact that at least 25 percent of Muslims are native black or white Americans. Muslim women are the targets of racial slurs, harassment, profiling for "security reasons," and patronizing behaviors to "encourage" them to "become empowered" (Jamil 2009). While many Muslim women have begun to wear hijabs to challenge these discriminatory behaviors and ideologies, the important point here is the curtailment of their cultural human rights through these ongoing discriminatory practices (al-Hibri 1999; Reed and Bartkowski 2000). Several Muslim organizations have been working very actively, like the Sikh groups, to raise the mainstream's consciousness about Islam and Muslims as a strategy for addressing discrimination. However, the need to remain vigilant about their surroundings inhibits these minority religious groups from enjoying the full range of freedoms that are the cornerstone of human rights documents.

Most Americans tend to place religion in a separate compartment from cultural practice. They think of religion as a set of practices that take place in homes or in churches on Sundays or designated holidays. But, as these cases show, such understanding of culture and religion only reflect the practices of the American mainstream. Religion and culture overlap for American Christians, too, but this overlap is rendered invisible because "American culture" remains unmarked.

The period after 9/11 has seen an increase in conflicts over these rights. UN Special Rapporteur on human rights of migrants Jorge Bustamante (2008) reported the worsening trend of xenophobia and racism toward migrants since those terrorist attacks. He lists "migrants who are, or are perceived to be, Muslim or of South Asian or Middle Eastern descent" (2008, 2) as one of the most vulnerable groups among the migrant population. Immigrants and their U.S. born descendents who exhibit features perceived to be of foreign or dangerous religious practices have become conflated with discussions about "national security" and consequently legitimized xenophobia and racism in the United States at the interpersonal level. The negligence of minority cultural and religious human rights by the state perpetuates institutional discrimination by violating a range of human rights. While hundreds of groups, including SALDEF and the Muslim Legal Defense and Education Fund, are working to claim human rights and address discrimination, in the end, the responsibility for ensuring these human rights depends on the rest of us, since the discriminatory barriers experienced by minority groups were not created by them. Our lack of engagement in these issues undermines the principle of the *human* rights for all, not simply for the privileged few.

Culture and Questions of Rights

Since the task of ensuring human rights falls on states, there is an ongoing debate about the extent to which Western democracies should accommodate minority cultural practices. The question of cultural human rights is related to these debates about granting cultural rights within states. In academic discourse, there are two distinct approaches to such cultural rights discussions. In a seminal book, Canadian scholar Will Kymlicka (1995) proposed that Western democracies ought to provide multicultural citizenship, that is, give minority groups special cultural rights to make them equal to the majority groups whose rights are assured by national constitutions. These special rights of minority cultural groups are to be worked out after a close examination of the contexts and the needs of particular groups. Most important, those special cultural rights are only to be given to those groups that are internally liberal, so that the group accommodates diversity among its members. Kymlicka further argued that only those cultures that do not violate criminal laws of a country could be granted these cultural rights. These discussions of multicultural citizenship come closest to the principles of cultural human rights. The proposal attempts to ensure people are able to freely practice their cultures without trampling on the rights of others (through criminal practices). Thus Sikh turbans and hijabs could be accommodated, as well as religious worship that spills out beyond religious institutions.

However, Kymlicka's arguments have been severely criticized on the grounds that assimilating with modern cultures is good for "traditional" cultural groups (i.e., cultures of people from Asia, Africa, Latin America). Scholars have argued that granting group rights undermines the edifice of individual rights that are central to Western democracies. More specifically, some scholars have argued that granting any minority groups special cultural rights is bad for women because it would allow a segment of male members to use "culture" as a tool to control women of that group (see Okin 1999).[15] Controversies over the freedom to wear hijabs are, very often, framed in terms of freeing women from controlling traditional practices.[16]

Two key points are raised through these debates. There is likely to be little support for cultural rights through states (or support for the more expansive and flexible notion of cultural human rights) as long as majority groups in nation-states subscribe to the ideology that Western ways of life are the standard to which all others should assimilate. In matters of religion, the guarantee of religious freedom in democratic constitutions often means that the mainstream pays little attention to the ways structures set up to ensure freedom of religion for Christianity may contribute to the barriers for minority cultural groups. Thus the ideology of assimilation drowns out any discussion of barriers to groups practicing their religions. The second point relates to the process through which cultural rights ought to be accommodated within established states. To what extent should structures within nation-states be changed to accommodate a diversity of cultural practice. Would this be accomplished through incremental changes? Earlier Jews struggled to achieve the freedom to practice their religion (Sarna and Dahlin 1997); should contemporary groups wait for generations to reach similar acceptance? But at a time when more groups are impatient about claiming their rights now, at a time when they have the resources to organize on transnational scales to claim their rights, such incremental progress does not meet human rights standards. Equally important, accommodating religions like Hinduism that are organized in very decentralized, noncongregational forms, or Sikhism, which requires practicing a visible religious identity at all times, would require significant legal and cultural changes. Whether this can be achieved remains an open question.

Conclusion

The brief discussion here presents some of the conflicts and challenges of ensuring cultural human rights through states. Culture is shaped by and lived through existing social structures, and cultural human rights have to be ensured through conventions on civil, political, antiracism, and antisexism human rights as well. Within the United States, the way the term religion is enshrined in the Constitution often prevents us from understanding the multifaceted nature of religio-cultural rights. We also often fail to see how these religio-cultural practices are used for racial profiling and discrimination, because these appear to be practices of "migrants" who are expected to assimilate over time, and become American like other migrants in U.S. history (e.g., Ignatiev 1995; Sacks 1997, irrespective of the different circumstances within which the current struggles are situated.

The concept of cultural human rights that encompasses the right to practice cultures and the right to nondiscrimination has the potential to fundamentally challenge how questions of "others'" cultures are accommodated within Western democracies such as the United States. Cultural human rights were written into the human rights documents to ensure that minority cultural groups were not subject to social and political forces that led to their extinction. The long experience of many colonized nations and indigenous groups with "civilizing," modernizing forces of colonialists led to their championing of cultural human rights in the UDHR. The question for us here is whether such cultural human rights ought to be respected. As we described here, even the right to practice religions, a right granted by the U.S. Constitution, is contingent on a series of political issues of the time. Cultural human rights are intended to address this contingency. In other words, the intention of cultural human rights is to safeguard minority religious groups from the demands of the majority that they—the minority groups—significantly alter their ways of life, or sacrifice their freedoms for the good of "all." So, from a human rights perspective, "culture" and "religion," cultural rights and civil rights, cannot be separated if we wish to ensure people can access their cultural human right to practice their religion.

In sum, cultural human rights are key components for imagining and composing lives of freedom and dignity, the principal objective of UDHR. Exercising cultural human rights requires that individuals and collectivities have the ability—through structural arrangements—to exercise agency. Since cultural human rights imply collectivities have rights, balancing the rights of individuals and such collectivities through states remains controversial and contested.

PART IV

POLITICAL AND CIVIL RIGHTS

When we consider political and civil rights we are generally referring to rights and freedoms in the public arenas of society and our relationship with the state. Individuals, as human beings, have a right to fair and equitable treatment by the state: we have the right to recognition as a person before the law, to equality before the law, and to the presumption of innocence until proven guilty; the right to freedom from arbitrary arrest and detention; the right to legal recourse when our rights have been violated, even when the violators of our rights may have been acting in some official capacity; the right to freedom from slavery or involuntary servitude, torture or degrading treatment; and the right to appeal a conviction in a court of law. In addition, individuals have the right to life, liberty, and freedom of movement; the right to freely choose whom to marry; the right to privacy and protection of that privacy by law; the right to freedom of thought, conscience, religion, opinion, and expression; and the right to freely associate with other individuals and to assemble. These suggest, as well, a right to resistance to a state that does not adequately protect these rights.

Such rights are included not only in the U.S. Constitution; they are among the rights included in the UDHR and the ICCPR. But what happens when there is an apparent national crisis, as appeared to be the case after the attacks on the World Trade Center and the Pentagon on September 11, 2001? Do concerns for national security trump political and civil rights? More fundamentally, what does "security" mean, and is it mutually exclusive with liberties and rights? Is there a necessary trade-off between security and rights? If so, whose rights will be compromised to reinforce whose security? Who defines a crisis? Who or what determines which rights must be suspended to defend national security, and whose rights must be taken away? Several chapters in this section explore these themes in examinations of the USA PATRIOT Act, Guantanamo Bay, and U.S. asylum and refugee policy.

Moreover, the notion of political and civil rights as human rights involves an exploration of the meaning of citizenship. Civil and political rights are dimensions of citizenship. The founders of the United States constructed a concept of citizenship based in part on race, class, and gender, where it was relegated to property owning white males. The masculinized notion of citizenship was defined in terms of the ability to be independent and materially self-sufficient, to participate in the public arena of governance, and to participate in the military defense of the nation. Citizenship thus defined rendered women, children, slaves, and people of color invisible, undeserving of the protections and rights of citizens, because they lacked the necessary prerequisites.

This presumption of the dimensions and requirements of citizenship was further based on an unquestioned assumption of a heteronormative society, one in which heterosexuality was without question "natural" and "normal." But what, then, does this mean about the rights of gays, lesbians, bisexuals, and transgendered individuals? And what does this mean for immigrants? Is there a difference in the status of "legal" immigrants and "illegal" immigrants? Do they have rights, or are they invisible and undeserving of human rights in their exclusion from citizenship? Are human rights "portable" regardless of where in the world one lives in the moment? Several chapters in this section take on these issues, focusing on immigration in North America, the status of "guest workers" in the United States, and the notion of sexual citizenship.

CHAPTER ELEVEN

Erosion of Political and Civil Rights: Looking Back to Changes Since 9/11/01: The Patriot Act

Christine Zozula

People dropping off their children at the University of Idaho's day care on February 26, 2003, were surprised to find the parking lot overflowing with federal, state, and local law enforcement officers. The officers waited for Sami Al-Hussayen, a thirty-four-year-old graduate student, to arrive with his children, so they could arrest him on suspicion of terrorism. The Federal Bureau of Investigation (FBI) became interested in Al-Hussayen when they noted his generous donations to various Islamic organizations. The FBI also found that Al-Hussayen worked as the webmaster for the website of the Islamic Assembly of North America, a group that has been investigated for terrorist associations but never listed as a terrorist organization. Al-Hussayen's phone line was tapped in early 2002 and in spring 2002 all his phone calls and emails were recorded. He was charged with providing material support to a terrorist organization and visa fraud (O'Hagan 2004).

Was Al-Hussayen a terrorist, or someone who practiced his faith as a model Muslim American? Coming from a wealthy family in Saudi Arabia, Al-Hussayen used his resources to generously donate to Muslim humanitarian associations. He volunteered his computer skills to maintain a website that educated people about the Islamic faith, and served as president of the Muslim Student Association at the University of Idaho. After the September 11 attacks he organized a blood drive for victims, attended peace vigils, and composed a letter on behalf of the Muslim Student Association condemning the attacks (O'Hagan 2004).

Al-Hussayen went to court on charges of visa fraud and terrorism: he violated his visa by not disclosing his volunteer activities as "work," and was charged with terrorism for providing "material support" in the form of computer expertise by acting as webmaster for the Islamic Assembly of North America. In terms of the visa fraud, his immigration lawyer Robert Pauw stated, "It was the first time anyone had been charged with a crime for failing to disclose volunteer charity work to the U.S. government" (O'Hagan 2004).

> Prosecutors charged that the sites helped terrorists raise funds and drum up recruits, but jurors said the evidence didn't support that. The defense called only one witness, a former CIA official who said the sites linked to the student appeared to be analytical and religious in nature, and not terrorist tools. (Russell 2004)

After being incarcerated for approximately one and a half years, Al-Hussayen was cleared of the terrorist charges and returned to Saudi Arabia to be with his wife and children.

Al-Hussayen's case illustrates how the Patriot Act allows for the violation of people's various rights in the name of national security: he was arrested publically at his place of work, his phone calls were tapped and recorded, and he was charged with terrorism and visa fraud for his volunteer work in the Muslim American community. The Patriot Act threatens the human rights of all U.S. citizens, as articulated in (for example) the UDHR and ICCPR to which the United States is a State Party. Specifically, the Patriot Act disregards the rights to free association and expression, freedom from discrimination, from arbitrary arrest and invasions of privacy, and the right to a fair trial. The rights of immigrants, Muslims, and people of Middle Eastern or South Asian descent are of particular concern, where application of the Patriot Act seems to affect these populations (and other populations of color) disproportionately. On the whole, this chapter critically examines the Patriot Act and its implications for human rights in the United States.

History

The Patriot Act is the common abbreviation for the USA PATRIOT Act: Uniting and Strengthening America by Providing Appropriate Tools Required to Intercept and Obstruct Terrorism. Assistant Attorney General Veit D. Dinh and Michael Chertoff drafted the Patriot Act. Both the House and the Senate passed it, and President George W. Bush signed it into law on October 26, 2001. Cole and Dempsey (2002) make the claim that "It is virtually certain that not a single member of the House read the bill for which he or she voted" (151). Despite the criticism and outcry against particular measures of the

Patriot Act, many controversial provisions were extended or made permanent in 2006 through the USA PATRIOT Reauthorization Act.

This is not the first time Americans enacted policy that limited rights in a time of crisis. During World War II, the United States placed 110,000 people of Japanese ancestry in internment camps in the name of national security. This measure was racist and xenophobic, as it targeted people on the basis of national origin without actual evidence of wrongdoing. During the Cold War, people suspected of holding communist beliefs could be subpoenaed to appear before the House Un-American Activities Committee, and imprisoned if they refused to answer questions about their organization or supply the names of people in it (Navasky 1980). This action targeted people based on the basis of their political beliefs, and wrongly asserted that people who held particular political beliefs threatened the United States.

The Patriot Act, then, is a type of legislation that is not new to recent American history: it is speedily enacted policy that brands a particular type of group as being unpatriotic or a threat to national security, thereby justifying the violation of rights. The U.S. government has officially recognized its error in the cases mentioned above. In 1988, the government issued an official apology and reparations to those in the Japanese internment camps. The Supreme Court ruled in favor of the rights of people who are politically affiliated with Communism, in *Scales v. the United States* (367 U.S. 203 (1961)) and *United States v. Robel* (389 U.S. 258 (1967)). In regard to the ruling on *Robel*, Chief Justice Earl Warren wrote, "It would indeed be ironic if, in the name of national defense, we would sanction the subversion of one of those liberties—the freedom of association—which makes the defense of the Nation worthwhile" (264).

State actors have not taken these hard-learned lessons to heart, as evidenced by the Patriot Act's criminalization of association with people and organizations deemed somehow dangerous by the state (with little or no explanation, let alone evidence), and the racist and xenophobic undertones of its discourse and implementation.

Rights Threatened Under the Patriot Act

Some measures of the Patriot Act could be construed as helpful steps toward reducing social ills without a tremendous infringement of already established rights. For instance, the Patriot Act strengthens the ability of law enforcement agencies to enforce laws on money laundering, improves visa processing procedures, and updates transportation and public building security procedures in order to keep pace with new technologies. However, some sections of the

Act unnecessarily grant permission to government agencies to undercut people's rights. The most problematic measures include sections that redefine terrorism, change reasonable expectations to privacy, and change the consequences of crime for immigrants.

Changes to the Definition of Terrorism

The Patriot Act presents a problematic conceptualization of "terrorism" that attempts to define who terrorists are, what kind of actions can constitute terrorist activity, and what the appropriate and legitimate consequences (state sanctions/punishment) of such activity should be. For example, Section 802 of the Patriot Act defines "domestic terrorism" as

(5) . . . activities that—
    (A) involve acts dangerous to human life that are a violation of the criminal laws of the United States or of any State;
    (B) appear to be intended—
        (i)   to intimidate or coerce a civilian population;
        (ii) to influence the policy of a government by intimidation or coercion; or
        (iii) to affect the conduct of a government by mass destruction, assassination, or kidnapping; and
    (C) occur primarily within the territorial jurisdiction of the United States.

While Section 802 makes explicit that the intention of the crime must be to influence a population or the government, it has the potential to brand actions unrelated to terrorist activity, such as political protest, as terrorism. Rackow (2002) argues that political groups with any connection to violence such as members of the National Rifle Association and antiabortion activists could be considered terrorists under Section 802. She writes:

the fact that a target is a member of a vocal political organization likely will play *some* role in establishing the basis for a court-ordered surveillance authorization. As long as the agent applying for surveillance authority can demonstrate some other justification beyond the target's involvement with the organization—such as being born abroad, being married to a noncitizen, or traveling to countries with which the United States does not have strong foreign relations—this may be enough to receive a grant of surveillance from the [Foreign Intelligence Surveillance Court]. (2002: 1690)

Furthermore, two people can make the determination that a group is a terrorist organization: the secretary of state and the attorney general. There is therefore no truly established, agreed-upon definition of terrorism. The ambiguous definitions of terrorists and terrorist acts thus enable the executive branch to conduct, in essence, witch hunts, persecuting individuals and groups at will.

Section 412 redefines terrorist activity to include solicitation of funds or other things of value for terrorist activity or a terrorist organization. Individuals may be charged with terrorist activity even if they are unaware that an association they support is considered terrorist. Tariq Ramadan, a leading scholar of Muslim identity, was denied admission to the country on the basis of Section 412. In 2004, Ramadan accepted a tenured position at the Joan B. Kroc Institute for International Peace Studies at the University of Notre Dame. Eight days before he was to move with his family to South Bend, Indiana, he was informed that his visa was revoked. The first reason stated by the government claimed that Ramadan endorsed terrorism. After Ramadan won a lawsuit that challenged this claim, he was still denied a visa, though the reason had changed: Ramadan donated to Palestinian humanitarian organizations between 1998 and 2002. The State Department claimed that his money funded Hamas, a terrorist organization, and that he reasonably should have known his donations funded Hamas. In a letter to the *Washington Post*, Ramadan (2006) stated:

> my donations were made between December 1998 and July 2002, and the United States did not blacklist the charities until 2003. How should I reasonably have known of their activities before the U.S. government itself knew? I donated to these organizations for the same reason that countless Europeans—and Americans, for that matter—donate to Palestinian causes: not to help fund terrorism, but because I wanted to provide humanitarian aid to people who desperately need it.

Tariq Ramadan was allowed back into the United States only after Hilary Rodham Clinton signed an order lifting his ban in early 2010.[1]

Justifying Detention of Immigrants

The redefinition of terrorist activity under sections 411 and 412 has allowed the United States to deport immigrants for crimes, humanitarian efforts, and expression of political dissent by categorizing such activities as related to terrorism. Sections 411 and 412 allow the government to deport immigrants to the United States based on their participation in terrorist groups, but as we have seen, the definition and application of terrorist activity is now quite vague and subjective. Section 412 allows the government to detain suspected terrorists for up to seven days without ever being charged with a crime. This enables the government to detain people on the basis of very weak evidence, or perhaps mere suspicion. The detention may continue indefinitely, so long as the secretary of state thinks that a person could potentially pose a threat to national security upon release. A report from Human Rights Watch in 2005 revealed that

> federal agents have swept through Muslim communities to pick up suspects often based on leads that, according to the Justice Department Inspector General's subsequent report, "were often quite general in nature, such as a landlord reporting suspicious activity by an Arab tenant." (Human Rights Watch 2005: 17)

The Patriot Act conflates any violent crime of immigrants with terrorism, which allows officials to refuse to give immigrants accused of violent crime, such as brawling, assault, domestic violence, their rights to an attorney, and rights to a swift trial. One's immigration status limits one from exercising rights that are extended to American citizens, such as posting bail or pursuing a fair trial. The Patriot Act then "sacrifices commitments to equality by trading a minority group's liberty for the majority's purported security" (Dempsey and Cole 2002: 152).

Increased Surveillance

The Patriot Act provides for increased state surveillance of all people within the United States. Section 214 alters the conditions under which the FBI can use wiretapping tools such as pen registers and trap and trace devices.[2] While the Foreign Intelligence Surveillance Act (FISA) previously allowed the FBI to use such devices, the FBI needed to specify the target of surveillance and demonstrate that the purpose of the device was intelligence gathering. Section 214 allows for the use of pen register and trap and trace devices even when the identity of the suspect is unspecified. Section 214 also expands the use of wiretaps without a warrant. Previously, such devices were reserved for investigations in which the "primary purpose" was intelligence gathering. Section 214 allows wiretaps for investigations in which intelligence gathering is a "significant purpose." This means that the primary purpose of the wiretap could be a criminal investigation, but so long as an agent claims a case serves some foreign intelligence gathering purpose, then the government can violate previously protected Fourth Amendment Rights. State authorities do not need to demonstrate probable cause that a crime has been committed, or is about to be committed, and there is no judicial oversight to ensure that the wiretaps are used legally (Rackow 2002).

Sections 216 and 206 present updated surveillance tactics to keep pace with changes in technology. Section 216 sets the terms for the tracking of Internet usage, which some have argued violates ones right to privacy, as previously the tracking of Internet usage was unregulated (Etzioni 2004). Section 216, however, does not have a safeguard to protect against the monitoring of communications of those who are not actively suspects of terrorism and permits the monitoring of publicly accessible computers. Section 206 allows for "roving wiretaps"—devices that can be installed on any communication tools a target might use. Section 206 states that the FBI can install devices without specifying the target and the explicit purpose of the surveillance. The language also states that the FBI can bug any device a target could *potentially* use. The FBI does not have to specify its target, nor demonstrate reasonable proof that a target will use a particular communication device before installation.

Section 215 of the Patriot Act allows the FBI to pursue records from libraries, bookstores, and so forth, to gain information for intelligence gathering purposes. This section further states that no person or entity may disclose that the FBI has requested such information. Section 215 changed both the type of information the FBI could request and the reasons for which it could request that information: "Previously, the FBI could get the credit card records of anyone suspected of being a foreign agent. Under the PATRIOT Act, the FBI can get the entire database of the credit card company" (Cole and Dempsey 2002: 167). The FBI does not have to demonstrate probable cause, and does not need to demonstrate that the records will help build a case against a suspect of terrorism. Solely stating that the records were sought for a terrorism or espionage investigation, rather than providing evidence, is now sufficient to procure records.

Blurring Intelligence and Crime Investigations

The Patriot Act also eliminates the separation between intelligence agencies and criminal agencies. While this move makes sense in terms of eliminating bureaucratic red tape, the Patriot Act does not make sufficient provisions for judicial oversight, nor does this move recognize the differences in training, purpose, and evidence that may be used in criminal trials in contrast with intelligence gathering.

Particularly disturbing is the employment of grand juries to gather information and evidence under the Patriot Act. A grand jury is a legal proceeding that typically precedes a formal criminal trial. The grand jury has great power, and the Patriot Act arguably allows for the abuse of that power (Cole and Dempsey 2002). A grand jury can compel anyone to testify under oath, and request that people produce documents and records without a warrant, under the immediate threat of potentially indefinite incarceration for failures to comply. Grand jury proceedings were relatively secret prior to the Patriot Act. Any evidence that the government gathered via grand jury had to satisfy all due process requirements—testimonies that were incorrect, misleading, or irrelevant were kept out of criminal proceedings. The Patriot Act allows intelligence gathering departments like the Central Intelligence Agency (CIA) to access grand jury records without the provisions of due process. The CIA can now easily garner information that was not subject to due process, and can use testimonies from the grand jury out of context—either willingly or unwillingly in order to make a case against or further investigate particular individuals or groups. In addition, the CIA is not beholden to report why it used information from the grand jury, nor in what capacity—meaning that there is little to no mechanisms for oversight.

Patriot Reauthorization

Despite multiple court cases and petitions by U.S. citizens and various activist groups, the Patriot Act was reauthorized on March 9, 2006. In the original document, many of the provisions were to be phased out of use before 2006. However, the PATRIOT Reauthorization Act made fourteen of the sixteen expired provisions permanent. Other provisions were extended through 2015, such as use of roving wiretaps and procurement of business and library records.

American citizens have not blindly accepted the provisions of the Patriot Act. In June 2004, librarians at the Deming branch of the Whatcom County Rural Library District in Washington State refused to let FBI agents access records without a subpoena. When agents returned with a subpoena, the library voted to take the case to court, and the FBI withdrew its request (Finan 2007). In 2006, the American Civil Liberties Union won a case against the National Security Agency, which claimed that warrantless wiretapping without judicial oversight violated the right to free speech (Finan 2007). That case has since been overturned, signaling a continued disconnect between state practices and ratified commitments to human rights outlined in such instruments as the UDHR and ICCPR. However, these examples testify to growing public resistance to the Patriot Act, and its trampling of civil and

political human rights many have come to expect in light of the U.S. ratification of existing human rights instruments.

Why Should You Care?

People feel that if they are not doing anything wrong, that they shouldn't care
about expanded surveillance powers, the blurred lines between criminal investigations and intelligence gathering investigations, and the expanded policing of
immigrants, Muslims, and people of Middle Eastern and South Asian descent.
However, many people who have done "nothing wrong" have been detained for
questioning, their possessions taken, and their lives turned upside down.

On September 21, 2001, government agents arrested Mohar Abdullah as
they surrounded his car in San Diego. He met with the FBI several times to
provide information on two people with whom he had once worked who
were under suspicion. Despite his cooperation with the investigation, he was
harshly treated and humiliated. In an interview with Human Rights Watch,
Abdullah described his experience:

> Five to six cars surrounded my car. The agents pulled out shot guns
> and told me to get out of the car or they will shoot me. They told me
> they were about to shoot me. I was dropping off a coworker and she
> fainted. They had to call an ambulance. I was shackled, surprised. I
> asked what's going on? I've been so helpful. But three guys told me
> to put my hands on the car, they patted me down and shackled me. I
> asked what am I arrested for? Am I charged with something? I am sup-
> posed to meet [the FBI agent who was questioning him] at 10. I got no
> answer. They shoved me against the car and handcuffed me . . . .They
> didn't tell me why I was arrested—they said they'd explain in the main
> office. They didn't read me Miranda rights.
>
> I got in the car. They were so disrespectful and so rude. They told
> me to "shut the fuck up." (Human Rights Watch 2005: 119)

Another person who was treated inhumanely because of a suspicion of terrorism was a visual artist and professor at SUNY Buffalo. On May 11, 2004,
Steven Kurtz woke up to find that his wife was not breathing. He called the
police, who found his wife dead of heart failure. The officers noticed petri
dishes full of harmless bacteria Kurtz was using for an art installation, and
informed authorities. The next day, as Kurtz drove to the funeral home, he
was arrested by the FBI, and held in custody for twenty-two hours while his
home was searched. Authorities

seize[d] his cat, his car, and with complete disregard for morals or human decency, the government seized his dead wife's body from the coroner. This seems so extreme that even the most hated and dangerous criminals would have to face such an uncompassionate ordeal. (Hillary and Kubasek 2007: 34)

Aside from the Patriot Act's sanctioning of extreme measures of detention and surveillance, which do not require probable cause or judicial oversight, the act also threatens to punish individuals for political dissent. A healthy democracy is one that provides for freedom of expression, without fear that statements that critique the practices of the government could amount to detention, abuse, or deportation: "When Americans are intimidated into keeping dissident views to themselves, our public discourse is constricted, the First Amendment is diminished, and democracy itself is under attack" (Chang 2002: 102).

This analysis here of the Patriot Act and its consequent abrogation of many civil and human rights as outlined by ratified international conventions like the UDHR and ICCPR highlights an important tension in the implementation of human rights to which so many observers point: that is, a seeming tension between sovereign security and human rights. Some might argue that in the post-September 11 world, when the United States faces severe security issues, it is imperative to exercise the sort of vigilance the Patriot Act facilitates. The loss of human rights is an otherwise unfortunate consequence; but national security must trump human rights. Critics of this point of view, however, make a persuasive case that the willingness to compromise human rights actually undermines sovereign security. Luban (2005) makes one of the more cogent and compelling cases to this end, arguing that security and human rights are not inconsistent at all, and thus do not require trade-offs between the two. To believe that we need fear the state less than terrorists, he argues, is to ignore that the state can make mistakes in judgment, can exercise decisions with malice in defining political opponents and dissidents as "enemies of the state," and can, and often does, fail to admit such mistakes. Empowering the state to unchecked seizures of individuals' human rights violates people's constitutional rights to due process (and presumption of innocence until proven guilty) and freedom from unreasonable search and seizure, runs the danger of permanent militarization of civilian existence, and courts the very real possibility of galvanizing more "home-grown" terrorists.

Finally, the existence of the Patriot Act raises some thought-provoking questions posed by Luban (2005) for those who believe that loss of human rights is a reasonable price to pay for national security: even if we might agree that the unfortunate price of security may be loss of human rights, how many rights must we be willing to lose in order to gain what measure of increased security? How will we know when we've given up enough? How do we calculate this equation at all? Most pointedly, Luban (2005: 256) asks: "how much of your own protection action bureaucratic errors or malice by the government—errors that can land you in jail indefinitely—are you willing to sacrifice in return for minute [or unspecified] increments in security?" That's a very good question we will all have to grapple with, now and in the foreseeable future.

CHAPTER TWELVE

U.S. Asylum and Refugee Policy: The "Culture of No"

Bill Frelick

The United States has the sovereign right to decide which foreigners it wants to give permission to enter or stay. Yet U.S. law also recognizes that refugees are people with well-founded fears of being persecuted if returned to their homelands and that they have certain rights under international law, most fundamentally the right not to be returned to face persecution. Thus, there is a tension between the sovereign rights of the U.S. government and the individual rights of the refugee. Refugee rights, in short, are the exception to governments' general sovereign discretion with respect to immigration. Governments have the right to deny entry or to deport. But when this is done to a refugee, it means return to persecution, torture or death. That is not allowed.

Expedited Removal

In 1996, the Illegal Immigration Reform and Immigrant Responsibility Act (IIRAIRA) created an expedited removal procedure for arriving noncitizens who are undocumented, have fraudulent documents, or who have a valid passport and nonimmigrant visa but appear to be intending to enter for some other reason than what is specified on their visa.[1] IIRAIRA authorized low-level immigration inspectors to order the removal of such allegedly improperly documented noncitizens without review by an immigration judge and mandated the detention of noncitizens subject to expedited removal, including asylum seekers (people claiming to be refugees).

People who flee persecution, particularly at the hands of their own governments, usually have difficulty obtaining valid travel documents (they need, after all, to procure them from the same authorities who are seeking to harm them) and often have to rely on forged documents to make their escape.[2] IIRAIRA made an exception to summary removal for a noncitizen able to convince an immigration inspector at the port of entry that he or she has a fear of return. But people who actually have fled persecution and fear return are often torture victims or otherwise traumatized; they generally arrive tired, afraid, confused, and ignorant of the applicable law and procedures. The expectation that they should be able to articulate, to uniformed authorities in a strange land, a convincing fear of return immediately upon arrival is inconsistent with the refugee reality—a reality filled with trepidation, uncertainty, and mistrust.

Nevertheless, immigration inspectors are supposed to recognize such people and refer them to asylum officers, officials in the U.S. Citizenship and Immigration Services (USCIS) in the Department of Homeland Security (DHS) who conduct interviews to determine if the asylum seeker has a "credible fear." Those found not to have a credible fear are subject to removal, though they may appeal to an immigration judge, who operates out of the Executive Office of Immigration Review (EOIR) in the Department of Justice. An immigration judge's decision on the appeal of a negative credible fear finding is not subject to further review.[3]

If the asylum officer determines that the person has "credible fear," the asylum seeker then has the opportunity to raise his or her fear of return as a defense against removal in an adversarial hearing before an immigration judge. A trial attorney represents the government from DHS's Bureau of Immigration and Customs Enforcement (ICE). The asylum seeker may have counsel present but only at his or her own expense.

ICE has discretion on whether to release asylum seekers who have passed their credible fear tests. Many remain in detention while they wait—often for months—for their immigration court hearings. Detention, often in remote locations, increases the difficulty for the asylum seeker to find legal representation or even the support and advice of friends and relatives, and detention, particularly when prolonged and in prison conditions, takes a psychological toll, which is often harder to bear for those who have experienced torture and abuse.[4]

Several studies have examined the impact of expedited removal on the right to seek asylum.[5] The most comprehensive study has been that of the U.S. Commission on International Religious Freedom (USCRIF), which had unprecedented access to data, ports of entry, and detention centers.[6] The study found that the greatest risk of error was not at the "credible fear" determination stage but rather in the arriving noncitizen's encounter with an immigration inspector in "secondary inspection." If an immigration inspector at passport controls thinks that the arriving noncitizen might be subject to expedited removal, the first inspector sends him or her to secondary inspection.

In 15 percent of cases observed, the USCIRF found that immigration inspectors in secondary inspection did not refer noncitizens who expressed a fear of return to asylum officers for credible fear interviews. Among those not referred for credible fear interviews were "aliens who expressed fear of political, religious, or ethnic persecution, which are clearly related to the grounds for asylum."[7] The USCIRF observed newly arrived noncitizens expressing a fear of return and found that in the majority of cases in which referrals were not made, "the inspector incorrectly indicated on the sworn statement that the applicant stated he had no fear of return."[8]

Although IIRAIRA mandated only expedited removal for improperly documented noncitizens identified by immigration inspectors at ports of entry (such as airports and border crossing points), it was expanded in November 2002 to apply to all undocumented boat arrivals (except Cubans) landing anywhere on the coast. It was expanded again in August 2004 to authorize border patrol agents to remove undocumented noncitizens for up to two weeks after arrival who have not proceeded more than one hundred miles from the border.[9]

Even while independent studies of expedited removal were showing that immigration inspectors at ports of entry were insufficiently trained or supervised to recognize arriving noncitizens with asylum claims, the George W. Bush administration expanded expedited removal well beyond ports of entry and empowered border patrol agents who operate along the border between land ports of entry to summarily remove noncitizens, as well. In announcing the expansion of expedited removal, the administration said that border patrol agents would receive a mere eight hours of training to recognize a protection claim and refer it to an asylum officer.[10]

Given this superficial training, border patrol agents may well not be correctly identifying asylum seekers among the 1.1 million undocumented noncitizens they apprehend per year[11] and properly referring them for credible fear interviews. That possibility is reinforced by Homeland Security secretary Michael Chertoff's August 2006 announcement that DHS had managed during the course of the previous year to "eliminate the previous policy of catch-and-release whereby most non-Mexicans who were caught at the border were released, and to reverse that and impose catch-and-remove—100 percent catch-and-remove for everybody caught at the border."[12] Is it conceivable that none of those people had protection claims?

One-Year Filing Deadline

IIRAIRA also narrowed access to asylum by creating significant new procedural bars, including the introduction of a one-year deadline to file an asylum claim.[13] The bar to asylum for applicants who fail to lodge a claim within one year of arriving has resulted in asylum officers referring large numbers of would-be asylum applicants directly to immigration court for removal proceedings without first considering the merits of their claims.[14]

The law makes exceptions to the filing deadline in cases of changed country conditions that would materially affect the asylum claim or extraordinary circumstances that prevented the timely filing of a claim. Such exceptions do not take into account, however, the time it takes asylum seekers to gain sufficient understanding and confidence in the asylum system to come forward and to find free or low-cost legal representation.

The effect of the one-year filing bar is to force asylum applicants who may, in fact, qualify as refugees under U.S. law (that is, that they indeed have a well-founded fear of persecution) to seek protection under higher legal standards under a provision of law called "withholding of removal" (which requires that the persecution can objectively be shown to be more likely than not to occur) or the provision of law that implements the Convention Against Torture (which only protects against torture that involves state agency). Consequently, this procedural bar to asylum means that the United States is able within its law to return a refugee with a well-founded fear of persecution simply for having failed to file a claim within one year.

Deporting Refugees

The granting of asylum is a matter of discretion but the prohibition on returning refugees to places where their lives or freedom would be threatened is mandated as a fundamental principle of international law. This principle, *nonrefoulement*, is established in Article 33 of the 1951 Convention Relating to the Status of Refugees and is reiterated in the "withholding of removal" section of the Immigration and Nationality Act, which prohibits the United States from returning a refugee to persecution.[15]

Article 33.2 of the Refugee Convention makes an exception to the principle of *nonrefoulement* for a refugee "who, having been convicted by a final judgment of a particularly serious crime, constitutes a danger to the community of that country." U.S. immigration law followed this exception with similar language.[16] UNHCR's Executive Committee interprets the "particularly serious crime" exception to nonrefoulement to apply only in "exceptional cases and after due consideration of the circumstances."[17] The UNHCR *Handbook on Procedures and Criteria for Determining Refugee Status* further elucidates this point, saying that Article 33.2 should be applied only in "extreme cases."[18] In reference to another exclusion clause in the Refugee Convention,[19] the *Handbook* states that "a 'serious' crime must be a capital crime or a very grave punishable act. Minor offenses punishable by moderate sentences are not grounds for exclusion."[20]

UNHCR wrote an advisory opinion on Article 33.2 saying, "It must . . . be shown that the danger posed by the refugee is sufficient to justify *refoulement*. The danger posed must be to the country of refuge itself; the danger must be very serious; and the finding of dangerousness must be based on reasonable grounds and therefore supported by credible and reliable evidence."[21]

Until 1990 judges had the discretion to decide what constituted "a particularly serious crime" and to weigh the seriousness of the crime against the likelihood and severity of persecution expected upon return. Beginning with the Immigration Act of 1990, however, which defined a particularly serious crime as an aggravated felony, Congress has dictated to judges the crimes that would exempt refugees from protection. Successive amendments to the Immigration and Nationality Act have expanded the definition and list of crimes that qualify as aggravated felonies for purposes of deportation until today the list includes what are in fact misdemeanors under criminal law.[22]

Mark McAllister, for example, a native of Northern Ireland, came to the United States as a juvenile with his parents in 1996. He came after unknown persons had repeatedly shot at his home. In addition, the Royal Ulster Constabulary regularly arrested, beat, and jailed his father. McAllister was convicted on three counts of possession with intent to distribute the drug known as ecstasy. After his conviction the immigration judge, Board of Immigration Appeals, and district court all ruled that his crime was an aggravated felony and a particularly serious one, barring him from withholding of removal.[23]

In addition, the courts have ruled that people who have been recognized by the United States as refugees but who subsequently adjust their status to that of permanent residents lose their protection as refugees and can be deported for even more minor crimes. Suwan, a Cambodian refugee living in Houston, Texas, with a wife and two young children, for example, was deported to Cambodia for two counts of indecent exposure. He committed these offenses, he said, because there was no toilet at the construction site where he was working and he was forced to urinate outdoors.[24] In another case involving a Bosnian refugee, Sejid Smriko, the BIA held that a person "admitted to the United States as a refugee [who] adjusted his status to that of a lawful permanent resident, is subject to removal on the basis of his crimes involving moral turpitude, even though his refugee status was never terminated."[25] Smriko's crimes involved two minor shoplifting offenses for which he was sentenced to a fine and a five-day suspended sentence, respectively, and a third conviction for receiving stolen property, which resulted in a year's probation. He was ordered deported to Bosnia.

Lack of Legal Representation for Asylum Seekers

Unlike the right to counsel that is guaranteed to those charged with crimes in the criminal justice system, noncitizens in removal proceedings have access to counsel only insofar as it is "at no expense to the government."[26] Andrew Schoenholz and Jonathan Jacobs conducted a study on the impact on asylum approval of the availability of legal representation and found that a represented asylum seeker in U.S. immigration courts is six times more likely to be granted asylum than an asylum seeker who appears pro se.[27]

Given the potentially serious consequences of deportation, particularly for a person claiming a fear of persecution upon return, and in view of the complexity of immigration and asylum law, the lack of legal counsel can be a matter of life or death for those who cannot afford counsel or for whom a pro bono representative is unavailable (and that is often the case, especially for noncitizens detained in remote locations).

In the landmark *Gideon v. Wainwright* case the Supreme Court held that indigent criminal defendants had the right to a court-appointed attorney because they could not otherwise be assured their Sixth Amendment right to a fair trial,[28] and subsequent rulings have expanded this right to certain civil proceedings as well.[29] In the context of removal proceedings, however, the Supreme Court held in *Ardestani v. INS* that noncitizens do not have a right under current U.S. law to a court-appointed attorney, but that the "broad purposes" of the law "would be served by making the statute applicable to deportation proceedings."[30] The Court added, "We are mindful that the complexity of immigration procedures, and the enormity of the interests at stake, make legal representation in deportation especially important."

Detention of Asylum Seekers

Under IIRAIRA all asylum seekers in the expedited removal process must be detained at least until the conclusion of their credible fear interviews.[31] Almost all of the detention facilities used for asylum seekers are no different from prisons used to incarcerate criminals. "Indeed, in some instances," said the USCIRF report, "actual criminal justice institutions—in this case, county jails—are operated as dual use facilities that simultaneously house asylum seekers and criminal offenders, side by side."[32] The report further found that "whether they were county jails, DHS run facilities, or private contract facilities, they were operated in more or less the same way." This included secure barriers, strip searches, twenty-four-hour surveillance lighting and the use of segregation or solitary confinement for disciplinary reasons. The report included interviews with asylum seekers in detention. One said:

> The whole detention system is there to break you down further. The time you spend there prolongs your trauma. And you are not even allowed to cry. If you do, they take you to isolation.[33]

Another said:

> I felt really isolated and humiliated. I felt like a person who had no value. At any time, the security guards made us do whatever they wanted. I felt traumatized by my treatment. My blood pressure went higher and my medical problems worsened there.

ICE parole decisions cannot be appealed; review is possible only through a habeas corpus petition. Immigration judges in turn have seen their discretion to grant eligible asylum seekers release on bond (as opposed to DHS release through parole) increasingly curtailed.

Conclusion and Recommendations

Determining which people claiming to be refugees should be granted asylum is a process that requires fairness and deliberation. At the end of the process, not everyone will be found to meet the standards for protection. People who are not otherwise authorized to stay and who are not in need of protection can certainly be compelled to go home. But asylum seekers should at least have access to refugee determination procedures; those procedures should be fair; and the standards people are expected to meet and the burden of proof for meeting them should be reasonable.

The following five "fixes" would go a long way toward repairing a system that has failed to give asylum seekers in the United States a fair chance to have their claims heard and decided to:

1. Create a system of government-funded, public-defender-like representation for noncitizens in removal proceedings.

2. Restore to immigration judges the authority to order the removal of arriving noncitizens so that such life-and-death decisions are taken out of the hands of low-level immigration inspectors and border patrol agents. If expedited removal is retained, authorize asylum officers to grant asylum at the time of the credible fear interview to arriving noncitizens who clearly meet the well-founded fear of persecution standard.

3. Amend the Immigration and Nationality Act to lift the one-year filing deadline for filing an asylum claim.

4. Amend the Immigration and Nationality Act to ensure that individuals whose lives or freedom would be threatened if returned to their home countries are provided protection from return to persecution unless they can reasonably be regarded as posing a genuine danger to the security of the United States or have been convicted of a crime that truly is serious within the meaning of the Refugee Convention and Protocol.

5. Detain asylum seekers only when necessary; subject them to review by an immigration judge or an independent authority; and promulgate regulations to establish uniform criteria for release so that ICE officials exercise parole authority more consistently. When detention of non-criminal asylum seekers is necessary, make it as humane as possible in nonprison-like facilities with access to legal assistance and separation of asylum seekers from criminal offenders.

CHAPTER THIRTEEN

The Border Action Network and Human Rights: Community-Based Resistance Against the Militarization of the U.S.-Mexico Border

Sang Hea Kil, Jennifer Allen, and Zoe Hammer

Media images of the U.S.-Mexico border[1] overwhelmingly portray an empty desert landscape in which border patrol agents hunt down and capture groups of migrant men attempting to cross the border. The setting is barren, lacking towns, communities, wildlife, families, churches, culture, commerce, or any form of political activity. These images, as Zoe Hammer discusses in her chapter (22) on the prison abolition movement, reduce the complexity of life on the border to a cat and mouse dynamic that encourages policymakers, media, and the general public to blame immigrants for the woes of an entire nation. These images also help to reassure the public that the "war on the border" is working (Kil forthcoming).

The reality of life on the border is something altogether different. There are 6.9 million residents living in cities and towns in the border counties that span the states of California, Arizona, New Mexico, and Texas (U.S./Mexico Border Health Commission 2006). Every day, people go to school, work, and church in this region. They shop, take walks, and engage in the daily routines typical of residents throughout the nation. Yet these millions of people live their lives in the midst of low-intensity warfare (Dunn 1996) in, as Hammer demonstrates later in this volume, one of the most highly politicized and misrepresented regions of the United States. Launched in 1994, an ongoing set of "deterrence through prevention" strategies (Massey, Durand, and Malone 2002) have taken a devastating toll on the rights and dignity of those that cross the border and those that call the region home (Kil and Menjívar 2006).

At the same time, the militarization of the U.S.-Mexico border has catalyzed a growing movement for social justice on the border and human rights in the United States (Hammer 2009).

This chapter introduces the work of Border Action Network (BAN), a grassroots, immigrant-led human rights organization based in southern Arizona that is building local power and political engagement, creating new visions of human rights, and forging coalitions of diverse border region social sectors. We begin by providing an overview of the relationship between militarized federal immigration policy and the dehumanization and criminalization of immigrants and border residents. We continue by describing the human rights vision of BAN. We end by describing BAN's strategies of community organizing, local campaigns, and policy advocacy. Throughout the chapter, we mainly use the term "rights" to refer to "community rights," in that a community can come together and create rights by organizing for their recognition and realization. While BAN also references the U.S. Bill of Rights and the UDHR, BAN recognizes that simply because these formal legal instruments exist, it does not necessarliy mean that these rights are applied when appropriate. The concept of community rights is an underutilized human rights framework that BAN creates organically, from the "bottom up," and insists that its recognition and creation be upheld and respected by the state and other political actors.

The Militarization of the Border

Global trade policies and the resulting economic migration motivate the rationale for a militarized border enforcement strategy. The use of a military paradigm, in rhetoric, technological weaponry, personnel, training, and posture along the border contribute to the criminalization of immigrants and their dehumanization. While no official counts have occurred so far, unofficially, human rights groups estimate that since 1994 more than 4,000 deaths have occurred due to border crossing attempts (http://www.nnirr.org/registrations/HR4437.htm). These deaths only increase as militarized border strategies escalate. However, rarely is the border region viewed as a terrain of human rights crisis. This section will provide some background information for understanding this border region as a human rights crisis.

In 1994, the federal government introduced the "prevention through deterrence" strategy, marking a new era of militarization in border enforcement (Dunn 2009). The intention was to push immigrants from safer, more urban crossing points into more dangerous and remote areas of the desert. Walls, fences, towers, roads, surveillance technologies, and lights were installed to increase border patrol visibility and mobility. Each border patrol sector launched its own "operation": "Operation Gatekeeper" in San Diego, "Hold the Line" in El Paso, "Rio Grande" in southeastern Texas, and "Safeguard" in Arizona. These "operations" expanded barriers spanning the 2,000-mile U.S. border with Mexico causing thousands of migrant deaths and injuries, creating chaos and havoc in border towns and cities, dividing and damaging the economies of binational communities, conveying a message of hostility toward our neighboring nation, creating lucrative new opportunities for transnational organized crime cartels and entrepreneurs, and severely damaging the natural environment.

Fourteen years later the current spending on border security and immigration enforcement is enormous. For example, in fiscal year 2008, spending exceeded $12 billion (DHS 2008). Despite these spending efforts, rates of immigration have increased (Massey, Durand, and Malone 2002). Border Patrol has tripled its ranks to more than 18,000 agents (Spagat 2008). Surveillance camera towers, connected to rooms full of monitors, dot the arid landscape and city centers. The DHS goal of 670 miles of pedestrian and vehicle walls is almost complete with 500 miles of fencing built by the end of 2008 ("Border Fence Project" 2008). Every year more women, men, and children lose their lives to the horrific toll of exposure and dehydration. In 2007, 237 dead bodies were found in the Arizona desert alone, though it may be impossible to know just how many more actually died (McCombs, Satter, and Marizco 2009).

As the United States attempts to control the border, it simultaneously commands global forces that continue to drive immigration. With trade agreements like NAFTA (North American Free Trade Agreement), CAFTA (Central American Free Trade Agreement,) and the (AFTA) Andean Free Trade Agreement taking a devastating toll on Latin American farming communities, people across the hemisphere are driven north out of need for basic survival (Delgado-Wise and Covarrubias 2007; McCarty 2007). While the intent of these free trade agreements among participating countries was to reduce barriers to trade between countries, thus freeing the flow of capital to cross borders, the result has also been to decouple capital from labor and inhibiting people's movement in the search for work through border militarization. From a human rights perspective, respect for the rights of immigrants before, during, and after the process of migration is essential, especially in light of these trade agreements that erode their ability to support themselves in their homeland. Bill Frelick's chapter provides details on the state's legal obligations toward immigrant and refugee populations.

Border enforcement, immigration, and global trade policies have failed on another level that is equally profound: they have resulted in the structural exclusion of immigrants and border communities from the legal rights guaranteed to all by the U.S. Constitution and formal human rights instruments. In this sense, immigrants occupy a "legal nonexistence" that helps the public to see immigrants as having no rights; human, civil, or otherwise (Kil and Menjívar 2006; citing Susan Coutin). Current practices function to systematically dehumanize immigrants and people of color, often literally depriving them of life—from the toleration of armed vigilantes patrolling the desert for migrants and systematic racial profiling perpetrated by federal and local law enforcement agents, to border patrol agents shooting at the backs of fleeing people and the polluting of border environments. These practices result not only in the unlawful and intolerable abuse and death of passing migrants, but also in the unnecessary harassment and physical endangerment of people of color that live near the border. Such political suppression has left entire communities feeling powerless to challenge unresponsive federal agencies. In many cases, local communities have come to accept this everyday human and civil rights crisis as the norm. So, while this strategy continues to fail to deter immigration, it succeeds quite well in creating an escalating human and civil rights crisis.

BAN and a Human Rights Framework

In response to the human rights crisis on the southern U.S./northern Mexican border, BAN formed in 1999 and works with immigrant families and border communities in rural and urban areas along the Arizona border with Mexico. BAN works to ensure that community rights are protected, human dignity is upheld, and that these communities are healthy and safe places for everyone to live. BAN is a membership-based human rights community organization that combines grassroots organizing, leadership development, policy advocacy, and litigation. Members pay an annual due and participate in one of several levels of leadership like human rights committee member, promoter, or abuse documenter.

BAN members work within immigrant and border communities, building a collective capacity to articulate and defend human and constitutional rights. BAN members organize diverse, immigrant-led coalitions to denounce rights violations and promote new policies that espouse human rights practices grounded in new visions of just communities. BAN's efforts tie grassroots community organizing to policy advocacy including utilizing the Organization of American States (OAS) and the UN mechanisms to promote human rights on the U.S.-Mexico border and beyond. The OAS is a unilateral forum for the nations of North and South America. It plays a role in carrying out mandates related to democracy, human rights, illegal drugs, and corruption established by the Summit of the Americas held each year.

Three factors seem to fuel and foster human and civil rights abuses in border regions. First, dominant ideology, reflected in media and policy discourse, presents border militarization as a natural and necessary national security measure. Second, immigrants are then constructed as criminals through laws and policies that specifically label their presence on U.S. soil as illegal. The criminalization of immigrants, like the criminalization of many low-income and poor communities of color in the United States, has been accomplished by crafting new laws, renaming agencies and operations, and developing policies and practices that frame immigrants as threats.[2] Third, the abusive treatment of immigrants (or those believed to be immigrants) is seen as less problematic where immigrants are abstracted or objectified, as statistics or ID numbers to be monitored, or as nonhuman animals to be controlled or contained.[3] The end result is that immigrants and their communities are hit hardest by the "war on the border" while also at the forefront of resisting and transforming the notion of border security into one that integrates human rights, community security, and economic vitality. Just as the one-size-fits-all approach to border security has failed to understand the complexity and dynamism of the unique border region, the response and transformation of the border needs to be rooted in complexity. BAN's approach, based on a unique, community-based vision of human rights, starts by challenging and redefining the notion of rights—who has them, who defines them, and how they are implemented.

In June 2006, BAN's community leaders came together to rethink and strategize around BAN's stated goals. From this discussion, the BAN leaders developed what has become the vision for the organization and for the communities in which BAN members live. This vision begins by asking the question, "what is needed for individuals and as communities to lead dignified lives?" While immigration reform and protection of constitutional rights on the border are indeed priorities, they are not the only ends of struggle. What this process revealed is that immigrant communities are not looking for "immigrant rights," they are looking for community rights that recognize immigrants not as "immigrants" but as human beings with hopes, dreams, needs, and a strong commitment to realizing the ideals of dignity and justice for all communities. BAN principles are

- Immigration reform
- Civil and constitutional rights
- Workers' rights

- Education
- Health care
- Housing
- Healthy communities
- Culture and language
- Human mobility
- Family unification
- Civic participation
- Justice, equality, and dignity

These principles guide BAN members and ensure that BAN's vision is more than just fighting, more than just legislative victories in the halls of Congress, and more than just isolated issues. This vision is one that sees immigrants as part of a society that they have helped transform into a more just place—breaking through the constraints of militarization, criminalization, and dehumanization. The BAN principles are human rights principles, not because the UN or the OAS says so, but because community members have decided to work together to articulate them based on their experiences with living on a militarized border. The significance of BAN's principles is that they are mainly "bottom-up" assertion of community rights.

Leadership Development and Community Organizing

Human rights training and education is at the center of the BAN human rights model. Members are largely immigrant women, men, and youth living in various communities across the 200-mile-long Arizona border—Douglas, Pirtleville, Naco, Bisbee, Sierra Vista, Nogales, Sahuarita, Summit, Tucson, Willcox, San Luis, and other areas. People get involved in the organization through family, friends, coworkers, their church, school, or neighbors. They come to their first meeting, event, or training typically because they or a loved one has been abused or mistreated because of their immigration status or their proximity to the U.S.-Mexico border. If members demonstrate a commitment to working with others to challenge these abuses, they are invited to participate in an intensive forty-hour training[4] in which they discuss and study the U.S. Constitution, the UDHR, the multiple processes of documenting human rights violations, the history of immigration to the United States, and immigration policy. Beyond these tools, the new "human rights promoters" (as they are called upon graduation) discuss how to put their education into action by helping to create the safety in their communities in which people not only know their rights, but also how to defend them. They denounce violations and work collectively to put into place new rights that expand the notion of equality and integrate dignity and justice into all border communities. To date, BAN's seventy human rights promoters have become recognized resources and leaders within their neighborhoods, schools, churches, and communities. Formalizing this new leadership, each promoter is tasked with forming a Human Rights Committee with other local community members.

A committee creates the safer space within a community where people can learn about their rights as well as get involved in local and national campaigns. But each committee is also tasked with charting the political and strategic course of the organization. Committees determine the priorities of the organization, elect the board of directors, evaluate the executive director, define local and national campaigns, and make all the political decisions. These committees are notably decentralized, mini-organizations that work together as a network to increase their overall strength, impact, safety and vision (thus, Border Action *Network*).

Local Campaigns

It is not enough to advocate and organize for national policy reforms, particularly not in a state like Arizona where anti-immigrant leaders, state laws, and local enforcement measures have terrorized communities for some time. Border communities must localize the struggle for human rights for it to be meaningful and measurable. BAN trains and deploys human rights promoters and committees to point to concrete successes in their own backyards to encourage those more hesitant to speak up.

One example of localizing the movement for human rights is an annual campaign launched by BAN to encourage community members to report incidents of violations of their human rights. Every year, more than one hundred trained volunteers fan out in their communities, knocking on doors, setting up tables in front of grocery stores and parks, and hit the airwaves to encourage people to tell BAN their stories of abuse. The message is clear: if abuse is to be stopped, then the stories must be told first. Putting pain to paper is not an easy process, but BAN members have learned that the written word speaks louder and lasts longer than verbal testimonies. Over the span of two to three months, volunteers document incidents that BAN staff turn into a report (protecting people's identity) that is presented back to communities so that people can see they are not alone in enduring abuse. Moreover, through local human rights committees, BAN tells communities that abuses by authorities should not be suffered alone, but put on the table, named, and then challenged collectively. The report is also presented to the agencies named as abusers, including the border patrol, U.S. Customs, local police and sheriffs, employers, housing authorities, and others. The report and community report-back process often leads to local campaigns designed to change law enforcement practices, increase government accountability, file lawsuits, and so forth.

Policy Advocacy

In terms of national advocacy, BAN has learned that it is easy to complain about national policy, to critique bills and proposals, and blast national leaders. The hard work is actually coming up with alternatives that BAN members can support and promote. BAN members, in conjunction with a border-wide process with other border immigrant community groups, developed a series of policy recommendations for immigration and border policy. These recommendations were developed through community consultations wherein promoters and other members conducted surveys in their communities to identify and prioritize solutions to the human rights crisis. The final product, grounded in BAN's human rights framework and principles, is practical, proactive, and profound: from increasing the oversight and accountability of border agencies, to requiring ongoing human rights and constitutional rights certification of agents.

BAN combines a number of strategies in order for these recommendations to be included in national policy. Delegations of BAN members travel to Washington, D.C., several times each year and lobby key congressional leaders for comprehensive immigration reform. These delegations have helped build relationships with lawmakers across party and regional lines. BAN has also worked to form broad multisector coalitions. Border community leaders build relationships with national advocacy organizations, write legislative language for use by policymakers, and increase the capacity of immigrant communities on the border to keep the pressure on policymakers. As a result, in 2006 five of the group's recommendations were included in both House and Senate immigration reform bills. It was the first time that human rights were included in border and immigration policy legislation.

Too often people use the UN and the OAS to talk about human rights abuses in order to highlight the atrocities outside the United States. In the United States, the general perception is that human rights violations or abuses typically occur in other, "less developed" countries. Citizens generally perceive the Bill of Rights and broader U.S. Constitution as sufficient to prevent human rights abuses from occurring domestically. In addition, human rights tend to be framed only as negative rights—especially under the norm set by the historical U.S. support of the ICCPR, as violations, abuses, or "a lack of." BAN uses a positive rights framework and discourse. BAN articulates what border communities need and deserve, which moves beyond violations and abuses in framing human rights. It strives to utilize the tools and forums these institutions provide to not only expose the human rights crisis on the border and in immigrant families, but also to bring the concept of human rights to the United States more broadly. Domestic social justice movements and policymakers alike have placed human rights in a box with the label of "international"—things that relate to people somewhere else. To open this box on our soil and integrate its contents domestically, we must combine education, local campaigns, and national policy in order to have human rights abuses investigated and prosecuted. In 2005, BAN filed a petition to the OAS charging the United States with violating the human rights of migrants and border communities in Arizona for their failure to prosecute border vigilante groups. In 2006, BAN traveled to Geneva to present findings to the subcommission on human rights regarding border vigilante and border agency violence. The organization also hosted a community meeting to present testimonies and recommendations from human rights committees to Jorge Bustamante, the UN special rapporteur on the human rights of migrants, during his visit in May 2007.

Conclusion

For human rights to gain widespread legitimacy, human rights instruments—while important tools to pressure and expose government abuses and neglect—are not and should not be enough. The vision for social change needs to come from those who are hit the hardest by human rights violations. Human rights are not a difficult concept for marginalized, criminalized, and dehumanized communities to embrace. Border residents and immigrants have lived the reality of policies that strip them of their humanity, lump them into boxes labeled "security threats," and completely ignore the complexities of these communities by relying on heavy-handed, unaccountable enforcement measures cloaked in "security." To talk about human rights as BAN's vision for change inherently recognizes the complexity of what it means to be human. Immigrant and border communities, and their mobilization for dignity and equality, will hopefully be a key force in the next mass movement in the United States: a human rights movement.

CHAPTER FOURTEEN

Sexual Citizenship, Marriage, Adoption, and Immigration in the United States

Katie Acosta

Carmen is a forty-three-year-old U.S. citizen of Dominican descent. She has lived in the United States most of her life but her parents live in the Dominican Republic. Ten years ago Carmen met Casandra during one of her trips to visit her parents. She describes their encounter as love at first sight. The two maintained a long-distance relationship for several years. Frustrated with the difficulties associated with a binational relationship, the couple decided that Casandra would immigrate to the United States, where Carmen eagerly awaited her arrival. Naive and ill-prepared for the difficulties that awaited them, Casandra left her family and moved to the United States. Casandra is now an undocumented citizen, struggling to make a living while having no legal right to remain in this country. Tired of waiting for more equal immigration rights to pass in this country, the couple decided to begin their family. Casandra gave birth to the couple's first child four years ago. She still does not have legal status in the United States and has not been able to visit her family in the Dominican Republic in more than ten years. While Carmen is a U.S. citizen, she has no legal connection to Casandra or the child they decided to bring into the world together. Even though second-parent adoption is legal in the state where they reside, the high cost associated with executing second-parent adoptions and Casandra's undocumented status have been huge barriers for them in trying to gain protection and recognition for their family.

Social policies in the United States are designed in a way that ignores the needs of families like this one. The state actively strives to reproduce a particular family form and in doing so excludes alternative families. This privileging adversely affects the sexual citizenship rights of gay and lesbian families and renders them partial citizens. Citizenship as employed here would assume the provision of equal rights and protections, as well as equal access to benefits for all those who fall under this category in order to facilitate equal participation in social and political processes (Phelan 2001). The state's unwillingness to respect and validate lesbian/gay/bisexual/transgendered (LGBT) individuals is made clear through an analysis of U.S. laws, particularly those concerning immigration and citizenship. Close analysis reveals the specific ways that citizenship is diminished for LGBT individuals in the United States, and how this contributes to their social disenfranchisement.

In this chapter, I address the current state of citizenship rights for gay and lesbian families. I survey U.S. policies on gay marriage, adoption, and immigration to highlight the interconnected nature of citizenship rights in this country. I use a human rights framework to argue that the state places gay and lesbian families in an exclusionary category outside the realm of the nuclear family. In doing so, the state sends a message that these families are less deserving of citizenship and therefore limits these family's prospects for full acceptance and inclusion as equal members of society.

In the United States, LGBT advocates have long been reluctant to frame the concerns of their communities within a human rights framework. Instead these advocates have privileged a civil rights framework as a platform from which to fight for equality. This may be because a human rights framework is often centered on rigid identity categories, whereas identities within this community are often seen as socially constructed and fluid rather than essential (Mertus 2007). Still, a human rights lens has been popular when addressing LGBT issues internationally, especially for advocates working to stop violence against LGBT individuals and their families. These advocates have used human rights violations against LGBT individuals as a basis from which to seek asylum or refugee status (Fairbairn 2005; Anker 2005). Such arguments are framed as the necessity of LGBT individuals to be granted asylum because they are a member of a social group that is actively persecuted in their country of origin.

While a human rights framework has been most used by those advocating for the cessation of violence and hate crimes against LGBT individuals, a human rights lens is still fruitful when critically analyzing other social policies. In this chapter, I argue that the human rights of gay and lesbian families are violated in the United States due to existing rigid and heteronormative laws that adversely affect their quality of life. In using a human rights frame as a platform from which to advocate for more inclusive social policies for gay and lesbian families, I shift the focus away from violence against and discrimination of LGBT individuals. Instead, I question another fundamental human right—the right to not be subject to interference on one's family, which has often been denied to gay and lesbian families in this country. Article 12 of the UDHR states that

> No one shall be subjected to arbitrary interference with his privacy, family, home or correspondence, nor to attacks upon his honour and reputation. Everyone has the right to the protection of the law against such interference or attacks.

Furthermore, I argue that gay and lesbian couples are denied the right to marry and their families lack the protection of the state as outlined in Article 16 of the UDHR. Article 16 states that,

(1)   Men and women of full age, without any limitation due to race, nationality or religion, have the right to marry and to found a family. They are entitled to equal rights as to marriage, during marriage and at its dissolution.

(2)   Marriage shall be entered into only with the free and full consent of the intending spouses.

(3)   The family is the natural and fundamental group unit of society and is entitled to protection by society and the State.[1]

The UDHR does not define a family, nor does it specify whether one has the right to marry one's same-sex partner. Rather, this declaration is contingent on how specific countries come to define these categories (Tahmindjis 2005). Thus the state is allowed to disregard LGBT human rights by relying on a heteronormative interpretation of these laws. In the United States, both Articles 12 and 16 have been interpreted so that the family to be protected is heterosexual. While men and women have the right to marry, this is interpreted as only possible for individuals marrying someone of the opposite sex. Such interpretations have resulted in the exclusion of gay and lesbian families from full citizenship rights.

Same-Sex Marriage

One of the most common human rights, which LGBT advocates have actively fought for, is the right for same-sex marriage. The advancements of LGBT advocates for gay marriage rights prompted the government to take action. The Defense of Marriage Act (DOMA) of 1996 defines marriage as between two individuals of the opposite sex for the purpose of the federal government. It also outlines that states are not obligated to honor same-sex marriages granted in another state (Harvard Law Review 2004). DOMA excludes same-sex couples from federal benefits, including retirement, federal tax deductions for married couples, federal health benefits, immigration, and federal employee life insurance (Merin 2002). As if the federal DOMA was not enough, many states have since passed DOMAs in their jurisdictions. They have done so as a preemptive measure to ensure that same-sex couples that marry in another state cannot have these marriages legally recognized in their state.

In response to these restrictions several states have passed legal alternatives to federally sanctioned marriages in order to provide same-sex couples with basic legal protections. Vermont, Hawaii, and California are among those states that have created civil unions or domestic partnerships for gay and lesbian citizens. In 2004, Massachusetts became the first state to allow same-sex couples to legally marry at the state level. This was a major development as it was the first time that same-sex couples not only receive the same benefits as their fellow heterosexual citizens; it was the first time their rights did not get lumped into an alternative category. As it stands in Massachusetts, same-sex couples have the same rights as heterosexual couples to take out a marriage license from the state where they reside (the neighboring state of Connecticut followed suit in 2008).

California also attempted to pass gay marriage; however, Proposition 8 that passed in California by a 4 percent margin overturned it months later in 2008. Ironically, even as marriage equality supporters have correlated the prohibition of gay marriage to the prohibition of interracial marriages decades earlier, African American and Latino/a Christian groups who voted against same-sex marriage ironically supported the passage of Proposition 8 (Monroe 2009). Such mishaps have created divisions between oppressed groups, and continue to threaten civil and human rights progress through fraction and a failure to see the connection between various movements.

Adoption Rights

The limitations placed on same-sex couples' right to marry not only leaves the couples without legal protections, but also affects the children that they bring into their relationships or those they conceive together. Adoption for same-sex couples can vary a great deal in the United States because adoption laws are regulated entirely by the state where one resides. While most U.S. states allow gays or lesbians to adopt children as individuals, several have explicitly prohibited same-sex couples from jointly adopting children. These states include Michigan, Utah, Arkansas, and Florida[2] (Polikoff 2000).

In 2008, Arkansas passed a bill banning same-sex couples from becoming foster parents (Taneff 2009). In recent years, several states including Ohio, Arkansas, Alabama, Indiana, Oregon, Tennessee, Texas, and Virginia have all introduced a ban on adoption by gay individuals (Bagby 2006). While these bans have been predominantly unsuccessful, they do signal the deep division within states regarding legitimating gay and lesbian families. Interestingly with the exception of Arkansas, most states that do not allow gay and lesbian couples to adopt children will allow them to foster these children. This is contradictory because states like Florida, Michigan, Arkansas, and Utah argue that it isn't in the best interest of the child to be raised by same-sex couples, yet allow these children to live with gay and lesbian foster parents indefinitely when a suitable, sexually conforming couple is not found.

Those same-sex couples that already have biological children have different options in legitimating (in the eyes of the law) their families. These families need a mechanism to recognize the nonbiological parent who participates in the raising of the child without legal protection. One way to create these protections is through second-parent adoptions. Second-parent adoption laws allow an individual to adopt his or her partner's biological child so that both parents are legally recognized (Gibson 1999). Second-parent adoptions are permitted in California, District of Columbia, Indiana, Vermont, Massachusetts, New York, Connecticut, Illinois, Pennsylvania, and New Jersey (Palmer 2003). Nebraska, Ohio, and Colorado do not allow second-parent adoptions. Without the protection of second-parent adoptions, those couples that cannot legally marry do not have the protections for their children in the event of a separation or death. Therefore, by not extending legal protections to gay and lesbian couples, the state is also denying these couples' children their human rights because of their parents' relationship.

Adoption law in the United States highlights one of the biggest problems with the partial citizenship of same-sex couples. By extension, other members of their families are adversely affected by their lack of protection.

Immigration Policies

Marriage and adoption laws in the United States demonstrate that the state actively regulates sexuality and promotes hegemonic heterosexuality. Immigration is just one avenue through which this reproduction is executed. U.S. immigration law privileges the heteropatriarchal family as the preferred candidates for citizenship (Luibheid 2002).

The most common avenue for immigration is through family reunification. U.S. citizens have the legal right to sponsor their spouses, children, and siblings for immigration to the United States. However, in order for one to sponsor a spouse, one's marriage must be legally recognized at the federal level. Marriages established at the state level are not honored for immigration purposes. Since DOMA has defined marriage as between one man and one woman, immigration policies essentially allow heterosexual U.S. citizens to sponsor their spouses and prohibit same-sex married couples from accessing this right. Same-sex binational partnerships[3] make up more than 6 percent of the gay and lesbian couples in the United States (Human Rights Watch/Immigration Equality, 2006). Forty-six percent of these couples are raising children under age eighteen in their homes. Thus, much like the couple described at the beginning of this chapter, these families are not only struggling to be legitimated as citizens in the United States, they are struggling to have their partnerships to one another recognized, and to have their relationships to the children they are raising legitimatized.

The family sponsorship aspect of immigration policies is designed in a way that encourages binational same-sex couples to emulate heterosexuals in their efforts to gain heteronormative citizenship rights (Stychin 2000). Thus, in order to gain equal citizenship same-sex couples must reproduce themselves according the rigid value system of our immigration policies, which legitimate not only heterosexuality but also monogamy and morality.

The United American Families Act (UAFA) (formerly known as the Permanent Partners Immigration Act) was introduced in February of 2000. This proposal was initiated at the federal level and would allow U.S. citizens to sponsor their foreign-born same-sex partners for immigration. This bill would allow the U.S. Citizenship and Immigration Services to recognize same-sex couples as a family form for the sake of immigration without affecting the institution of marriage. This bill has been reintroduced every year since 2000 but unfortunately has not been passed.

While the UAFA holds potential for reuniting binational same-sex couples, it fails to challenge the heteronormative institution of marriage. Rather what UAFA achieves, much like civil unions and second-parent adoptions, is to create a separate category for gay and lesbian families that exists outside the realm of the privileged heteronormative family. Undoubtedly such policies have real-life implications for nonnormative families who are vulnerable without the protections provided by these rights. Still, to the extent that policies such as civil unions, second parent-adoptions, and same-sex immigration rights exist in a category outside of the norm, they do very little for encouraging citizenship and active participation of gay and lesbian families in the larger society.

Conclusion

In this chapter, I have surveyed the current status of three separate social policy issues. It is, however, important to note that what these social policies look like on paper is distinct from how they are executed in practice. Thus, a more thorough analysis of sexual citizenship and human rights issues would address not only whether both federal and state laws exist to protect gay and lesbian families, but also how effectively these laws are executed on the ground.

While I have provided a succinct account of the citizenship rights of gay and lesbian families it is also important to note that citizenship isn't just rooted in equal rights. Providing equitable rights for gay and lesbian families is only the first step for creating full citizenship. More important than having equitable rights is being able to participate in the community as an equal citizen (Phelan 2001). This analysis of federal and state laws allows us to better grasp how little the state respects alternative family forms. This chapter further highlights the ways that the state produces the types of citizens it deems most valuable and excludes those it does not accept.

As this analysis shows the underlying presumption of many human rights instruments and much of human rights discourse is heteronormativity. Future work in this area should use an intersectional approach to understanding sexual citizenship and human rights concerns. A middle-class lesbian couple may share an inability to marry with a poor lesbian couple, but the middle-class couple has the means to create other legal contracts to protect their family. Such an option may not be available to working lesbians who are struggling to make ends meet. To that end it is important that future work in the area of human rights and sexual citizenship addresses how the policies affect individual's lives and that the effects of these policies will vary according to race, class, and immigrant status.

CHAPTER FIFTEEN

Do Human Rights Endure Across Nation-State Boundaries? Analyzing the Experiences of Guest Workers

Shweta Majumdar Adur

When I stepped into my man camp that is provided in the yard of Signal International, I just surprised that, because in my twenty years of experience, I didn't dream of such a situation, because there is twenty-four peoples in a room, like I think it's a pigs in a cage. It is too hard to live there, because somebody is sneezing, somebody is snoring, and somebody is making sound, and we cannot even go to bathroom without spending hours. There is only two bathrooms and four toilets. And we are struggling very well. And in the mess hall we are not getting good food even. And they are saying that this is Indian good. And when we make complain, the camp manager said to us that, "You are living in slums in India. It is better than that slums."

—Indian guest worker

The Cost of the "American Dream"

In 2006, Signal International, a subcontractor for mammoth defense contractor Northrop Grumman—a marine construction company on the Mississippi Gulf Coast, recruited around 500 men from across India. The company needed extra workers to make up for the shortage of skilled labor following Hurricane Katrina. The men recruited reported that they had paid $20,000 to recruiters in exchange for promises of a green card and a prosperous life in the United States—a chance to realize the "American Dream." For many, the $20,000 had meant their life savings, for others it meant selling off their lands and for still others a life plunged in debt. Upon arriving, however, the workers were given ten-month temporary H2B visas under the guest worker program instead of green cards. And instead of an affluent lifestyle they found themselves living in appalling surroundings, working in "slave like conditions" and being kept under constant surveillance.[1]

They lived like that for eighteen months before walking out of their jobs and reporting Signals International as a human trafficker. Early in 2008, with the help of local immigrant rights activists, one hundred Indian guest workers undertook a perilous journey largely on foot from Louisiana to Washington, D.C. They described it as their Satyagraha,[2] a quest and a demand for truth. On May 14, 2008, they launched their hunger strike to demand temporary legal status in the United States, Congressional hearings into abuses of guest workers, and talks between the U.S. and Indian governments to protect future guest workers. The hunger strike lasted 29 days and was suspended only upon assurances of support and solidarity from U.S. Congress members and leaders from labor, civil rights, and religious communities. Nearly three years later (as this goes to print) the Indian workers continue to live on American soil still waiting for justice and the restoration of their dignity.

The plight recounted by the Indian guest workers in the Gulf Coast is probably one among many tales recounted by guest workers who cross national borders in search of a better life and better wages. Instead, they often find themselves in precarious situations compelled to endure gross violations of their human rights. As guest workers, these individuals have fewer avenues left open in their quest for justice. In the absence of citizenship entitlements in the host countries, there is little that the governments of the host countries are obligated to do for them. Plus, once guest workers have voluntarily left the jurisdiction of the countries where they have citizenship rights there is also little that the governments of these countries are required to do for them. A great deal is left open to binational political will, initiative, and dialogue. In such situations, political inertia exhibited by both governments frequently leaves migrants and guest workers fending for themselves in a treacherous "no mans land."

Their only hope in such circumstances would seem to be the transnational civil society and formal human rights instruments for protection (Das Gupta 2006). The growing power of the transnational civil society in the era of globalization has led many scholars to argue that migrants, as "postnational citizens," should seek protection from the transnational civil society, guided in theory by the UN and international law, including formal human rights instruments. Postnational citizenship, in its broadest sense, is defined as membership in a transnational world protected by the principles of the human rights framework. In effect, the concept suggests that migrants qualify for protection against human rights violations, even in the absence of national citizenship rights (Soysal 1994).

At the same time, enthusiasm about the promises and potentials of post-national citizenship must be tempered. Although migrants and guest workers can evoke human rights principles and law to advance their claims, the success of these struggles is nevertheless variable and not guaranteed. Ultimately much is left to political will and the inclination of host countries (member states) to abide by and enforce human rights obligations to which they are party.

The case of Indian guest workers in the United States is a telling illustration of the struggles faced by those forced into such a legally ambiguous state of being. Though the workers' plight has been made more visible by the NGOs working with them, their claims are still unmet. "Post-national citizenship" in this context has afforded few, if any, benefits to the guest workers, as they remain strung in the liminal space between the disenfranchisement they face in the host countries and the human rights they are entitled to as post-national citizens in a transnational world. To this end, this chapter questions the effectiveness of the formal human rights paradigm in protecting guest worker rights in the United States, where the guest worker program is particularly problematic in this regard.

In this chapter, I explore various facets of the guest worker program in the United States. First, I will articulate the relevance of human rights discourse in the contemporary world and enumerate the conditions that have led to the rise of post-national citizenship. Then, I will examine how the guest worker program works. In doing so, I will show how certain stipulations built into the guest worker programs make workers vulnerable to human rights abuses. Finally, I will evaluate the efficacy of the human rights paradigm in the era of globalization. I conclude that although the human rights discourse offers alternative avenues for protest and contestation, there is little that can be done as long as nation-states back greedy corporations and recruiters that deploy clauses outlined within the guest worker program to exploit foreign workers.

The Relevance of Human Rights in the "Post-National" World

Theorists of postnational citizenship define ways in which new forms of civic participation in the era of globalization are displacing traditional national citizenship. The national model of citizenship emerged as the hallmark feature of European modernity made possible by new structural conditions of modern industrial society—industrial, bureaucratic, media, and educational infrastructures (Tambini 2001; Sassen 2005).

The institutionalization of national citizenship became as much the pre-occupation of the modern nation-state as the sovereign will of the nation became the edifice for the state's legitimacy. From the point of view of the citizen, the institution of national citizenship became the legitimizing basis for the allocation of resources, rights, entitlements and responsibilities. In contemporary times, the structures of global capitalism and flexible capital have posed a grave threat to the sovereignty of the state and the sanctity of national citizenship (see also Armaline and Glasberg 2009). Easy mobilization and relocation of capital has made it possible for corporations to speedily shift production to places where costs of production—social, environmental, and labor—are the cheapest. Frequent capital flights have in effect left states struggling with shrinking budgets. Consequently, states have coped with the financial crisis by cutting back on welfare measures such as subsidized health care and education. Services that hitherto were among the entitlements of citizenship have now become increasingly commoditized and privatized. This trend has particularly hurt the poorest of citizens, who can neither rely on the state nor afford the competitively priced privatized services. The exigencies of global capitalism have thus created a disconnect between the state and its poor citizens, as the state is no longer capable of providing for its citizens as it may have done in the past (Sassen 1996; Tambini 2001).

The diminished capacity of the welfare state, increased capital mobility coupled with austerity packages enforced by global institutions provide an impetus to labor mobility as people relocate to find better lives and livelihoods (though the latter is neither as free or as footloose as the former). Migrants from poverty-stricken developing-peripheral nations are often forced to migrate to the wealthier industrial/postindustrial/core nations in search of gainful employment (Bacon 2008; Sassen 1996; Das Gupta 2006).

The intensity and frequency of labor migration has further increased the relevance of human rights principles and formal instruments that theoretically promise blanket protections to all migrants regardless of their race, sex, class, caste, religion, nationality, language, social origin, and so on. As Das Gupta (2006, 19) notes, "in this transnational complex, migrants want rights to mobility rather than to rootedness and citizenship" and that is exactly what the formal human rights regime offers.

For example, Article 28 of the UDHR states that, "everyone is *entitled to a social and international order* in which the rights and freedoms set forth in this Declaration can be fully realized." Commenting on the importance of transnational discourses such as the human rights paradigm, Soysal (1994) argues that politicians and policymakers," find it much harder to deny social and civil rights—those directly linked to the person, such as individual liber-

ties and a minimum standard of living—to new groups of people, even if they
do not belong to the formal national polity" (Soysal 1994, cited in Bloemraad 2004: 396). Hence proponents of postnational citizenship argue that in
the era of globalization, individuals may attain rights, protection and membership within states that are not their own (Soysal 1994). As a result, the
national no longer has primacy but coexists with the transnational, mutually
reinforcing and reconfiguring each other (Soysal 1994).

Are guest workers in the United States then "post-national citizens"? Do
they then reap aforementioned benefits of "post-national citizenship"? To
answer these questions, it is first important to understand the contours of the
guest worker program in the United States.

The Guest Worker Program

The effects of the economic-political changes we discussed in the last section
are most evident in the case of "guest workers" in the United States. As noted
above, the disparate levels of wealth between the core-periphery nations often
"push" workers to seek employment in the industrialized and postindustrial
world. In many countries, guest worker programs have been institutionalized
to provide temporary legal employment to migrants (Attas 2006).

The United States offers similar provisions. The most significant guest
worker program in the United States was known as the "Bracero Program."
The program was launched in 1942 and lasted until 1964, admitting 4.6 million Mexicans to work in U.S. agriculture. It was introduced to make up for
the wartime deficit in agricultural labor, but continued beyond the war as
agricultural stakeholders sought to retain cheap labor. The program was
finally suspended in 1964 in reaction to public outcry against reports of
human rights abuses of Mexican workers (Pastor and Alva 2004).

Currently, the guest worker program operates under the H2 and H1 visa
categories. The H1-B category consists of skilled workers who must hold
an undergraduate degree or its equivalent to qualify. Typical H1-B occupations include architects, engineers, computer programmers, accountants,
doctors, and college professors. In the case of H1-B workers, employers
can petition the government to adjust the guest workers status from temporary to permanent resident or immigrant. Under the immigration provisions outlined, H1-B workers are allowed to bring spouses and children
to the United States. Typically, spouses of H1-B workers are not allowed
to work on dependent visa status. The only exception to the rule occurs if
the spouses have their own H1-B status. The children of H1-B workers are
allowed to attend local schools. The H1-B visa is valid for three years upon

which it must be renewed. Typically an H1-B worker is allowed to work for the maximum of 6 years.

The H2 category belongs to seasonal workers and currently operates at two levels—H-2A for agricultural work, and H-2B for nonagricultural work. In the H-2A program, the agricultural employer must attest that domestic workers are unavailable at the prevailing wage rate before they can contract out positions to migrant workers. Though the H-2A program provides legal protections for foreign farm workers—such as a guarantee of at least three quarters of the total employment hours promised, free housing, transportation compensation, medical benefits, and legal representation—many of these protections exist only on paper. H-2B workers, on the other hand, have even fewer rights or protections. In the case of H-2B workers, as well, employers must first certify that demand is temporary and they were unable to find U.S. nationals to fulfill the spots before they can advertise to recruit abroad (Pastor and Alva 2004).

Between the H1-B and the H2-B programs, arguably it is the H2 program that is most exploitative and renders immigrants vulnerable to human rights abuses.[3] The guest worker program then identifies two conditions— first, states actively distinguish between citizens and immigrants. In doing so, states disenfranchise and deny immigrants basic entitlements by defining them as temporary workers even as they bring them in to perform crucial labor. Second, immigration policies in the United States hierarchically distinguish temporary workers, thereby normalizing the differential treatment of each category (Das Gupta 2006; Franz 2007).

With this historical context in mind, in the following section we will explicate how the stipulations built into the guest worker program make workers vulnerable to human rights abuses in the United States.

Examining the Conditions of Exploitation

Provisions inscribed in the guest worker program leave the workers vulnerable to exploitation and human rights abuses. The legal provision of the guest worker program essentially ties the guest worker to one employer. During the period of H2-A or H2-B visa status a guest worker is not entitled change jobs or employers. Left at the mercy of their employers, workers are often afraid of complaining as complaints or protests often lead to job loss and deportation. Hence, they become subject to low wages, poor working and living conditions, and lack of freedom to unionize or to find alternative employment (Bacon 2008; Franz 2007; Attas 2000). For example, the guest worker program establishes a minimum wage rate. Still, wherever it is adhered to, the minimum standard often becomes the maximum standard that the worker can reasonably expect will be honored. In 2006, for example, the minimum wage for a farm worker was set at $8 per hour (Bacon 2008).

Guest workers also suffer poor living conditions—mainly housing and food. The H2-A visa mandates that growers provide housing to workers they bring into the country—at least in theory. Often, housing, if provided at all, is overcrowded with poor sanitary conditions. Today in most parts of California, growers are no longer willing to house the workers who harvest their crops. In the fall of 2000, amid negotiations proposing expansion of guest worker programs, big agribusinesses proposed getting rid of the requirement (Bacon 2008: 86). As a result, "at harvest times it is common to see cars parked on the outskirts of farm worker towns, families sleeping beside them" (85).

The housing conditions provided to the Indian H2-B guest workers profiled at the beginning of the chapter were equally poor, if not worse. Workers reported that they were crammed like "sardines in a jar" in windowless bunkhouses that measured 36 by 24 feet and held 24 bunk beds. The workers could only lie in the beds, as there was no space between the bunk beds to even sit up. There were only two showers, one television, and no privacy. Armed guards, barricades, and fences prevented the workers from fleeing.[4] Food was allegedly stale and cold. And, ironically, the workers *paid $35 per day* out of their wages to stay in the labor camps Signal set up inside the yard (Bacon 2008, 172). Unlike H1-B workers, H2-B guest workers lack familial support, as they are not typically allowed to bring their families with them. Loneliness coupled with dehumanizing conditions and constant threat of deportation makes life incredibly hard for them.

Trapped in such situations, workers lose their power to bargain, strike, and engage in collective action because of the threat of job loss and deportation. For guest workers being without a job violates the conditions of their visas and renders them subject to immediate deportation. Nevertheless, it does not mean that workers have always acquiesced to their oppression. But protests have also met with swift retribution as the scales are often tipped in favor of the employers. Historically the Bracero Program has been replete with examples where dissenting workers and organizers suffered severe sanctions from the employers.

In the case of Indian guest workers, history seems to repeat itself. The news of Indian guest workers organizing, with the help of Mississippi Immigrant Rights Alliance (MIRA) and New Orleans Workers' Center for Racial Justice (NOWCRJ), met with swift reprisal from the company authorities as they handed out termination letters to the dissenters. The *New York Times* editorial, "A Bitter Guest Worker Story," published on February 4, 2010, notes that

> the company—according to court testimony by its own officers— sought guidance from Immigration and Customs Enforcement (ICE) on how to fire "chronic whiners" who were threatening to organize broader protests. The agency replied, according to one official: "Don't give them any advance notice. Take them all out of the line on the way to work; get their personal belongings. Get them in a van and get their tickets and get them to the airport and send them back to India." The private deportation failed after workers' advocates organized a protest at the shipyard gates. In an internal e-mail message 10 days later, a shipyard official disclosed that the agency had promised to go after workers who had left their jobs, "if for no other reason than to send a message to the remaining workers that it is not in their best interests to try and 'push' the system.

Relatively hopeless, helpless, and heavily indebted, one worker disappeared while another attempted to commit suicide upon hearing the news (Bacon 2008: 173).

Currently, investigations are underway and as of June 2010, the federal government has decided to grant special visas to about 150 Indian metalworkers.[5]

Human Rights Norms: The United States as Gold Standard?

Detailed accounts by workers indicate that their human rights were clearly violated by their employers and recruiters. The federal Equal Employment Opportunity Commission (EEOC) determined in September that there was "reasonable cause" to believe the Indian guest workers at Signal had faced discrimination and a work environment "laced with ridicule and harassment" (Preston 2010).

Many of these violations were possible because of problematic provisions embedded in the guest worker program. The Indian workers reported that they were kept in "slave-like conditions," even though servitude in any form is a clear violation of the ICCPR, to which the United States is party (Articles 2-5 are relevant here). Moreover, Article 5 in the UDHR states that "no one shall be subjected to torture or to cruel, *inhuman or degrading treatment* or punishment." Yet, the living conditions workers described were clearly degrading and inhuman. Further, Article 7(2) in ICESCR asserts that every worker is entitled to a "decent living for themselves and their families in accordance with the provisions of the present Covenant."

The workers' experiences violate the various provisions enshrined under Article 23 of the UDHR. Article 23(1) states that "everyone has the right to work, to free choice of employment, to just and favorable conditions of work and to protection against unemployment." The workers were clearly denied just and favorable conditions of work as they lived cramped in a single room with guards watching over them. The dehumanization they suffered in the hands of recruiters and employers violates provisions under Article 23(3) that states that "everyone who works has the right to just and favorable remuneration ensuring for himself and his family an existence worthy of human dignity, and supplemented, if necessary, by other means of social protection." The fact that the guest worker visas tie workers to one and only one employee violates the right to the free choice of employment and subjects workers to a work environment in which wages can be below subsistence and thus inconsistent with human dignity.

Finally, Article 23 (4) states, "everyone has the right to form and to join trade unions for the protection of his interests." However, the fact that workers essentially depend on their employers to maintain a "legal" status implicitly results in the loss of their power to bargain, strike, and engage in collective action. Workers often suffer excesses out of the fear of losing their jobs, which would in turn mean deportation. Where the focus here so far has been on broadly accepted international human rights instruments, the UN Convention on the Protection of the Rights of All Migrant Workers and Members of Their Families (MWC) is worth mentioning. It suggests some level of international consensus on the need to explicitly address the conditions of migrant workers, and those who might be constructed as "transnational" or "post-national" citizens. Still, the MWC has a long way to go in terms of ratification. Most of the ratifications are from primarily countries of origin of migrants (Mexico, Philippines, Sri Lanka, Nicaragua, etc.). So far none of the western/migrant receiving countries have ratified the treaty, and this includes the United States. Thus, where guest worker protection is most needed, governments seem least interested in seriously committing to their protection.

As evident from this discussion, human rights discourse has been critical in shaping the language of resistance. The question that follows from this discussion asks whether human rights norms have really been beneficial for this group of postnational citizens —citizens of India but guest workers in the American soil? Has it made much difference for their disenfranchisement? As is typical, there is no simple or straight-cut answer to the question.

On the one hand, the growing relevance of human rights discourse in the era of globalization has led to the creation of "transnational social justice organizations" that act as vanguards of human rights by compelling states and markets to act in compliance. The guest workers' struggle also relies on similar structures of support. NGOs like NOWCRJ have been at the forefront of organizing the workers. Various other labor and civil rights organizations have been supporting their campaign, including Jobs with Justice, the Southern Poverty Law Center, and the American Federation of Labor and Congress of Industrial Organizations (AFL-CIO). The workers, backed by NOWCRJ and the Southern Poverty Law Center, have also filed a federal antiracketeering lawsuit against their recruiters. The outcome is, however, undetermined, as the lawsuit is ongoing. The organizational support enabled the workers to launch a momentous protest. The "Satyagraha" and the ensuing hunger strike got the workers much-needed public visibility and the attention of diplomats and state officials. It also exposed the corruption and exploitation embedded in the guest worker programs. All over the United States marches and vigils were organized on the day of the hunger strike to express solidarity with the workers' cause.

On the other hand, there have been few tangible gains as political will in this matter has been, at best, sluggish. The fact that 150 metal workers were granted special visas from the federal government reiterates the significance of the civil society and the human rights networks, but also raises important questions. In the two years that have transpired, workers have remained unemployed in the United States, uncertain what the future holds for them, while their families back home deal with the burden of debt and loan sharks. It's hard to imagine the uncertainties, hopelessness, and emotional distress that this might have meant and continues to mean to guest workers. Finally, unless the problematic provisions inherent in the guest worker program are redressed, this one-time accommodation may mean little to other guest workers on American soil.

The proponents of post-national citizenship and enthusiasts of the formal human rights regime must reckon with its limitations. Not all migrants come in with equal status and make equal claims on the state. Even under the scope of legal migration, immigration policies distinguish between the desirable and undesirable migrants. In this case, the guest workers are clearly at the bottom of the hierarchy as undesirable migrants (note: H1-B workers are relatively better off but not in absolute terms[6]). Thus, the enforcement of human rights norms requires substantial political commitment. And as the provisions enshrined in the guest worker program show, political will does not always conform to the moral and legal standards enshrined by human rights instruments. The issue of immigrant and migrant rights as transnational citizens also highlights the tension between international human rights instruments and sovereign rights of individual member states to establish and enforce law. This tension is largely to blame for the wide open door to the sorts of human rights abuses to which guest workers are subjected. The Indian guest workers have come a long way, but the final decision in the case is unknown. Will the verdict reiterate the successful empowerment of postnational citizens or reinforce the disempowerment of guest workers? This is something that remains unsettled.

PART V

___

CONVENTION ON THE ELIMINATION OF ALL FORMS OF RACIAL DISCRIMINATION

The International Convention on the Elimination of All Forms of Racial Discrimination (ICERD) was established in 1966. The United States has signed and ratified the convention, indicating agreement with its principles defining all forms of racism as violations of human rights. (However, as did many other party states, the U.S. filed a reservation keeping ICERD from becoming "the law of the land," suggesting that the treaty is incompatible with U.S. sovereignty.) But how well does the U.S. conform to those principles? Issues of racialized discrimination have already appeared throughout this volume. For example, previous chapters have explored racism in the context of predatory lending and economic justice, housing rights in New Orleans, education rights under No Child Left Behind, cultural rights of Native Americans, national security policies, and immigration rights.

In this section, the chapters focus centrally on questions of racism, raising several critical questions about human rights. For example, racism is commonly considered an interpersonal expression of individuals' prejudices, suggesting that all that must be done is to change individuals' attitudes in order to eliminate racism. But such a perspective is ahistorical: it ignores the centuries of laws and practices that have served to embed racism into the very fabric of institutions, so that individuals' personal attitudes are less relevant than how the institutions are organized and operate. How are institutions arranged so that they reproduce racialized inequality despite what individuals may or may not believe? This question requires a shift in perspective, from one of individual attitudes and behaviors to one of structural arrangements concerning how society is organized.

Questions of racism also raise issues of citizenship and human rights. Who is defined as a citizen, and by what criteria? What rights may be lost when one is defined and treated as a non-citizen or a second-class citizen? What actions of resistance have challenged the definition of racialized citizenship to alter institutional arrangements that reproduce racism?

Additionally, children are often all but invisible in questions of rights, with the possible exception of labor rights. Children are commonly ignored as citizens, often placing them below the human rights radar and excluding them from discussions of their own rights. This is particularly the case for children who become ensnared in the juvenile justice system. The chapter here explores the caging of children, where racism is reproduced through the aggressive coercion of youth of color, often in the name of public safety and child protection. When does "protection" of children become a violation of human rights? How might a human rights discourse be applied to understanding state-sponsored institutional racism in juvenile justice and possible alternatives?

CHAPTER SIXTEEN

From International Platforms to Local Yards: Standing Up for the Elimination of Racial Discrimination in the United States

Bandana Purkayastha, Aheli Purkayastha, and Chandra Waring

In April 2009, the United States refused to participate in the Durban Review Conference, which was set up to assess the progress made by countries on combating racism. This review conference was a follow-up to an earlier conference that was held in Durban in 2001, on eliminating all forms of racial discrimination. The 2001 Durban Conference, attended by ten thousand people from around the world—state delegates, NGOs, and others—reignited a global discussion on the principles of ICERD, which was enshrined as part of the UN human rights instruments in 1965. The U.S. position on ICERD, which it signed in 1994, as well as its lack of participation in the review conferences, offers us one starting point for understanding how human rights are refined, challenged, and claimed.

According to U.S. State Department's Robert Wood, the U.S. refusal to participate in the Durban Review Conference was based on its concern about the document that was being negotiated to serve as a template for the conference (Wood 2009). The United States objected to the length of the document (i.e., it was too long, and it ought to be shorter than the document produced in an earlier conference at Durban in 2001). According to Wood, the Durban Review Conference document also contained a troubling phrase "defamation of religion," which raised U.S. official concern about how this would be interpreted at the conference. The United States was also worried that only one country (Israel) would be singled out for racism. Finally, the United States expressed concern that the issue of reparations for slavery might be raised again. The mainstream U.S. media, however, described the U.S. objections in terms of refusal to support an anti-Semitic platform, since Iranian president Mahmoud Ahmadinejad, who had publicly denied the Holocaust, was to be one of the speakers. Members of Congress were divided; some felt the United States ought to participate in the conference, introducing resolutions (e.g., Res. 1361) in favor of U.S. participation, while others opposed it (Congressional Research Reports for People 2009).[1]

Earlier, in 2001, the United States had walked out of the World Conference Against Racism, Racial Discrimination, Xenophobia and Related Intolerance, Durban, South Africa (WCAR, the Durban Conference) after three days because of what it viewed as too much time spent by other governments on criticizing Israel's treatment of Palestinians. The Durban Conference raised a number of other "controversial" issues including reparations for slavery and colonialism. The final document, however, did not contain any reference to Israel nor did it uphold the initial calls for reparations (see Durban document[2]). Among other issues, the declaration emphasized racism suffered by people of African and Asian descent, indigenous populations, and migrants; and it linked racism to economic and political inequalities, as well as armed conflict. The Durban declaration stated that the Holocaust must never be forgotten, and expressed concern about the increase in anti-Semitism and Islamophobia.

If we simply rely on the official U.S. statements and reports in the mainstream media, we might conclude that the primary U.S. role at these conferences was to lead the rest of the world in identifying and protesting racism and xenophobia. But the picture is far more complicated. Anti-Semitism that the United States officially protested—including statements and accounts that deny the Holocaust—are indeed examples of racism, and need to be vigorously challenged. However, these conferences (WCAR, Durban Review) have raised international consciousness about the multifaceted nature of racism, and the variety of groups who are subjected to structural and interpersonal racism. These conferences have generated political pressure on governments to produce internationally transparent records of their progress on eliminating racial discrimination. By using one type of racism to distance its self from these conferences, the United States has avoided engaging with multifaceted racism within its borders.

Racism in the United States:
International Platforms and Local Yards

Numerous scholars and activists have documented historical and contemporary forms of racism within the United States.[3] From centuries-long efforts to eliminate indigenous people or contain them within reservations, slavery, residential and other forms of segregation, stratified access to economic and social resources, forced internment, and bracero programs, U.S history is replete with examples of racism against groups who are socially constructed as non-white or "less than" American. A range of institutional arrangements, interactions, and ideologies has contributed to such racial discrimination. Other chapters of this book, for instance, discuss contemporary racial profiling, curtailment of immigrants' rights, violations of indigenous rights, unequal access to education, unequal access to housing, predatory lending, and caging of children, and document a variety of ways in which structural and interpersonal racism continues to systematically marginalize people based on their membership in racially defined (minority) groups. At the same time, groups have organized against racism; any account of the human rights enterprise against racism is an account of claiming rights, winning and losing claims, and reorganizing again and again in a long journey to claim human rights with or without reference to signed, ratified, or enforced international conventions.

In this chapter we focus on two contemporary, but not widely recognized, types of effort to combat racial discrimination. We focus on the efforts of organized groups to develop a report on racism in the United States, and we examine how racism and the challenges to racism play out on college campuses. We begin this discussion by looking at international-level activism against racism as U.S.-based activist groups collectively challenge the U.S. official report on its effort to eliminate racial discrimination. We discuss how the report is created and how activist groups reframe the ways in which racism in the United States is understood at the international level. The second part of the discussion focuses on the local level. We analyze the nature of racism on college campuses and some actions to combat racism as students claim their human right to be in an arena free from racial discrimination. We discuss these two levels in order to show that the human rights enterprise to eliminate racism occurs (and has to occur) at different levels, in different ways, through the efforts of different groups, in order to address everyday behaviors and perceptions as well as policies and institutional structures that sustain racism.

ICERD and the United States:
Engagements in the International Arena

The U.S. Report on Combating Racism

The United States signed onto ICERD (or CERD) in 1966, and ratified it in 1994.[4] As a signatory, the United States is obligated to submit reports on its progress to combat racism, and it has produced two reports on this subject. The 2007 report is discussed below.

ICERD developed its principles on the elimination of racism based on the original UDHR emphasis on the dignity and equality inherent in all human beings. ICERD defines racial discrimination as

> any distinction, exclusion, restriction or preference based on race, colour, descent, or national or ethnic origin which has the purpose or effect of nullifying or impairing the recognition, enjoyment or exercise, on an equal footing, of human rights and fundamental freedoms in the political, economic, social, cultural or any other field of public life. (Art. 1)

It calls on governments to ensure to all human beings fullest access to political, civil, cultural, social, and economic human rights, including through protection measures. Along with legal measures and programs, states are expected to set up immediate measures to use education, culture, and information resources to help eliminate prejudice and discrimination. States are also expected to file regular reports on the progress of their actions; a review committee consisting of selected members of nations is supposed to examine the reports and assess progress. However, in order to get this convention passed, ICERD followed the process used for the other instruments. It offered a compromise to states that were wary of signing onto the whole instrument: states are allowed to formally express reservations, that is, a state can formally announce it will not participate in sections of ICERD.[5]

The U.S. CERD 2007 report provides the country's official position on combating racism. Briefly, the United States claims that its constitutional guarantees against nondiscrimination are a sufficient measure to combat racism. On page 1, the report points out:

> As described in that Report, the United States Constitution; the constitutions of the various states and territories; and federal, state, and territorial law and practice provide strong and effective protections against discrimination on the basis of race, color, ethnicity, and national origin in all fields of public endeavor and with regard to substantial private conduct as well. These protections, as administered through executive action and the judicial system, continue to apply.

The U.S. report highlights the constitutional guarantees of civil rights to all people in the nation, and it highlights its current administrative structure for combating racism. It explains the structure of DHS, and on page 13 states:

> Within DHS [Department of Homeland Security], Congress established an Office for Civil Rights and Civil Liberties, led by the DHS Officer for Civil Rights and Civil Liberties who reports directly to the Secretary of Homeland Security. The Office is charged with investigating allegations of abuses of civil rights, civil liberties, and discrimination on the basis of race, ethnicity, and religion by employees or officials of the Department of Homeland Security. (13)

This 2007 report points out that people are well informed of their political and civil rights since these are debated in the media and the information is disseminated through different channels, especially the Internet. Acknowledging remaining challenges, especially subtle and, sometimes, overt discrimination against marginalized groups, the report connected this to attitudes of people, as well as a lack of awareness of government programs. The report identified bias crimes against Arab and Muslim populations and the impact of changing demographics due to legal and illegal immigration. In other words, the report pointed to the *structural attempts to eliminate* racism, and identified personal *prejudice*, or inability of groups to take advantage of existing programs, as the reason for some of the remaining challenges. Overall it claimed:

> the United States has made significant progress in the improvement of race relations over the past half-century. Due in part to the extensive constitutional and legislative framework that provides for effective civil rights protections, overt discrimination is far less pervasive than it was in the early years of the second half of the Twentieth Century. As the United States continues to become an increasingly multiethnic, multi-racial, and multi-cultural society, many racial and ethnic minorities have made strides in civic participation, employment, education, and other areas. (15)

This generally positive official assessment, and the stated reasons for continuing racism in the United States—that racial discrimination is primarily an outcome of prejudiced behavior or the victims' lack of awareness of government programs—is not shared by all who read the report in the United States. In fact, large numbers of scholars and activist groups that have been working, sometimes for many decades, to turn the spotlight on structural racism, are very critical of the identified causes (and effects) in the U.S. official report.

These activist groups have collectively issued a "shadow" report to the UN based on their own experiences in combating racism across different arenas of U.S. society.

U.S. Activists and the Shadow Report

Shadow reports are created by NGOs to challenge official reports that are submitted by countries. Such reports have become important to the human rights enterprise since NGOs have been given a formal role in UN deliberations to ensure assessment bodies hear from sources other than governments about the progress in human rights. Thus, the shadow report provides an opportunity to groups that are working within a country to come together and provide a critical assessment of the state of human rights within their country.

The key organizing entity for the shadow report on racism in the United States has been the Human Rights Network (www.ushrnetwork.org/about_us). It serves as a conduit for an array of U.S. organizations ranging from university-based centers, activist organizations with very long histories of civil rights struggles, such as the NAACP, to newer organizations such as the American Muslim Voice; the network includes well-recognized organizations such as the ACLU to smaller organizations such as Southwest Workers Union, and Coalition on Anti Asian American Violence. Their websites indicate the array of issues they address and the diverse strategies they use to achieve their objectives. Consequently, the shadow report, which combines the input from diverse organizations, distills their insights from their ongoing work and emphasizes the multifaceted nature of racism.

The construction of the shadow report reflects a coming together of diverse activist agendas to develop the indicators of multifaceted racism. The types of racism identified by the shadow report are a distillation of a series of meetings and negotiations between multiple activist groups around the country over a couple of years. The website http://www.hrpujc.org/CERDShadowReporting.html provides an example of the process of producing a shadow report. A lead organization, such as New York City's Urban Justice Center Human Rights Project, organizes a large number of community groups. Part of this organizing consists of making the global and national documents available to the organizations via their website. These documents shape some of the language in which the injustices are expressed. Then a series of meetings are scheduled through the year for organizations to come together to identify injustices and prepare a report such as *Race Realities in NYC* featured on the Urban Justice Center website. These local reports are sent to the U.S. Human Rights Network to compile in the shadow report on racism in the United States.

The 2008 Shadow Report's description of racism includes structural racism, immigrant rights, issues of the indigenous people, hate groups, police brutality, prisons, access to civil justice, voting rights, housing discrimination, homelessness, health, education, and a range of other issues.[6] Thus it focuses on structural and interpersonal forms of racism and identifies the shortcomings of the U.S. official report. This gap—the areas of disagreement between the two reports—becomes part of the data at the international level on the progress of a country toward eliminating racism.

A key point of the shadow report is that the United States' constitutional or statutory laws do not meet the ICERD standards on combating racism. For example, the ICERD recognizes that discrimination results not just from deliberate acts on the part of the government but also from actions and laws that have a differential impact on different racial groups. ICERD requires that both types of discrimination be eliminated. The shadow report points out that U.S. law, with a few exceptions, always considers the intent to discriminate (e.g., in hate crimes) as an important precursor for understanding discrimination, whereas ICERD emphasis is on the effect. The ICERD also demands that governments take action to eliminate racial discrimination in the enjoyment of the right to work, the right to housing, the right to medical care, and the right to education—a range of economic and social human rights that are not recognized under U.S. domestic law. Equally important, the Shadow Report emphasizes that the United States has been, especially since September 2001, subjecting immigrants and refugees to systematic violations of their human rights. This matter parallels Christine Zozula's (chapter 11) discussion of the erosion of political and civil rights in the post-9/11 context. From immigration raids, racial profiling in a variety of spheres, and systematically denying immigrants their right to access jobs, housing, education, and health care, a new series of discriminatory measures have been institutionalized in the United States in the twenty-first century. Thus, according to the shadow report, the United States has failed to make significant progress to combat de jure and de facto racism.

The activist organizations do not stop with the ICERD shadow reports. The consequences of racism, evident through lack of proper housing, education, access to jobs, health care, and political and civil rights are brought to the international arena through other actions. Such actions include meeting the UN Special Rapporteurs on poverty or housing as they visit the United States (see, e.g., Barret Katuna's chapter on the report on poverty in the United States), and filing complaints with the Inter-American Court (Ford Foundation 2004). These different actions create a tapestry of human rights enterprise to eliminate racism.

These shadow reports are a crucial tool in the quest for human rights. They provide a conduit for recording the experiences of groups whose views are not represented in the official reports. Thus, these reports provide a way for those whose human rights are violated to publicize their experiences to the world. These shadow reports also generate international discussions and put pressure on the U.S. government to respond to these charges. While countries can ignore the mandates of UN human rights councils, such collective "airing of grievances" carry the potential for diluting a state's status in international arenas, and consequently their ability to sway international opinion on specific matters. Thus, organizations get together to create such shadow reports because they understand such "naming and shaming" tactics provide an additional means to hold the United States accountable on behalf of the people who are not well-served by the existing structures and provisions lauded in the U.S. official report.

College Students and Contemporary Racism

The problems of racism are not wholly addressed through the efforts of organized groups that focus on the government and other macro-level entities. Racist institutional arrangements, interactions, and ideologies are sustained because people do not "see" how racism works; they are, therefore, not inclined to act to address racism.[7] In this section we focus on college students who are likely to learn about racism in college classrooms. By and large, many college students train to participate in these local, regional, and international activist efforts. So the way that they speak, act, and respond to issues of racism affects not only their surrounding community but also what they do after college.

Since K-12 schools continue to be segregated on race/class lines in the United States, many students encounter people of different races/classes as peers for the first time in college. With the growing emphasis on "race" and gender issues in many courses, many more students, compared to the previous generation, have begun to study racism. In the classroom, students use sophisticated terms such as "privilege" and "systems of oppression" to describe racism, and the majority of college students identify that racism still exists.

However, Aheli Purkayastha and Chandra Waring's research on college students from the eastern United States in 2008 shows that despite becoming very conversant with the language in which racism is discussed, students continue to associate "racism" with the Jim Crow type racist actions constituted of lynching, legal segregation, and overt forms such as racial slurs and epithets. Thus, when asked about the possibility of racism within their own communities—their friends, families—students often protest or resist the idea that they might play a part in sustaining the contemporary system of racism. For instance, during our research a twenty-one-year-old female European American student at a very well-known liberal arts college admitted that racism still exists, but when asked for a specific example, she paused and replied: "I mean, it bothers me that people are treated differently because of the color of their skin or their personal history. Um. But it's something that I don't see a lot, I don't think about it often." For this student, "race" is relegated to the classroom where she can "think" about it; outside the classroom, she doesn't "see" it, so she doesn't have to think or do anything about it. She does not consider the fact that she is privileged because she doesn't have to "see it"or "think about it," unless she wishes to do so.

When asked about subtle, covert forms of racism within their community, students often protest and resist the idea that racism occurs in their social life. While these students rarely use explicitly racist, or racially charged language—indeed many find it abhorrent—they also fail to pay attention to the forms of contemporary racism. When asked "how do you think that people of color have been treated in this society," the (same) student's response was

Um, I think that those who [pause] those who are not as wealthy as others I feel are looked down upon and treated differently whereas those who are extremely wealthy or well educated are treated as members of society, whereas their fellow brethren, I guess I should say, are treated differently.

While we do not think that she intentionally means to insinuate that all people of color are poor, she nonetheless draws upon the long-existing ideologies about racial minorities—as poor, under-educated—to describe how people of color are treated. This conflation of poverty and race is the staple of "culture of poverty" perspectives that, in effect, blame poor uneducated people for being negatively affected by structural discrimination. The implication is that if people tried harder, they would be upwardly mobile in society, and, consequently, as this student points out, they would be accepted. It is necessary to understand this statement in context of her entire interview. She had just said, "it bothers me that people are treated differently," effectively implying that "I'm not racist because it bothers me that people are treated differently." But like many students, her awareness of racism emerges out of a "colorblind" perspective, that is, she did not recognize her role in perpetuating a racial stereotype because she used color-neutral language to do so. The interviews showed that the problem does not lie in understanding that racism exists, but rather connecting the contemporary forms of racism to their daily lives.

The respondent in this study initially communicated in "front stage"[8] language by acknowledging that racism still exists and that it "bothers" her. It is politically correct to recognize the fundamentally different history that African Americans and other Americans of color have experienced in the United States. On the other hand, once probed about how racism directly shapes the lives of Americans of color, this same student clings to racist ideologies, which conflate economic background with race, more specifically, *poverty* with *people of color*. It is safe to assume that this student did not receive messages about all people of color being impoverished from courses that deconstruct the concept of "race." Therefore, it is possible that this student received these racist messages from the "backstage." As Picca and Feagin (2007) contend, European Americans are racially socialized in markedly different ways in all-white settings: "whites often do interactive racial performances differently in places where there are multiracial populations (the *frontstage*) as compared with their interactive racial performances in places where only whites are present (the *backstage*)" (2007, xi, emphasis original).[9]

Waring's research with black/white biracial Americans reveals similar patterns of racist language in informal settings (i.e., outside the classroom) on U.S. college and university campuses. For example, a black/white biracial female named Christina, who attended a well-known college in New England, recalled experiences in her sorority when some of her sorority sisters—and friends—would make explicitly racist statements couched in an intentionally deracialized, yet essentially, hyperracialized manner. In other words, Christina's friends would make racist remarks about African Americans and then exclude Christina from being a member of the African American community. In doing so, her friends would to try to dismiss Christina's potential anger by deracializing her (e.g., removing her from being black), yet in reality, they were making Christina's race (as a racial "other" because she is not perceived as white) more apparent by first, uttering the comment and, subsequently, attempting to explain why Christina is exempted from negative stereotypes of black individuals. These situations simultaneously highlight Christina's blackness while attempting to make her blackness (conveniently) disappear. On some occasions, her sorority sisters would "slip up" and say things that "they didn't mean to say in front of [her]," including using the notoriously racist "n word" while driving with Christina in the backseat.

Like one time we were driving and she missed the turn and she said "Oh Nigger!" Apparently, using the word "nigger" is like "I made a mistake." And she was like "Oh my God, I'm sorry, Christina!" And I'm like "Why would you say that anyway? Why would that be something that you think is okay [to say] in general?" So it's stuff like that. Or [some white friends would say] "Oh, I would never date a black guy, no offense, Christina." I'm like "I don't give a shit." But you don't have to—I'm not offended, I don't care who you date.

While this language is undeniably racist, the fact that a friend who is also a sorority "sister" spoke it complicated the situation for Christina, who had to interact with this individual at sorority functions for the duration of her college career. Because this remark was not an *intentional* racial slur, how should Christina have responded? What would the ramifications of her response be in her sorority community? Because the overwhelming majority of the members of her Greek organization are white, is it even worth mentioning to the executive board, which is also predominately white and, consequently, may not understand? What impact will this have on Christina's friendships with her other white peers in the sorority? Because she is half black instead of "full black," would she be taken seriously if she lodged a complaint about this incident?

These are the types of questions students of color (and biracial students) have to ask themselves when enduring forms of racial discrimination, racist comments, and other forms of racism "in their own back yard." And, most important, they have to keep wrestling with these questions in different arenas of their lives. While such incidents appear to be far removed from human rights issues, these everyday, *cumulative experiences* violate the fundamental principle of the human rights charter—the ability to enjoy and exercise, "on an equal footing, of human rights and fundamental freedoms in the political, economic, social, cultural or any other field of public life" (UDHR, Art.1).

In *fully* understanding racism and joining in the effort to combat racism, college students must be *willing* to understand racism as a system and understand the role that they play within the system. When students understand racism they can join in multiracial coalitions to protest racism. For instance when the Jena 6 incident happened, nationwide student protests followed.[10] On the other hand, incidents around hateful speech are often viewed as ambiguous forays into First Amendment rights issues when students fail to link such speech to racism.

An example covered by a college newspaper illustrates this "grey area" and the type of on-campus activism that can challenge racial discrimination.[11] A college group proposed to bring a band called Ching Chong Song to a campus on the East coast. The Asian students group on that campus initiated the protests and complaints—pointing out that such terms are racially charged stereotypes used against Asian origin people in the United States for centuries—and other student groups of color joined in the protest very quickly. The combined group began to "raise consciousness" about the racist overtones of the name of the band, and asked that the invitation be rescinded.[12] In the discursive conflict that followed, a representative of the band claimed that the students of color were being unreasonably sensitive to the name of the band and that, in Germany, the words Ching Chang Chong was the equivalent of "rock, paper, scissors." She also pointed out that as a gay student who grew up in a poor, second-generation household, she was sensitive to language, and the students of color needed to come and talk to her or listen to her band instead of protesting. As the controversy continued, an administrator publicly supported the students by writing to the newspaper to explain why it was important to listen to the protesting students. The editors of the newspaper defended their right to publish the letters as part of their mission to protect First Amendment rights, when a few students labeled some of the letters to the editor as hate speech. In the end, the invitation to the band was rescinded, and, according to the archives of the newspaper, the band later changed their name.[13]

On-campus activism emerged at another Northeastern university after a series of sexist and racist cartoons were printed in the campus daily newspaper in Spring 2008. The racist cartoon depicted an extraordinarily tall black male basketball player with a paper in his hand that read the number 88. It was implied in the drawing that the basketball player did not receive the score 88 on an academic assignment, rather this was how much he scored on the basketball court. Furthermore, the cartoon insinuated that it was quite *unlikely* that this student-athlete would receive an 88 on any academic work because this student-athlete's skills and talent were relegated to the athletic realm. This cartoon—which draws upon notoriously racist ideologies of African Americans as intellectually inferior and physically or athletically superior to European Americans— was intended to be a joke, apparently the idea that someone might momentarily confuse an academic grade with a game statistic is supposed to be comical. However, the person in the cartoon was not merely an arbitrary portrayal of any athlete; it was an exaggerated depiction of a black male basketball player, an image that historically and presently is saturated with social meanings and expectations.

A series of on-campus activists, such as students and organizations that are social justice-oriented, collectively sponsored an event that spoke out against the racist and sexist cartoons from the campus newspaper. The event was comprised of students, faculty, and staff explaining how the comments were "offensive" and "hurtful," and that a university community should condemn "jokes" of this nature. It included a slide show of a series of cartoons and statistics of acts of violence in order to explain how "harmless" comics, pictures, and articles go beyond the printed page and influence the lives of marginalized individuals. This event was followed by other measures taken by student activists, such as meeting with the editor of the newspaper and contacting the funding board. Finally, students, faculty, and staff witnessed the fruits of their labor. The campus newspaper staff was mandated to attend an event in which journalists explained the ethical responsibilities of journalism. Additionally, there was a discussion of "regulating" the content of the comics section and, lastly, the cartoonist who was responsible for creating the most racist and sexist "jokes" eventually resigned, although this individual did not publically state the reasons for his resignation. However, and perhaps most notably, no member of the administration of this college engaged in the conversation or therefore spoke out against the racist rhetoric that was spewing from the pages of an institutionally funded newspaper.[14]

Linking the Worlds of the Global and the Local

Incidents on college campuses, such as those described above, are far removed from ICERD and human rights activism against racism. Yet, the two are intertwined. These college-based incidents reveal contemporary cultural understandings of racism, as well as behavior—irrespective of their intention—and institutional settings that contribute to sustaining racism in this country. As the U.S. Shadow Report points out, racial discrimination is very much about the consequences of unintentional action *and* inaction of individuals. Thus, the ability of students to understand contemporary racism—their ability to address their racist behaviors—becomes very crucial to the process of eliminating racism.

The college incidents exemplify the type of problem the shadow report identifies in the U.S. official report. ICERD recognizes that discrimination results not just from deliberate acts on the part of the government, but also from actions and laws that have a differential impact on different racial groups. But, U.S. laws narrowly defines "cognizable racial discriminate" by requiring the intent to discriminate. If we assume that the person who named the band Ching Chong, or the person who drew the cartoon of the basketball player, did not intend to discriminate, legally this would fall through the cracks of the U.S. system. Thus, as human rights activists have pointed out, the United States needs to improve its human rights record by addressing the *effects*, across all arenas of social life, rather than the intent of practices, if it is to meet the standards of ICERD. Furthermore, the shadow report points out that "racial discrimination in American society often arises from the interactions, public and private, over time and across domains" so that it would be difficult to eliminate racism if we simply dismiss these types of incidents on college campuses as one-time issues. Racial discrimination has to be understood as a continuum, ranging across multiple arenas, appearing sometimes as unintentional practices, and at other times as overt incidents and structured discrimination. Cultural understandings, interpersonal behavior, and structural racism have to be addressed in order to move toward a human rights-oriented society.

And much like activist groups that are part of the Human Rights Network, the college groups act, in their own "yards," to publicize racism—raise consciousness about racism--while working to create structural solutions to racial discrimination. The shadow reports produced by the Human Rights Network and the discussions, meetings, and written exchanges on college campuses, are all part of the human rights enterprise continuum to eliminate racism.

Last Words

The United States refusal to participate in the 2009 racism conference has been presented as a one-dimensional issue—this country's refusal to support an anti-Semitic platform—in the media. But, as this and other chapters demonstrate, this account simply ignores the larger story of racism and antiracist organizing that shapes the United States today. The work of groups who organize on campuses, in communities, in places of work, and through the legal system, reveal a whole range of ways in which people and groups in the United States continue to challenge existing structural, cultural, and interpersonal racism. But we have to pay attention to their work—especially the multifaceted definition of racism—if we wish to understand the state of human rights in the United States. Such informed action is what ICERD wishes to achieve through its call to states to use education, information, and all other related resources to make people aware of racism, so that many more people are committed to eliminating racism.

CHAPTER SEVENTEEN

Caging Kids of Color: Juvenile Justice and Human Rights in the United States

William T. Armaline

Any conversation of human rights dilemmas in the United States would be incomplete without mention of the U.S. criminal and juvenile justice systems, particularly with regard to the practice of incarceration (Davis 2003; Herivel and Wright 2003)—that is, the caging of human beings. Where a great deal of existing research[1] focuses on adult prisons and the practice of caging people more broadly, I will illustrate the stark contrast between current juvenile justice policies and practices in the United States, and the standards set by numerous human rights instruments[2] on the treatment of young people before the law. Given limited space, I will focus on the disproportionate caging of young people of color—particularly African American and Latino/a youth. Moreover, I illustrate how the disproportionate incarceration of youth of color, and the array of oppressive practices that define juvenile incarceration directly violate human rights instruments to which the United States is party. I will conclude with a brief conversation on how some grassroots organizations have mounted successful civil and human rights campaigns to resist the systematic coercion and oppression of young people of color by the U.S. police state.

We need not look far to find the complete disregard for the civil or human rights of young people before the law in the United States. In the spring of 2009, Wilkes-Barre, Pennsylvania, county judge Mark Ciavarella was found "receiving kickbacks from the operators of two secure juvenile facilities in exchange for shutting down the county's [less punitive] public detention center; then sentencing youths to the private facilities" (Kelly 2009: 1). In short, Judge Ciavarella was taking bribes from the local private prison industry to railroad young people, often without legal representation, into private cages for profit. In his first two years on the bench (1997-1999) carceral placements of juvenile offenders in Ciavarella's district rose 50 and 118 percent (Kelly 2009). This is not simply an illustration of the despicable acts of a corrupt judge. It exemplifies the extent to which young people can be exploited by states and their carceral systems gone unchecked.

However, the U.S. criminal and juvenile justice systems do not target and exploit all populations equally. As we take a closer look at the imprisonment of adults and juveniles in the United States, we find a great deal of consistency in the extent to which people of color, particularly African Americans, are disproportionately incarcerated. As we take a look at numerous human rights instruments that the United States has signed and ratified, such as ICERD or CAT, we find measures against which the U.S. police state might be checked, and fundamental reforms might be constructed.

Caging People of Color in the United States

Of the 2.2 million incarcerated adults in the United States, over half are African Americans, yet African Americans represent only 12.3 percent of the total U.S. population (Street 2003). African American males in their twenties experience an incarceration rate *25 times higher than the total population.* Institutionalization and surveillance of African American males has become so pervasive and consistent that on any given day, 30 percent of African American males ages ten to twenty-nine are "under correctional supervision"—jail, prison, probation, or parole. Research also suggests that over one fourth of all African American men and one in ten Latinos who were teens by the late 1990s are likely to be incarcerated in state or federal prison for at least a year of their life (see Street 2003; Davis 2003; Western 2007 for all the above). When we consider the intersectional effects of gender, we find that African American women continue to experience the highest imprisonment growth rate (78 percent in the late 1990s) (Western 2007; Mauer 1999).

The massive racial disparities found in the adult prison system are closely paralleled in the U.S. juvenile justice system, where youth of color are disproportionately found. In the United States, "youth of color make up 35 percent of the American population but 62 percent of youth in juvenile detention. African American youth, who comprise just 16% of the general population, make up 38 percent of those doing time in local and state correctional facilities" (NCCD 2007: 2). This all comes as no surprise given the interconnectedness of the adult and juvenile justice systems, and the general ideological dominance of imprisonment as the answer to "fighting crime" (Feld 1999, 2003;

Davis 2003; Sudbury 2005; Davey 1995, 1998). In fact, scholar/activist Mike Males (2002) details the contemporary social construction of youth as, inaccurately, the source of violent crime and reason for public fear and reactionary measures—such as mass imprisonment and an aggressive police state. In actuality, "the percentage of crime committed by youth today remains well below that of 1965. . . . There is no grounds, in short, for branding today's youth as uniquely criminal compared to past generations; just the opposite conclusion would be warranted when all serious crime is assessed" (Males 2007: 1).

Perhaps nowhere has the criminalization of young people, particularly youth of color, been as pervasive as in California, with an infamously large and powerful adult and juvenile prison industry. We find, not surprisingly, that massive racial disparities of juvenile incarceration are present. Of the nearly 2,000 youth caged in California's youth prisons, 87 percent are people of color—overwhelmingly African American and Latino/a. Though African Americans are only 6 percent of California's total population, they comprise 31 percent of the state's incarcerated youth. Similarly, Latino/as comprise 36 percent of the state population and 55 percent of California's incarcerated juveniles. As a common feature, nearly all the youth imprisoned by California's Department of Juvenile Justice (DJJ, formerly California Youth Authority or CYA), were from "low income backgrounds."[3] It seems that national- and state-level (California, for example) data reflect a particular focus on behalf of the formal justice system on the caging of poor kids—particularly kids of color. This is not a new finding by any means (Hagen, Shedd, and Payne 2005; Ayers 1998; Bortner and Williams 1997). However, before moving forward to the implications of targeting young populations of color for incarceration, it is important to address common narratives that suggest such data reflect "something else" besides racial discrimination and a manifestation of institutional or systemic racism[4] more broadly.

Is It Really About Race?

Common Myth(s): African Americans and other populations of color are disproportionately imprisoned because they (A) commit more crimes, and would otherwise pose a threat to society, or (B) because they are simply poor, and what we observe in terms of racial disparities are completely reducible to socio-economic variables.

To quickly address point (A), a great deal of research challenges the claim that African Americans' and Latino/as' disproportionate rate of imprisonment and state sanction is simply from their committing more crimes. Several scholars have pointed to measures presenting considerable evidence of racial disparities in rates of arrest, imprisonment, and capital punishment where nearly all other variables (type of crime, criminal history, and so forth) remained constant (Blumstein 1982; Tonry 1995, 1996; Mauer 1999; Western 2007). We see similar findings in the area of juvenile justice from a report by the National Council on Crime and Delinquency (NCCD 2007; Bernstein 2007: 1):

> African-American youths are 4.5 times more likely, and Latinos 2.3 times more likely, than white youths to be detained for identical offenses. About half of white teenagers arrested on a drug charge go home without being formally charged and drawn into the system. Only a quarter of black teens arrested on drug charges catch a similar break. When charges are filed, white youths are more likely to be placed on probation while black youth are more likely to get locked up. Unequal treatment didn't stop upon entry into the juvenile justice system . . . African-American youths are more likely than whites to be charged, tried, and incarcerated as adults. African Americans comprise 58 percent of youths charged and convicted as adults and sent to adult prisons.

From these and similar reports we find evidence that racial disparities in youth incarceration cannot be explained sufficiently by the assumption that these youth simply commit more crimes. Furthermore, in comparison to the criminal justice system for adults, the juvenile system consists of more points of intervention and decision-making, where racial and other forms of discrimination might take place at the hands of state institutions and actors (Feld 1999, 2003).

To address the second point, we should first recognize that there are clear connections between socioeconomic variables, such as poverty, and the rates and chances of imprisonment. Marxist criminological scholarship (Rusche and Kircheimer 1939; Melossi and Pavarini 1981; Spitzer 1975) has for some time pointed to the correlation between socioeconomic class and chances of imprisonment. Perhaps the most common study of this nature (though not explicitly "Marxist" per se) was Reiman's (1998) classic illustration of the ways in which affluent individuals are able to navigate the criminal justice system such that they have several ways out before being sentenced to prison, while impoverished populations are led on a "fast-track" to prison. Such important scholarship draws attention, for example, to the fact that over 80 percent of

U.S. prisoners could not afford a private attorney at the time of trial (Herivel and Wright 2003). It is without question that one's socioeconomic position significantly shapes one's relationship to and potential experiences with the (adult) criminal or juvenile justice system. But even for Reiman (1998), the choice to emphasize class in his work as central (versus race) was, in his own words, a difficult one.

Not unlike Reiman, other scholars have begun to recognize race and racism as relatively autonomous and important variables for explaining manifest patterns of incarceration in the United States. As Hagen, Shedd, and Payne (2005: 383) note of the race-class debate:

> Although leading conflict theorists of crime such as Chambliss and Seidman (1971: 475) framed their foundational hypotheses in class terms, more recently Chambliss (2000: 75) emphasizes that intense surveillance of black neighborhoods, the relative absence of surveillance of white neighborhoods, and differences in punishments for white and black offenders reinforce perceptions that the system is racist in ways designed to more specifically oppress black people.

As a reaction to these and other historical and contemporary patterns in U.S. criminal and juvenile justice, it is no surprise that there is some agreement among scholars (Bobo and Johnson 2004: 152; Davis 2003; Brewer and Heitzeg 2008) that U.S. criminal justice policies and practices are deliberate attempts to control and dominate populations of color. The most common examples pointed out in this scholarship have to do with the policies and outcomes of the failed "war on drugs."

Maybe the best empirical examples to illustrate the development of modern racial disparities of imprisonment for adults and juveniles are the policies defining the contemporary "war on drugs" and their effects. From the beginning of the drug war, and especially throughout the 1980s and 1990s, empirically inaccurate controlling images (Collins 2000; Gray 2000) were constructed of African Americans and Latino/as as the face of the drug problem. Indeed, "one [national] study found that when asked to imagine a typical drug user, over 95% of survey respondents pictured an African American" (Beckett et al. 2005: 436). Furthermore, as a result of harsh penalties for crack cocaine offenses (versus cocaine offenses, for example), increased policing of nonwhite urban communities, and increased minimum sentencing policies across the board, even now, "nearly 80% of those currently serving time in state prison for drug offenses are black or Latino" (437). This is important, where the majority of illicit drug users are white (for youth and adults), and the largest rises in drug overdose deaths are among white, middle-aged adults (Gray 2000).[5]

Again, historical and statistical research on incarceration suggests that young people of color, all other things equal, are more likely to be policed and caged by the juvenile justice system. But what does this mean for young populations of African Americans and Latino/as who are systematically targeted? What are these kids exposed to in the caged experience? As a closer look reveals, juvenile prisons are abusive environments, where common practices such as forceful restraint, imprisonment of youth with adult populations, use of chemical weapons (excessive use of mace, for example), and extended solitary confinement all violate international human rights standards and instruments. Furthermore, the discrimination against young people of color, and the vastly disproportionate caging of kids of color as a partial result, can be seen as a direct violation of international human rights law according to ICERD.

The Explicit Caging of Kids of Color as a Violation of Human Rights

Human rights instruments generally hold states responsible for the protection and pursuit of human rights practice (Donnelly 2003). These instruments provide a standard by which we might find some consensus on the rights and agency of incarcerated youth. Specifically, human rights instruments were designed from a liberal social contract perspective, where states are expected to "respect, protect, and fulfill" the human rights of those under their jurisdiction. Though it is problematic to suggest their universal and ultimate truth, human rights instruments help to evaluate juvenile justice policies in relation to international legal standards on the rights of all youth.

Several human rights organizations are challenging the disproportionate caging of youth of color as a violation of international human rights standards. Over the past ten years, several states have faced suits over the widespread abuse of young detainees—mostly African American and Latino/a youth—incarcerated in their facilities. Organizations such as Human Rights Watch and Amnesty International have been documenting these abuses as violations of human rights and international law for some time now. In 2000, Human Rights Watch issued a letter and report to the governor of South Dakota, outlining the abuse in the state's juvenile prison facilities that would soon appear as a formal suit filed by the state's Youth Law Center. As they note (HRW 2000),

Juvenile rights groups, parents of youth in detention, and the children themselves have charged that guards shackle youth in spread-eagled fashion after cutting their clothes off (a practice known as "four-pointing"), chain youth inside their cells ("bumpering"), and place children in isolation twenty-three hours a day for extended periods of time. Girls held in the State Training School report that they have been strip-searched by male guards, sprayed with pepper spray while naked, and handcuffed spread-eagled to their beds. In all facilities, children also report that they are forced to endure grossly inadequate mental health care, glaring deficiencies in education, and other substandard conditions of confinement.

These practices are not unique to South Dakota. In a similar suit (2004) that will be revisited shortly, the CYA, now DJJ, was publicly indicted on charges that detainees were excessively restrained, maced (some facilities had reports of hundreds of macings in a single month), sexually abused, physically abused (including staging "friday night fights" between detainees for the gambling pleasure of guards), and assigned to solitary confinement (23-hour cell lock-down) for months or even years at a time.[6]

The UN Rules for the Protection of Juveniles Deprived of Their Liberty "specify general standards for the treatment of children deprived of their liberty in any form of detention or imprisonment ordered by a judicial or other public authority. They cover a wide range of matters including the provision of education and medical care, limitations on the use of force and independent inspections of facilities" (Amnesty International 1998: 4). The practices detailed above are arguably against constitutional rights against "cruel and unusual punishment," and are explicitly in violation of international standards set by the UN rules on juvenile detainees (to which the United States is party). According to Rule 67,

> All disciplinary measures constituting cruel, inhuman or degrading treatment shall be strictly prohibited, including corporal punishment, placement in a dark cell, closed or solitary confinement or any other punishment that may compromise the physical or mental health of the juvenile concerned.

All the above conditions are violated on a regular basis in juvenile prisons and detention facilities across the United States, as illustrated in the South Dakota and California systems. As will be suggested shortly, a human rights discourse might aid in resisting these practices, and the caging of young people more broadly. However, we should return first to the central point of this chapter: that young people of color are systematically targeted by the juvenile justice system and exposed to these abuses in carceral facilities. To examine the human rights implications of the disparate incarceration of youth of color, we can look to ICERD.

The United States signed ICERD in 1965, and finally ratified the treaty, ironically, in 1994 amid the now notoriously racist welfare reform movement (Roberts 2002; Neubeck and Cazenave 2001) and a climax in the growth of U.S. prison populations thanks to the "war on drugs" and implementation of harsh minimum sentencing structures such as "three strikes" measures (Western 2007). ICERD obliges states to eradicate all forms of racial discrimination in state policies—not simply in their discourse, but in their resulting practices and measurable effects. As Fellner and Mauer (1998: viii) explain,

> ICERD wisely does not impose the requirement of discriminatory intent for a finding of discrimination. *It requires states parties to eliminate laws or practices which may be race-neutral on their face but which have "the purpose or effect" of restricting rights on the basis of race.* Regardless therefore, of whether they were enacted with racial animus . . . they unnecessarily and unjustifiably create significant racial disparities in the curtailment of an important right. (emphasis added)

As clearly demonstrated thus far, the U.S. juvenile justice system (or the many state systems taken on the whole) demonstrates the restriction of "rights on the basis of race" on a grand scale. First, the rights of young people of color are violated by their being systematically targeted for state sanction by the criminal and juvenile justice system, resulting in their disproportionate rates and levels of confinement. Second, once in the cage, these youth suffer unspeakable abuses, which also fall under the category of violating both civil and human rights law on the treatment of young detainees. ICERD in particular might be a "legitimate" legal tool for combating and challenging the disparate incarceration of African American and Latino/a youth, and systemic racism more broadly, due to its emphasis on systematic *effects* rather than issues of "racist intent," and the like.

Further, the language of ICERD reflects a proper (supported) conceptualization of contemporary systemic racism, in that we know it to operate largely through overlapping, subtle, seemingly "colorblind" or "race neutral," institutionalized policies and practices (Bonilla-Silva: 2003). Comparatively speaking, U.S. civil law on racial discrimination requires a finding of "intent"—often absent from modern manifestations of racism and racially oppressive policies that no longer tend to reflect explicitly "racial" discourse (Feagin 2000; Neubeck and Cazenave 2001). Where ICERD is also a binding international treaty (human rights instrument) to which the United States is party, a human rights discourse might be useful for those who seek to resist the oppressive caging of young people of color in the United States.

Human Rights and Resistance

Two recent movements, the Raise the Age Campaign in Connecticut and the Books Not Bars (BNB) movement in California, might serve as illustrations of how civil and human rights laws and standards can be employed to resist the caging and abuse of young kids of color. One of the major blemishes on the U.S. human rights record is the history of trying, sentencing, and, until 2005, executing children as adults. Both Human Rights Watch and Amnesty International have issued numerous reports on the incarceration of juveniles for life without parole, the housing of juveniles with adult populations, and the trying of juveniles "as adults" in adult courts—all violations of international human rights.[7]

Until recently, three states—Connecticut, North Carolina, and New York—automatically tried and sentenced youth sixteen or older as adults *regardless of offense*. Recently, the Raise the Age Campaign CT (partnered with the Connecticut Juvenile Justice Alliance) mounted a successful campaign to end the practice there. As also reflected in the arguments posed in this chapter, the Raise the Age Campaign highlights that their efforts are in part a response to racial and class disparities. In Connecticut, "children of color from cities are disproportionately represented in the system and once inside are treated more severely than their white, suburban peers."[8] The Raise the Age CT campaign recognized that while these disparities were part of their argument against current juvenile justice practices, their campaign needed a more universal popular appeal for success: "juvenile justice reform, therefore, could have become a quixotic appeal [for the white community] to invest in 'somebody else's kid.'" The Campaign aimed at ending Connecticut's dubious distinction as having one of the worst records on racial and ethnic disparity of incarceration, and on incarcerating children as adults. Following the suicide of a seventeen-year-old who had been tried and incarcerated as an adult for a parole violation in 2005, Connecticut governor Jodi Rell agreed to a dialogue on ending the practice of automatically trying kids as adults. In 2007, the state legislature passed the Raise the Age legislation that ended trying sixteen- and seventeen-year-olds as adults in 2010.

Similarly, it took the suicide of detainees in solitary confinement for a suit finally to be won against the former CYA for its systematic abuse of young detainees. In 2004, Durrel Feaster and Deon Whitfield (both African American) were found dead in their cells at California's Preston Youth Prison after having been kept in solitary confinement (23-hour cell lockdown) for extended periods. BNB, an organization stemming from the Ella Baker Center for Human Rights (headquarters in Oakland, California) joined in organizing parents of detainees, former detainees, community members, and professional medical experts, to file suit against the former CYA for their systematic targeting of youth of color, their horribly abusive practices, their manifest failure to reduce recidivism or crime, and their massive public expense. Though the suit succeeded in exposing abusive practices of the CYA, setting the stage for stopping the construction of new juvenile "supermax" facilities, and exposing the massive incarceration of largely poor, kids of color, BNB and their allies continue to fight a state system that continues many of their systematic abuses of young detainees.

As an organization, BNB illustrates the problem it seeks to address and current progress:

> With a 70% recidivism rate and a cost of $252,000 per ward, per year, DJJ is the nation's most expensive, least effective juvenile justice system. . . . Since we launched the campaign in 2004, the youth prison population has fallen from 5200 to 1900—a drop of more than 60%. (BNB 2009)

As apparent in the name, BNB employs a discourse on the rights of all children to an education, pointing out that the state of California spends a great deal more money on cages and policing than on schools. Their policy position is well suited for current conditions in California, where public schools and universities are being decimated under massive state and federal budget shortfalls.

Though both organizations have seen significant success, they face a long fight when it comes to fundamentally changing the racial oppression exercised through the almost explicit caging of African American and Latino/a youth. We might learn from their employment of a fundamental rights discourse for young people, their employment of broad coalitions to affect change, and their willingness to engage in public demonstrations and civil disobedience to think about resistance strategies moving forward. As we look at the challenges ahead, we might consider the use of explicit human rights instruments, such as ICERD, to provide legal "legitimacy" to any agenda seeking to resist racial oppression—even when somewhat hidden behind seemingly "race-neutral" policies and institutions.

PART VI

CONVENTION ON THE ELIMINATION OF ALL FORMS OF DISCRIMINATION AGAINST WOMEN

The United States has still not ratified the Convention on the Elimination of All Forms of Discrimination Against Women (CEDAW), which was established in 1979. Citing concerns about issues such as marriage and abortion, the U.S. has resisted joining the scores of nations that have agreed to end gendered discrimination. Instead, the U.S. has chosen to assert sovereign rights over international agreements concerning women's human rights. The notion of women's rights raises the question of citizenship, and highlights a history in which women, like slaves and children, have frequently been treated as property of adult men rather than as full citizens. While this is certainly evolving, and women now have more citizenship rights than a century ago, there remains a great deal more to be done for women to be seen as full citizens.

Chapters in this section explore several key issues concerning women's rights in the U.S. For example, one chapter examines the foundations of women's rights in the U.S., asking why their rights have not been framed as human rights. Another chapter interrogates the question of violence against women in the context of a culture of violence. Still another chapter pursues the question of sex trafficking as a human rights issue.

Together, these chapters raise the question: why are women's rights not often defined as human rights? What are the notions of citizenship, culture, and "humanness" that hinder the public discourse of women's rights as human rights? How have people resisted, challenged, and subverted formal and informal expressions of women as second-class citizens?

CHAPTER EIGHTEEN

"What Lies Beneath": Foundations of the U.S. Human Rights Perspective and the Significance for Women

Tola Olu Pearce

Women's struggle for equality with men is a recurring theme in most societies, since gender regimes have been the norm for centuries. In oral tradition it is codified in myths, songs, stories, and annual rituals. Documents reveal similar activities in countries where writing has existed for some time. For Western societies some of the earliest records date back to the fifteenth century indicating legal struggles in France (Fraser 2006). In the pursuit of equality, numerous strategies, arguments. and practices have been harnessed even though conflicts have existed between categories of women in different social locations as so well articulated by racial minorities in the United States (Beale 1969; Collins 1998; Glenn 2002; Mills 1997; Romero 2002). Building on this long tradition and the success of earlier struggles, women's embrace of the human rights perspective is an important strategy that gained momentum during the last quarter of the twentieth century. It is yet another chapter in the push for equality still denied—all the laws, structures, and activities that "guarantee" gender equality notwithstanding. Indeed, as Lorber argues, "the revolution that would make women and men truly equal has not yet occurred" (Lorber 2005: 4). This is not to deny that everywhere *some* women are more equal than *some men*, but such women are expected to know their place within their own group—be it upper class, white, or professional—as is true for women in other categories: lower class, Latina, or blue collar.

Given the interlocking dimensions of all gender systems, the employment of a human rights framework appears to be the best strategy for the final leap to close disparities of power and resources along lines and in the construction of gender. I would argue that through a human rights framework women might aspire beyond mere equality, since we now understand that in order to gain equality for women more substantive changes are required than hitherto envisaged; in institutions and relationships for example, including our relationship to the earth itself. As noted by Donnelly, human rights activists seek "to make real the world that they envision" (2003, 21). The goal of women's rights is now embedded in a larger vision for our species. This vision includes important factors affecting the human condition: our frailty as humans; the requirements of human reproduction; aging; need for adequate food, water, and shelter; the limits of the earth and its resources and environment; death; etc). For many, the human rights model seeks to bring about major shifts in our human and nonhuman relationships. Women's equality is a piece of the puzzle, but a piece that both feeds on and is essential to the vision.

Although I am interested in the promise of a human rights framework or political platform for achieving equality, in this chapter I examine what lies beneath this platform in the United States. I examine two foundational pillars that support the agenda but hinder the transformations that now appear within reach. The roots of American society lie in liberal individualism and capitalism. Both have affected mainstream discourses on human rights and, more importantly, the state's stance: its disinterest in accommodating dissenting views or in allocating resources to alter the condition of vulnerable groups. Further, the interconnections between these two important foundations cause additional complications for women.

Liberalism and Human Rights

Liberalism is the foundation of the American perspective on "rights" and rights-holders were constructed as rational individuals. In this narrative, autonomous individuals established the state whose duty it is to protect rights. In keeping with this focus on the individual, the dominant ideology of individualism further emphasizes privacy, self-improvement, and personal freedoms. As many feminists have pointed out, women were not originally perceived as rational individuals and thus not part of the liberal public protected by state laws. Prominent scholars like Locke supported the public/private divide relegating women to the private sphere; they were unable to obtain the legal, civil, and political rights available to men in the public sphere (Pateman 1988; Phillips 1993). Historically, much of women's fight for equality in the West has been influenced by attempts to gain these rights in the public sphere. Fraser (2006) catalogues the struggle for education, paid employment, the right to publish, inherit, own property, retain custody of children, vote, hold public office, and so forth.

Many legal struggles have been won, but the public/private divide remains a powerful construct and leaves women in an ambiguous position as citizens in the United States and other nations. Although Nash (2001) traces liberalism's development in Britain, much of this history is relevant to the United States; one might even argue that the emphasis on the individual's responsibility in handling the divide is even stronger in the United States. Nash discusses the many phases through which liberalism has passed: classical, progressive, welfare, and neo. Her overall argument is that within each context it is not clear whether women are able to gain more rights by pursuing a gender-neutral or gendered stance in the public or in the private sphere. For instance, during the progressive era some argued that gender-neutral "individuals" in public would be in a better position to gain the rights available to men. Others assumed that women emerging *as women* in public would be able to use the female experience to lift society and obtain a better deal for everyone. Again, women could fight to be neutral individuals in private and gendered in public.

This "undecidability" of the female condition exists for each stage of liberalism. Nash suggests that it allows feminists wiggle space to craft a variety of solutions in both the public and private spheres. She notes that "Feminism has made considerable gains for women since the seventeenth century by reconfiguring the terms of liberalism around the undecidability of women on which its principal binary opposition between public and private depends. Furthermore, given that citizenship is liberal . . . it is also important to understand what liberalism has effectively permitted in this respect" (Nash 2001: 166). She wonders whether a more optimistic outcome could be in the offing if women are able to use liberalism with greater productive effect. Perhaps. But some of the problems that have surfaced with neoliberalism in the twenty-first century appear quite problematic for women. In the United States, in particular, the state encourages lower-class women, single mothers, and professional women to work but is not eager to assist with programs for family life in the private sphere. Mothers on welfare, historically constructed (and in the case of African Americans, racialized) as "welfare queens" (Neubeck and Cazenave 2001) are expected to seek employment with little assistance. Welfare reform during the Clinton administration, namely the rise of TANF (1996), merely turned impoverished singe mothers into low-wage or temporary workers for capital. Employers under TANF and welfare to work programs are not required to provide health insurance and other benefits available to regular workers. On the other end of the spectrum, professional women often quit work to take care of children, the sick, or parents and extended family members, again with little help from the state. Impoverished women and mothers are often constructed as "individuals" to cope within the public and private sphere, reflecting the hegemonic (albeit poorly supported) belief that personal responsibility is paramount in determining one's condition in capitalist societies such as the United States.

In opposition to the focus on the individual, critical sociological perspectives suggest that individuals must always be understood within social and environmental contexts. Clearly, contexts, systemic influences, and the society/individual nexus matter (Pearce 2001) if one wishes to interpret and analyze complex social systems and social phenomena (such as the role of gender and patriarchy in constructing society, the human condition, and notions of "rights"). As Robertson (1978, 169) points out, there is a tendency in the United States:

> to operate in associational rather than systemic terms is clear from pre-republic times, but even clearer from the founding of the Republic; such a tendency to see society as an association of individuals or relatively autonomous units, rather than a system prevailing over the individuals, being largely embodied in the constitution.

Focusing on the individual/context nexus of the period of late modernity, Bauman (2001) believes that while risks and contradictions continue to be socially produced, the necessity of coping with them is being individualized. It is clear he feels that individuals should not be expected to shoulder all the weight of socially produced risks and contradictions. Such expectations are untenable. Bauman goes on to argue that too much emphasis on individualization makes individuals skeptical about the meaning of the "common good," thus weakening the very concept of citizenship in the public sphere. I would argue that in such an environment, a woman's freedom to make choices as she navigates the public spheres of institutional life (such as work, politics, economy, education, etc.) and private spheres of family soon become overwhelming and not cause for much optimism.

Merry (2006b) reveals just how overwhelming this decision-making can be in her study of domestic violence in a small city in Hawaii. To become a human rights subject, a woman must enact a new role, moving from intimate relational positions of wife, mother, or daughter-in-law to an entirely different position that is largely "shaped by the discourses of autonomy, choice and reasonable behavior, not by love, anger, hurt and ambivalence" (400). Many women vacillate because it is unnerving and often dangerous to navigate the unfamiliar "rights bearer" identity. Again, they are not always fully protected by officials in the public sphere, many who themselves are not fully convinced of the need for these new rights for women. Battered women find that they are unable to do what is expected, since "Becoming an entitled person in this situation depends on being the rational person who follows through, leaves the batterer, cooperates with the prosecuting case, and does not provoke violence, take drugs or drink or abuse children" (402).

The continued emphasis on the sufficiency of first generation human rights to address these issues has been criticized by several scholars (Blau and Moncada 2006; Neubeck 2006; Roberts 1997). The refusal to ratify instruments such as ICESCR and CEDAW allows the state to decide what problems women must shoulder alone. This can be quite confusing, for within the liberal public the same lone mother is treated as both an abstract individual (a gender neutral worker—no paid maternity leave) and a "woman" (a welfare mother of underage children). Thus insofar as females are different from the male individual of liberal thought they must struggle to justify the rights they seek. But given these differences, the human rights enumerated in the second and third generation conventions are necessary to allow women full access to the political and civil rights operating in the liberal public as Roberts (1997) and others have pointed out.

This discussion of difference touches on the paradox of liberalism highlighted by Mehta (1999). He notes that while insisting on its superior universalistic tenets, liberalism has in practice been staunchly exclusionary. Pointing to the works of Locke, James Mill, John Stuart Mill, and others in their discourse on India, Mehta reveals that liberalism has always had problems accepting the unfamiliar. The granting of rights, seen as "natural" for English males, required that other types of individuals and societies meet certain standards. Thus, while liberalism professes to embrace everyone, "The limiting point of this perimeter is a form of alterity beyond which differences can no longer be accommodated. The alterity can take many forms" (67). According to Mehta, a wide array of characteristics have been conjured up to deny the other any claim to liberalism's rights: individual capacities (lacking rational abilities), stage of societal development (primitive), identities (race), and so forth.

Mehta addresses this problem in liberalism by pointing out that while the claim to rights is progressive, what needs to change is liberalism's gatekeeping role. It must drop the constant demand that others meet a priori conditions. He makes an important comparison between liberal thought and Gandhi. While scholars of liberalism saw rights (and progress) in terms of evolutionary development along a political continuum, Gandhi saw progress as the development of "an ethical relationship that an individual or a community has with itself, with others, and with its deities" (Mehta 1999: 81). One might then argue that the human rights project is basically a struggle to develop new codes to alter human relationships. Defining women's rights as human rights is central to this project.

Finally, digging into the cultural roots of mainstream perspectives on human rights in the United States does not assume there's an immutable core to cultures. Change occurs all the time. According to Bayart, culture "is less a matter of conforming or identifying than of making: making something new with something old, and sometimes also making something old with something new; making self with the other" (Bayart 2005: 96). Much of culture is negotiation and different subgroups (women, sexual and racial minorities) do not necessarily draw the same conclusions as the powerful from cultural ideologies, texts, or symbols. The "political plasticity" of cultural forms becomes obvious when new cultural interpretations gain ascendancy. In today's global political environment there are significant challenges from women's groups, both within and outside of the US, that were not contenders for interpretations in the past (either due to their illiteracy, colonized status, or dormant activism). Challenges to dimensions of liberalism are growing.

Capitalism and the Human Rights Perspective

Liberalism's promise of universalism and, yet, exclusionary practices, are not the only problems blocking the implementation of women's human rights. The impact of capitalism on women's lives has been under scrutiny for some time. From its inception, capitalism was made possible by deliberate economic policies constructed by leaders and rulers to facilitate the birth of the new economic system. Polanyi (1944/1957) painted a disturbing picture of the rise of industrial capitalism in England. To begin with, there were major transformations in social life when labor became a commodity at the service of a budding factory system at the end of the eighteenth century. The Poor Laws and other economic "reforms" devastated whole communities and the lives of ordinary people were "*awful beyond description* . . . indeed, human society would have been annihilated but for counter protective moves" (79, emphasis added). Such a serious indictment of the early capitalist system is arguably still relevant.

Western societies are proud of many dimensions of modernity, but for some sociologists including Bauman (2000, 2001, 2004) Bourdieu (1998), and Pieterse (2000) the underside of capitalism is a major component of Western modernity. As capitalism evolved through different stages it left its imprint on modernity, affecting different segments of society in different ways. Industrial, imperial/colonial, and now global capitalism have required shifts in the way the liberal individual connects with others and builds communities. For Bauman, the move from industrial capitalism to global capitalism is a move from "heavy" capitalism and "solid" modernity to "light" capitalism and "liquid" modernity (2000). Under "heavy" capitalism labor and capital were bonded in an uneasy relationship with capital attempting to immobilize labor to curb constant worker turnover or flight. Workers were therefore in a position to make some demands on capital. The Fordist system was mindful of the need for a strong healthy workforce. A welfare system also had to be established for the unemployed who could be called on to work at any time (Bauman 2001).

This conceptual truce began to unravel with global capitalism and the neoliberal construction of policies: particularly the deregulation and liberalization policies of the 1980s and 1990s. The emphasis on finance as the motor for growth freed capital from labor. As manufacturing declined, both workers and the unemployed were left in weaker positions. The former became an obstacle to higher profits and the outsourcing of production to cheaper labor markets was viewed as an excellent solution. The latter had truly become redundant and welfare systems were targeted for dismantling. Thus Bauman states that with global capitalism "keeping the 'underclass' alive and well defies all rationality and serves no visible purpose" (2001: 89). Now, segments of the U.S. population and others around the globe are on a conveyor belt to dumping sites (prisons) or waste heaps (urban ghettos or cemeteries). This speaks directly to the issue of human rights. One needs to ask, if people have human rights by virtue of being human, do these rights still hold when humans become "waste"? The economic rules designed by global financial institutions are causing immense damage given the end product: populations as waste.

But beyond the economic anxieties resulting from informalization, casualization, and unemployment, Bauman discusses the sociopsychological problems that mount because of the uncertainties generated around work. Increasingly it becomes difficult for individuals to use the liberal public sphere as a space for mutual problem solving since social progress itself becomes deregulated and privatized (Bauman 2004: 112). As Fullerton and Robertson have discussed in their chapter on labor rights, each individual is made responsible, *in an unprecedented way*, for her/his own progress. Indifference soars, or as Pateman argues, we have developed "the contract of mutual indifference" (Pateman and Mills 2007: 155). But for Bauman, this indifference is a rational response to anxiety-ridden economic environments, where extreme individualization has taken hold.

Feminist economists have long argued that women's relationship to capitalist markets differs from men's (Brush 2003; Folbre 2001. Unpaid homemakers produce goods, services, and socialized human beings who are raised ready to serve society. This "free" labor increases the profit margins of capital. Also, working women tend to be paid less than their male counterparts. When the captains of economic globalization demand that states reduce public spending on social services (health care, childcare, elder care, etc.) much of the private burden falls on women as care-workers. Attempts to claim economic and social human rights in order to obtain resources are easily rebuffed as claims for special treatment. Many of the jobs available for women cannot sustain poor families. Living on "disease-crime-and-drug infested mean streets" (Bauman 2001: 116) in a nation where government policies result in increased wealth for the few and widening income gaps calls attention to the absence of second generation human rights in the United States. The constant push for individual solutions disproportionately affects those with few resources to solve their problems. (This is evident in the chapter on the aftermath of Katrina). It is not enough to call on the generosity of charitable populations. Humanitarian charity is assistance that does not address the claim to "rights." Rights *institutionalize* the long-term access to a better life by working through the economic, political, and social systems in ways that cannot be addressed through humanitarian charity.

The Combined Impact

Any discussion of the foundations of human rights in the United States must be mindful of the fact that other phenomena exist. For instance, much has been written about the nation's Judeo-Christian roots and its democratic foundation. Nonetheless, we cannot ignore the significance of economic systems on our lives. Social relations are now embedded in the economic system. Polanyi wrote that since

> the organization of labor is only another word for the forms of life of the common people, this means that the development of the market system would be accompanied by a change in the organization of society itself. All along the line, human society had become an accessory of the economic system. (1944, 1957: 79)

On the question of combined impact, the issue is to review how capitalism has interacted with liberalism. Analyzing such developments is in fact one of the tasks that Bauman set himself in his numerous publications. Under global capitalism for instance, the sense of insecurity among individuals who no longer feel in control of their lives or communities as promised by liberal individualism is growing, and Bauman argues that

> the political economy of uncertainty is good for business. It makes the orthodox, bulky, unwieldy and costly instruments of discipline redundant—replacing them not so much with the self-control of trained, drilled and disciplined objects, as with the inability of privatized and endemically insecure individuals to act in a concerted way.—As far as eliciting passive submission to the rules of the game, or to a game without rules, is concerned, endemic uncertainty from the bottom to the top of the social ladder is a neat and cheap, yet highly effective substitute for normative regulation, censorship and surveillance. (2001: 119–20)

Since no one knows what human nature really entails, human rights scholars and activists argue that we need to build environments that enable rather than suppress the ability of humans to lead dignified lives. We need to take seriously lessons from the experiences and theories of others as opposed to the ideas emanating from those advantaged by global capitalism and liberal individualism. One example is that theorizing about the lives, experiences and relationships of women has for some time now emphasized human connectedness as opposed to individualization. As Rothman (2000) and Marshall (2005) argue, all humans begin within an organic unit, as part of the mother's body and remain in close relationship with the adults responsible for their welfare (Kahn 1995). While the bulk of childcare is usually the mother's, the size and shape of the care group depends on race, culture, class, historical period, and so forth. No newborn or infant would survive physically (or emotionally) without this care group.

Such theorizing is important in helping us grapple with our understanding of what humans are or need to become. However, much of this work is still at the micro-level. But Sjoberg, Gill, and Williams (2001) draw attention to successive levels of interaction. They make the case that insofar as organizational structures embody power relations, these units are moral in nature and must therefore be held accountable within human the rights discourses. Further, particular organizations are to be judged as "fundamentally flawed with regard to sustain human rights principles, and consequently need to be reconstituted" (33). The rules that are set up within organizations (community, national, global) form the context within which humans flourish or decline. They discuss how global institutions such as transnational corporations, World Trade Organization (WTO), World Bank, and IMF structure social life. From this it is clear that the liberal individual is up against formidable forces beyond her/his reach. The liberal model of associational individuals is unable to deal with social environments that are structured by global financial organizations. Banding together to protest against one's government, as advocated by Locke and others, is not likely to be very effective in an age when governments are pondering over their own power vis-à-vis these global institutions. But a critical sociological perspective would insist that these institutions must be held accountable as somehow subject to moral and analytical critique. In other words, the role of international financial institutions and the effect they have on human rights *must become part of the human rights conversation*. How else can we begin to re-embed the economy into society?

Conclusion

The 1990s argument that "women's rights are human rights" was viewed in many feminist circles as a major boost in the struggle for women's equality. Many problems could be brought under this umbrella and the necessary linkages made between disparate issues. Further, the human rights discourse draws attention to the need for a broader overhaul of society based on a dream of a better future. While there is no doubt that progress has been made in obtaining women's human rights, longstanding issues exist. This chapter has been concerned with two of the important foundations on which the U.S. human rights platform rests. The theoretical significance of capitalism and liberal individualism cannot be ignored as women move forward in the quest for human rights. It is increasingly clear that aspects of these foundations must now be challenged and reconstituted if real progress is to be made. Presently, the situation has become critical since the macroeconomic policies that ushered in globalization brought both the United States and the global economic systems to near collapse in 2008.

The official U.S. perspective on human rights is under intense pressure from many groups including the UN family of agencies, NGOs, and feminist networks. For example, the U.S.-based advocacy network, Women's Environment and Development Organization (WEDO), provides leadership in addressing social, political, economic, and environment injustices. WEDO is particularly concerned with building global connections and confronting uncooperative institutions and governments. The many problems it addresses go beyond first generation human rights to more comprehensive matters. In 2000, WEDO worked with more than a dozen U.S. women's organizations to produce *Women's Equality: An Unfinished Agenda*, a report condemning the macroeconomic policies at home and abroad that have been responsible for impeding women's progress (Moghadam 2005). To date, WEDO still has a full agenda, working with organizations such as the International Network on Economic Social and Cultural Rights, Women's Rights in Development, Development Alternatives with Women for a New Era and WIDE-globalizing for Gender Equality.

In addition to women's networks, new associations like Sociologists Without Borders (Sociologos sin Fronteras; SSF) are increasingly being founded on human rights platforms. SSF is the brainchild of Alberto Moncada in Spain, but has a U.S. chapter headed by Judith Blau and is dedicated to challenging, among other things, the official U.S. human rights perspective, market fundamentalism, and the subordination of any group. Further, sociology as a discipline draws attention to the fact that in pursuing social justice, all organizations and institutions, and not just the state, must be evaluated for their perspective on power and accountability. From micro-level household and familial structures to community organizations and global institutions, a tremendous amount of work needs to be done to uncover what impedes the construction of a human rights enabling environment. The twenty-first-century version of the American Dream will need to incorporate the human rights platform, and discard the more obsolete dimensions of social Darwinism held captive to harmful aspects of capitalism and liberal individualism.

CHAPTER NINETEEN

Sex Trafficking: In Our Backyard?

Ranita Ray

Trafficking in persons is a form of racism that is recognized as a contemporary form of slavery and is aggravated by the increase in racism, racial discrimination, xenophobia and related intolerance. The demand side in trafficking is created by a globalized market, and a patriarchal notion of sexuality. Trafficking happens within and across borders, largely in conjunction with prostitution.

—World Conference Against Racism, Durban, 2001

On February 2002, the police raided a house on 1212$^1/_2$ West Front Street in Plainfield, New Jersey, and found four girls between the ages of fourteen and seventeen. They were all Mexican nationals without documentation. They were not prostitutes working for profit or a paycheck, they were sex slaves. They were captives to the traffickers. The house was the equivalent of a nineteenth-century slave ship, with door less bathrooms, bare, putrid mattresses, and a stash of penicillin, morning after pills, and misoprostol, an antiulcer medication that can induce abortion. The girls were rented out for sex for as little as fifteen minutes at a time, dozens of times a day. They were pale, exhausted, and malnourished.

—Peter Landesman, "The Girl Next Door"

The place Landesman describes is one of what law-enforcement officials say are hundreds of active stash houses in major cities like New York, Los Angeles, Atlanta, and Chicago, where underage girls and young women from dozens of countries are trafficked and held captive. Some of them have been enticed by promises of legitimate jobs and a better life in America; some have been abducted; others have been bought from or abandoned by their impoverished families. However, the scope of U.S. laws to address the sex trafficking epidemic suggests that it is essentially a global problem and not an American one. For instance, in the Trafficking Victims Protection Act of 2000—the first U.S. law to recognize that people trafficked against their will are victims of a crime, not illegal immigrants—the U.S. government rates other countries' records on human trafficking and can apply economic sanctions on those that are not making efforts to improve them. Another piece of legislation, the Protect Act, which president George W. Bush signed into law in 2003, makes it a crime for any person to enter the United States, or for any citizen to travel abroad, for the purpose of sex tourism involving children (Landesman 2004).

This chapter examines sex trafficking as a violation of human rights and explores its prevalence in the United States. It attempts to analyze the inherent gendered and racial nature of modern sex trafficking. And, it discusses some organized efforts to combat sex trafficking in the United States.

Sex Trafficking as Human Rights Violation

Sex trafficking is linked to sexual violence and is recognized as a human rights issue in CEDAW—often described as an international bill of rights for women. CEDAW defines discrimination against women as "any distinction, exclusion or restriction made on the basis of sex which has the effect or purpose of impairing or nullifying the recognition, enjoyment or exercise by women, irrespective of their marital status, on a basis of equality of men and women, of human rights and fundamental freedoms in the political, economic, social, cultural, civil or any other field."[1] Forced trafficking of women and their subsequent commoditization as objects for the sex market is undeniably a gross violation of their basic human rights. Furthermore, Article 2 of the ICCPR states that "Each State Party to the present Covenant undertakes to respect and to ensure to all individuals within its territory and subject to its jurisdiction the rights recognized in the present Covenant, without distinction of any kind, such as race, color, sex, language, religion, political or other opinion, national or social origin, property, birth or other status," while the ICCPR also articulates the right to freedom from slavery and torture.[2] Sex trafficking—arguably a form of slave trade—essentially treats women and children as objects or commodities to be traded and sold. Hence it is also an issue of social and civil rights, and of marginalization and invisibility of females and children.

Sex trafficking: In Our Own Backyard?

In the popular imagination, sex trafficking is a problem of other countries. Yet, sex trafficking is as prevalent in the United States as anywhere else in the world. The United States ranks as the world's second largest destination and market (after Germany) for women and children trafficked for sexual exploitation. Between 100,000 and 300,000 children are exploited annually by the sex industry in the United States (Klueber 2003). The U.S. government estimates that 50,000 women and children are trafficked each year into the United States from nearly every source country of the world. Immigration and Naturalization Service (INS) has discovered more 250 brothels in 26 different cities that probably involve trafficking (Richard 1999). In looking at organized resistance, efforts seem to be significantly affected by whether or not host countries have ratified CEDAW, and the United States is yet to ratify it.

One case that is particularly illustrative of the patterns of sex trafficking in the United States, and the ways women are moved quickly from place to place, occurred in Atlanta, Georgia, in March 1998. Original reports indicated that FBI agents raided a house in Atlanta in which they found eight girls, ages fifteen and sixteen, being held in prison-like conditions (*United States v. Yong Hui McCready et al.* 1999). This brothel turned out to be only one in a nationwide network that operated in fourteen states. Later reports indicated that there were 500-1,000 trafficked women between ages of thirteen and twenty-five, many of them minors, who passed through Atlanta. The average time they spent in the city was two weeks, because male buyers ("customers") demanded sex with different women (*United States v. Ninh Vinh Luong et al.* 1999), and also because owners wanted to avoid detection by the police (Raymond, Hughes, and Gomez 2001).

Another case involved the Cadena family from Veracruz, Mexico, who trafficked at least twenty Mexican women—one as young as fourteen—into the United States for purposes of prostitution. The women, lured with promises of economic opportunities, were transported through Texas and then kept in trailers transformed into mobile brothels located near migrant workers' camps in Florida and South Carolina. The women lived in brutal conditions. Prosecutors said that many were compelled to have sex with 130 men per week, beaten, raped, and forced to undergo abortions. They were told that they would be released after paying off debts of around $3,000 for having been smuggled into the country (Wilson 1998).

In July 1999, fifteen Americans were arrested on charges of running a prostitution ring out of Minneapolis, Minnesota. The FBI released a 44-count indictment charging offenders with forcing teenage girls into prostitution, maintaining control over them with repeated rapes, beatings, and death threats. According to the FBI, the ring had been operating for seventeen years, getting progressively larger, with operations in 24 states and two Canadian provinces (Rosario 1999).

Despite numerous instances of sex trafficking and sex slavery, there is little systematic research on contemporary trafficking in the United States (Raymond, Hughes and Gomez 2001). The United States has been less visible as a site for transnational and domestic trafficking in women because research on sex trafficking in the United States has been inadequate. Statistical data on trafficking, racial profiles of victims, profiles of customers, the number of women trafficked into the country, and estimates advanced by governmental and nongovernmental agencies are difficult to verify mainly because incidents reported are in isolation from one another and the "who," "what," and "why" of trafficking into the United States has not been manifest. This lack of information can also be attributed to the separation of international sex trafficking from domestic sex trafficking or prostitution (Wijers and Lap-Chew 1997; Skrobanek, Boonpakdee, and Janthakeroo 1997). The 1949 UN Convention for the Suppression of the Traffic in Persons and of the Exploitation of the Prostitution of Others recognized the inconsistency of isolating the international problem of sex trafficking from the various forms of commercialized sex within nation-states. Trafficking for sexual exploitation is, for the most part, trafficking for prostitution. Domestic trafficking is, for the most part, trafficking for prostitution. Additionally, traffickers rely on local and existing sex industries, whether women are trafficked domestically or internationally. Separating international trafficking from domestic trafficking and prostitution can also create the impression that trafficking is an immigration crime rather than a human rights violation. Traffickers and victims of trafficking can be U.S. citizens and residents, or foreign nationals (Raymond, Hughes, and Gomez 2001).

Furthermore, the portrayal of sex trafficking as a series of discrete policy problems for "developing" economies "out there," effectively erases from view the international system's complicity in sex trafficking and its impact on the "advanced" economies "in here." It obscures the real power politics and the construction of identities along racial, gender, class, and cultural lines, which often result in sex trafficking (Agathangelou and Ling 2003).

The Gendered and Racial Nature of Sex Trafficking

Because the overwhelming majority of trafficked persons are women, trafficking is usually considered to be a gendered issue, and the partial result of patriarchy. It is rarely analyzed from the perspective of race discrimination. There has been little discussion of whether race, or other forms of discrimination, contributes to the likelihood of women and girls becoming victims of trafficking. However, when attention is paid to which women are most at risk of being trafficked, the link of this risk to their racial and social marginalization becomes clear.[3] Thus, even though the associations between contemporary sex trafficking and racism are not immediately clear, they are nonetheless undeniable. As UN High Commissioner for Human Rights Mary Robinson put it,

> Trafficking is . . . inherently discriminatory. In the case of trafficking into the global sex industry, we are talking about men from relatively prosperous countries paying for the sexual services of women and girls—and sometimes men and boys—from less wealthy countries. This is more than a labor rights issue or an issue of unequal development. It is a basic human rights issue because it involves such a massive and harmful form of discrimination. (World Conference Against Racism 2001).

Race and racial discrimination constitute a risk factor for trafficking and also determine the treatment that women experience in the sex market. Demand in the sex market is related to the marginal identity of those who are trafficked (Batsyukova 2007). It constitutes a risk factor for trafficking since women who are the victims of sex trafficking are already marginalized in a variety of ways. The intersection of race, class, gender, and nation already put them in a disadvantaged position and increase their vulnerability. For instance, where white women make sixty or seventy cents to the dollar of white men, women of color earn even less by comparison (World Conference Against Racism 2001). It is no coincidence then that most who are targeted for sex trafficking are considered "prostitutes of color" coming from poor, weak economies (even if many of those who are trafficked are well educated) (Agathangelou and Ling 2003). Racism increases the vulnerability of minority women and girls to sexual exploitation, and keeps them trapped in the sex industry through limiting their alternative opportunity structures and paths to safely exit the trade (Nelson 2003). Racist ideology also contributes to the demand in the region or country of destination of particular populations of sexual slaves and popular racial stereotyping are used in the sex industry to market women. Minority women are more sexualized and culturally less dominant, which makes them more vulnerable to sex trafficking. For instance, Asian females—stereotyped as females who are willing to do anything to please men—are in demand by sex traffickers (Espiritu 1997; Purkayastha and Majumdar 2009).

Race and racial discrimination also determine the treatment of women in the sex industry. Since these women are treated as commodities, it becomes

easy to deny them rights because they are not seen as fully human or full societal participants. And this becomes especially the case for women and girls
of color, where their gender and race connote forms of inferiority in patriarchal, racist societies. Buying women from different races and nationalities
gives men the illusion of experiencing the "different" or "exotic." Men come
to expect stereotypical behavior from the women they buy in prostitution.
Further, trade is, in part, conducted on the Internet, where discourse between
customers and providers (traffickers) reveal, not surprisingly, cruel, racist,
misogynist attitudes and treatment of the women and girls in the sex industry. The more sophisticated search engines allow buyers to search images
based on race and ethnicity (Raymond, Hughes and Gomez 2001). Prejudice
and poverty make women of color vulnerable to all kinds of exploitation; the
sex business combines the worst of it.

U.S. Responses to Sex Trafficking

The U.S. federal government has taken a firm stance (in theory) against
human trafficking both within and across its borders. Under the Trafficking
Victims Protection Act of 2000, U.S. law recognizes that people trafficked
against their will are victims of a crime, not illegal immigrants. An important aspect of the U.S. effort is to strengthen law enforcement's ability to
investigate, prosecute, and punish violent crimes committed against children, including child sex tourism and the commercial sexual exploitation
of children. To this effect, another important piece of legislation was the
Protect Act (Prosecutorial Remedies and Other Tools to End the Exploitation of Children Today Act of 2003). It was passed by Congress in April 2003
and signed into law by former President George W. Bush. The act serves as
a historic milestone for protecting children while severely punishing those
who victimize young people. Of particular note, the Protect Act allows law
enforcement officers to prosecute American citizens and legal permanent
residents who travel abroad and commercially sexually abuse minors without having to prove prior intent to commit this crime. The law also strengthens the punishment of these child sex tourists. If convicted, child sex tourists
now face up to thirty years imprisonment, an increase from the previous
maximum of fifteen years.

The United States now also offers 5,000 visas a year to trafficking victims
to allow them to apply for residency since only a legal status in this country will make victims feel secure enough to come forward with information
about traffickers and other victims (Landesman 2004). Further, the Victims
of Trafficking and Violence Protection Act of 2000 allowed for greater statu-

tory maximum sentences for traffickers, provided resources for protection of and assistance for victims of trafficking, and created avenues for interagency cooperation. It also allows many trafficking victims to remain in the United States and apply for permanent residency under a T-1 Visa. Since the criminal status of the trafficked women and children make them doubly vulnerable to this predatory practice. State policies like deportation, jail, and foster care hinder victims from lodging complaints with the police (Landesman 2004).

At a global level international NGOs such as Human Rights Watch and Amnesty International have called on the United States to improve its measures aimed at reducing trafficking. They recommend that the United States more fully implement the UN Convention Against Transnational Organized Crime Protocol to Prevent, Suppress and Punish Trafficking in Persons, especially Women and Children and for immigration officers to improve their awareness of trafficking and support the victims of trafficking. Several state governments have taken action to address human trafficking in their borders, either through legislation or prevention activities. For example, Florida state law prohibits forced labor, sex trafficking, and document servitude, and provides for mandatory law enforcement trainings and victim services. A 2006 Connecticut law prohibits coerced work and makes trafficking a violation of the Connecticut RICO Act.[4]

The Trafficking Victims Protection Act of 2000 identifies the role of local NGOs as being vital to the U.S. effort in resisting sex trafficking. Under the provision of this act the U.S. government is required to engage in extensive outreach to NGOs, which are often the first point of contact with trafficking victims. However, the scope for NGO resistance is rather bleak. Given the dire needs of victims and the lack of funding, the few understaffed organizations are overwhelmed with direct services as well as advocacy work. Still, only a few nonprofit organizations have been relatively successful in their battle against sex trafficking (Foo 2002). For instance, Shared Hope International, founded in 1998 by former Representative Linda Smith, is a nonprofit organization that exists to rescue and restore women and children in crisis. It is part of a worldwide effort to prevent and eradicate sex trafficking and slavery through education and public awareness. For over a decade, Shared Hope International has worked diligently around the world and in the United States, partnering with local groups to help women and children escape the sex trade by offering a place of refuge and a chance for a new future. Shared Hope uses a three-pronged strategy of prevention, rescue, and restoration, which also addresses ending the demand for women and especially children in the commercial sex industry, as well as performing field research and making policy recommendations on state and federal levels (Bergin 2009).

Another organization, Women Against Slavery, founded in 2009 by an international group of women operating in both Canada and the United States, is a grassroots, consciousness-raising organization dedicating to raising awareness of human trafficking and related issues. The group focuses on education as a primary means of combating human trafficking.[5]

Redefining Sex Trafficking and Its Victims

The primary challenge lies in redefining sex trafficking. Human rights legislation against trafficking must apply to both international women and women of the United States; otherwise there is a risk of depriving all women of recourse, remedy, and redress. The key element of the offense of trafficking, contained in the new UN Protocol's definition of trafficking, focuses on the exploitation, not the transport or movement of a victim across a border. American women who have been domestically trafficked within the United States should also be protected by anti-trafficking legislation. Focusing only on international trafficking as an actionable risk can lead to stereotyping trafficking as an immigration problem. Consequently, foreign victims of trafficking will be treated as immigration criminals, and trafficking will be regarded as a crime against the state rather than a crime against the person (Raymond, Hughes, and Gomez 2000).

CHAPTER TWENTY

The U.S. Culture of Violence

Stacy A. Missari

The most insidious myth about women's rights is that they are trivial or secondary to the concerns of life and death. Nothing could be farther from the truth: sexism kills. There is increasing documentation of the many ways in which being female is life-threatening.

—Charlotte Bunch

On June 23, 1999, Simon Gonzales drove to the Castle Rock Police Station at 3:20 a.m. and opened fire. Gonzales was killed in the shootout, but he was not the only fatality on the scene. Officers found the bodies of his three young daughters, whom he had shot to death at point blank range. Gonzales's trip to the police department was not his first contact with the police that day, however. His estranged wife, Jessica, had called the police earlier that day to inform them that he was in violation of her restraining order when he did not drop off the girls at the specified time. When her daughters were still missing a few hours later, she called the police three more times before driving to the police department herself. Following her daughters' murders, Jessica Gonzales sued the town of Castle Rock, the police department, and three individual officers with whom she had spoken for failure to adequately enforce her restraining order. Both the U.S. District Court of Colorado and the U.S. Supreme Court concluded that Gonzales did not have the constitutional right to protection (Leung 2005).

Although the Gonzales case may not be representative of the "typical" domestic violence case, the conclusions of the U.S. District and Supreme

Courts have important consequences for the use of restraining orders, which are the primary tools battered women use to keep themselves safe from their abusers. This case is especially striking because Gonzales did not stop after being denied justice at the highest levels in the United States. Gonzales, along with the ACLU and the Columbia Law School Human Rights Clinic, brought a petition to the Inter-American Commission on Human Rights, making it the first individual complaint of a human rights violation against the United States by a domestic violence survivor (Lenahan 2008).

The *Gonzales* case illuminates the fundamental inadequacies of the United States' approach to domestic violence intervention. Although organized struggles against domestic violence have a two-hundred-year history in the United States (Schneider 2000; Pleck 1987; Gordon 1988), in the past fifteen years the U.S. government been virtually absent in the movement to define violence against women as a human rights violation. Despite the government's acknowledgement of violence against women as a social problem warranting federal intervention with the passage of the Violence Against Women Act (VAWA) in 1994, the United States remains the only industrialized country that has not ratified CEDAW, which is internationally accepted as the most comprehensive declaration to end discrimination against women to date. CEDAW stands to address gender-based discrimination against women and in all areas of public and private life including: politics, education, employment, law, health care, and the family. CEDAW addresses the connection between women's equality and domestic violence, a link feminist activists have affirmed for years. Not only does CEDAW "spell out the meaning of equality [for women] . . . but also an agenda for action by countries to guarantee the enjoyment of those rights" (CEDAW 1992).

This chapter will explore the prevalence of systematic violence against women in the United States and the various struggles surrounding intervention, specifically, the passage and use of VAWA and the reservations of ratifying CEDAW. Although the battered women's movement has helped unprecedented numbers of women escape violence, domestic violence law and policy has an ambivalent and often contentious history in the United States. This chapter will demonstrate how the United States continues its "cultural complicity" (Schneider 2000, 5) regarding violence against women by failing to address the problem in a comprehensive way, thus failing to fully ensure the human rights of women.

Domestic Violence as a Social Problem

In terms of the most dangerous places for women to be, nowhere else can compare to the home. Women are far more likely to be abused in their own home than by an anonymous attacker, despite media coverage suggesting otherwise. The United States has among the highest rates in the industrial world for rape, domestic violence, and spousal murder. Domestic violence is the leading cause of injury to women in the nation, affecting nearly 4 million women a year (Kimmel 2008), and between 25 and 50 percent of all women over age eighteen will experience domestic violence at some point during their lives (Tjaden and Thoennes 2000). Despite these staggering statistics, the United States is rarely included in discussions of cultures that need human rights intervention. However, the sheer numbers of women affected by domestic violence, sexual assault, and stalking tell a different story about "our" culture.

Domestic violence is defined as a pattern of behavior in an intimate relationship that includes physical, verbal, and psychological acts used to maintain control over an intimate partner (Parmley 2004). Rather than individualized random acts of violence, the structure of an abusive relationship is frequently described as a "cycle of violence." Along with physical, emotional, and sexual abuse, batterers typically isolate their victims from family and friends, physically and emotionally intimidate them on a daily basis, and create a situation of economic dependence (Stephens, Hill, and Gentry 2005).

Domestic violence should not solely be examined at the micro-level, however. As law professor Donna Coker notes, individual batterers do not act alone (1999: 39). In order to fully understand the nature and prevalence of battering we need to examine the social structures that support domestic violence in the United States, including: "widespread denial of its frequency or harm, economic structures that render women vulnerable, and sexist ideology that holds women accountable for male violence and for the emotional lives of families, and that fosters deference to male familial control" (39). Understanding domestic violence in this comprehensive way stands in contrast to the individualized accounts of domestic violence that dominate popular media.

From Chastisement to Human Rights: The Evolution of Domestic Violence Intervention in the United States

Although the cycle of violence may be strikingly similar, the ways that activists have addressed a woman's right to physical integrity has taken many different forms throughout history. Often, more radical feminist agendas have been muted to allow for social change to take place through formal channels. In the nineteenth century, the split between marriage reformers and activists in the temperance movement characterized this process. Both groups saw wife beating as problematic. Whereas the temperance movement saw alcohol as the cause, feminists saw the hierarchical structure of marriage and divorce laws as the chief facilitator of violence against women (Schneider 2000).

Through the rest of the nineteenth and early twentieth centuries, the critique of patriarchy subsided and the first formal social agencies to deal with family violence were created, primarily as aids to children. Societies for the Prevention of Cruelty to Children (SPCCs) were founded by members of the upper class and were often used as places of refuge for women experiencing domestic violence who would make claims based on the safety of their children. SPCCs served a different purpose, though, and were largely a mechanism of social control of "disorderly" immigrant families who were a threat to middle class values and national stability (Gordon 1988; Felter 1997). The involvement of formal agencies like the SPCCs signaled a turning point in domestic violence intervention as a problem of state concern. Domestic violence was added to the list of the problems associated with poor immigrant communities that warranted formal intervention (Felter 1997).

Throughout the first half of the twentieth century, child welfare agencies provided the only institutional support for battered women. However, many women remained ambivalent about the individual "right" to freedom from violence throughout this period. Given the choice of protesting beatings while risking the loss of their homes and livelihoods, many women chose to stay with abusive husbands. It was not until (certain) women had the possibility of independence from their husbands from employment outside the home, divorce, and remarriage, birth limitation, and government aid to single mothers did the concept of the entitlement to freedom from violence become realized (Gordon 1988: 256).

It was not until the 1960s when consciousness-raising groups began defining violence against women in political terms that the first battered women's shelter opened in 1971. Shelters received funding from the Social Security Administration, taxes on marriage licenses, and the Concentrated Employment and Training Act during the 1970s (Pleck 1987). But despite increased funding from the state and federal governments, the majority of shelters still relied on grants and donations for the bulk of their funding. By 1980, only 15 states had passed laws to directly fund shelters and fewer than half of all shelters received any money from the state (Schechter 1982).

Federal Intervention: The Violence Against Women Act

Despite the passage of the Family Violence Prevention Services Act and Victims of Crime Act in 1984, the United States still lacked comprehensive legislation to adequately fund and address the prevention and intervention of domestic violence on a national scale. Discussions of such a policy were initiated in 1990 when the VAWA was introduced by then-senator Joseph Biden. Feminist organizations, along with a coalition of civil rights and workers' rights groups organized to lobby Congress in favor of the bill (Gelb 2003).

Four years of witness testimony and data gathering by Congress provided support for federal intervention. The data that showed that domestic violence has a significant effect on women's ability to participate fully in the national economy as workers and consumers. Homicide is the leading cause of death for women at work, almost half of all victims of rape lose their jobs, and batterers frequently harass their partners at work (Goldscheid 2000: 116-17). Gender-based violence not only costs millions in health care costs per year, but also costs employers an estimated $3 to $5 billion as a result of absenteeism due to domestic violence annually (Biden 2000: 22).

When the bill was passed in 1994, it allocated $1.8 billion over six years to address domestic violence, rape, sexual assault, and stalking. VAWA also provided funds for the implementation of educational programs for local communities, youth, service providers, police officers, and court personnel as well as a national domestic violence hotline. Grants for victim services, temporary shelters, and the adoption of mandatory reporting were also earmarked for states (Meyer-Emerick 2002; Biden 2000). Unlike previous legislation that only addressed gender violence in the workplace, VAWA covers violence against women in public (especially, public transit), in the home, and in the courts. VAWA also recognizes the scope and risks of stalking and the potential barriers to redress for battered immigrant women (Meyer-Emerick 2002; Heger 2000).

Whereas the allocation of funding was accepted as a necessary step in the prevention and intervention of violence against women, the civil rights provision of VAWA has encountered much resistance. The civil rights remedy, codified in Section 13981 of VAWA, provided a federal civil remedy for victims of domestic violence. The provision allowed victims of crimes motivated by gender to sue for damages in federal court and authorized courts to issue injunctions based on gender-motivated crimes.

In addition to the federal civil remedy, the Equal Protection Clause was invoked in support of VAWA to address gender bias in the court system, where women have had difficulty gaining effective redress of their claims of domestic violence and sexual assault (e.g., Das Gupta 2007). Section 5 of the Fourteenth Amendment authorizes Congress to enact legislation to enforce the constitutional guarantee of equal protection of the laws (U. S. Constitution) and data gathered by Congress prior to the passage of VAWA that illuminated the need for such a remedy. Long-standing gender and marriage norms were largely to blame for persistent formal bias in the court system. Until 1990, seven states did not recognize marital rape as a prosecutable offense and twenty-six states had laws that prosecuted marital rape only in instances of physical injury. Ten states barred battered women from suing their spouse under "interspousal tort immunity." In addition to formal barriers, state task forces also reported widespread informal biases in courts regarding attitudes toward victims of domestic violence and sexual assault. Reports documented that unlike victims of similar crimes, the "spotlight of suspicion [is] on the victim" when it comes to female victims of domestic violence and sexual assault (Biden 2000: 34).

Examples of informal bias and victim blaming in state courts were not isolated to a few discriminatory judges or police officers. Despite a traditional antipathy toward federal intervention in state law, especially with respect to family law, 41 attorneys general signed a statement saying "the problem of violence against women is a national one, requiring federal attention, federal leadership, and federal funds" (Biden 2000: 13). VAWA sought to alleviate this entrenched bias by requiring domestic violence training for state judges and court personnel. Additionally, states were now required to honor protective orders issued in other states (Meyer-Emerick 2002).

Challenges to VAWA

Congress's authority to enact the civil remedy in VAWA was challenged following the Supreme Court opinion in *United States v. Lopez* (1995). The *Lopez* opinion called into question the limits of federal power to restrict gun possession on school grounds under the Gun-Free School Zones Act and became the first time in sixty years that use of the Commerce Clause had been invalidated (Goldscheid 2000). The *Lopez* resolution questioned the "breadth of commerce power and VAWA's constitutionality" (Lemos 1998: 1254) and this stricter standard was applied to cases of gender-motivated violence.

In *United States v. Morrison* (2000), Antonio Morrison and James Crawford, who were members of the school's football team, allegedly assaulted their fellow student at Virginia Tech, Christy Brzonkala. After the University found insufficient evidence to sanction Crawford and dismissed the punishment of Morrison, Brzonkala filed federal suit against Morrison, Crawford, and the school citing a violation of §13981 of the Violence Against Women Act and Title IX of the Education Amendments of 1972.

On appeal, the Fourth Circuit Court, sitting en banc, found the federal civil remedy in §13981 unconstitutional, citing the decision in *Lopez* (Lemos

1998; Biden 2000; Goldscheid 2000). The Supreme Court affirmed the decision of the Fourth Circuit Court, concluding that the powers granted under
the Commerce Clause cannot be used to regulate private conduct that does not
directly involve commerce. Supporters of VAWA have criticized this decision
noting that "nowhere has this Court been more sensitive to Congress's discretion in exercising its Commerce Clause authority, as here [with VAWA]" (Biden
2000: 12). Unlike gun possession, which may affect access to education and
thus restrict participation in the marketplace, violence against women has been
demonstrated to hinder women's full participation in the market.

Domestic Violence on the International Stage: CEDAW

Although the Violence Against Women Act has been called the "most significant piece of legislation ever enacted on the subject of domestic violence
against women" (Brooks 1997, 65), the United States has been less willing to
adopt international standards in regard to the commitment to end gender-
motivated violence. Domestic violence in and of itself does not constitute a
human rights violation and states cannot be held responsible for the actions
of private individuals. However, domestic violence constitutes a human rights
violation when a state systematically fails "to enforce laws equitably across
gender lines" (Thomas and Beasley 1993: 46). This standard could certainly
be upheld given the extensive data gathered on the biases of state and federal
courts and law enforcement. Despite the passage of VAWA, the millions of
women who are affected by domestic violence each year are a testament to
the lack of state and federal commitment to truly addressing the underlying
causes of domestic violence.[1]

Despite the tireless work of domestic violence coalitions, battered wom-
en's shelters, and feminist organizations across the country, an explicit guarantee of women's right to equality and freedom from violence still does not
exist. This lack of Constitutional support for equality of women is demonstrated over and over again—in the unavailability of Congressional authority for cases of domestic violence, the U.S. reservations against CEDAW, the
resolution in the Gonzales lawsuit—and the list goes on. CEDAW, in particular, in Article 2(a), which calls for "Constitutions and laws to embody
the principle of equality," would remedy this hole in the U.S. Constitution.
However, in the almost thirty years since its drafting, CEDAW has had more
reservations than any other human rights convention, which some scholars
argue is because the international community as a whole regards women's
rights as secondary to other traditional human rights concerns (Mayer 1996).

President Carter signed CEDAW in 1980 and introduced it to the Senate Foreign Relations Committee before leaving office. However, the Reagan and Bush administrations did not support ratification and the Convention on remained pending for the next twenty-five years. The Clinton administration supported CEDAW and submitted it to the Senate Foreign Relations Committee in 1994, which was then chaired by Senator Jesse Helms. Despite the administration's support, Clinton submitted CEDAW with substantial reservations, understandings, and declarations (RUDs). In terms of reservations, the United States specifically opposed any federal regulation of private conduct, combat assignments, comparable worth, and paid maternity leave. The United States' refusal to regulate private conduct coupled with the declaration of a "non-self-executing provision" (Blanchfield 2006, 5) essentially rendered any mandates that would be imposed by the ratification of CEDAW powerless (the U.S. has employed "non-self-executing" reservations in nearly every binding human rights instrument to which it is party).

CEDAW was never brought to a full Senate vote in 1994 but was reintroduced in 2002 when Biden became chair of the Senate Foreign Relations Committee. Opposition to CEDAW during this stage of consideration was understood to hinge on the assumption that the Constitution is the superior guarantor of rights to American citizens. However, the right to vote in the Nineteenth Amendment is the only place where women's rights are explicitly guaranteed and are not subject to interpretation or the political climate of the day.

As women's rights were thrust onto the international stage in the 1980s and 1990s, the United States became more and more isolated from the international legal system (Mayer 1996: 746). This American exceptionalism is demonstrated by the staunch U.S. commitment to certain standards such as the right to privacy and freedom from government intrusion, above others, such as freedom from violence. While other countries have balanced certain constitutional rights with new international standards, the United States has shown to be virtually unyielding in its "smug complacency about inferior . . . domestic rights standards" (766).

While commitment to constitutionalism has been the official position that the United States has taken against CEDAW, others have argued that constitutionalism is a "veil" that hides the true objections to CEDAW—that ratifying the Convention would radically disrupt the status quo as well as women's traditional role in society (Mayer 1996; Powell 2005). Catherine Powell suggests that:

Rather than dwell on the poetics of the veil as a symbol of women's oppression in Afghanistan and other parts of the Muslim world . . . American women could benefit from considering that,

today, Afghanistan has ratified CEDAW, while the United States has
not. (2005: 337)

Throughout the 1990s and 2000s, conservative and religious groups, with
powerful allies in the U.S. government, viewed CEDAW's commitment to
equality as an attack on traditional gender roles. Opponents argue that the
ratification of CEDAW will destroy traditional family values by legalizing
abortion,[2] "undercut parental rights, and lead to gender re-education, homo-
sexual rights, and legalized prostitution" (Blanchfield 2006, 10).

The Future of VAWA and CEDAW:
The End of Domestic Violence?

Whether reservations to CEDAW center on a commitment to the Constitution or more controversially, a commitment to the status quo (Mayer 1996),
something as integral as the right to live a life free of violence, is not something that should be left to political whims. The prospects for CEDAW ratification may begin to improve during the Obama administration, however, the
same issues that have hampered other guarantees of equality still pervade the
Senate. The ratification of CEDAW is the first step, but compliance to international conventions without a means of enforcement may allow the pervasive
culture of violence against women in the United States to continue.

Despite cutbacks in funding for VAWA and resistance to CEDAW in
the last ten years, the election of Senator Biden as vice president might provide a window of opportunity for supporters of VAWA and increased attention to violence against women as an important area of policy. Biden also
introduced the International Violence Against Women Act in 2007 and is
a supporter of the ratification of CEDAW. With the passage of these bills,
the causes of domestic violence may be addressed in a comprehensive way
through increased education about women's second-class status around the
world, rather than singular attention on criminal intervention. These changes
may also influence the definition of "success" of domestic violence intervention, not solely in terms of leaving the abusive relationship, but not going
back, securing safe housing and an adequate income.

As Biden noted on his website, the passage of VAWA represents "the
beginning of a historic commitment to women and children victimized by
domestic violence and sexual assault."[3] With increased attention from human
rights groups to domestic violence, the commitment to truly eradicating violence against women may be realized.

PART VII

HUMAN RIGHTS AND RESISTANCE IN THE
UNITED STATES

Although the United States was a leader in spearheading international human rights efforts following World War II, and the development of international human rights instruments, it has not necessarily been among the leaders in implementing and enacting human rights. Moreover, the conceptualization of human rights and related initiatives, interpretations, and implementations are not solely topics of formal legislation and state practices. Indeed, much happens in the human rights enterprise that occurs from the bottom up, through local efforts on the ground, without the state itself, and often in fact challenging the state's inaction or obstruction of the implementation of human rights.

The chapters in this section examine non-state movements in the human rights enterprise, often by those with relatively little power against the state. For example, one chapter explores the prisoners' rights movement, in which those whose very rights have been taken away by the state still organize and agitate against the assumption that incarceration necessarily means one is subhuman and thus not subject to human rights. Another chapter explores the efforts by local communities to establish themselves as Human Rights municipalities. These efforts can result in substantial changes in the formal arrangements of local governments, and in many ways imply the way for statewide and national models of similar efforts. The human rights enterprise is not a set of formal laws and international treaties determined by the state as an elite, top-down dictate: it is often a more democratic, bottom-up process of shaping, defining, and challenging the meaning of human rights and their practice.

Finally, we conclude with an examination of the original question that framed this volume: while the United States was a leader in the development of international human rights accords, is it the "gold standard" of human rights practices among the world's many nations? Is the record of human rights implementation and practice among the very best in the world, or is there much work still to be done? What happens when the state fails to implement and enforce the human rights instruments that it has ratified? What is the role of the human rights enterprise in filling that void and empowering people in their claims to human rights? The final chapter in this volume assesses these questions, the answer to which has already been suggested by the previous chapters. We have come so far, and still have so very far to go, right in our own backyard.

CHAPTER TWENTY-ONE

Building U.S. Human Rights Culture from the Ground Up: International Human Rights Implementation at the Local Level

Chivy Sok and Kenneth J. Neubeck

Since 1945, the United States has provided critical leadership in shaping human rights institutions and treaties. It was U.S. leadership that helped to found the UN and, in its Charter, formally codified "human rights." The United States, led by Eleanor Roosevelt as Chair of the first UN Human Rights Commission, played a major role in giving the world a "common standard of achievement" in the form of the UDHR. This core document, unanimously adopted by the UN General Assembly on December 10, 1948, promoted the drafting and adoption of important human rights treaties.

Under the U.S. Constitution, all international treaties—including human rights treaties—become the "supreme law of the land" when signed by the president and approved by a vote of two-thirds of the U.S. Senate. When the United States ratifies a human rights treaty, it has a legal obligation to respect, protect, and fulfill the fundamental rights that it addresses. The United States has ratified some key treaties, such as ICCPR, CAT, and CERD. Yet it has not ratified others, including CEDAW, and CRC.

Without a doubt, America has, albeit selectively, championed human rights. But its promotion and protection of human rights has been outwardly directed, supporting others when politically expedient while ignoring, chastising, or threatening to punish others for criticizing the U.S. record. The government has failed to recognize and apply the human rights framework to conditions within the United States, even as it has condemned other nations' governments for human rights violations.

Human rights violations happen in America on a daily basis. Under the George W. Bush administration, for example, due process was suspended in the name of fighting terrorism and individuals have been jailed for years without access to a lawyer. Torture by U.S. authorities became "legal" when a law professor turned Department of Justice official penned a series of memos that provided justification for using draconian methods such as "waterboarding" to extract information from detainees. (Waterboarding, a technique that simulates drowning, is widely recognized internationally as torture.) In some states, prison officials still allow the shackling of women during childbirth. Nearly 500,000 children are laboring in some of the most dangerous conditions picking the very fruits and vegetables that may end up in our grocery stores. Capital punishment is applied to black men at a much higher rate than white men for committing comparable crimes. People of color continue to face persistent discrimination in a variety of areas, specifically in their access to health, quality education, labor protection, and so forth. Professional women are still earning less for performing the same job as men. The list of violations is a long one, as already illustrated in several chapters of this volume.

People in the United States are starting to resist the lack of initiative being taken at the federal level to address international human rights within this nation. Addressing human rights violations at home is as critical as promoting human rights abroad. Concerted efforts are needed to require U.S. governmental bodies at the local, state, and national levels to meet its international obligations and facilitate human rights practice within the United States. As we will see, resistance to the failure to address human rights at home is increasingly occurring at the grassroots local level. This article examines the local implementation of international human rights by the people of San Francisco, which, as a city, led by example when it adopted a local ordinance grounded in CEDAW principles, and offers some examples of efforts in other cities that San Francisco inspired.

Breaking the Path for Others:
The San Francisco CEDAW Ordinance

As mentioned above, the United States still has not ratified a number of key human rights instruments, including CEDAW, a comprehensive treaty supporting women's rights as human rights. This is a glaring omission and prevents women from using this very powerful legal tool to advance the dignity and rights of women and girls in the United States. A group of extraordinary San Francisco women activists decided to change this after returning home from the 1995 World Conference on Women in Beijing. In 1996, the Women's Institute for Leadership Development (WILD) for Human Rights, led by Krishanti Dharmaraj, was established and the women went to work to get the city and county of San Francisco to adopt the first local CEDAW Ordinance in the United States.

In its detailed manual based on the San Francisco experience, *Making Rights Real: A Workbook on the Local Implementation of Human Rights* (WILD 2006), WILD for Human Rights outlines basic steps taken to implement CEDAW at the local level. Below, we offer a summary of the San Francisco experience.

It begins with partnerships and education. Building a partnership and a coalition of supporters from diverse stakeholders was critical to creating support for the implementation of CEDAW in San Francisco. No one organization or individual can take on such a task without broad support. WILD for Human Rights was the lead organizer and provided the bold vision of bringing CEDAW home. Critical to the success of this trailblazing ordinance was WILD's partnership with key governmental and nongovernmental institutions. These included Amnesty International USA Western Region (AIUSA), The Women's Foundation of California (TWF), and the San Francisco Commission on the Status of Women (COSW). COSW was particularly critical because it was the one local governmental body that had a mandate to address issues affecting women and girls. More important, COSW had access to other officials and knowledge of the process necessary to facilitate the passing of a local CEDAW ordinance.

Equally important to the implementation process was doing the education and organizing to raise awareness of human rights in general and CEDAW in particular. For eighteen months, WILD for Human Rights, partner organizations, and dedicated volunteers organized monthly workshops and seminars for diverse groups of community members and organizations. They helped participants to understand the history and contents of CEDAW and how it might be used to improve the lives of women and girls. This intensive education process reached local providers serving women and girls, activists working on a multitude of social issues, officials working in the city government, and local unions. The education process was important for building a coalition of knowledgeable supporters who could put pressure on the city's legislative body, the San Francisco Board of Supervisors, and the mayor to support the initiative. The organizers also worked to educate and secure support from key local politicians and political leaders, such as Barbara Kaufman, a conservative lawmaker who was also the president of the board of supervisors.

After eighteen months of intensive organizing and education, the organizers staged a two-hour public hearing before the board of supervisors on October 30, 1997. Holding public hearings as a strategy is not new to human rights advocates. Women from all over the world have used this type of forum to voice their experiences, especially violations inflicted upon them, and to have their demands heard. For the San Francisco organizers, a public hearing was a

> means of educating policymakers and other decision makers about the human rights of women and girls in San Francisco and of holding them accountable for protecting these rights. The hearing facilitated a public exchange of ideas and demands among community members, service providers, advocates, and city officials. It highlighted the relevance of CEDAW in people's lives and the systematic discrimination faced by women (WILD 2006: 67).

The hearing brought diverse women's voices speaking about a range of issues affecting their lives, including discrimination, employment, access to credit, affirmative action, sexual harassment, family violence, health, reproductive rights, and political participation and public life. Through their stories and testimonies, the women were able to demonstrate the need for CEDAW. The following day, the board of supervisors passed a resolution calling on the federal government to ratify CEDAW and made a commitment to implement CEDAW locally.

Four months later, on March 2, 1998, board of supervisors president Kaufman introduced the CEDAW ordinance to the board, stating, "San Francisco must take a leadership role in protecting women's human rights. We cannot wait for the U.S. Government to do so" (WILD 1998). On April 13, the Board unanimously passed the ordinance and it became law on April 14 when Mayor Willie Brown signed it at the conclusion of the Mayor's Summit for Women. "San Francisco is showing the way in protecting the rights of all women. The U.S. is the only industrialized country in the world that has yet to ratify CEDAW. We are moving forward on CEDAW to set an example for the rest of the nation. It is long overdue" (Office of the Mayor of San Francisco 1998).

What Does the San Francisco CEDAW Ordinance Mean for Women and Girls?

CEDAW addresses major areas in which women face persistent discrimination—education, employment, equal pay for equal work, maternity leave, health, economic benefits such as access to loans and credit, social institutions such as marriage, sexual exploitation, and trafficking, equality before the law and equal access to legal institutions, the need to change social and cultural practices that perpetuate discrimination, reproductive rights, and participation in political and public life. The treaty provides clear standards for governments and holds them accountable for implementing policy measures so that women may achieve full equity.

The San Francisco ordinance is not an exact replication of the international treaty. In a localized form, the city adopted CEDAW's definition of discrimination and some of its core principles, and created a human rights implementation process tailored to the structure and operations of San Francisco government. Below are highlights of the ordinance.

Definition matters. The San Francisco CEDAW Ordinance adopted CEDAW's definition of discrimination against women:

> Discrimination against women shall include, but not be limited to, any distinction, exclusion or restriction made on the basis of sex that has the effect or purpose of impairing or nullifying the recognition, enjoyment or exercise by women, irrespective of their marital status, on a basis of equality of men and women, of human rights and fundamental freedoms in the political, economic, social, cultural, civil or any other field.

By adopting this definition, the ordinance accepted the need to address both intentional and unintentional discrimination. This is a radical departure from U.S. legal tradition in that victims of discrimination typically react to discrimination only after it has happened, usually through filing formal complaints or law suits, and must show that it was intentional. The human rights approach requires governments at all levels to address discrimination proactively and to look not only at intentional discrimination, but also unintentional discrimination and the detrimental effects it has on specific vulnerable populations such as women and girls.

Moreover, the San Francisco ordinance goes one step farther by addressing not only gender but also racial discrimination. In 2000, an amendment was added to the ordinance to include the definition of racial discrimination contained in CERD.

> Racial discrimination shall mean any distinction, exclusion, restriction or preference based on race, color, descent, or national or ethnic origin which has the purpose or effect of nullifying or impairing the

recognition, enjoyment or exercise, on an equal footing, of human rights and fundamental freedoms in the political, economic, social, cultural or any other field of public life.

This amendment also recognizes both intentional and unintentional discrimination, but with the emphasis on race, color, descent, national and ethnic origin, and other identities. Why is this important? When we scan human rights violations in the United States, such as police brutality, juvenile detention practices, lack of access to health care, unequal educational opportunities, or low-wage workers' inhumane conditions, we find huge disparities between the treatment of whites and people of color. By adopting the CERD definition, the San Francisco ordinance recognizes the theoretical concept of intersectionality (implicitly), and the pragmatic need to address discrimination against women and girls of color.

Mandate, implementing body, and budget support. San Francisco's CEDAW Ordinance mandated human rights education for public officials with a view to "integrating gender equity and human rights principles into all [city] operations, including policy, program and budgetary decision-making." The ordinance called for the establishment of a CEDAW task force, a temporary implementing body composed of government representatives and community members with knowledge and expertise in international human rights, health, employment, violence against women, and other women's issues. The San Francisco Commission on the Status of Women provided administrative services to the task force. From 1998 to 2002, the CEDAW task force had responsibility for the implementation of the local human rights ordinance. After this period, power and responsibilities transferred to the Commission.

Impacts of the San Francisco CEDAW Ordinance. Adopting an ordinance based on human rights principles does not mean that changes will happen immediately. In social justice work, changes may be slow and incremental. The San Francisco CEDAW ordinance is no exception. But it is clear from the experience of San Francisco that such an ordinance, if persistently and consistently applied, can generate meaningful changes toward greater equity. Here we examine concrete examples of these beneficial changes.

In the course of the implementation process, six city agencies participated in "gender analysis" of their programs, budgets, and employment practices to evaluate and to take proactive steps to eliminate discrimination against women: The Department on the Status of Women (DOSW); the Arts Commission; the Department of the Environment; the Department of Public Works; the Adult Probation Department; and the Residential Rent Stabilization and Arbitration Board. Let us look at some of the impacts that doing such gender analysis had on city government operations.

Process matters. The Residential Rent Stabilization and Arbitration Board (rent board) conducted a gender analysis and submitted its first report to the CEDAW Task Force in 2000. This is a case that demonstrates that the process of implementation can catalyze systemic change. As part of the reporting and review process, the task force asked about client demographics to understand who the rent board served and the level of client satisfaction. Emily Murase, who now serves as the executive director of the DOSW, recalls the Board's reaction. We "were met with blank stares." The Board had not kept these records and was not able to analyze gender impact.

The CEDAW task force recommended that the rent board collect disaggregated data to understand the gender impact of its policies and practices. Here, disaggregated data means not just how many clients does the board serve and how satisfied are they, but a detailed breakdown of who the board serves, and whether there is a pattern of who is satisfied and who is not, and why. "Steps must be taken to ensure that disaggregated data is collected and reported to the public. It is impossible to analyze trends or evaluate the affect of services on women and men if this information does not exist" (San Francisco Rent Board 2000). In response, the Board went back and modified their evaluation form in order to collect gender information (San Francisco Rent Board 2002). To some, this may seem insignificant. But in human rights work, it is essential. As Murase noted in one of her presentations, "Perhaps the biggest lesson we learned was the importance of disaggregated data. Drilling down to this level of detail is essential to understand patterns of discrimination and to recommend policy change" (Murase 2005).

Use of city grants and contracts to increase gender equity and diversity. The Department of the Environment is an excellent example of how city grants and contracts with non-city government organizations can be used to promote gender equity in those organizations without incurring additional costs. During the review of its first gender analysis in 2006, for example, the CEDAW task force recommended that the department "integrate gender concerns into the development of evaluation measures and include gender in the RFP [Request for Proposals for grants or contracts] process." As part of its strategy, the department "will require grantees to submit a final report which will include information on gender and diversity of the staff positions which were created as a result of the Department of Environment funding" (San Francisco Department of the Environment 2000.) Considering the fact that the department gives out approximately $1.4 million in grants annually to a variety of organizations in San Francisco, this change can have positive impact well beyond city government if implemented consistently.

Work-life policies. Perhaps one of the most notable impacts of the San Francisco ordinance is promoting family-friendly policies and work-life balance. Women face one of the toughest dilemmas when it comes to balancing their work and family obligations, whether it is taking care of children or of their elders. Currently, the United States does not offer paid leave for new parents. As of January 2009, U.S. lawmakers were still trying to introduce legislation on paid parental leave for federal employees (Pianin 2009). As a nation, we are a long way from national family-friendly workplace policies. But San Francisco moved ahead.

The gender analysis reporting and review process revealed in black and white the realities and challenges faced by city employees. "City employees were being squeezed by the double burden of childcare for young children and eldercare for aging parents" (Murase 2005). No policies existed on telecommuting or flexible work schedules. This affected a large percentage of women, as well as men who were single parents. The city's DOSW, in collaboration with others, embarked on a citywide survey on work-life policy in 2001. The findings were encouraging.

> The survey found that departments with flexible work-life policies cited this as a strength that also helped with morale, customer service, job retention and recruitment, and improved performance. Most departments viewed the benefits of these practices as far outweighing the concerns. (San Francisco Department on the Status of Women 2001)

Today, the city's actively promotes both flexible work schedules and telecommuting in its departments (San Francisco Department on the Status of Women 2007: 20). Furthermore, the DOSW worked with lawmakers to pass new city legislation on paid parental leave in 2002. This is no small accomplishment. Professor Debra Liebowitz, who authored an evaluation report for WILD, attributed these policy changes to the ordinance.

> The CEDAW Ordinance was a driving force to bring the issue of employees' needs around work-life balance to the fore. Indeed, the CEDAW Ordinance catalyzed attention to the issue city-wide and also facilitated specific policy changes within individual departments. (Liebowitz 2008: 9)

Inspiring and strengthening the human rights movement in the United States. The impact of the CEDAW Ordinance is not limited to San Francisco. On the contrary, it has inspired initiatives and actions around the country. As Krishanti Dharmaraj, the co-founder of WILD for Human Rights stated during the historic adoption of the ordinance in 1998, "San Francisco may be the first city, but it will not be the last" (WILD for Human Rights 1998). Many advocates have found this model of localizing human rights affirming. Sarah Albert, cochair of the Working Group on the Ratification of CEDAW, said it best:

> San Francisco is a model and a pioneer in how the United States can use the treaty to provide equal rights for women. It says to the rest of the country that this is not some wild UN treaty that came in from outer space. This is relevant. (Veseley 2002)

New York Advocates Organize to Implement Human Rights GOAL

Inspired by the success of the San Francisco's 1998 CEDAW ordinance, human rights advocates in New York City launched a campaign in 2002 to accomplish a similar feat. The New York City Human Rights Initiative (NYCHRI) is a citywide coalition of organizations that includes social justice advocacy groups, grassroots community organizations, service providers, and unions. Today, there are over 100 members of the coalition, whose lead coordinating organization is the Human Rights Project of New York's Urban Justice Center.

Human rights advocates in New York City were determined to pursue the implementation of treaties that would address both gender and racial discrimination from the start. In embracing both CEDAW and CERD, the goal of the NYCHRI is that of eliminating gender and racial discrimination in civil, political, social, economic, and cultural spheres (www.nychri.org).

Systemic gender and race inequalities have been pressing human rights issues in New York City, but typically different organizational actors in the social justice community have addressed such issues. The human rights framework demands and draws much of its strength from the way in which it fosters collaboration and mutual support among groups that are often divided and separated along identity politics lines. By adopting a strategy of addressing both forms of inequality simultaneously, NYCHRI showed its intention to break down the issue silos separating social justice groups right from the start.

New York City currently has a very broad human rights ordinance, although it is in reality a civil rights ordinance. It prohibits discrimination against a long list of protected classes in housing, employment, and public accommodations and gives the city some local enforcement powers. In 2004, NYCHRI proposed that the city government adopt a new ordinance that would strengthen and expand upon its existing one, which only reacts to complaints. They called it the Human Rights in Government Operations Audit Law or Human Rights GOAL.

The ordinance was introduced into the New York City Council in December 2004 and was assigned to the Council Government Operations Committee. It became the subject of a major public hearing in April 2005, in which many coalition members and their allies testified on its behalf. The measure, however, did not have the support of New York mayor Michael Bloomberg. NYCHRI advocates believe that he viewed it as unnecessary, duplicating existing antidiscrimination efforts, and an added expense. With the lack of mayoral support, Human Rights GOAL did not have strong enough support among members of the City Council to be brought up for a Council vote.

After some revision, Human Rights GOAL was resubmitted to the City Council in March 2008, shortly after the City agreed to pay over $21 million to settle a federal class action discrimination suit for race and national origin discrimination in hiring in its Parks Department. Advocates of the measure took care to note that had Human Rights GOAL been in place, such discrimination would very likely have been addressed proactively, either prevented or eliminated when detected, and saved the city taxpayers $21 million.

The Council failed to act on Human Rights GOAL in 2008, and the bill was again submitted in June 2010. The fate of the latest Human Rights GOAL proposal is unclear at this writing, given that in October 2008 the City Council approved an ordinance allowing Mayor Bloomberg to run for an unprecedented third four-year term in 2009. But advocates and supporters of GOAL remain highly optimistic and believe that by continuing their education and organizing efforts the ordinance will in time be adopted and implemented.

Eugene, Oregon, Works to Implement a Human Rights City Framework

The idea of local human rights implementation in Eugene took hold in 2006 with the City of Eugene Human Rights Commission. The Commission, established by ordinance, consists of a diverse group of community members appointed by the City Council to advise the mayor and council on human rights issues in the City. Historically, "human rights" was viewed by the Commission solely in conventional "civil rights" terms, and essentially referred to the right of protected classes to be free from or to have access to legal recourse in response to discriminatory treatment. The Commission, an advisory body, had no anti-discrimination enforcement powers under the ordinance establishing it. Not only was the principal focus of the Commission on what amounted to civil rights violations, but its stance on these violations—and that of city government—was essentially reactive rather than proactive.

In 2006, inspired by San Francisco's implementation of CEDAW and the local implementation ordinance proposed in New York City, the commission decided to explore the desirability and feasibility of the Eugene city government adopting international human rights principles and standards across its operations (www.humanrightscity.com). The 2006-2008 work plan included an item calling for the commission to determine what other locales were doing with regard to local implementation efforts and to open up conversations on the topic of human rights implementation with city staff and community groups.

Over the course of 2007, a "Human Rights City" subcommittee of the Commission gathered information on local implementation elsewhere and networked with national organizations who were working to implement human rights in the United States. Subcommittee members began to conduct human rights workshops for small groups of city employees and managers from various city departments to acquaint them with international human rights principles and the concept of local implementation. The subcommittee organized a public symposium on human rights in the United States and a community-wide workshop that focused on local implementation of human rights in Eugene. The mayor and other elected officials, city staff, and representatives attended the workshop from a wide range of social justice groups, social service organizations, religious groups, and educational institutions. The subcommittee also engaged in outreach to local civic organizations such as the City Club of Eugene and utilized media outlets to promote awareness. In her 2008 State of the City address, Eugene's mayor Kitty Piercy expressed the hope that Eugene would become "an official human rights city" and later issued a mayoral proclamation calling for implementation of human rights principles.

Members of Eugene's NGOs are lending their support. In late 2008, several local human rights advocates in Eugene developed a coalition composed of some thirty community organizations. The newly established Community Coalition for Advancement of Human Rights pledged to partner with the Human Rights Commission on securing City Council support for implementation of the human rights city concept, which is now a goal on the Commission's 2009-2010 work plan. Both the Commission and coalition members wish to see the human rights framework applied to a broad range of human rights challenges in the city, including chronic homelessness and hunger, insufficient physical and mental health care, racial discrimination, threats to the city's immigrant population, and inadequate citizen-based police oversight. While they will look to San Francisco, New York, and other local initiatives for ideas and inspiration, the Eugene experience promises to evolve at its own pace and in its own way.

Conclusion: Building a Strong U.S. Human Rights Movement Through Local Implementation

The concept of human rights is not new to the United States. The July 4, 1776, Declaration of Independence referred to humanity's "inalienable rights to life, liberty, and the pursuit of happiness," which it said government must secure. This Declaration, along with the Bill of Rights to the U.S. Constitution, heavily influenced the modern notion that all people, everywhere, have basic rights that must be respected if they are to live free and with dignity. The concept of human rights is not, as some critics of human rights treaties would have it, a foreign idea. But full implementation of internationally recognized human rights within the United States has yet to occur. In response, a number of organizations are collaborating to "bring human rights home" and have formed the "U.S. human rights movement" for this purpose.

The U.S. human rights movement is diverse in terms of geography and composition, as is readily seen in the membership composition of the nation-wide U.S. Human Rights Network (www.ushrnetwork.org). The network is a broad coalition of over three hundred national, regional, state, and local social justice organizations that support implementing human rights in the United States. The various organizations involved in the network address such topics as the protection of civil liberties, abolition of capital punishment, immigration reform, homelessness and affordable housing needs, health care, environmental deterioration, as well as the rights of indigenous peoples, the LGBTQ population, workers, prisoners, people with disabilities, impoverished families, women, children, and people of color.

One of the best ways to support the U.S. human rights movement is by educating about, organizing around, and seeking to implement human rights at the local level. The impact of such activities can be beneficial, regardless of the outcome. There is no one exact model for implementing human rights in each locale. San Francisco was a highly successful process that resulted in an adoption of a local ordinance to drive change. And it is still a work-in-progress. The New York City effort, while inspiring, has yet to succeed in securing the political support to pass an ordinance. The city of Eugene's human rights initiative is still nascent and undergoing its own organic evolution.

There is a lot of room for creativity in implementing human rights at the local level, and ultimately how it will occur will be subject to the will of people in communities. Strategies and process may differ, but the goal remains the same: localize human rights so that every citizen, every household, and every community can benefit from this transformative framework.

CHAPTER TWENTY-TWO

Critical Resistance and the Prison Abolitionist Movement

Zoe Hammer

The United States Prison Boom

The incarceration rate in the United States has increased by more than 400 percent since the mid-1980s. As this massive expansion has taken place, we have been encouraged by media, politicians, and popular culture to believe that our society builds prisons as a response to crime. Prisons, we are told, remove dangerous individuals from society; individuals who have chosen to break our rules, and thus threaten our collective safety. This unexamined assumption has become axiomatic in public discourse—a form of "common sense." However, research, experiential insight, and analysis offered by prison abolitionist scholars and activists in recent decades challenges this common sense, allowing us to understand that prisons not only do not keep our communities safe, they actually create the social problems they claim to solve.

Critical Resistance (CR) is a grassroots prison abolition organization with chapters around the United States and a national office in Oakland, California. Formed in 1998, CR uses a multipronged set of strategies, including decarceration and decriminalization, organizing to reduce prison populations in various ways such as decriminalizing drug addiction and sex work; ending prison building, including closing existing facilities and stopping the construction of new prisons and jails; and the development of alternatives to incarceration, organizing new practices that do not rely on the use of imprisonment.[1]

The scholar activists who contributed to the founding of CR—former prisoners, prisoners and their loved ones, grassroots social justice organizers, and critical scholars from many fields—have conducted extensive research and analysis that demonstrates and explains why and how the U.S. prison system has exploded, and how its massive growth impacts communities and produces and perpetuates dynamics of inequality, poverty, and systemic injustice in the United States.

Abolitionist Analysis

With 5 percent of the world's population and 25 percent of its prisoners, the United States has the world's highest incarceration rate.[2] A thirty-year prison building project, accompanied by waves of new criminal legislation, vast increases in the numbers, surveillance capacities, and interpenetrating functions of police, border patrol, and other law enforcement units keep this rate of incarceration growing (Parenti 2000). The contemporary U.S. prison boom is the result of many social forces, including: changing state spending priorities since the early 1980s favoring punishment and militarism over social spending and safety nets; vigorous economic development in some places at the expense of growing poverty in others; the disproportionate political influence of corporate interests; and mass consent born of a national history of racist violence (Davis 1995; Gilmore 1997, 1998/99, 2007; Davis 2003).

One thing the prison boom is not a result of is increasing crime rates. U.S. crime rates have not gone significantly up or down since the early 1970s. The expansion of the U.S. prison system is enabled primarily through policy shifts, including: the increasing criminalization of everyday behaviors and of whole segments of the U.S. population, as well as a radical increase in the duration of prison sentences wrought by mandatory minimums; the abolition of parole; and other "tough on crime" measures such as three and even two strikes laws. This means that many more behaviors have been defined as criminal in recent years, and also that people convicted of crimes serve much longer sentences than ever before.

A combination of racial profiling practices, racially targeted surveillance, and the practice of "sweeping," which occurs primarily in communities of color, along with incredible racial disparities in sentencing (70 percent of arrests are white, 70 percent of prisoners are people of color) means that U.S. incarceration practices are not only clearly racist, but that they also create, rely on, and perpetuate racism and systemic racial disparity (Davis 1995; Gilmore 1997, 1998/99, 2007; Davis 2003).

The impacts of the prison boom have come down hard on poor communities of color, particularly in regions, cities, and towns with high rates of unemployment and a lack of available job opportunities, dividing families, locking up tens of thousands of children, parents, and young adults, often for decades, and using incarceration as the only solution for race and poverty related problems such as criminalization, homelessness, and the untreated addictions and illnesses of the uninsured and workless.

As for the future, the children of people who have served time are eight times more likely to go to prison than other kids. This escalation of prison expansion threatens to create what Mike Davis has called, "a permanently incarcerated class" (Davis 1995).

Antiprison organizers point out ways that prisons operate socially and politically as a way of "disappearing" social problems; displacing accountability for social inequity and injustice onto targeted individuals deemed to be "criminals" (Davis and Shaylor 2001). The result is that the public is led to understand social problems as the outcome of millions of discrete individual acts, instead of seeing them as the consequences of social systems, attitudes, and institutions. CR aims to reverse this individualized understanding of social problems and promote creation of a more just society, supporting grassroots social transformation through abolitionist organizing strategies and social justice movement building. Ists mission statement reads:

> Critical Resistance seeks to build an international movement to end the Prison Industrial Complex by challenging the belief that caging and controlling people makes us safe. We believe that basic necessities such as food, shelter, and freedom are what really make our communities secure. As such, our work is part of global struggles against inequality and powerlessness. The success of the movement requires that it reflect communities most affected by the PIC. Because we seek to abolish the PIC, we cannot support any work that extends its life or scope.

Abolition Exposes the Limits of Human Rights Principles

Prison abolition and human rights activists agree that access to basic necessities and freedoms are preconditions for building safe, egalitarian communities of empowered individuals. However, the abolitionist view goes further, demonstrating that the use of prisons to solve social problems is literally antithetical to the goals of social justice. The concept of universal human rights that guarantee political freedom and protect people from unfair treatment is based, in part, on the notion that "all men (sic) are created equal." Ironically, the idea of universal human equality is a product of the Enlightenment, the emergence of the nation state and capitalism (Ishay 2007: 475)—systems of

control, cultural and economic production, and social reproduction impli-
cated in slavery, colonialism, industrialization, imperialism, militarism,
genocide, and today, the U.S. prison system. These social orders and practices
produce unequal groups of people, rather than a mass of equal individuals—
groups with disparate access to basic necessities and freedoms. Overlapping
social inequalities such as economic class, race, gender, sexuality, citizenship, and many others shape and severely challenge the ability of people living within states to define and fulfill their basic human, social, and political
needs—processes that are essential to the fulfillment of what we think of as
rights. As Hannah Arendt explains, "Our political life rests on the assumption that we can produce equality through organization, because man can act
in and change and build a common world, together with his equals and only
with his equals" (Arendt 1973, 375).

Human rights advocates and activists seek to solve social problems by
defining the conditions that would be necessary to maximize individual
equality, and so ensure that society is as fair and democratic as possible, but
the solutions to inequality and suffering offered by human rights principles
and declarations do not recognize or address the role of prisons in producing
radical, systemic social inequality.

While it is considered to be a violation of human rights to imprison a
person without a fair trial, to lock people up for expressing political dissent,
or to torture or starve a prisoner, the right of the state to cage human beings
remains unchallenged by the UDHR, or any other document elaborating the
principles of human rights. Hence, the use of incarceration to enforce laws,
including human rights law, undermines the goal of social equality. Prison
abolitionists confront this problem by analyzing the state as a complex and
contradictory set of capacities (Gilmore and Gilmore 2008).

Abolition as Intervention in Contemporary
Understandings of the State

Many activists reject human rights advocacy as a social change strategy
because the human rights framework fails to critically analyze or challenge
the social role of the state. Not everyone, however, agrees that the state's ability to imprison people is the problem. Neoliberals believe that concerns over
human rights, imposed through the state in the form of social spending and
corporate regulation (such as tax-supported projects like public education
and enforcement of labor rights) hinder the ability of capitalism to produce
profit, which neoliberals see as the ultimate social good. In this view, the state
is an obstacle to human progress, defined as capital accumulation. Neoliberal

doctrine sees human suffering as an unfortunate but reasonable price to pay in the pursuit of expanding wealth. This stance is fundamentally incompatible with the principles of human rights, which prioritize human well being over profit, insisting that dignity and equality are the foundation of social justice, and essential to the eradication of mass violence, poverty, and unnecessary suffering.

Neoliberal activists see the state as an impediment to profit accumulation, yet rather than turn their backs on the flawed institution, they have embarked on a thirty-year strategy coordinating efforts promoting new laws and policies, rolling back social spending and corporate regulation, and launching a media and communications blitz delegitimizing the state's capacity to provide social safety nets and expand opportunities as well as tax and regulate corporations (Gilmore 1997, 1998; Harvey 2005; Gilmore and Gilmore 2008). However, as abolitionist scholars Gilmore and Gilmore explain, while neoliberals have successfully framed the state as "the problem" and claim to be "shrinking the state," the reality is that they have actually succeeded in shifting budget priorities from select forms of social and environmental well-being to the construction of new prisons (Gilmore and Gilmore 2008). For prison abolitionists and many other activists organizing for social justice, this increasing capacity of the state to imprison people is the problem. Yet, among social justice activists, there is disagreement over how to confront the state's exploding capacity to lock people up.

"How Can We Ask a State That Is Responsible for So Much Suffering, Injustice, and Brutality to Protect Our Rights?"

Many "antistate anticapitalists" believe that fighting the oppressive powers of capitalism using appeals to rights increases the power of the state to control human action, and thus increases its capacity to continue to perpetuate the unjust social impacts of capitalism, such as poverty, racism, sexism, and environmental destruction. In this view, everything the state does always automatically supports, and never contradicts, the purposes of corporations and their ability to exploit people and the natural world, always privileging profit over justice and equality. This rejection of rights appeals as a strategy shares the goals of human rights activists, yet rejects the very idea of rights, seeing any form of political engagement with the state as inherently supportive of an intrinsically oppressive institution.

Neoliberal and antistate anticapitalist political stances are quintessential opposites in their political priorities, and in their views of capitalism as a social force, yet they share a view of the state as a static, uncontradictory concentration of power that either always hinders capitalist development or always seamlessly supports the oppressive system of global capitalism. For this reason, people who share this particular antistate anticapitalist view of the state also reject approaches to social justice organizing, such as prison abolition, that identify the state as a strategic site of intentional struggle and potential social transformation—in part because the state has been successfully framed, through both neoliberal and antistate anticapitalist ideologies, as "the problem" (whether one defines the problem as obstacles to capitalism or capitalism itself).

In addition to the belief that the state is utterly corrupt (whether one is struggling to free capitalism from humanity or free humanity from capitalism), the notion, prominent in popular and academic discourse since the early 1990s, that the state is a weak and disappearing social formation has served trends, in right, center, and left popular movements, that believe building alternative practices while ignoring the state is the only viable strategy for building a just society. The idea here is that turning our organizing efforts away from the state will make it go away. Prison abolition, with its analysis of the rise of the prison industrial complex under neoliberal globalization, suggests quite the opposite.

Prison abolition activists share key aspects of the intentions of human rights advocates, seeking to remake society in ways that enable communities to articulate and solve the problems and suffering engendered by systemic social inequalities. It also shares the analysis of anticapitalist social justice advocates, recognizing the oppressive and violent social impacts resulting from cooperation between capitalism and the state. However, prison abolition analysis and tactics offer an alternative approach, critically analyzing the specific ways in which the state (A) remains a very powerful force of social control and a producer of social inequality and human suffering, and (B) operates in contradictory ways that offer opportunities for effective opposition.

Starting with the perspectives of people most affected by prisons—the two million plus people who live in cages in the United States and their loved ones and communities—CR makes it clear that ignoring the state will not and has not made it go away—quite the opposite. While claiming to shrink the state, neoliberal political campaigns and strategies have (A) promoted the widespread abandonment of the nation's most vulnerable communities by supporting the withdrawal of public for support for necessities, such as education, health care, and affordable housing, and (B) rallied widespread consent for massive prison expansion. CR's efforts to reduce prison populations combine decriminalization campaigns designed to change laws criminalizing identities and behavior, such as antigang policies and laws criminalizing sex work, citizenship status, and addiction, and coalition-building projects aimed at reversing the budget priorities of government with community organizing projects that seek new ways to solve social problems without relying on prisons and policing. CR also uses a combination of strategies to stop construction of new prisons developed in collaboration with the California Prison Moratorium Project (CPMP). Urban organizers build coalitions in rural towns sited for new prison construction, exposing the negative social, environmental, and economic impacts of prisons and rallying local communities against them. Through this process, CR developed an innovative legal argument, framing prison sitting as a form of environmental racism, since prisons harm the environment and, like toxic waste incinerators, are most often built in poor communities of color. In this way, CR and CPMP distinguish between the capacity of the state to incarcerate and destroy the environments of poor people of color, and the capacity of social justice organizers to shift government priorities and transform state capacities in ways that have begun rolling back the growth and reach of the expanding prison system.

Prison abolition critiques and challenges the state and global capitalism, while sharing the fundamental goals of human rights activism. Because abolitionist analysis understands the state as both powerful and contradictory, abolitionists combine multiple strategies that begin with the principle that social justice work must never support or extend the life or scope of the prison industrial complex.[3] This means that abolitionist strategies cannot support any rights scheme that relies on the threat and practice of imprisonment to ensure the freedom and dignity of one individual or group at the expense of another. At the same time, the abolitionist understanding of the state has the potential to extend the vision and reach of human rights goals, offering both analysis and strategies that truly challenge the foundations of social inequality.

CHAPTER TWENTY-THREE

Human Rights in the United States: The "Gold Standard" and the Human Rights Enterprise

William T. Armaline, Davita Silfen Glasberg, and Bandana Purkayastha

Human Rights in the United States: Strategies and Implications

Contributions to this volume clearly demonstrate that the United States is far from the "gold standard" for international human rights practice. However, as several chapters illustrate, there are ongoing, successful struggles to combat human rights violations, define and develop concepts of human rights and fundamental human dignity, and—most important—to realize human rights practice in the United States. Our goal here is not to conduct or publish scholarship simply for scholarship's sake, but we will take this opportunity in the conclusion to discuss what we think are some implications of this collection of work for human rights scholars, advocates, and activists.

As suggested by the notion of a human rights enterprise, we might first recognize that struggles to define and realize fundamental human rights and dignity in the United States include struggles outside of and potentially against states and the formal human rights regime as manifested in international law and official IGO/NGO advocacy networks. Those interested in the study of or engagement in social movements to (re)define and achieve human rights practice in the United States should consider such a broad range of possibilities for action strategy, organizing, and scholar-activism. As pointed out by several authors in this volume, human rights struggles often include confronting and resisting the state and other powerful international players such as multinational corporations. Because of the inability for international law to effectively constrain and direct the actions of the U.S. government and other powerful states on its own, formal human rights instruments typically provide a legitimate discourse to accompany social movements such that their demands cannot be completely dismissed, and they carry the ideological force of international consensus.

Where we see formal human rights instruments and discourse put to good use in such movements in the United States, discourse is often not enough to inspire or force changes in policy, practice, or relevant social conditions. As should be manifest in this volume, contemporary movements for social justice and human rights in the United States (and elsewhere) tend to be movements "from below" (Armaline and Glasberg 2009), also typically in conflict with powerful state and private interests and actors. For this reason, we join several of the authors here in suggesting that struggles to realize human rights practice typically require various forms of resistance— particularly direct action, civil disobedience, and grassroots organizing and the formation of coalitions or networks to give voice and teeth to movements from below. It seems at this point somewhat naïve to think that, for example, the concentrated power of the corporate owning class (whose power is also heavily concentrated in and through the state) will somehow yield, or be suddenly legislated away from above, to allow for the realization of economic human rights and the reasonable redistribution of wealth and resources such rights would require, without significant pressures from people willing to assert their right to such resources. Of course, U.S. history seems to bear this out. Whether we observe antiracist, feminist, sexual liberation, LGBT rights, indigenous rights, labor/anticapitalist, or immigrant rights movements (many of which are/were simultaneously human rights movements) in the United States, they have typically been driven by relatively grassroots resistance movements from below. To be blunt, U.S. history is not one of generous rulers granting privilege to the less powerful out of generosity or notions of responsibility to international law/consensus or the supposed social contract between state and citizen. The elimination of formal racial segregation, the fights for women's rights to work and political participation, and the often taken-for-granted rights to labor standards such as the eight-hour day and the right to collective bargaining were long, hard, bloody struggles *against* the state and other coalitions of the powerful. They required, again, more than liberal appeals to the supposed responsibilities of states to provide for social change and the prioritization of (for example) human rights standards and practice over other concerns or agendas.

We do not mean to suggest here a false binary for the success of the human rights enterprise, where groups struggling for human rights practice in the United States must somehow choose whether to work in or outside of the formal state and international legal frameworks to achieve their goals. Again, as demonstrated in this volume, many successful struggles opt to draw from both strategies simultaneously (an approach we explicitly support). However, we would insist that a human rights enterprise without significant elements and mechanisms for resistance outside of and potentially against these frameworks (and their support structures, such as the police state) would be ill informed by history and destined for failure. For human rights scholars, advocates, and activists, this requires constant critical reflection on the *actual* relationships between (for example) state and society, rather than their theoretical connections. It requires organizing, action, and research that refine and develop strategies and mechanisms for achieving human rights practice in the face of very real, relatively massive power differentials, typically through forms of resistance such as direct action and civil disobedience.

It might be useful to conceptualize the human rights enterprise as something other than a pluralistic project of states that somehow accurately and sufficiently represent the interests of the governed, or as a project reduced to codifying particular rights into national or international law. Instead, it seems more prudent and empirically accurate to conceptualize the human rights enterprise as a democratization movement against structured, imposed hierarchies, where the struggle to define and realize universal human rights practice might be better defined as a struggle between more or less powerful groups and the mechanisms that ensure power and resources for the very few. What are human rights, if not statements of how power and resources must be minimally distributed among the world's peoples? In this sense, efforts to realize human rights practice might be explicitly designed to target the ever-increasing consolidation of power and resources that defines contemporary human civilization, particularly in the United States where, for example, wealth disparity continues to grow beyond nearly all international comparison.

Just as conditions in the United States reflect significant challenges for human rights and social justice movements, opportunities emerge, as well. As demonstrated in several of the contributions here, the exercised rights to (for example) free speech, assembly, and due process provide significant sociopolitical space for movements to gather the support and momentum required for social change. Where it is unlikely that outside influences will or could somehow force social change upon the United States, as the largest military (and to some extent) economic power in world history in the near future, human rights scholars, advocates, and activists should recognize their duty to alter policy, practice, and social structure in the United States from within—by whatever means, upon critical reflection, seem appropriate and effective.

NOTES

Chapter 1. Sweatshirts and Sweatshops: Labor Rights, Student Activism, and the
Challenges of Collegiate Apparel Manufacturing

1. Notably, there is considerable theoretical and legal debate over the scope of the
right to freedom of association. Debate centers on whether freedom of association
extends either to the right to collective bargaining or to strike. For examples of related
case law, see Atelson, Compa, Rittich, Sharpe, and Weiss (2008), particularly chap. 8.

2. In Dine (2005), see especially chap. 4 on "Relationship Between Companies and
Human Rights Law," and chap. 5 on "Corporate Social Responsibility."

3. For details on the range of actual corporate practice on human rights, see UNHRC
(2007a), especially sections IV and V.

4. For related analysis of contemporary union organizing efforts, see Esbenshade
(2004) and Bronfenbrenner (2007).

5. Past FLA board representatives have included Nike, New Era, Pennsylvania State
University, University of Maryland, National Consumers League, and Human Rights
First.

6. For an in-depth organizational history of USAS, see Featherstone and USAS
(2002).

7. For example, in 2005, two high school students contacted several original organizers of the 1960s-era organization Students for a Democratic Society (SDS) from
Michigan State University. Within a year they had more than one hundred chapters and
launched a successful national convention (http://studentsforademocraticsociety.org).
A group of college students, in turn, formulated the first student-organized think tank
named the Roosevelt Institute Campus Network (http://www.rooseveltcampusnetwork.
org/about-us). And in 2003, the Campus Anti-War Network was founded in opposition
to the invasion of Iraq; websites accessed March 7, 2011.

8. http://www.facebook.com/press/info.php?statistics, accessed October 23, 2010.

9. These schools (University of Connecticut, Duke University, Georgetown University, Indiana University, University of Maine-Farmington, Santa Clara University, Smith
College, University of Wisconsin-Madison) are all WRC members.

10. The turnout of people under age 30 rose in 2008 for the third consecutive
presidential election. Approximately 23 million people in this age cohort voted—an
increase of 3.4 million over the turnout in 2004, between 52 and 53 percent. Full data
analysis available from the Center for Information and Research on Civic Learning and
Engagement (CIRCLE), Jonathan M. Tisch College of Citizenship and Public Service,
Tufts University, under "Youth Voting" via http://www.civicyouth.org/?page_id=241,
accessed March 7, 2011.

11. In Reich (2007), see especially chaps. 5 and 6.

12. http://altagraciaapparel.com.

Chapter 2. Labor Rights After the Flexible Turn: The Rise of Contingent Employment and the Implications for Worker Rights in the United States

1. Contingent work may be broadly defined as "any job in which an individual does not have an explicit or implicit contract for long-term employment or one in which the minimum hours worked can vary in a nonsystematic manner" (Polivka and Nardone 1989: 11). Contingent workers may be defined as "persons who do not expect their jobs to last or who reported that their jobs are temporary . . . [excluding] persons who do not expect to continue in their jobs for personal reasons such as retirement or returning to school" (Bureau of Labor Statistics 2005: 1-2).

2. James Allan Davis and Tom W. Smith, General Social Survey, machine-readable data file. Principal Investigator, James A. Davis; Director and Co-Principal Investigator, Tom W. Smith; Co-Principal Investigator, Peter V. Marsden, NORC ed. Chicago: National Opinion Research Center, producer. Storrs, Conn.: Roper Center for Public Opinion Research, University of Connecticut, distributor. 1 data file (51,020 logical records) and 1 codebook (2,552 pp.).

Chapter 3. Preying on the American Dream

1. In 2007, UN Special Rapporteur on poverty Arjun Sengupta reported his findings on poverty in the U.S. based on his fact finding mission to the U.S. in 2005 (Sengupta 2007).

2. Not all subprime lending is intended to be predatory. However, predatory lending appropriates the logic and rationale for subprime lending to profit from economic injustice.

3. U.S. Senate, Community Reinvestment Act, Hearings Before Committee on Banking, Housing, and Urban Affairs, 100th Cong., 2nd sess., March 22-23, 1988.

Chapter 4. Food Not Bombs

1. The U.S. Department of Agriculture defines "food-insecure" as "At times during the year, these households were uncertain of having, or unable to acquire, enough food to meet the needs of all their members because they had insufficient money or other resources for food. Food-insecure households include those with *low food security* and *very low food security*" (2009).

2. All names of people and places have been changed to protect anonymity.

Chapter 5. The Long Road to Economic and Social Justice

1. ACORN filed for bankruptcy in March 2010, ending its forty-year activism for economic and social rights including housing, voter registration, and living wages. ACORN became the subject of controversy after some conservative activists publicized a video where two ACORN workers, in two cities, appeared to advise sting operators claiming to be prostitutes to make false claims about their work on forms. In the maelstrom that followed, ACORN lost its federal funding and was stripped of its status as a

valid community organization for census outreach purposes. Even though a congressional inquiry cleared ACORN of all charges of fraud, and federal judges ruled that the ban against ACORN's federal funding was unconstitutional, the group was no longer able to survive its financial losses (Lorber 2009). This chapter, which focuses on ACORN just after the 2008 elections, continues to offer lessons about the power of stories grounded in local contexts—stories that resonate, and those that ultimately fail to garner support among the public—and the importance of the claims of the poor on societies remains relevant even with the bankruptcy of ACORN.

Chapter 6. Hurricane Katrina and the Right to Food and Shelter

1. As of December 31, 2010, FEMA was still threatening to fine individuals who had not yet returned their trailers (Burdeau 2010).

2. Within a month after the fifth anniversary of Hurricane Katrina, FEMA gave $100 million to Jefferson Parish to repair streets (Rainey 2010) and $14.4 million to St. Bernard Parish to rebuild the parish civic center (Warren 2010). Under President Obama's leadership, the U.S. government is beginning to confront the poverty of New Orleans without the institutional bandages that overlook the root of the systemic problem (Nolan 2010).

Chapter 8. Health and Human Rights

1. An odd feature of this insurance system is that it did not grow out of a societal commitment to provide health care on a national basis, as is the case in most other affluent industrial nations. Instead, it grew out of a World War II wage freeze, which led employers in a number of major industries to find another way to increase employee compensation so they could attract and retain workers. Their strategy was to pay for their workers' health insurance. This mode of access to health care was flawed from the start since it not only did not evolve from any commitment to a national system of health care but is reliant on insurers that have a primary need to show a profit. Even initially it didn't cover everyone since some employers, especially those with low-wage workers, did not provide this benefit and it never reached those unemployed or not employed full-time.

Chapter 9. We Are a People in the World: Native Americans and Human Rights

1. *Shoshone Tribe of Indians of the Wind River Reservation v. United States*, 11 Ind. Cl. Comm'n (1962): 387–416.

2. The oversight committee created to address claims concerning the Convention on the Elimination of All Forms of Racial Discrimination.

Chapter 10. Reflections on Cultural Human Rights

1. Much of the media discourse and scholarly literature tend to describe Latino and Asian American immigrants as new immigrants to the U.S. In fact Latinos, especially people of Mexican origin, have been present in this geographical area since before the national boundaries of the U.S. were established. Asian-origin migrants predate more recognized "established" migrants such as the Irish or Italians, since Asian-origin groups

have been migrating to the U.S. in large numbers since the mid-nineteenth century. A range of laws and policies mostly banned the migration of Latino and Asian groups until the 1960s. Hence they appear as "new" migrants to people who are unaware of this earlier history (see Takaki 1989 for more on this subject).

2. To most Americans, the term "religion" connotes faith-based practices in designated institutions. We use the term "religio-cultural practices" here to indicate that the boundary between the practice of religion and of culture more generally cannot always be drawn with precision. Through the rest of the chapter we use the term "religion" as a way to problematize the U.S. mainstream understanding of religion. As we discuss later, the mainstream definition of religion does not describe diverse understandings of faith-based or spiritual practices. Nor does it help us to understand the specific challenges minority groups face when they claim cultural human rights.

3. In its simplest form the term "culture" refers to a group's values, norms, world-views, and the practices that shape the ways they see the world and the right ways to live in it. Such cultural practices—for instance religious practices—are dynamic, responding to the social-structural context in which they are situated (Narayan and Purkayastha 2009). Exactly what is perceived as an important part of a group's culture varies according to the situated context in which a group is placed and which group holds the power to define a culture in that context. A group with power in a society to practice their culture in the way they wish to—often the dominant majorities in society—can take their culture for granted; the ways their cultural norms, values, and worldviews shape their structural context become mostly invisible to themselves. But groups that do not have the power to freely practice their cultures, who constantly have to try to fit in with the structures preset according to the dominant group's cultural beliefs and practices, are very much aware of their culture. These cultural minority groups have to struggle to practice their cultures, and as they do so, they remain "culturally visible" to the dominant group. Cultural human rights, then, are as much about cultural practices as they are about the structured relationship between groups with unequal power within specific contexts.

4. Claude (1955) has argued that the UN chose to emphasize the rights of all individuals without reference to their membership in particular groups. Lauren (2003) offers a different view.

5. While the terms majority and minority are often used in the United States to denote racial groups, for example, a white majority and various nonwhite minority groups, in the case of cultural human rights the designation of majority and minority cultural groups can cross racial lines. At one level, people of all racial backgrounds who practice Christianity are less likely to encounter structural barriers to practicing their religion since the laws relating to religious freedom are based on what is normal for Christians. People who belong to religious minority groups, with different beliefs and expectations about religious practices, are more likely to encounter significant barriers when their practices do not resemble the social-structural organization of Christianity. However, as we discuss in this chapter, racialization processes create distinctions between religious practices based on who are the worshippers, so the questions of cultural minority groups ultimately reflect the ways in which phenotypes and cultures (in

this case, marked religious practices) are intertwined to create racial distinctions (see also Purkayastha 2010).

6. We are well aware that there are other patterns for ensuring cultural rights in other countries. Constitutions of countries like India guarantee a series of rights to cultural minorities, on the grounds of religion, regional cultures, and so on. The discussion of those differences and their relative efficacy or merits is outside the scope of this chapter. For one set of discussions on granting religious rights, see Bhargava 1998.

7. While this chapter focuses on religions, a similar case can be made about the right to maintain languages. The battles over Spanish and other languages in public places exemplify some of the same points we raise here.

8. The scholarly discussion on marketing multicultural products has focused on the power of markets to co-opt and profit from items associated with groups, while draining them of their cultural significance. The substantive point of these discussions is that cultural items are available for consumption, but such consumption does not alter the structured power inequalities between powerful and marginalized groups. (For more on this subject see, e.g., Davila 2001; Halter 2000; Purkayastha 2005.)

9. There is a significant debate about the ways in which states ought to accommodate minority cultures. The contours of that debate are not within the purview of this chapter, though we touch on a portion of it at the end of this chapter. Interested readers should see Bhargava, Bagchi, and Sudharshan (1999), Kymlicka (1995), or Willett (1998) for an overview of the debates.

10. These local officials range from planning and zoning compliance officers to residential life officers in universities who ban the use of joss sticks or candles for individual prayers in rooms (citing these as fire hazards and asking students to go to formal places of worship to pray).

11. "Flying While Sikh," http://www.sikhcoalition.org/LegalAirTravel.asp, accessed May 9, 2009.

12. "Racial Profiling," http://www.sikhnet.com/daily-news/sikhs-shun-san-francisco-airport-alleging-religious-profiling, accessed May 9, 2009.

13. "California Governor vetoes AB 504 'kirpan' bill," http://sikhsindia.blogspot.com/2009/10/california-governor-vetoes-ab-504.html, accessed March 3, 2011.

14. The term hijab has now become the catchall for a range of apparel from a cover for the head and neck to an all-enclosing cover over clothes that allows only slits for the eyes. The head cover—often a scarf—is more widely adopted in the United States.

15. Okin expressed the concern that multicultural citizenship would allow control of women by men of their cultural communities, under the guise of "cultural practice" to go undetected, and that granting special cultural rights to minority groups should not be permitted. Instead, she argued that since most minority cultures, compared to Western cultures, treat their women badly, many of these cultures should simply be allowed to "die" to address the oppression of women. In this argument, others' "cultures" are conceptualized as traditional, illiberal practices of non-Western societies, and she juxtaposes it with the modern, liberal Western regimes.

16. For instance, the rapidly growing popularity of cosmetic surgery, as well as a range of eating disorders, in the U.S. are marked by women in other countries as evi-

dence of American cultural pressure on women to develop particular kinds of bodies. Similarly, the high level of intimate partner violence against women in the U.S. is seen as an indicator of continuing oppression of women.

Chapter 11. Erosion of Political and Civil Rights

1. However, another scholar who was critical of U.S. policies, Adam Habib of South Africa, was allowed entry into the United States in 2010 after intensive lobbying by several organizations including the ACLU and American Sociological Association, http://www.asanet.org/press/20100120_Habib_Decision.cfm.

2. A pen register is a device that is attached to a phone and registers all numbers dialed from the phone. A trap and trace device records all numbers of incoming calls.

Chapter 12. U.S. Asylum and Refugee Policy: The "Culture of No"

1. One such case involved eighty-one-year-old Haitian pastor Rev. Joseph Dantica, who arrived with valid travel documents at Miami International Airport on October 29, 2004. He was subjected to mandatory detention because he said that he was seeking asylum. He died five days later while in U.S. immigration custody. See "Pastor's Death in Custody Is Probed" (2004).

2. The UNHCR *Handbook on Procedures and Criteria for Determining Refugee Status Under the 1951 Convention and the 1967 Protocol Relating to the Status of Refugees* (UNHRR 1992; hereafter UNHCR *Handbook*) presumes that legitimate refugees generally do not carry valid passports and provides guidance for recognizing the exceptional cases of people with valid passports who are, indeed, refugees. See pages. 47-50.

3. 8 C.F.R. § 1003.19 (h)(2)(i)(B).

4. Physicians for Human Rights/Bellevue/NYU Program for Survivors of Torture (2003).

5. See U.S. GAO (2000); Center for Human Rights and International Justice (2000).

6. U.S. Commission on International Religious Freedom (= USCIRF) Report (2005).

7. USCIRF Report, 1: 41.

8. Ibid., 6.

9. U.S. DHS (2004).

10. Swarns (2004), A11.

11. DHS (2007).

12. DHS, Office of the Press Secretary (2006).

13. INA § 208(a)(2)(B).

14. Since the filing deadline was implemented in 1996-2008, about 74,000 asylum cases have been denied or referred for removal proceedings in immigration court because of the one-year filing bar.

15. INA § 241(b)(3)(A).

16. Ibid., (3)(ii).

17. UNHCR Executive Committee Conclusion No. 7 (1977), http://www.unhcr.org/41b041534.html.

18. UNHCR *Handbook*, para. 154. The U.S. Supreme Court has determined that although the *Handbook* is not legally binding on U.S. officials, it nevertheless provides

"significant guidance" in construing the 1967 Protocol (*INS v. Cardoza-Fonseca*, 480 U.S. 421, 439, n. 22; 107 S.Ct. 1207, 1217 (1987)).

19. Article 1F(b) excludes from refugee status persons who "committed a serious non-political crime outside the country of refuge."

20. UNHCR *Handbook*, para. 155.

21. Unpublished letter from Thomas Albrecht, Deputy Regional Representative, UNHCR, Washington, D.C., January 6, 2006, on file with author.

22. See Human Rights Watch (2007), 53.

23. *McAllister v. Ashcroft*, 2004, U.S. Dist. LEXIS 29598 (D.N.J. July 21, 2004), discussed Human Rights Watch (2007), 81

24. Ibid., 54.

25. *In re Sejid Smriko*, 23 I&N Dec. 836 (BIA 2005).

26. 8 U.S.C. § 1362 (2001).

27. Schoenholtz and Jacobs (2002), 743.

28. *Gideon v. Wainwright*, 372 U.S. 335, 344 (1963).

29. *In re Gault*, 387 U.S. I, 41 (1967) and *Vitek v. Jones*, 445 U.S. 480, 100 (1980).

30. *Ardestani v. INS*, 502 U.S. 129 (1991) at 138.

31. INA § 235(b)(1)(B).

32. USCIRF Report, 2: 189.

33. Ibid., 190.

Chapter 13. Border Action Network (BAN) and Human Rights: Community-Based Resistance Against the Militarization of the U.S.-Mexico Border

1. Dr. Kil points out that that there is more than one "United States" on this planet, so that the use of U.S. reinforces USA American solipsism.

2. The following are important examples of this criminalization process: the renaming of the Immigration and Naturalization Service the "Department of Homeland Security" with a redefined mission to protect the country from terrorists, the implementation of Operation Streamline, a practice of mass trials charging nearly 100 immigrant men and women every day with federal crimes, ICE (immigration and customs enforcement) raids on homes and places of business where local law enforcement personnel participate as ICE agents, government toleration of racist vigilante groups with names like Cochise County Concerned Citizens, American Border Patrol, Ranch Rescue, and Minutemen, and the passage and implementation of state laws that create criminal penalties for the mere act of not having proper immigration paperwork.

3. Examples of this dehumanization process: (1) Border agencies regularly use acronyms like OTM (other than Mexican), UDA (undocumented alien), LPR (legal permanent resident), USC (U.S. citizen). These acronyms reduce an individual's humanity to legal or citizenship status. (2) Border Patrol posts signs and billboards throughout the border region boasting statistics of how many people and drugs have been apprehended by their sector over the last quarter, month, or other time increment. This reduces immigrants to numbers. (3) Systematic use of physical and psychological abuse by border enforcement against migrants and border residents sends a message that border agents are above the rule of law that everyone else is subject to. (4) Armed civilian groups

patrolling the border and the groups' rise in national prominence have created an image of migrants as huntable prey

4. This training curriculum was originally developed by the Border Network for Human Rights.

<h3 style="text-align:center">Chapter 14. Sexual Citizenship, Marriage, Adoption,
and Immigration in the United States</h3>

1. Taken from http//www.un.org/Overview/rights.html#atop.

2. It is unclear what rights for gay and lesbian couples interested in adopting children will look like in the years to come in Florida. In November 2008, the ban on same-sex couple adoptions in Florida was overturned and deemed a violation of equal rights ("Miami Judge Rules Against Florida Gay Adoption Ban"). Furthermore, in September 2010, Florida's District Court of Appeals ruled that Florida must stop enforcing the gay adoption ban ("Florida Overturns Gay Adoption Ban"). It is unclear whether the case will go to the Supreme Court.

3. Binational same-sex partnerships are lesbian and gay couples where one partner is a U.S. citizen and the other is not (Human Rights Watch/Immigration Equality 2006). Chapter 15. Do Human Rights Endure Across Nation-State Boundaries?

<h3 style="text-align:center">Chapter 15. Do Human Rights Endure Across Nation-State Boundaries?</h3>

Epigraph: "Indian Guestworker Slits Wrists After Being Fired for Complaining About Squalid Work Conditions" (2009), Transcript of an Interview by Democracy Now describing living conditions Indian guest workers endured upon moving to the U.S., http://www.democracynow.org/2007/3/15/indian_guestworker_slits_wrists_after_being.

1. BBC 2008, "Indian Men in U.S. 'Slave' Protest."

2. Satyagraha is a philosophy and practice of nonviolent resistance developed by Mohandas Gandhi. Satyagraha was the bedrock of Gandhi's campaigns against the British Raj in India.

3. H1-B visa status also imposes several unique restrictions on workers in the host countries that undermine their freedoms and liberties. H1-B workers belong to the more literate echelons of the society more aware of their rights; they have relatively better pay and are allowed to bring their families.

4. http://neworleans.indymedia.org/news/2008/03/12261.php.

5. http://www.nytimes.com/2010/06/29/opinion/29tue3.html.

6. As mentioned above, typically H1-B workers are better off than workers in the H2 category, but they are still subject to unique limitations. For example, spouses/dependents of H1-B workers cannot work in the United States until they get their own H1-B visa, which can take months. H1-B status is also tied to employment status. An H1-B worker who is laid off has about 30-60 days to find another job or leave the country.

Chapter 16. From International Platforms to Local Yards

1. Countries including Canada, Australia, Italy, and Sweden also refused to participate in the Durban Review Conference.

2. World Conference Against Racism, Racial Discrimination, Xenophobia and Related Intolerance, Durban, South Africa, Declaration, 2001 (Durban Document), http://www.un.org/durbanreview2009/pdf/DDPA_full_text.pdf, accessed May 9, 2009.

3. The literature on this subject is too vast to enumerate here. Among some key sociological studies over the last few decades are Bonilla-Silva (1996); Espiritu (1989); Glenn (2002); Feagin and Sikes (1994); Segura and Zavella (2007); Baca Zinn and Dill (1984).

4. Arguably, other instruments—such as the ICCPR that the U.S. signed in 1977 and ratified in 1992, and the CAT signed in 1988 and ratified it in 1994—also attempt to ensure equal and humane treatment of those who are treated as "others" by states and dominant majority groups within states.

5. The United States, for instance, has filed a reservation, among other matters, against Article 22, which states that if two state parties are in dispute, and the matter does not get resolved, the dispute can be taken to the International Court of Justice (ICJ). The U.S. reservation states that if another country is in a dispute with the U.S., the other party can apply to ICJ only after seeking U.S. permission to do so.

6. CERD Shadow Report, 2009, http://www.ushrnetwork.org/cerd_shadow_2008, accessed May 9. The chapters in this book also document how racism affects people's ability to access a variety of human rights.

7. A whole body of sociological work addresses colorblind racism (see Bonilla-Silva 1996) that shore up racist ideologies, behaviors, and institutional arrangements (e.g., Essed 1991; Feagin and Sikes 1994; Picca and Feagin 2007).

8. These findings are consistent with Picca and Feagin's (2007) assertion that most white Americans "adhere, at least at an abstract level, to the equality-and-justice framing of society" and that in the past fifty years, "the public face of the United States has been that of a nonracist society that appears to live up to these equality-and-justice ideals" (viii). However, a critical lens of racial realities in the U.S. illustrates that "subtly racist cognitions, images, emotions and inclinations" currently exist due to a prevalent racist framework that denigrates black Americans and other Americans of color. Picca and Feagin argue that overt racist emotions and inclinations have been substantially relegated to the "backstage." Borrowing Goffman's theoretical framework of the "frontstage" as public and the "backstage" as private, they define the "backstage" as all-white environments and the "front stage" as multiracial arenas. The "backstage" is where racist thoughts and interpretations are reproduced and perpetuated among friends and relatives, to do so is no longer appropriate (i.e., "politically correct") on the "frontstage" or in the public domain.

9. Furthermore, Aheli Purkayastha, who conducted the research, is a person of color, which may have influenced the manner the European American student responded to the questions. If the interviewer had been a European American (or appeared to be), the student might have slipped deeper into "backstage" language that is more explicitly racist.

10. This was an incident in Louisiana in 2006, when six black students were arrested for beating a white student. The incident followed months of racial tension, including hanging a noose on a certain tree to warn black students from sitting under it.

11. We could have chosen many other incidents, but we picked this because it represents a case where an administrator took a public stand. This incident is representative of many similar incidents across college campuses over speakers who deny, minimize, or downplay racism, and deny the Holocaust or genocide of Native Americans.

12. A part of this controversy is recorded in the letters to the editor (bi-co news.com).

13. Ching Chong song archives. www.biconews.com, accessed May 9, 2009.

14. The incidents described here are not isolated. For additional examples of students of color experiencing racism on American college and university campuses, see, among others, Aries 2008; Feagin and Sikes 1994; Lewis 2003; Lopez 2005; Kibria 2002; Purkayastha 2005; Swail, Redd, and Perna 2003; Valverde and Castenell 1998.

Chapter 17. Caging Kids of Color: Juvenile Justice and Human Rights in the United States

1. See, e.g., Davis 2003; Western 2007; Brewer and Heitzeg 2008; Mauer 1999; Human Rights Watch 2009.

2. These instruments include the UDHR, the two covenants (ICCPR, ICESCR), various international conventions (such as CRC and ICERD), regional human rights treaties, and regulatory bodies assigned to each—meant for implementation, information dissemination, and enforcement.

3. Books Not Bars (BNB) 2009,
http://www.ellabakercenter.org/page.php?pageid=2, accessed July 20, 2010.

4. Unfortunately, a discussion of racism theory is beyond the scope of this chapter. For more on these concepts that define racism as a structural social system of privilege and oppression, see, for example, Feagin 2001, 2006; Neubeck and Cazenave 2001.

5. YouthFacts 2009, www.youthfacts.org, accessed July 10, 2010.

6. BNB and WITNESS, 2004, *System Failure* (documentary film),
www.ellabakercenter.org/page.php?pageid=44, accessed July 20, 2010.

7. For these and other similar reports on the human rights of incarcerated juveniles in the United States, please see www.hrw.org and www.amnesty.org.

8. Raise the Age Campaign CT, 2009, www.raisetheagect.org, accessed July 10, 2010.

Chapter 19. Sex Trafficking: In Our Backyard?

Epigraph: NGO Forum, Declaration and Programme of Action, World Conference Against Racism, Racial Discrimination, Xenophobia and Related Intolerance, Durban, South Africa, August 31–September 7, 2001.

1. Division for the Advancement of Women, Convention on the Elimination of all Forms of Discrimination Against Women, 2007, http://www.un.org/womenwatch/daw/cedaw/text/econvention.htm, accessed January 31, 2009.

2. UNHCR, 2004, http://www2.ohchr.org/english/, accessed November 11, 2010.

3. A substantial body of literature documents the sexualization of African American, Latino, and Asian women (e.g., Espiritu 1997; Purkayastha and Majumdar 2009; Raymond, Hughes, and Gomez 2001).

4. Initiative Against Sexual Trafficking (IAST), http://www.iast.net/, accessed November 11, 2010.

5. UN Children's Fund (UNICEF), http://www.unicef.org/protection/index_exploitation.html, accessed November 11.

Chapter 20. The U.S. Culture of Violence

The author would like to thank Leslie Levin and Jon Bauer and the editors of this volume for their invaluable input and suggestions.

Epigraph: Charlotte Bunch, "Women's Rights as Human Rights" (1990: 488).

1. While this chapter focuses on some of the major issues that affect all women in the U.S., depending on a woman's racial status, citizenship—immigrant or native—status, religion, age, sexual preference, many other factors intersect to further complicate a woman's ability to access help from the state (e.g., Abraham 2000; Schilt and Westbrook 2009).

2. CEDAW never explicitly mentions abortion, and supporters note that countries in which abortion is illegal (Ireland, Rwanda) have ratified CEDAW (Blanchfield 2006).

3. Joe Biden Senate Website, "Domestic Violence," 2008, http://biden.senate.gov/issues/issue/?id=975b0cf4-ce25-42cc-b63d-072fb81e8618, accessed December 7.

Chapter 22. Critical Resistance and the Prison Abolitionist Movement

1. Critical Resistance, 2009, http://www.criticalresistance.org/article.php?id=3, accessed April 2.

2. Bureau of Justice Statistics, 2009, http://www.ojp.usdoj.gov/bjs/, accessed April 29

3. Critical Resistance, 2009.

REFERENCES

Abraham, Laurie Kaye. 1993. *Mama Might Be Better Off Dead: The Failure of Health Care in Urban America*. Chicago: University of Chicago Press.

Abraham, Margaret. 2000. *Speaking the Unspeakable: Marital Violence Among South Asian Immigrants in the United States*. New Brunswick, N.J.: Rutgers University Press, 2000.

ACORN. 2009. "Recent Highlights." http://www.acorn.org/index.php?id=12442, accessed April 20.

ACORN Pennsylvania. 2000. "Equity Strippers: The Impact of Subprime Lending in Philadelphia." http://www.acorn.org/news/releases, accessed May 18.

Agathangelou, Anna and Ling L. H. M. 2003. "Desire Industries: Sex Trafficking, UN Peacekeeping, and the Neo-Liberal World Order." *Brown Journal of World Affairs* 10: 133–48.

Akers, Donna. 1999. "Removing the Heart of the Choctaw People: Indian Removal from a Native Perspective." *American Indian Culture and Research Journal* 23: 63–76.

Al-Hibri, Azizah. 1999. "Is Western Patriarchal Feminism Good for Third World/Minority Women?" In *Is Multiculturalism Bad for Women?* ed. Joshua Cohen, Matthew Howard, and Martha Nussbaum, 41–46. Princeton, N.J.: Princeton University Press.

Alonzo, Angelo A. and Arthur B. Simon. 2008. "Have Stethoscope, Will Travel: Contingent Employment Among Physician Health Care Providers in the United States." *Work, Employment & Society* 22: 635–54.

America, Richard, ed. 1990. *The Wealth of Races: The Present Value of Benefits from Past Injustices*. New York: Greenwood Press.

American Civil Liberties Union-North Carolina. 2010. "The United Nations Human Rights Treaty System." http://www.acluofnorthcarolina.org/?q=human_rights, accessed November 9.

American Sociological Association. 2009. "Statement Affirming and Expanding the Commitment of the American Sociological Association." Adopted by the Council, August 13. http://www.asanet.org/index.cfm, accessed November 9, 2010.

——. 2010. "State Department Ends Unconstitutional Exclusion of Scholar from United States; A Victory for Academic Freedom South African Professor Adam Habib to Be Allowed to Reapply for U.S. Visa." January 20. http://www.asanet.org/press/20100120_Habib_Decision.cfm, accessed November 15, 2010.

American Staffing Association. 2007. "Fact Sheet: Increasing Average Tenure to 13.5 Weeks, Staffing Employer Turnover Decreased in 2007." http://www.americanstaffing.net/statistics/pdf/turnover_rates.pdf, accessed October 23, 2008.

——. 2008. "Staffing Statistics." http://www.americanstaffing.net/statistics/facts.cfm, accessed October 25, 2010.

Americans United for Separation of Church and State. 2007. "San Diego School Cancels Prayer Break for Muslim Students." www.thefreelibrary.com/San+Diego+public+school+cancels+prayer+break+for+Muslim+students-a0168748587, accessed May 9, 2009.

Amnesty International. 1998. *Betraying the Young: Human Rights Violations Against Children in the U.S. Justice System.* AMR 51/57/99. New York: Amnesty International.

Amster, Randal, Abraham DeLeon, Luis Fernandez, Anthony Nocella II, and Deric Shannon. 2009. *Contemporary Anarchist Studies: An Introductory Anthology of Anarchy in the Academy.* London: Routledge.

Andreopoulos, George and Richard Pierre Claude. 1997. *Human Rights Education for the Twenty-First Century.* Philadelphia: University of Pennsylvania Press.

Anker, Deborah. 2005. "Refugee Law, Gender and the Human Rights Paradigm." In *Passing Lines, Sexuality and Immigration,* ed. Brad Epps, Keja Valens, and Bill Johnson Gonzalez. Cambridge, Mass.: Harvard University Press.

Annan, Kofi A. 2005. *In Larger Freedom: Towards Development, Security and Human Rights for All.* New York: UN Department of Public Information.

Anyon, Jean. 1997. Ghetto Schooling: *A Political Economy of Urban Educational Reform.* New York: Teacher's College Press.

Appelbaum, Eileen. 1992. "Structural Change and the Growth of Part-Time and Temporary Employment." In *New Policies for the Part-Time and Contingent Workforce,* ed. Virginia L. duRivage, 1–14 Armonk, N.Y.: M.E. Sharpe.

Arbour, Louise. 2006. "Foreword." In *Development as a Human Right: Legal, Political, and Economic Dimensions,* ed. Bård A. Andreassen and Stephen P. Marks, iii–v. Cambridge, Mass.: Harvard University Press.

Arendt, Hannah. 1973. *The Origins of Totalitarianism.* New York: Harcourt.

Aries, Elizabeth. 2008. *Race and Class Matters in an Elite College.* Philadelphia: Temple University Press.

Armaline, William T. and Davita Silfen Glasberg. 2009. "What Will States Really Do for Us? The Human Rights Enterprise and Pressure from Below." *Societies Without Borders* 4: 430–51.

Arriola, Elvia. 1996. "LatCrit Theory, International Human Rights, Popular Culture and the Faces of Despair in INS Raids." *University of Miami Inter-American Law Review* 28: 245–62.

Atelson, James, Lance Compa, Kerry Rittich, Calvin William Sharpe, and Marley S. Weiss. 2008. *International Labor Law: Cases and Materials on Workers' Rights in the Global Economy.* St. Paul, Minn.: Thompson West.

Attas, Daniel. 2000. "The Case of Guest Workers: Exploitation, Citizenship and Economic Rights." *Res Publica* 6, 1: 73–92.

Avery, Robert B. and Michael S. Rendall. 2002. "Lifetime Inheritances of Three Generations of Whites and Blacks." *American Journal of Sociology* 107: 1300–1346.

Ayres, William. 1998. *A Kind and Just Parent: The Children of Juvenile Court.* Boston: Beacon Press.

Baca Zinn, Maxine and Bonnie Thornton Dill, eds. 1994. *Women of Color in U.S. Society.* Philadelphia: Temple University Press.

Bacon, David. 2008. *Illegal People: How Globalization Creates Migration and Criminalizes Immigrants.* Boston: Beacon Press, 2008.

Bagby, Dyana. 2006. "Only One State Now Facing Adoption Ban." *Houston Voice*, February 24, 6.

Banks, James. 2009. "Human Rights, Diversity and Citizenship Education." *Educational Forum* 73: 100–110.

Barker, Kathleen and Kathleen Christensen. 1998. *Contingent Work: American Employment Relations in Transition.* Ithaca, N.Y.: Cornell University Press.

Batsyukova, Svitlana. 2007. "Prostitution and Human Trafficking for Sexual Exploitation." *Gender Issues* 24: 45–50.

Bauman, Zygmunt. 2000. *Liquid Modernity.* Cambridge: Polity Press.

———. 2001. *Individualized Society.* Cambridge: Polity Press.

———. 2004. *Wasted Lives: Modernity and Its Outcasts.* Cambridge: Polity Press.

Bayart, Jean-François. 2005. *The Illusion of Cultural Identity.* Chicago: University of Chicago Press.

BBC. 2006. "Superdome Reopens in New Orleans: The Stadium That Symbolised New Orleans' Suffering During Hurricane Katrina Last Year Has

Reopened." *BBC News*, September 26. http://news.bbc.co.uk/2/hi/americas/5380242.stm, accessed December 22, 2008.

——. 2008 "Indian Men in U.S. 'Slave' Protest." March 28. http://news.bbc.co.uk/2/hi/south_asia/7316130.stm.

Beale, Frances M. 1969. "Black Women's Manifesto; Double Jeopardy: To Be Black and Female." Pamphlet submitted to Third World Women's Alliance, New York. http://www.Hartford-hwp.com/archives/45a/196.html, accessed September 17, 2007.

Beckett, Katherine, Kris Nyrop, Lori Pfingst, and Melissa Bowen. 2005. "Drug Use, Drug Possession Arrests, and the Question of Race: Lessons in Seattle." *Social Problems* 52: 419–41.

Bendix, Richard and Bryan Turner. 1998. *Max Weber: An Intellectual Portrait*. New York: Routledge.

Bergin, Mark. 2009. "Shame of the Cities." *World Magazine*, February 28.

Bernstein, Nell. 2007. *Racism of the Juvenile Justice System Revealed*. San Francisco: New American Media.

Beyerstein, Lindsay and Larisa Alexandrovna. 2007. "Human Trafficking of Indian Guest Workers Alleged in Mississippi Shipyard; Contractor Defends 290-Man Camp." *Raw Story*, April 13. http://rawstory.com/news/2007/Human_trafficking_of_Indian_guest_workers_0412.html, accessed February 17, 2009.

Bhargava, Rajeev, ed. 1998. *Secularism and Its Critics*. New Delhi: Oxford University Press.

Bhargava, Rajeev, Amiya Kumar Bagchi, and R. Sudharshan, eds. 1999. *Multiculturalism, Liberalism and Democracy*. New Delhi: Oxford University Press.

Biden, Joseph. 2000. "The Civil Rights Remedy of the Violence Against Women Act: A Defense." *Harvard Journal of Legislation* 37: 1–43.

Birn, Anne-Emanuelle. 2008. "Special Section: Health and Human Rights: Historical Perspectives and Political Challenges. Introduction." *Journal of Public Health Policy* 29: 32–41.

"A Bitter Guest Worker Story." 2010. Editorial, *New York Times*, February 4. http://www.nowcrj.org/press/alliance-of-guest-workers/2410-the-new-york-times-a bitter-guest-worker-story/, accessed October 18.

Blanchfield, Luisa. 2006. "The Convention on the Elimination of All Forms of Discrimination against Women (CEDAW): Congressional Issues." *CRS Report for Congress*: 1–12.

Blattberg, Charles. 2007. "The Ironic Tragedy of Human Rights." In *Women of Color in U.S. Society*, ed. Maxine Baca Zinn and Bonnie Thornton Dill. Montreal: McGill-Queen's University Press.

Blau, Judith and Alberto Moncada. 2005. *Human Rights: Beyond the Liberal Vision*. Lanham, Md.: Rowman & Littlefield.

———. 2006. *Justice in the United States: Human Rights and the U.S. Constitution*. Lanham, Md.: Rowman & Littlefield.

Bloemraad, Irene. 2004. "Who Claims Dual Citizenship? The Limits of Postnationalism, the Possibilities of Transnationalism, and the Persistence of Traditionalism." *International Migration Review* 38: 389–426.

Bluestone, Barry and Bennett Harrison. 1982. *The Deindustrialization of America*. New York: Basic Books.

Blumstein, Alfred. 1982. "On Racial Disproportionality of the United States Prison Populations." *Journal of Criminal Law and Criminology* 73: 1259–81.

Bobo, Lawrence and Devon Johnson. 2004. "A Taste of Punishment." *DuBois Review* 1: 151–80.

Boling, Dee and David Adler. 2008. "Report Stresses Need for Better Access to Fresh, Healthy Food in New Orleans, Current Supply Lags Far Behind National Average." New Orleans Food Policy Advisory Committee, March 18.

Bonilla-Silva, Eduardo. 1996. *White Supremacy and Racism in the Post Civil Rights Era*. Boulder, Colo.: Lynne Rienner.

———. 2003. *Racism Without Racists: Color-Blind Racism and the Persistence of Racial Inequality in the U.S.* Lanham, Md.: Rowman & Littlefield.

Bortner, M. A. and Linda Williams. 1997. *Youth in Prison: We the People of Unit 4*. New York: Routledge.

Boulard, Garry. 2008. "Three Years Later: After the Devastation of Katrina, Gulf-State Lawmakers Are Optimistic But Sobered by the Work That Remains." *State Legislatures* 34: 22–25. http://www.no-hunger.org/news/FPAC-pr/FPAC%20Press%20Release%203-1808.pdf.

Bourdieu, Pierre. 1998. "The Essence of Neoliberalism." *Le Monde diplomatique.* http://monddiplo.com/1998/12/08bourdieu?var_recherche=Bourdieu, accessed March 17, 2006.

Bowen, Wiliam and Derek Bok. 1998. *The Shape of the River: Long Term Consequences of Considering Race in College and University Admissions*. Princeton, N.J.: Princeton University Press.

Bradley, Jeanette. 2000. *The Community Guide to Predatory Lending Research*. Durham: Community Reinvestment Association of North Carolina.

Brewer, Rose and Nancy Heitzeg. 2008. "The Racialization of Crime and Punishment: Criminal Justice, Color-Blind Racism, and the Political Economy of the Prison Industrial Complex." *American Behavioral Scientist* 51: 625–44.

Bridges, William. 1994. *Job Shift: How to Prosper in a Workplace Without Jobs.* New York: Perseus.

Bronfenbrenner, Kate. 2007. *Global Unions: Challenging Transnational Capital Through Cross Border Campaigns.* Ithaca, N.Y.: ILR/Cornell University Press.

Brooks, Rachelle. 1997. "Feminists Negotiate the Legislative Branch: The Violence Against Women Act." In *Feminists Negotiate the State: The Politics of Domestic Violence,* ed. Cynthia R. Daniels, 65–81. Lanham, Md.: University Press of America.

Brown, Michael K., Martin Carnoy, Elliot Currie, Troy Duster, David B. Oppenheimber, Marjorie Shultz, and David Wellman. 2003. *Whitewashing Race: The Myth of a Color-Blind Society.* Berkeley: University of California Press.

Browne, Irene, Cynthia Hewitt, Leann Tigges, and Gary Green. 2001. "Why Does Job Segregation Lead to Wage Inequality Among African Americans? Person, Place, Sector, or Skills?" *Social Science Research* 30: 473–95.

Brush, Lisa. 2003. *Gender and Governance.* Walnut Creek, Calif.: Altamira.

Bullard, Robert D., Paul Mohai, Robin Saha, and Beverly Wright. 2007. *Toxic Waste and Race at Twenty: 1987–2007.* Cleveland: United Church of Christ.

Bunce, Harold L., Debbie Bruenstein, Christopher E. Herbert, and Randall M. Scheessele. 2001. "Subprime Foreclosures: The Smoking Gun of Predatory Lending?" In *Housing Policy in the New Millennium Conference Proceedings,* ed. Susan M. Wachter and R. Leo Peene, 257–72. Washington, D.C.: U.S. Department of Housing and Urban Development.

Bunch, Charlotte. 1990. "Women's Rights as Human Rights: Toward a Re-Vision of Human Rights." *Human Rights Quarterly* 12: 486–98.

Burdeau, Cain. 2010. "New Orleans Moves to Get Rid of Last FEMA Trailers." USATODAY, December 31. http://www.usatoday.com/news/nation/2010-12-31-new-orleans-fematrailers_N.htm, accessed March 7, 2010.

Bureau of Labor Statistics. 2005. "Contingent and Alternative Employment Arrangements, February 2005." http://www.bls.gov/news.release/archives/conemp_07272005.pdf, accessed November 7, 2010.

———. 2008. "Issues in Labor Statistics, December 2008: Involuntary Part-Time Work on the Rise." http://www.bls.gov/opub/ils/pdf/opbils71.pdf, accessed November 7, 2010.

Bush-Clinton Katrina Fund. 2009. "Bush-Clinton Katrina Fund Announces Grant to Community Foundation of Acadiana for Hospital Aid." http://

www.bushclintonkatrinafund.org/index.php?src=news&submenu=Media&srctype=detail&category=Press%20Releases&refno=34, accessed January 7.

Bustamante, Jorge. 2008. "Report of the Special Rapporteur on the Human Rights of Migrants: Mission to the United States of America." UN General Assembly, Human Rights Council. A/HRC/7/12/Add.2. http://daccessdds.un.org/doc/UNDOC/GEN/G08/112/81/PDF/G0811281.pdf?OpenElement, accessed February 2, 2009.

Butler, C. T. Lawrence and Keith McHenry. 2000. *Food Not Bombs*. Tucson, Ariz.: Sharp Press.

Campbell, Tom. 2006. Rights: *A Critical Introduction*. New York: Routledge.

Cappelli, Peter, Laurie Bassi, Harry Katz, David Knoke, Paul Osterman, and Michael Useem. 1997. *Change at Work*. New York: Oxford University Press.

Carmalt, Jean M. 2006. "Hurricane Katrina and Violations of ICCPR Articles 6 and 26: A Response to the Third Periodic Report of the United States of America." Report submitted by U.S. Human Rights Network to 87th Session of the Human Rights Committee, Geneva.

Carré, Françoise J. 1992. "Temporary Employment in the Eighties." In *New Policies for the Part-Time and Contingent Workforce*, ed. Virginia L. duRivage, 45–88. Armonk, N.Y.: M.E. Sharpe.

Center for Human Rights and International Justice. 2000. "Report on the First Three Years of Expedited Removal." University of California, Hastings College of Law, May.

Chambliss, William. 2000. *Power, Politics, and Crime*. Boulder, Colo.: Westview.

Chambliss, William and Robert Seidman. 1971. *Law, Order, and Power*. Boston: Addison-Wesley.

Chang, Nancy. 2002. *Silencing Political Dissent: How Post-September 11 Anti-Terrorism Measures Threaten Our Civil Liberties*. New York: Seven Stories Press.

Chomsky, Noam. 2009. *Powers and Prospects: Reflections on Human Nature and the Social Order*. Boston: South End Press.

Cincotta, Gail. 2000. Testimony Before the U.S. House of Representatives Committee on Banking and Financial Services, May 24. http://www.financialservices.house.gov/, accessed November 9, 2010.

Clapham, Andrew. 2007. *Human Rights: A Very Short Introduction*. Oxford: Oxford University Press.

Claude, Inis. 1955. *National Minorities: An International Problem*. Cambridge, Mass.: Harvard University Press.

Cobble, Dorothy Sue. 2003. *The Other Women's Movement: Workplace Justice and Social Rights in Modern America.* Princeton, N.J.: Princeton University Press.

Cohen, Roberta. 2006. "Human Rights at Home." Statement delivered on behalf of Brookings-Bern Project on Internal Displacement, Harvard University Kennedy School of Government, Boston.

Coker, Donna. 1999. "Enhancing Autonomy for Battered Women: Lessons from Navajo Peacemaking." *UCLA Law Review* 47: 1–111.

Cole, David and James X. Dempsey. 2002. *Terrorism and the Constitution: Sacrificing Civil Liberties in the Name of National Security.* Washington, D.C.: First Amendment Foundation.

Cole, Mike. 2006. "Introduction: Human Rights, Equality and Education." In *Education, Equality and Human Rights: Issues of Gender, "Race," Sexuality Disability and Social Class*, ed. Mike Cole, 1–17. London: Routledge.

Collins, J. Michael. 2000. "Analyzing Trends in Subprime Originations: A Case Study of Connecticut." Washington, D.C.: Neighborhood Reinvestment Corporation.

Collins, Patricia Hill. 2000. *Black Feminist Thought.* 2nd ed. New York: Routledge.

———. 1998. *Fighting Words: Black Women and the Search for Justice.* Minneapolis: University of Minnesota Press.

Compa, Lance. 2008. "Labor's New Opening to International Human Rights Standards." *WorkingUSA: The Journal of Labor and Society* 11: 99–123.

Congressional Research Reports for People. 2009. "The 2009 U.N. Durban Review Conference: Follow-Up to the 2001 U.N. World Conference Against Racism." opencrs.com/document/RL34754/2008-11-20, accessed May 9.

Connelly, Catherine E. and Daniel G. Gallagher. 2004. "Emerging Trends in Contingent Work Research." *Journal of Management* 30: 959–83.

Cowan, Jane, Marie-Benedicte Dembour, and Richard Wilson, eds. 2001. *Culture and Rights: Anthropological Perspectives.* Cambridge: Cambridge University Press.

Darder, Antonia, Rodolfo Torres, and Marta Baltodano. 2009. *The Critical Pedagogy Reader.* New York: Routledge.

Darity, William A., Jr. and Samuel L. Myers, Jr. 2001. "Racial Economic Inequality in the USA." In *The Blackwell Companion to Sociology*, ed. Judith R. Blau, 178–95. Malden, Mass.: Blackwell.

Das Gupta, Monisha. 2006. *Unruly Immigrants: Rights, Activism, and Transnational South Asian Politics in the United States.* Durham, N.C.: Duke University Press.

Das Gupta, Shamita, ed. 2007. *Body Evidence: Intimate Violence Against South Asian Women in America*. New Brunswick, N.J.: Rutgers University Press.

Davey, Joseph Dillon. 1995. *The New Social Contract: America's Journey from Welfare State to Police State*. Westport, Conn.: Praeger.

———. 1998. *The Politics of Prison Expansion: Winning Elections by Waging War on Crime*. Westport, Conn.: Praeger.

Davies, Lynn. 2000. *Citizenship Education and Human Rights Education: Key Concepts and Debates*. London: British Council.

Davila, Arlene. 2001. *Latinos, Inc.* Berkeley: University of California Press, 2001.

Davis, Angela. 2003. *Are Prisons Obsolete?* New York: Seven Stories Press.

Davis, Angela and Cassandra Shaylor. 2001. "Race, Gender, and the Prison Industrial Complex: California and Beyond." *Meridians* 2: 1–25.

Davis, Mike. 1995. "Hell Factories in the Field: A Prison Industrial Complex." *The Nation* 260: 229.

Day, Richard J. F. 2005. *Gramsci Is Dead: Anarchist Currents in the Newest Social Movements*. Ann Arbor, Mich.: Pluto Press.

De Cleyre, Voltairine. *The Voltairine de Cleyre Reader*. Ed. A. J. Brigati. Oakland, Calif.: AK Press, 2004.

DeLeon, Abraham. 2006. "The Time for Action Is Now! Anarchist Theory, Critical Pedagogy, and Radical Possibilities." *Journal for Critical Education Policy Studies* 4. http://www.jceps.com/?pageID=article&articleID=67, accessed January 5, 2010.

———. 2008. "Oh No, Not the 'A' Word! Towards an Anarchism for Education." *Educational Studies* 44: 122–41.

———. 2009. *Review of Pedagogy and Praxis in the Age of Empire: Towards a New Humanism* by Peter McLaren and Nathalia Jaramillo (Rotterdam: Sense, 2007). *Workplace: A Journal for Academic Labor*. http://m1.cust.educ.ubc.ca/journal/index.php/workplace/article/viewFile/55/deleon, accessed January 5, 2010.

Delgado, Gary. 1986. *Organizing the Movement: The Roots and Growth of ACORN*. Philadelphia: Temple University Press, 1986.

Delgado-Wise, Raul and Humberto Márquez Covarrubias. 2007. "The Reshaping of Mexican Labor Exports Under NAFTA: Paradoxes and Challenges." *International Migration Review* 41: 656–79.

"Indian Guestworker Slits Wrists After Being Fired for Complaining About Squalid Work Conditions." 2009. Democracy Now transcript. http://www.democracynow.org/2007/3/15/indian_guestworker_slits_wrists_after_being, accessed February 17.

Denton, Nancy. 2001. "Housing as a Means of Asset Accumulation: Good Strategy for the Poor?" In *Assets for the Poor: The Benefits of Spreading Asset Ownership*, ed. Thomas M. Shapiro and Edward N. Wolff. New York: Russell Sage.

Department of Homeland Security (DHS). 2008. "DHS Announces $12.14 Billion for Border Security & Immigration Enforcement Efforts." http://www.dhs.gov/xnews/releases/pr_1201803940204.shtm, accessed May 12, 2009.

Dewan, Shaila. 2008. "Resources Scarce, Homelessness Persists in New Orleans." New York Times, May 28. http://www.nytimes.com/2008/05/28/us/28tent.html, accessed January 7, 2009.

Dine, Janet. 2005. *Companies, International Trade, and Human Rights*. Cambridge: Cambridge University Press.

Diner, Hasia R. 1984. *Erin's Daughters in America: Irish Immigrant Women in the Nineteenth Century*. Baltimore: Johns Hopkins University Press.

DiTomaso, Nancy. 2001. "The Loose Coupling of Jobs: The Subcontracting of Everyone?" In *Sourcebook of Labor Markets*, ed. Ivar Berg and Arne L. Kalleberg, 247–70. New York: Kluwer Academic/Plenum.

Dodoo, F. Nii-Amoo and Baffour K. Takyi. 2002. "Africans in the Diaspora: Black-White Earnings Differences Among America's Africans." *Ethnic and Racial Studies* 25: 913–41.

Donnelly, Jack. 2003. *Universal Human Rights in Theory and Practice*. 2nd ed. Ithaca, N.Y.: Cornell University Press.

Douzinas, Costas. 2007. Human Rights and Empire: *The Political Philosophy of Cosmopolitanism*. New York: Routledge, 2007.

Dunn, Timothy. 1996. *The Militarization of the U.S.-Mexico Border, 1978–1992: Low-Intensity Conflict Doctrine Comes Home*. Austin: CMAS Books, University of Texas.

———. 2009. *Blockading the Border and Human Rights: The El Paso Operation That Remade Immigration Enforcement*. Austin: University of Texas Press.

duRivage, Virginia L., ed. 1992. *New Policies for the Part-Time and Contingent Workforce*. Armonk, N.Y.: M.E. Sharpe, 1992.

Dyson, Michael Eric. 2005. *Come Hell or High Water: Hurricane Katrina and the Color of Disaster*. New York: Basic Civitas.

Earthworks. 2007. Special Places at Risk: Mt. Tenabo Nevada. http://www.earthworksaction.org/MountTenabo.cfm, accessed February 28, 2009.

Environmental Protection Agency (EPA). 2009. "Basic Information About Food Scraps." http://www.epa.gov/epawaste/conserve/materials/organics/food/fd-basic.htm, accessed April 23.

Esbenshade, Jill. 2004. *Monitoring Sweatshops: Workers, Consumers, and the Global Apparel Industry.* Philadelphia: Temple University Press.

Espiritu, Yen. 1997. *Asian American Women and Men: Labor, Laws, and Love.* Thousand Oaks, Calif.: Sage.

Essed, Philomena. 1991. *Understanding Everyday Racism: An Interdisciplinary Approach.* London: Sage.

Etzioni, Amitai. 2004. *How Patriotic Is the Patriot Act?* New York: Routledge.

Fadiman, Anne. 1997. *The Spirit Catches You and You Fall Down: A Hmong Girl, Her American Doctors, and the Collision of Two Cultures.* New York: Noonday Press, 1997.

Fairbairn, Barrie. 2005. "Gay Rights Are Human Rights: Gay Asylum Seekers in Canada." In *Passing Lines, Sexuality, and Immigration,* ed. Brad Epps, Keja Valens, and Bill Johnson Gonzalez. Cambridge, Mass.: Harvard University Press.

Feagin, Joe R. 2000. *Racist America: Roots, Current Realities, and Future Reparations.* New York: Routledge.

———. 2006. *Systemic Racism: A Theory of Oppression.* New York: Routledge.

Feagin, Joe R. and Melvin P. Sikes. 1994. *Living with Racism: The Black Middle Class Experience.* Boston: Beacon Press.

Featherstone, Liza and United Students Against Sweatshops. 2002. *Students Against Sweatshops: The Making of a Movement.* London: Verso.

Feld, Barry. 1999. *Bad Kids: Race and the Transformation of the Juvenile Court.* New York: Oxford University Press.

———. 2003. *Juvenile Justice Administration.* New York: Oxford University Press, 2003.

Fellner, Jamie and Marc Mauer. 1998. *Losing the Vote: The Impact of Felony Disenfranchisement Laws in the United States.* Washington, D.C.: Human Rights Watch/ Sentencing Project.

Felter, Elizabeth. 1997. "A History of the State's Response to Domestic Violence." In *Feminists Negotiate the State: The Politics of Domestic Violence,* ed. Cynthia R. Daniels, 5–20. Lanham, Md.: University Press of America.

Finan, Christopher M. 2007. *From the Palmer Raids to the Patriot Act: A History of the Fight for Free Speech in America.* Boston: Beacon Press.

Fishel, Julie. 2006/7. "Symposium: Lands, Liberties, and Legacies: Indigenous Peoples and International Law: Application of International Law to the Problems of Indigenous Peoples: United States Called to Task on Indigenous Rights: The Western Shoshone Struggle and Success at the International Level." *American Indian Law Review* 31: 619.

Flippen, Chenoa A. 2001. "Racial and Ethnic Inequality in Homeownership and Housing Equity." *Sociological Quarterly* 42: 121–49.

Flores, Glenn. 2005. "The Impact of Medical Interpreter Services on the Quality of Health Care: A Systematic Review." *Medical Care Research Review* 62: 255–99.

"Florida Overturns Gay Adoption Ban." 2010. *Huffington Post*, September 22.

Flowers, Nancy. 2003. *A Survey of Human Rights Education.* Hamburg: Bertelsmann.

Folbre, Nancy. 2001. *The Invisible Heart: Economics and Family Values.* New York: New Press.

Foo, Laura Jo. 2002. *Asian American Women: Issues, Concerns, and Responsive Human and Civil Rights Advocacy.* New York: Ford Foundation.

Ford Foundation. 2004. "Close to Home: Case Studies of Human Rights Work in the United States." http://www.fordfound.org/pdfs/impact/close_to_home.pdf, accessed December 23, 2009.

Fox News. 2007. "Controversy over Foot Washing." http://www.foxnews.com/story/0,2933,265913,00.html, accessed May 9, 2009.

Franz, Barbara. 2007. "Guest Workers and Immigration Reform: The Rise of New Feudalism in America?" *New Political Science* 29: 349–70.

Fraser, Arvonne. 2006. "Becoming Human: The Origins and Development of Women's Human Rights." In *Women's Rights*, ed. Bert Lockwood, 3–56. Baltimore: Johns Hopkins University Press.

Freire, Paulo. 2000. *Pedagogy of the Oppressed.* New York: Continuum, 2000.

Freund, David M. P. 2007. *Colored Property: State Policy and White Racial Politics in Suburban America.* Chicago: University of Chicago Press, 2007.

Fullerton, Andrew S. and Michael Wallace. 2007. "Traversing the Flexible Turn: U.S. Workers' Perceptions of Job Security, 1977–2002." Social Science Research 36: 201–21.

Gabhruji. 2008. "U.S. Sikh Held, Turban Snatched over Kirpan." www.sikhnet.com/discussion/viewtopic.php?f=2&t=390&hilit=&sid=fefef59afc86fce76f5eeaaa47d76abb, accessed May 9, 2009.

Gabin, Nancy. 1990. *Feminism in the Labor Movement: Women and the United Auto Workers, 1935–1975.* Ithaca, N.Y.: Cornell University Press. 1990.

Gardner, Tiffany M. 2008. "Rebuilding Sustainable Communities for Children and Their Families After Disasters." National Economic and Social Rights Initiative, November. http://www.nesri.org/fact_sheets_pubs/GardnerRebuildingSustainableCommunitiesConfernceNov2008.pdf, accessed January 9, 2009.

Gelb, Joyce. 2003. *Gender Policies in Japan and the United States: Comparing Women's Movements, Rights and Politics*. New York: Palgrave Macmillan.

Gelderloos, Peter. 2006. "A Critical History of Harrisonburg Food Not Bombs: Culture, Communication, and Organization in an Anarchist Soup Kitchen." *Social Anarchism* 39: 64–70.

Gibson, Jeffrey G. 1999. "Lesbian and Gay Prospective Adoptive Parents: The Legal Battle." *Human Rights* 26, 2 (Spring).

Gilmore, Ruthie. 1998/99. "Globalisation and U.S. Prison Growth: From Military Keynesianism to Post-Keynesian Militarism." *Race and Class* 40: 171–88.

———. 2007. *Golden Gulag: Prisons, Surplus, Crisis, and Opposition in Globalizing California*. Berkeley: University of California Press.

Gilmore, Ruthie and Craig Gilmore. 2008. "Restating the Obvious." In *Indefensible Space: The Architecture of the National Security State*, ed. Michael Sorkin. New York: Routledge.

Glenn, Evelyn Nakano. 2002. *Unequal Freedom: How Race and Gender Shape American Citizenship*. Cambridge, Mass.: Harvard University Press.

Global Security. 2009. "Worldwide Military Expenditures." http://www.globalsecurity.org/military/world/spending.htm, accessed April 23.

Goering, John and Ron Wienk, eds. 1996. *Mortgage Lending, Racial Discrimination, and Federal Policy*. Washington, D.C.: Urban Institute Press.

Goldscheid, Julie. 2000. "*United States v. Morrison* and the Civil Rights Remedy of the Violence Against Women Act: A Civil Rights Law Struck Down in the Name of Federalism." *Cornell Law Review* 86: 109–39.

Goldstein, Deborah. 1999. *Understanding Predatory Lending: Moving Toward a Common Definition and Workable Solutions*. Cambridge, Mass.: Joint Center for Housing Studies of Harvard University.

Gonos, George. 1997. "The Contest over 'Employer' Status in Postwar United States: The Case of Temporary Help Firms." *Law & Society Review* 31: 81–110.

———. 1998. "The Interaction Between Market Incentives and Government Actions." In *Contingent Work: American Employment Relations in Transition*, ed. Kathleen Barker and Kathleen Christensen, 170–91. Ithaca, N.Y.: Cornell University Press, 1998.

———. 2001. "Fee-Splitting Revisited: Concealing Surplus Value in the Temporary Employment Relationship." *Politics & Society* 29: 589–611.

Gordon, David M. 1996. *Fat and Mean: The Corporate Squeeze of Working Americans and the Myth of Managerial Downsizing*. New York: Free Press.

Gordon, Linda. 1988. *Heroes of Their Own Lives: The Politics and History of Family Violence, Boston 1880–1960*. New York: Penguin.

Gordon, Neve. 2004. *From the Margins of Globalization: Critical Perspectives on Human Rights.* Lanham, Md.: Lexington Books, 2004.

Gottfried, Heidi. 1992. "In the Margins: Flexibility as a Mode of Regulation in the Temporary Help Service Industry." *Work, Employment, and Society* 6: 443–60.

Graham, Laurie. 1995. *On the Line at Subaru-Isuzu: The Japanese Model and the American Worker.* Ithaca, N.Y.: Cornell University Press.

Gray, Mike. 2000. *Drug Crazy: How We Got into This Mess and How We Can Get Out.* New York: Routledge.

Grim, John. 1996. "Cultural Identity, Authenticity, and Community Survival: The Politics of Recognition in the Study of Native American Religions." *American Indian Quarterly* 20: 353–77.

Grodsky, Eric and Devah Pager. 2001. "The Structure of Disadvantage: Individual and Occupational Determinants of the Black-White Wage Gap." *American Sociological Review* 66: 542–67.

Gruenstein, Debbie and Christopher E. Herbert. 2000. *Analyzing Trends in Subprime Originations and Foreclosures: A Case Study of the Atlanta Metro Area.* Washington, D.C.: Neighborhood Reinvestment Corporation, 2000.

Habitat for Humanity. "New Orleans Area Habitat for Humanity Continues to Build and Provides Homes for 84 New Families in 2008: Affiliate Looks Forward to Building an Additional 100 Homes in 2009." http://www.habitatnola.org, accessed January 10, 2009.

Hafner-Burton, Emilie M. and Kiyoteru Tsutsui. 2005. "Human Rights in a Globalizing World: The Paradox of Empty Promises." *American Journal of Sociology* 110: 1373–1411.

Hagen, John, Carla Shedd, and Monique Payne. "Race, Ethnicity and Youth Perceptions of Criminal Injustice." *American Sociological Review* 70, 3 (June 2005): 381–407

Halter, Marilyn. 2000. *Shopping for Identity: The Marketing of Ethnicity.* New York: Shocken.

Hammer, Zoe. 2010. "The Architecture of Fear: Common Sense and the U.S.-Mexico Border Wall." In *Entertaining Fear: Rhetoric and the Political Economy of Social Control*, ed. Catherine Chaput, M. J. Braun, and Danika M. Brown. New York: Peter Lang.

Hampton, Tracy. 2007. "Food Insecurity Harms Health, Well-Being of Millions in the United States." *Journal of the American Medical Association* 298: 1851–53.

Hanifa, Aziz. 2009. "U.S.: Sikhs in Army Sore at Order on Turbans." www.

rediff.com/news/2009/apr/15sikhs-in-us-sore-at-order-on-turbans.htm, accessed May 9.

Hansen, Stephen A. 2002. "The Right to Take Part in Cultural Life: Toward Defining Minimum Core Obligations Related to Article 15 (1) (A) of the International Covenant on Economic, Social and Cultural Rights." In *Core Obligations: Building a Framework for Economic, Social and Cultural Rights*, ed. Audrey R. Chapman and Sage Russell, 279–303. Antwerp: Intersentia.

Hardt, Michael and Antonio Negri. 2000. *Empire*. Cambridge, Mass.: Harvard University Press.

Harjo, Suzanne Shown. 1992. "Native Peoples' Cultural and Human Rights: An Unfinished Agenda." *Arizona Law Journal* 24: 321–28.

Harris, Cheryl. 1993. "Whiteness as Property." *Harvard Law Review* 106: 1709–95.

Harrison, Bennett. 1994. *Lean and Mean: Why Large Corporations Will Continue to Dominate the Global Economy*. New York: Guilford Press.

Harrison, Bennett and Barry Bluestone. 1988. *The Great U-Turn: Corporate Restructuring and the Polarizing of America*. New York: Basic Books.

Harvey, David. 2005. *A Brief History of Neoliberalism*. New York; Oxford University Press.

Hatton, Erin. 2007. "The Temp Industry and the Transformation of Work in America." Ph.D. Dissertation, University of Wisconsin-Madison.

———. 2008. "The Making of the Kelly Girl." *Journal of Historical Sociology* 21: 1–25.

Heger, David. 2000. *The Violence Against Women Act of 1994*. National Violence Against Women Prevention Research Center. http://www.musc.edu/vawprevention/policy/vawa.shtml, accessed November 3, 2008.

Henson, Kevin D. 1996. *Just a Temp*. Philadelphia: Temple University Press.

Henry J. Kaiser Family Foundation. 2008. *New Orleans Three Years After the Storm: The Second Kaiser Post-Katrina Survey*. Kaiser Commission on Medicaid and the Uninsured and Public Opinion and Survey Research Program. http://www.kff.org/kaiserpolls/upload/7789.pdf, accessed December 22.

Herivel, Tera and Paul Wright. 2003. *Prison Nation: The Warehousing of America's Poor*. New York: Routledge.

Hertel, Shareen. 2009. "Human Rights and the Global Economy: Bringing Labor Rights Back In." *Maryland Journal of International Law* 24: 283–95.

Hertel, Shareen and Lanse Minkler. 2007. "Economic Rights: The Terrain." In *Economic Rights: Conceptual, Measurement, and Policy Issues*, ed. Shareen Hertel and Lanse Minkler, 1–35. New York: Cambridge University Press.

Hickey, Tom. 2006. "'Multitude' or 'Class': Constituencies of Resistance, Sources of Hope." In *Education, Equality and Human Rights: Issues of Gender, "Race," Sexuality Disability and Social Class*, ed. Mike Cole, 180–201. London: Routledge.

Hillary, Heather and Nancy Kubasek. 2007. "The Remaining Perils of the Patriot Act: A Primer." *Journal of Law in Society* 8, 2: 1–74.

Hirsch, Arnold R. 2000. "'Containment' on the Home Front: Race and Federal Housing Policy from the New Deal to the Cold War." *Journal of Urban History* 26: 158–89.

Hirsch, Barry and David MacPherson. 2010. "Union Membership and Coverage Databases from the CPS." http://www.unionstats.com., accessed November 7.

Hood, Ernie. 2005. "Dwelling Disparities: How Poor Housing Leads to Poor Health." *Environmental Health Perspectives* 113: 311–17.

Human Rights Watch. 2000. "South Dakota: Stop Abuses of Detained Kids: A Letter to South Dakota Governor William Janklow." http://www.hrw.org/en/news/2000/03/05/south-dakota-stop-abuses-detained-kids-0, accessed July 10, 2010.

———. 2005. *Witness to Abuse: Human Rights Abuses Under the Material Witness Law Since September 11*. New York: Human Rights Watch.

———. 2007. *Forced Apart: Families Separated and Immigrants Harmed by United States Deportation Policy*. 19, 3(G). New York: Human Rights Watch, July.

Human Rights Watch/Immigration Equality. 2006. "Family, Unvalued, Discrimination, Denial and the Fate of Binational Same-Sex Couples Under U.S. Law 2006. United States." Human Rights Center of Chapel Hill & Carrboro. http://www.humanrightscities.org/, accessed November 9, 2010.

Hursh, David. 2008. *High-Stakes Testing and the Decline of Teaching and Learning: The Real Crisis in Education*. Lanham, Md.: Rowman & Littlefield.

Ignatieff, Michael. 2005. "Introduction: American Exceptionalism and Human Rights." In *American Exceptionalism and Human Rights*, ed. Michael Ignatieff, 1–26. Princeton, N.J.: Princeton University Press.

Ignatiev, Noel. 1995. *How the Irish Became White*. New York: Routledge.

"Indian Men in U.S. 'Slave' Protest." BBC. http://news.bbc.co.uk/2/hi/south_asia/7316130.stm

Ishay, Micheline. 2007. "Introduction." In *The Human Rights Reader: Major*

Political Speeches, Essays and Documents from the Bible to the Present, ed. Micheline Ishay. New York: Routledge.

Josephides, Lisette. 2003. "The Rights of Being Human." In *Human Rights in Global Perspective: Anthropological Studies of Rights, Claims and Entitlements*, ed. Richard Wilson and Jon Mitchell, 229–50. London: Routledge.

Kahn, Robbie. 1995, *Bearing Meaning: The Language of Birth*. Urbana: University of Illinois Press.

Kalleberg, Arne L. 2000. "Nonstandard Employment Relations: Part-Time, Temporary and Contract Work." *Annual Review of Sociology* 26: 341–65.

———. 2003. "Flexible Firms and Labor Market Segmentation: Effects of Workplace Restructuring on Jobs and Workers." *Work and Occupations* 30: 154–75.

Kalleberg, Arne. L., Barbara. F. Reskin, and Ken Hudson. 2000. "Bad Jobs in America: Standard and Nonstandard Employment Relations and Job Quality in the United States." *American Sociological Review* 65: 256–78.

Katz, Bruce. 2006. "Concentrated Poverty in New Orleans and Other American Cities." *Chronicle of Higher Education* 52: 48.

Kauffman, Matthew and Lisa Chedekel. 2004. "As Colleges Profit, Sweatshops Worsen." *Hartford Courant*, December 12.

Kaur, Valarie. 2010. *Divided We Fall: Americans in the Aftermath, a Documentary*. Video, New Moon Productions.

Kelly, John. 2009. "Zero Tolerance Breeds Zero Justice." *Youth Today* 18: 1, 26.

Khan, Irene. 2005. "Understanding Corporate Complicity: Extending the Notion Beyond Existing Laws." Remarks of the Secretary General of Amnesty International at a Business Human Rights Seminar. London, December 8. http://www.amnesty.org/en/library/asset/POL34/001/2006/en/4c856377-fa0a-11dd-b1b0-c961f7df9c35/pol340012006en.html, accessed March 7, 2011.

Kibria, Nazli. 2002. *Becoming Asian American: Second Generation Chinese and Korean Identities*. Baltimore: Johns Hopkins University Press.

Kil, Sang Hea. Forthcoming. "Immigration and 'Operations': The Militarization (and Medicalization) of the USA-Mexico Border." In *Traversing Transnationalism: The Horizons of Literary and Cultural Studies*, ed. Ronit Frenkel, Paolo Frassinelli, and David Watson. Amsterdam: Rodopi Press.

Kil, Sang Hea and Cecilia Menjívar. 2006. "The 'War on the Border': The Criminalization of Immigrants and the Militarization of the U.S.-Mexico Border." In *Immigration and Crime: Ethnicity, Race, and Violence*, ed. Ramiro Martinez, Jr., and Abel Valenzuela, Jr., 164–88. New York: New York University Press.

Kimeldorf, Howard and Judith Stepan-Norris. 1992. "Historical Studies of Labor Movements in the United States." *Annual Review of Sociology* 18: 495–517.

Kimmel, Michael. 2008. *The Gendered Society.* 3rd ed. New York: Oxford University Press.

Kipke, Michele D., Ellen Iverson, Deborah Moore, Cara Booker, Valerie Ruelas, Anne L. Peters, and Francine Kaufman. 2007. "Food and Park Environments: Neighborhood-Level Risks for Childhood Obesity in East Los Angeles." *Journal of Adolescent Health* 40: 325–33.

Klueber, S. A. 2003. "Trafficking in Human Beings: Law Enforcement Response." M.A. thesis. University of Louisville.

Kmec, Julie A. 2003. "Minority Job Concentration and Wages." *Social Problems* 50: 38–59.

Kotlowitz, Alex. 2009. "All Boarded Up." *New York Times Magazine*, March 8.

Künnemann, Rolf. 2002. "The Right to Adequate Food: Violations Related to Its Minimum Core Content." In *Core Obligations: Building a Framework for Economic, Social and Cultural Rights*, ed. Audrey R. Chapman and Sage Russell, 279–303. Antwerp: Intersentia.

Kupers, Terry and Don Sabo. 2001. *Prison Masculinities.* Philadelphia: Temple University Press.

Kurasawa, Fuyuki. 2007. *The Work of Global Justice: Human Rights as Practices.* Cambridge: Cambridge University Press.

Kymlicka, Will. 1989. *Liberalism, Community, and Culture.* Oxford: Oxford University Press.

———. 1995. *Multicultural Citizenship: A Liberal Theory of Minority Rights.* New York: Oxford University Press.

Landesman, Peter. 2004. "The Girl Next Door." *New York Times*, January 24.

———. 1999. "Theorizing Indigenous Rights." *University of Toronto Law Journal* 49: 281–84.

Larson, Nicole I., Mary T. Story, and Melissa C. Nelson. 2009. "Neighborhood Environments: Disparities in Access to Healthy Foods in the U.S." *American Journal of Preventive Medicine* 36: 74–81e10.

Lauren, Paul Gordon. 2003. *The Evolution of International Human Rights: Visions Seen.* 2nd ed. Philadelphia: University of Pennsylvania Press, 2003.

Leary, Virginia. 1992. "Postliberal Strands in Western Human Rights Theory: Personalist Communitarian Perspectives." In *Human Rights in Cross-Cultural Perspectives: A Quest for Consensus*, ed. Abdullahi Ahmed An-Na'im, 105–32. Philadelphia: University of Pennsylvania Press.

Leipziger, Deborah. 2010. *The Corporate Responsibility Code Book.* Sheffield: Greenleaf.

Lemos, Judi. 1998. "The Violence Against Women Act of 1994: Connecting Gender-Motivated Violence to Interstate Commerce." *Stanford Law Review* 21: 1251–76.

Lenahan, Jessica. 2008. "Protection from Domestic Violence Is a Human Right." http://blog.aclu.org/2008/10/22/protection-from-domestic-violence-is-a-human-right/, accessed December 14.

Lerner, Steve. 2007. "Pensacola, Florida: Living Next Door to Mount Dioxin and a Chemical Fertilizer Superfund Site." Collaborative on Health and the Environment. http://www.healthandenvironment.org/articles/homepage/2628.

Leung, Rebecca. 2005. "*Gonzales v. Castle Rock*: Supreme Court to Decide If Mother Can Sue Her Town and Its Police." CBS News. http://www.cbsnews.com/stories/2005/03/17/60minutes/main681416.shtml, accessed January 31, 2009.

Levi, Margaret. 2003. "Organizing Power: Prospects for the American Labor Movement." *Perspectives on Politics* 1, 1: 45–68.

Lewin, Tamar. 2007. "Some U.S. Universities Install Footbaths for Muslim Students." *International Herald Tribune*, April 27. www.masnet.org/news.asp?id=4180, accessed May 9, 2009.

Lewis, Amanda. 2003. *Race in the School Yard: Negotiating the Color Line in Schools and Communities.* New Brunswick, N.J.: Rutgers University Press.

Lichtenstein, Nelson. 2002. *State of the Union: A Century of American Labor.* Princeton, N.J.: Princeton University Press.

Liebowitz, Debra. 2008. *Respect, Protect, Fulfill: Raising the Bar on Women's Rights in San Francisco.* San Francisco: WILD for Human Rights.

Lipsitz, George. 2006. *The Possessive Investment in Whiteness: How White People Profit from Identity Politics.* Philadelphia: Temple University Press, 2006.

Looking Horse, Carol Anne. 1992. "Our Cathedral Is the Black Hills." In *Messengers of the Wind*, ed. Jane Katz. New York: Ballantine.

Lopez, Ian Haney. 1996. *White by Law: The Legal Construction of Race.* New York: New York University Press.

Lopez, J. Derek. 2005. "Race-Related Stress and Sociocultural Orientation Among Latino Students During Their Transition into a Predominately White, Highly Selective Institution." *Journal of Hispanic Higher Education* 4: 354–65.

Lorber, Janie. 2009. "Report Finds ACORN Broke No Laws." *New York Times*, December 23. http://thecaucus.blogs.nytimes.com/2009/12/23/acorn-broke-no-laws/, accessed October 28, 2010.

Lorber, Judith. 2005. *Breaking the Bowls: Degendering and Feminist Change.* New York: Norton.

Lord, Richard. 2005. *American Nightmare: Predatory Lending and the Foreclosure of the American Dream.* Monroe, Me.: Common Courage Press.

Luban, David. 2005. "Eight Fallacies About Liberty and Security." In *Human Rights in the "War on Terror"*, ed. Richard Ashby Wilson, 242–57. New York: Cambridge University Press.

Luibheid, Eithne. 2002. *Entry Denied: Controlling Sexuality at the Border.* Minneapolis: University of Minnesota Press.

Lynd, Staughton and Andrej Grubacic. 2008. *Wobblies and Zapatistas: Conversations on Anarchism, Marxism and Radical History.* Oakland, Calif.: PM Press.

MacDorman, Marian F. and T. J. Mathews. 2008. "Recent Trends in Infant Mortality in the United States." NCHS Data Brief 9. Washington, D.C.: U.S. Department of Health and Human Services, October.

Mackinnon, Catharine A. 2006. *Are Women Human? And Other International Dialogues.* Cambridge, Mass.: Belknap Press of Harvard University Press.

Males, Mike. 2002. *Framing Youth: Ten Myths About the Next Generation.* Monroe, Me.: Common Courage Press.

———. 2007. "Youth Crime, 2006—Get Ready for Distortions." http://www.youthfacts.org/crim2006.html, accessed July 7, 2009.

Mann, Jonathan M. 1997. "Medicine and Public Health, Ethics and Human Rights." *Hastings Center Report* (May–June–): 6–13.

Marshall, Jill. 2005. *Humanity, Freedom and Feminism.* Aldershot: Ashgate.

Martin, Phillip. 2000. "Guest Worker Programs for the 21st Century." Washington, D.C.: Center for Immigration Studies. www.cis.org/articles/2000/back400.html, accessed February 17, 2009.

Massey, Douglas, Jorge Durand, and Nolan Malone. 2002. *Beyond Smoke and Mirrors: Mexican Immigration in an Era of Economic Integration.* New York: Russell Sage.

Mauer, Marc. 1999. *Race to Incarcerate.* New York: Sentencing Project/New Press.

May, Elaine Tyler. 1990. *Homeward Bound: American Families in the Cold War Era.* New York: Basic Books.

Mayer, Ann Elizabeth. 1996. "Reflections on the Proposed United States Reservations to CEDAW: Should the Constitution Be an Obstacle to Human Rights?" *Hastings Constitutional Law Quarterly* 23: 727–823.

McAdam, Doug. 1982. *Political Process and the Development of Black Insurgency, 1930–1970.* Chicago: University of Chicago Press.

McAdam, Doug, John D. McCarthy, and Mayer N. Zald. 1996. *Comparative Perspectives on Social Movements: Political Opportunities, Mobilizing Structures and Cultural Framings.* New York: Cambridge University Press.

McBean, A. Marshall and Marian Gornick. 1994. "Differences by Race in the Rates of Procedures Performed in Hospitals for Medicare Beneficiaries." *Health Care Financing Review* 15: 77–90.

McCall, Leslie. 2001. "Sources of Racial Wage Inequality in Metropolitan Labor Markets: Racial, Ethnic, and Gender Differences." *American Sociological Review* 66: 520–41.

McCarty, Dawn. 2007. "The Impact of the North American Free Trade Agreement (NAFTA) on Rural Children and Families in Mexico: Transnational Policy and Practice Implications." *Journal of Public Child Welfare* 1: 105–23.

McCombs, Brady, Andrew Satter, and Michael Marizco. 2009. "Total Border Deaths by Calendar Year." *Arizona Daily Star.* http://regulus.azstarnet.com/borderdeaths/, accessed March 14.

McGrath, Donald M. and Lisa A. Keister. 2008. "The Effect of Temporary Employment on Asset Accumulation Processes." *Work and Occupations* 35: 196–222.

McKinlay, John B. and Sonja M. McKinlay. 1977. "The Questionable Contribution of Medical Measures to the Decline of Mortality in the United States in the Twentieth Century." *Milbank Memorial Fund Quarterly* 55: 405–28.

McLaren, Peter. 2006. *Life in Schools: An Introduction to Critical Pedagogy in the Foundations of Education.* Upper Saddle River, N.J.: Allyn & Bacon.

Mehta, Chirag and Nik Theodore. 2001. "The Temporary Staffing Industry and U.S. Labor Markets: Implications for the Unemployment Insurance System." Paper presented at America's Workforce Network Research Conference, Washington, D.C., June 25–26.

Mehta, Uday. 1999. *Liberalism and Empire.* Chicago: University of Chicago Press.

Meintjes, Garth. 1997. "Human Rights Education as Empowerment: Reflections on Pedagogy." In *Human Rights Education for the Twenty-First Century*, ed. George J. Andreopoulos and Richard Pierre Claude, 64–79. Philadelphia: University of Pennsylvania Press.

Melossi, Dario and Massimo Pavarini. 1981. *The Prison and the Factory: Origins of the Penitentiary System.* Totowa, N.J.: Barnes and Noble.

Merin, Yuval. 2002. *Equality for Same-Sex Couples: The Legal Recognition of Gay Partnerships in Europe and the United States.* Chicago: University of Chicago Press.

Merry, Sally Engle. 2006a. *Human Rights and Gender Violence: Translating International Law into Local Justice.* Chicago: University of Chicago Press.

———. 2006b. "Rights Talk and Experience of the Law: Implementing Women's Human Rights to Protection from Violence." In *Women's Rights*, ed. Bert Lockwood, 393–430. Baltimore: Johns Hopkins University Press.

Mertus, Julie. 2007. "The Rejection of Human Rights Framing: The Case of LGBT Advocacy in the U.S." *Human Rights Quarterly* 29: 1036–64.

Meyer-Emerick, Nancy. 2002. "Policy Makers, Practitioners, Citizens: Perceptions of the Violence Against Women Act of 1994." *Administration & Society* 33: 629–62.

Meyerowitz, Joanne, ed. 1994. *Not June Cleaver: Women and Gender in Postwar America, 1945–1960.* Philadelphia: Temple University Press, 1994.

"Miami Judge Rules Against Florida Gay Adoption Ban." 2008. *Gay and Lesbian Times*, December 4.

Millhollon, Michelle. 2008. "Food Banks Ask $15 Million from State." http://www.2theadvocate.com/news/17412139.html, accessed January 10.

Mills, Charles W. 1997. *The Racial Contract.* Ithaca, N.Y.: Cornell University Press.

Moghadam, Valentin. 2005. *Globalizing Women.* Baltimore: Johns Hopkins University Press.

Mohr, Clarence L. and Lawrence N. Powell. 2007. "Through the Eye of Katrina: The Past as Prologue? An Introduction." *Journal of American History* 94: 693–94.

Monroe, Irene. 2009. "Proposition 8 and Black Homophobia." *Gay and Lesbian Review* 16, 1: 6.

Morris, Michael D. and Alexander Vekker. 2001. "An Alternative Look at Temporary Workers, Their Choices, and the Growth in Temporary Employment." *Journal of Labor Research* 22: 373–90.

Mortgage Bankers' Association. 2008. "Delinquencies and Foreclosures Increase in Latest MBA National Delinquency Survey." http://www.mbaa.org/NewsandMedia/PressCenter/64769.htm, accessed September 5.

Murase, Emily M. 2005. "CEDAW Implementation Locally: Lessons from San Francisco." Paper presented at the Eighth International Women's Policy Research Conference, Washington, D.C., June.

Narayan, Anjana and Bandana Purkayastha. 2009. *Living Our Religions: Hindu and Muslim South Asian American Women Narrate Their Experiences.* Sterling, Md.: Kumarian Press.

Nash, Kate. 2001. "Feminism and Contemporary Liberal Citizenship: The Undecidability of 'Women.'" *Citizenship Studies* 5: 255–68.

National Community Reinvestment Coalition (NCRC). 2007. "Income Is No Shield Against Racial Differences in Lending: A Comparison of High-Cost Lending in America's Metropolitan Areas." http://www.ncrc.org/images/stories/mediaCenter_reports/ncrc%20metro%20study%20race%20and%20income%20disparity%20july%2007.pdf, accessed November 7, 2010.

National Council on Crime and Delinquency. 2007. *And Justice for Some: Differential Treatment of Youth of Color in the Justice System.* Oakland, Calif.: NCCD. www.nccd-crc.org/nccd/, accessed July 1, 2009.

National Research Council. 2004. *Monitoring International Labor Standards: Techniques and Sources of Information.* Washington, D.C.: National Academies Press.

Navasky, Victor S. 2003. *Naming Names.* New York: Hill and Wang.

Needham and Company. 2010. "Yahoo! Inc. (YHOO)—Buy: Yahoo May Not Regret Paying for Facebook." http://www.needhamco.com/Research/Documents/CPY25924.pdf, accessed October 23.

Nelson, Kathryn E. 2003. "Sex Trafficking and Forced Prostitution: Comprehensive New Legal Approaches." *Houston Journal of International Law* 24, 3: 551–78.

Neubeck, Kenneth J. 2006. *When Welfare Disappears: The Case for Economic Human Rights.* New York: Routledge.

Neubeck, Kenneth J. and Noel Cazenave. 2001. *Welfare Racism: Playing the Race Card Against America's Poor.* New York: Routledge.

New Orleans Area Habitat for Humanity. 2011. "Projects." http://www.habitat-nola.org/projects/index.php, accessed March 7.

Nolan, Bruce. 2010. "Hurricane Katrina 5th Anniversary Ceremonies Mourn What Is Lost, Rejoice at What Is to Be." *Times-Picayune*, August 29. http://www.nola.com/katrina/index.ssf/2010/08/president_barack_obama_visits.html, accessed October 22.

Norrell, Brenda. 2008a. "Barrick Gold Blocks Western Shoshone Access to Ceremonial Grounds." *Narcosphere: Reporter's Notebook.* http://narcosphere.narconews.com/notebook/brenda-norrell/2008/12/barrick-gold-blocks-western-shoshone-access-ceremonial-grounds, accessed January 5, 2009.

———. 2008b. "Barrick Gold Ready to Carve up Western Shoshone Sacred Mountain." *Narcosphere: Reporter's Notebook.* http://narcosphere.narconews.com/notebook/brenda-norrell/2008/11/barrick-gold-ready-carve-western-shoshone-sacred-mountain, accessed January 5, 2009.

Nozick, Robert. 1974. *Anarchy, State, and Utopia.* New York: Basic Books, 1974.

O'Connor, Alice, Chris Tilly, and Lawrence D. Bobo. 2001. *Urban Inequality: Evidence from Four Cities*. New York: Russell Sage.

Office for Democratic Institutions and Human Rights. 2009. *Human Rights Education in the School Systems of Europe, Central Asia and North America: A Compendium of Good Practice*. http://www.ohchr.org/Documents/Publications/CompendiumHRE.pdf, accessed January 10, 2010.

Office of the Mayor of San Francisco. 1998. *Mayor Brown Signs Historic Legislation at Summit for Women*. Press Release, April 14.

Office of the United Nations High Commissioner for Human Rights. 2004. "Status of Ratifications of the Principal International Human Rights Treaties (2004)." http://www.unhchr.ch/pdf/report.pdf, accessed February 2, 2009.

Ofstead, Cynthia. 1999. "Temporary Help Firms as Entrepreneurial Actors." *Sociological Forum* 14: 273–94.

O'Hagan, Maureen. 2004. "A Terrorism Case That Went Awry," *Seattle Times*, November 22.

Okin, Susan Moller. 1999. "Is Multiculturalism Bad for Women?" In *Is Multiculturalism Bad for Women?* ed. Joshua Cohen, Matthew Howard, and Martha C. Nussbaum, 7–24. Princeton, N.J.: Princeton University Press.

The Opportunity Agenda. 2007. "Human Rights in the U.S.: Findings from a National Survey." In *Human Rights in the U.S.: Opinion and Research with Advocates, Journalists, and the General Public*. http://www.opportunityagenda.org.

Osler, Audrey. 2002. "Education for Human Rights and Citizenship in a Multicultural Society: Making a Difference." *Citizenship, Social and Economics Education* 5: 5–16.

Osterman, Paul. 2000. "Work Organization in an Age of Restructuring: Trends in Diffusion and Effects on Employee Welfare." *Industrial and Labor Relations Review* 53: 179–96.

Palmer, Tiffany. 2003. "Family Matters, Establishing Legal Parental Rights for Same-Sex Parents and Their Children. *Human Rights, Journal of the Section of Individual Rights & Responsibilities* 30: 3, 9.

Parenti, Christian. 2000. *Lockdown America: Police and Prisons in the Age of Crisis*. London: Verso.

Parker, Robert E. 1994. *Flesh Peddlers and Warm Bodies: The Temporary Help Industry and Its Workers*. New Brunswick, N.J.: Rutgers University Press.

Parmley, Angela M. Moore. 2004. "Violence Against Women Research Post VAWA: Where Have We Been, Where Are We Going?" *Violence Against Women* 10: 1417–30.

"Pastor's Death in Custody Is Probed." 2004. *Miami Herald*, December 10.

Pastor, Manuel and Susan Alva. 2004. "Guest Workers and the New Trans-nationalism: Possibilities and Realities in the Age of Repression." *Social Justice* 31: 92–112.

Pateman, Carole. 1988. *The Sexual Contract*. Stanford, Calif.: Stanford University Press.

Pateman, Carole, and Charles Mills. 2007. *Contract and Domination*. Malden, Mass.: Polity Press.

Pearce, Tola Olu. 2001. "Human Rights and Sociology: Some Observations from Africa." *Social Problems* 48: 48–56.

Peck, Jamie and Nik Theodore. 2007. "Flexible Recession: The Temporary Staffing Industry and Mediated Work in the United States." *Cambridge Journal of Economics* 31: 171–92.

Pfeffer, Jeffrey and James N. Baron. 1988. "Taking the Workers Back Out: Recent Trends in the Structuring of Employment." *Research in Organizational Behavior* 10: 257–303.

Phelan, Shane. 2001. *Sexual Strangers: Gays, Lesbians, and Dilemmas of Citizenship*. Philadelphia: Temple University Press, 2001.

Philips, Anne. 1993. *Democracy and Difference*. Cambridge: Polity Press.

Physicians for Human Rights/Bellevue NYU Program for Survivors of Torture. 2003. *From Persecution to Prison: The Health Consequences of Detention for Asylum Seekers*. Boston: Physicians for Human Rights; New York: Bellevue NYU Program.

Pianin, Eric. 2009. "Bill Would Grant Federal Workers 4 Weeks Paid Parental Leave." *Washington Post*. January 23. http://voices.washingtonpost.com/federaldiary/2009/01/bill_would_grant_federal_worke.html, accessed November 11, 2010.

Picca, Leslie H. and Joe R. Feagin. 2007. Two Faced-Racism: *Whites in the Backstage and Frontstage*. New York: Routledge.

Pieterse, Jan Nederveen. 2000. "Globalization North and South." *Theory, Culture & Society* 17: 129–37.

Piore, Michael J. and Charles F. Sabel. 1984. *The Second Industrial Divide*. New York: Basic Books.

Pleck, Elizabeth. 1987. *Domestic Tyranny: The Making of Social Policy Against Family Violence from Colonial Times to the Present*. Chicago: University of Chicago Press.

Polanyi, Karl. 1944/1957. *The Great Transformation*. Boston: Beacon Press.

Polikoff, Nancy D. 2000. "Recognizing Partners But Not Parents/Recognizing Parents But Not Partners: Gay and Lesbian Family Law in Europe and the United States. *New York Law School Journal of Human Rights* 17: 711–51.

Political Base. 2009. "Food Not Bombs." http://www.politicalbase.com/

groups/food-not-bombs/14163/, accessed April 23.

Polivka, Anne E. 1996. "A Profile of Contingent Workers." *Monthly Labor Review* 119: 10–21.

Polivka, Anne E., and Thomas Nardone. 1989. "On the Definition of 'Contingent Work.'" *Monthly Labor Review* 112: 9.

Polletta, Francesca. 2006. *It Was like a Fever: Storytelling in Protest and Politics.* Chicago: University of Chicago Press.

Powell, Catherine. 2005. "Lifting Our Veil of Ignorance: Culture, Constitutionalism, and Women's Human Rights in Post-September 11 America." *Hastings Law Journal* 57: 331–84.

Preston, Julia Preston. 2010. "Suit Points to Guest Worker Program Flaws." *New York Times.* February 1.

Print, Murray, Carolina Ugarte, Concepción Naval, and Anja Mihr. 2008. "Moral and Human Rights Education: The Contribution of the United Nations." *Journal of Moral Education* 37: 115–32.

Purkayastha, Bandana. 2005. Negotiating Ethnicity: *Second-Generation South Asian Americans Traverse a Transnational World.* New Brunswick, N.J.: Rutgers University Press.

———. 2009. "Transgressing the Sacred-Secular, Private-Public Divide." In *Living Our Religions: Hindu and Muslim South Asian American Women Narrate Their Experiences*, ed. Anjana Narayan and Bandana Purkayastha, 23–46. Stirling, Md.: Kumarian Press.

———. 2010. "Interrogating Intersectionality: Contemporary Globalization and Racialized Gendering in the Lives of Highly Educated South Asian Americans and Their Children." *Journal of Intercultural Studies* 31: 29–47.

Purkayastha, Bandana and Shweta Majumdar. 2009. "Sex Trafficking in South Asia." In *Globalization and Third World Women: Exploitation, Coping, and Resistance*, ed. Ligaya Lindio-McGovern and Isidor Wallimann, 185–204. Farnham: Ashgate.

"QuickStats: Life Expectancy Ranking at Birth, by Sex-Selected Countries and Territories, 2004." 2008. *Morbidity and Mortality Weekly Report* 57 (April 4): 346–48.

Rackow, Sharon. H. 2002. "How the USA Patriot Act will Permit Governmental Infringement upon the Privacy of Americans in the Name of 'Intelligence' Investigations." *University of Pennsylvania Law Review* 150, 5: 1651–96.

Rainey, Richard. 2010. "Jefferson Parish Gets $100 Million from FEMA to Fix Damaged Streets." Nola.com, October 5. http://www.nola.com/politics/index.ssf/2010/10/jefferson_parish_gets_100_mill.html.

Ramadan, Tariq. 2006. "Why I'm Banned in the USA." *Washington Post*, October 1.

Ramos, Damien and Robert Caldwell. 2008. "Indian Shipyard Workers Accuse Their Employer of Human Trafficking and Forced Labor." *Neworleans.Indymedia.org*, March 11. http://neworleans.indymedia.org/news/2008/03/12261.php, accessed February 17, 2009.

Randall, Vernellia R. 2002. "Racial Discrimination in Health Care in the United States as a Violation of the International Convention on the Elimination of all Forms of Racial Discrimination." *University of Florida Journal of Law and Public Policy* 14: 45–91.

Ranjeet, Bidya. 2009. "At the Cross Roads of Religions: The Experiences of a Newar Woman in Nepal and the U.S." In *Living Our Religions: Hindu and Muslim South Asian American Women Narrate Their Experiences*, ed. Anjana Narayan and Bandana Purkayastha, 81–96. Sterling, Md.: Kumarian Press, 2009.

Ransom, Roger and Charles Sutch. 1990. "Who Pays for Slavery?" In *The Wealth of Races: The Present Value of Benefits from Past Injustices*, ed. Richard F. America, 31–54. Westport, Conn.: Greenwood Press.

Ratcliff, Kathryn Strother. 2002. *Women and Health: Power, Technology, Inequality, and Conflict in a Gendered World*. Boston: Allyn and Bacon.

Ratcliff, Richard E. 1980. "Banks and Corporate Lending: An Analysis of the Impact of the Internal Structure of the Capitalist Class on the Lending Behavior of Banks." *American Sociological Review* 45: 553–70.

Raymond, Janice G., Donna M. Hughes, and Carol J. Gomez. 2001. *Sex Trafficking of Women in the United States: International and Domestic Trends*. Kingston, R.I.: Coalition Against Trafficking in Women.

Reed, Jen'nan Ghazal and John Bartkowski. 2000. "To Veil or Not to Veil." *Gender & Society* 14: 395–417.

Reich, Robert. 2007. *Supercapitalism: The Transformation of Business, Democracy, and Everyday Life*. New York: Knopf.

Reiman, Jeffrey. 1998. *The Rich Get Richer and the Poor Get Prison: Ideology, Class, and Criminal Justice*. Washington, D.C.: American University Press, 1998.

Richard, Amy O'Neill. 1999. *International Trafficking in Women to the United States: A Contemporary Manifestation of Slavery and Organized Crime*. DCI Exceptional Intelligence Analyst Program. Washington, D.C.: Central Intelligence Agency.

Robert Wood Johnson Foundation. 2009. "Getting Rid of the Poisonous Effects of Lead in Children's Homes"; "Talking to Latinos About Diabetes, Using Words They Can Understand"; "Helping Asian Americans Fight for the Right to Quality Health Care." http://www.rwjf.org/, accessed November 9.

Roberts, Dorothy. 1997. *Killing the Black Body: Race, Reproduction, and the Meaning of Liberty*. New York: Pantheon.

———. 2002. *Shattered Bonds: The Color of Child Welfare*. New York: Basic Books.

Robertson, Roland. 1978. *Meaning and Change*. New York: New York University Press.

Robeyns, Ingrid. 2006. "Three Models of Education: Rights, Capabilities and Human Capital." *Theory and Research in Education* 4: 69–84.

Robinson, Mary. 2005a. "Connecting Human Rights, Human Development, and Human Security." In *Human Rights in the War on Terror*, ed. Richard Wilson, 308–16. Cambridge: Cambridge University Press.

———. 2005b. "What Rights Can Add to Good Development Practice." In *Human Rights and Development: Towards Mutual Reinforcement*, ed. Philip Alston and Mary Robinson, 25–41. Oxford: Oxford University Press.

———. 2006. *A Voice for Human Rights*. Philadelphia: University of Pennsylvania Press.

Rochon, Thomas R. 1998. *Culture Moves: Ideas, Activism, and Changing Values*. Princeton, N.J.: Princeton University Press.

Rogers, Jackie Krasas. 2000. *Temps: The Many Faces of the Changing Workplace*. Ithaca, N.Y.: Cornell University Press.

Romero, Mary. 2002. *Maid in the USA*. New York: Routledge.

Rosario, Ruben. 1999. *Stolen Youth: Prostitution Takes Its Price*. Saint Paul, Minn.: Pioneer Press.

Ross, Stephen L. and John Yinger. 2002. *The Color of Credit: Mortgage Discrimination, Research Methodology, and Fair-Lending Enforcement*. Cambridge, Mass.: MIT Press.

Rothman, Barbara Katz. 2000. *Recreating Motherhood*. New Brunswick, N.J.: Rutgers University Press.

———. 2001. *The Book of Life*. Boston: Beacon Press.

Rubin, Beth A. 1996. *Shifts in the Social Contract: Understanding Change in American Society*. Thousand Oaks, Calif.: Pine Forge Press.

Rupp, Leila and Verta Taylor. 1987. *Survival in the Doldrums: The American Women's Rights Movement, 1945 to the 1960s*. New York: Oxford University Press.

Rusche, George and Otto Kirchheimer. 1939. *Punishment and Social Structure*. New York: Columbia University Press.

Russell, Betsy Z. 2004. "Sami Al-Hussayen on His Way Home: He Travels to Saudi Arabia After Months in Jails." *Spokesman Review*, July 22.

Sacks, Karen Brodkin. 1998. *How Jews Became White Folks and What That Says About Race in America*. New Brunswick, N.J.: Rutgers University Press.

Salazar, Milagros. 2006. "Peru: Indigenous People, Ignored Even by the Statistics." InterPress Service News Agency. http://ipsnews.net/news.asp?idnews=35058, accessed September 20, 2008.

San Francisco Department of the Environment (DOSW). 2000. "Gender Study Report—Department of the Environment." http://www.sfgov.org/site/dosw_page.asp?id=20442&mode=text, accessed November 11, 1010.

San Francisco Department on the Status of Women. 2001. "The San Francisco Department on the Status of Women Announces the Release of Its Work-Life Report." Press Release, October 18. http://www.sfgov.org/site/cosw_page.asp?id=10800, accessed November 11, 2010.

———. 2007. "Convention on the Elimination of Discrimination Against Women (CEDAW) Gender Analysis Report." http://www.sfgov.org/site/dosw_page.asp?id=66144, accessed November 11, 2010.

San Francisco Rent Board. 2000. "Rent Board Gender Analysis 2000." A http://www.sfgov.org/site/dosw_page.asp?id=20444&mode=text, accessed November 11, 2010.

———. 2002. "Rent Board Progress Report—March 2002." Report to the San Francisco Commission on the Status of Women. http://www.sfgov.org/site/dosw_page.asp?id=20445&mode=text, accessed November 11, 2010.

Sansani, Inbal. 2003. "American Indian Land Rights in the Inter-American System: *Dann v. United States*." *Human Rights Brief* 10, 2.

Sarna, Jonathan and David Dahlin. 1997. *Religion and State in the American Jewish Experience*. Notre Dame, Ind.: University of Notre Dame Press.

Sartwell, Crispin. 2008. *Against the State: An Introduction to Anarchist Political Theory*. Albany: State University of New York Press.

Sassen, Saskia. 1996. *Losing Control? Sovereignty in an Age of Globalization*. New York: Columbia University Press.

———. 2005. "The Repositioning of Citizenship and Alienage: Emergent Subjects and Spaces for Politics." *Globalizations* 2: 79–94.

Satcher, David and Eve J. Higginbotham. 2007. "The Public Health Approach to the Elimination of Disparities in Health." Paper presented at Public Health Summit 2007, Morehouse School of Medicine, Atlanta, April.

Savage, Charlie. 2006. "Bush Shuns Patriot Act Requirement: In Addendum to Law, He States Oversight Laws Are Not Binding." *Boston Globe*, March 24.

Scarberry, Susan. 1982. "Land into Flesh: Images of Intimacy." *Frontiers*: 24–28.

Schechter, Susan. 1982. *Women and Male Violence: The Visions and Struggles of the Battered Women's Movement*. Boston: South End Press.

Schilt, Kristen and Laurel Westbrook. 2009. "Doing Gender, Doing Heteronormativity: 'Gender Normals,' Transgender People, and the Social Maintenance of Heterosexuality." *Gender & Society* 23: 440–64

Schneider, Elizabeth. 2000. *Battered Women and Feminist Lawmaking*. New Haven, Conn.: Yale University Press.

Schoenholtz, Andrew I. and Jonathan Jacobs. 2002. "The State of Asylum: Representation: Ideas for Change," *Georgetown Immigration Law Journal* 16 (Summer).

Segura, Denise and Patricia Zavella. 2007. *Women and Migration in the U.S.-Mexico Borderlands: A Reader*. Durham, N.C.: Duke University Press, 2007.

Seidenberg, Steven. 2008. "Homing in on Foreclosure: Lawyers Are Finding Aggressive Defenses Against Foreclosure Actions: And Courts Are Listening as Never Before." *American Bar Association Journal* 94 (July): 54. http://www.abajournal.com/magazine/article/homing_in_on_foreclosure/, accessed November 7, 2010.

Seidman, Gay. 2007. *Beyond the Boycott: Labor Rights, Human Rights, and Transnational Activism* New York: American Sociological Association/ Russell Sage.

Sekaran. Sharda. 2006. "Human Rights of Hurricane Survivors: Challenges and Potential for a Human Rights Response to Hurricane Katrina." November. National Economic and Social Rights Initiative. http://www. nesri.org/fact_sheets_pubs/Challenges% 20and%20Potential%20for% 20a%20HR%20Response%20to%20Hurricane%20Katrina.pdf, accessed January 9, 2009.

Sen, Amartya. 1999. *Development as Freedom*. New York: Anchor.

Sengupta, Arjun K. 2002. "On the Theory and Practice of the Right to Development." *Human Rights Quarterly* 24: 837–89.

———. 2007. "Extreme Poverty and Human Rights: A Mission Report on the United States." UN Human Rights Council Centre for Development and Human Rights, January 6. http://papers.ssrn.com/sol3/papers. cfm?abstract_id=961230, accessed November 9, 2010.

Shapiro, Thomas M. 2001. "The Importance of Assets." In *Assets for the Poor: The Benefits of Spreading Asset Ownership*, ed. Thomas M. Shapiro and Edward N. Wolff, 11–33. New York: Russell Sage.

Shultz, Marjorie and David Wellman. 2003. *Whitewashing Race: The Myth of a Color-Blind Society.* Berkeley: University of California Press.

Silko, Leslie Marmon. 1996. *Yellow Woman and a Beauty of the Spirit: Essays on Native American Life Today.* New York: Touchstone.

Sjoberg, Gideon, Elizabeth A. Gill, and Norma Williams. 2001 "A Sociology of Human Rights." *Social Problems* 48: 11–47.

Skrobanek, Siriporn, Nattaya Boonpakdee, and Chutima Janthakeroo. 1997. *The Traffic in Women: Human Realities of the International Sex Trade.* New York: Zed Books.

Smedley, Brian, Adrienne Y. Stith, and Alan R. Nelson, eds. 2003. *Unequal Treatment: Confronting Racial and Ethnic Disparities in Health Care.* Washington D.C.: National Academies Press.

Soysal, Yasemin Nuhoglu. 1994. *Limits of Citizenship: Migrants and Postnational Membership in Europe.* Chicago: University of Chicago Press.

Spagat, Elliot. 2008. "Border Patrol Struggles to Keep New Agents." *New Mexico Daily Lobo*, August 8. http://www.dailylobo.com/, accessed March 12, 2009.

Spitzer, Steven. 1975. "Toward a Marxian Theory of Deviance." *Social Problems* 22: 638–51.

Spring, Joel. 2000. *The Universal Right to Education: Justification, Definition, and Guidelines.* Mahwah, N.J.: Erlbaum.

———. 2010. *American Education.* New York: McGraw-Hill.

Stephens, Debra Lynn, Ronald Paul Hill, and James W. Gentry. 2005. "A Consumer-Behavior Perspective on Intimate Partner Violence." *Journal of Contemporary Ethnography* 34: 36–67.

Stewart-Harawira, Makere. 2005. *The New Imperial Order: Indigenous Responses to Globalization.* London: Zed Books, 2005.

Straus, Anne. 1982. *The Structure of the Self in Northern Cheyenne Culture. In Psychosocial Theories of the Self*, ed. Benjamin Lee. New York: Plenum Press.

Street, Paul. 2003. "Color Blind." In *Prison Nation: The Warehousing of America's Poor*, ed. Tara Herivel and Paul Wright, 30–40. New York: Routledge.

Stychin, Carl. 2000. "A Stranger to Its Laws: Sovereign Bodies, Global Sexualities, and Transnational Citizens." *Journal of Law and Society* 27: 601–25.

Sudbury, Julia. 2005. *Global Lockdown: Race, Gender, and the Prison Industrial Complex.* New York: Routledge.

Sunstein, Cass R. 2005. "Why Does the American Constitution Lack Social and Economic Guarantees?" In *American Exceptionalism and Human Rights*, ed. Michael Ignatieff, 90–110. Princeton, N.J.: Princeton University Press.

Sutherland, J. J. 2008. "New Orleans Wants FEMA Trailers Out of Town." July 19. National Public Radio. http://www.npr.org/templates/story/story.php?storyId=92677156, accessed January 7, 2009.

Swail, Watson Scott, Kenneth E. Redd, and Laura W. Perna. 2003. *Retaining Minority Students Higher Education: A Framework for Success.* Association for the Study of Higher Education Report 30. San Francisco: Wiley Subscription Services.

Swarns, Rachel L. 2004. "Threats and Responses: Immigration; UN Report Cites Harassment of Immigrants Who Sought Asylum at American Airports." *New York Times,* August 13.

Sweet, Stephen and Peter Meiksins. 2008. *Changing Contours of Work: Jobs and Opportunities in the New Economy.* Thousand Oaks, Calif.: Pine Forge Press.

Tahmindjis, Phillip. 2005. "Sexuality and International Human Rights Law, a Global View." *Journal of Homosexuality* 48: 9–29.

Tait, Vanessa. 2005. *Poor Workers' Union: Rebuilding Labor from Below.* Boston: South End Press.

Takaki, Ronald. 1993. *A Different Mirror: A History of Multicultural America.* New York: Little, Brown.

___. 1989. *Strangers from a Different Shore: A History of Asian Americans.* Boston: Little Brown.

Talpur, Parveen, 2009. "Islam Through a Mosaic of Cultures." In *Living Our Religions: Hindu and Muslim South Asian American Women Narrate Their Experiences,* ed. Anjana Narayan and Bandana Purkayastha, 65–80. Sterling, Md.: Kumarian Press.

Tambini, Damian. 2001. "Post National Citizenship." *Ethnic and Racial Studies* 24: 195–217.

Taneff, Thomas. 2009/10. "Arkansas Adoption Ban, How Will It Affect the Kids?" *Outlook Weekly,* December 25–January 7.

Taylor, Peter. 1984. *The Smoke Ring: Tobacco, Money and Multinational Politics.* New York: Random House.

Theodore, Nik. 2003. "Political Economies of Day Labour: Regulation and Restructuring of Chicago's Contingent Labour Markets." *Urban Studies* 40: 1811–28.

Theodore, Nik and Jamie Peck. 2002. "The Temporary Staffing Industry: Growth Imperatives and Limits to Contingency." *Economic Geography* 78: 463–93.

"They Pushed Back." 2010. Editorial, *New York Times,* June 28. http://www.nytimes.com/2010/06/29/opinion/29tue3.html, accessed October 18.

Thomas, Dorothy Q. and Michelle E. Beasley. 1993. "Domestic Violence as a Human Rights Issue." *Human Rights Quarterly* 15: 36–62.

Tilly, Chris. 1996. *Half a Job: Bad and Good Part-Time Jobs in a Changing Labor Market*. Philadelphia: Temple University Press.

Tjaden, Patricia and Nancy Thoennes. 2000. *Full Report of the Prevalence, Incidence, and Consequences of Violence Against Women: Findings from the National Violence Against Women Survey*. Washington, D.C.: U.S. Department of Justice.

Tonry, Michael. 1995. *Malign Neglect: Race, Crime and Punishment in America*. New York: Oxford University Press.

———. 1996. *Sentencing Matters*. New York: Oxford University Press.

Turner, Bryan S. 2006. *Vulnerability and Human Rights*. University Park: Pennsylvania State University Press.

Turner, Scott. 2010. "Anarchist Theory and Human Rights." In *New Perspectives on Anarchism*, ed. Nathan Jun and Shane Wahl, 133–48. Lanham, Md.: Lexington Books.

UNESCO. (n.d.). "Human Rights and Education." http://www.unesco.org/en/human-rights-education/d, accessed January 5, 2010.

United Nations. 2006. *Report on the Sub-Commission on the Promotion and Protection of Human Rights on its Fifty-Eighth Session*. 2006.

———. 2008. "Press Conference by Special Rapporteur on Adequate Housing [Raquel Rolnik]." UN Department of Public Information News and Media. http://www.un.org/News/briefings/docs/2008/081024_Rolnik.doc.htm, accessed January 13, 2009.

———. 2009. "UN Experts Call for Protection of Housing Tights of Hurricane Katrina Victims." UN News Centre. http://www.un.org/apps/news/story.asp?NewsID=25782&Cr=housing&Cr1=, accessed January 8.

UN Committee on the Elimination of Discrimination Against Women (CEDAW). 1992. Introduction. http://www.un.org/womenwatch/daw/cedaw/text/econvention.htm#intro, accessed March 7, 2011.

UN Human Rights Council (UNHRC). 1992. *Handbook on Procedures and Criteria for Determining Refugee Status under the 1951 Convention and the 1967 Protocol relating to the Status of Refugees*. January 1.

———. 2006. [First] Interim Report of the Special Representative of the Secretary General on the issue of human rights and transnational corporations and other business enterprises [John G. Ruggie], Report submitted to UN Human Rights Commission, 62nd sess., February 22 (E/CN.4/2006/97).

———. 2007a. "[Second] Interim Report of the Special Representative of the Secretary General on the issue of human rights and transnational corpo-

rations and other business enterprises [John G. Ruggie], Report submitted to UN Human Rights Council, 4th sess., February 19 (A/HRC/4/35).
———. 2007b. Addendum on "State responsibilities to adjudicate corporate activities under the United Nations core human rights treaties: an overview of treaty body commentaries," submitted in conjunction with the [First] Interim Report of the Special Representative of the Secretary General on the issue of human rights and transnational corporations and other business enterprises [John G. Ruggie], Addendum submitted to the UN Human Rights Council, 4th sess., February 13 (A/HRC/4/35/Add.1).
———. 2008. "[Third] Interim Report of the Special Representative of the Secretary General on the issue of human rights and transnational corporations and other business enterprises [John G. Ruggie], Report given at the UN Human Rights Council, 8th sess., April 7 (A/HRC/8/5).
U.S. Commission on International Religious Freedom. 2005. *Report on Asylum Seekers in Expedited Removal.* Vol. 1, *Findings and Recommendations*; vol. 2, *Expert Reports.* Washington, D.C.: The Commission, February.
U.S. Committee on the Elimination of Racial Discrimination (CERD). 2007. Periodic Report of the United States of America to the UN Committee on Elimination of All types of Racial Discrimination. www.state.gov/documents/organization/83517.pdf, accessed May 9, 2009.
U.S. GAO. 2000. *Illegal Aliens: Opportunities Exist to Improve the Expedited Removal Process.* Washington, D.C., September 1. GAO/GGD-00-176.
U.S. Department of Agriculture. 2009. "Food Security in the United States: Key Statistics and Graphics." http://www.ers.usda.gov/Briefing/FoodSecurity/stats_graphs.htm, accessed April 13, 2009.
U.S. Department of Commerce, Bureau of the Census. 2005. "Contingent Work Supplement [computer file]" Washington, D.C.: Department of Commerce; Ann Arbor, Mich.: Inter-University Consortium for Political and Social Research [distributor].
———. 2004. *Statistical Abstract of the United States, 2003.* Washington, D.C.: Government Printing Office.
U.S. Department of Homeland Security (DHS), Customs and Border Patrol. 2004. "DHS Announces Expanded Border Control Plans," August 10. http://www.dhs.gov/vnews/releases/press_release_0479.htm, accessed July 18, 2007.
———, Office of the Press Secretary. 2006. "Remarks by Secretary of Homeland Security Michael Chertoff . . . on the Secure Border Initiative." August 23. http://www.dhs.gov/xnews/releases;pr_1158351672542.shtm, accessed July 19, 2007.

———. 2007. "DHS Budget in Brief, FY 2008." http://www.dhs.gov/xlibrary/assets/budget_bibfy2008.pdf, accessed July 13.

———. 2008. "Border Fence Project Surpasses 500-Mile Mark: Pedestrian, Vehicle Fence Installed Along the Border in California, Arizona, New Mexico and Texas." http://cbp.gov/xp/cgov/home.xml, accessed March 13.

U.S. Department of Housing and Urban Development. 2000. "Unequal Burden: Income and Racial Disparities in Subprime Lending in America." April. http://www.huduser.org/portal/publications/fairhsg/unequal.html, accessed November 7, 2010.

U.S. Department of Housing and Urban Development-U.S. Treasury National Predatory Lending Task Force. 2000. *Curbing Predatory Home Mortgage Lending.* June. Washington, D.C.: HUD.

U.S. Department of State, Bureau of Consular Affairs. 2008. "Destination USA. Secure Borders. Open Doors." http://travel.state.gov/, accessed October 23, 2008.

U.S./Mexico Border Health Commission. 2006. "The U.S./Mexico Border: Demographic, Socio-Economic, and Health Issues Profile 1." http://www.borderhealth.org/index.php, accessed March 14, 2008.

Unity Council. "Fruitvale Transit Village Project." 2009. Federal Highway Administration: Environmental Justice. www.fhwa.dot.gov, accessed November 9, 2010.

Valverde, Leonard A. and Louis A. Castenell. 1998. The *Multicultural Campus: Strategies for Transforming Higher Education.* Walnut Creek, Calif.: AltaMira.

Van Arsdale, David. 2008. "The Recasualization of Blue-Collar Workers." *Labor: Studies in Working-Class History of the Americas* 5: 75–99.

Vednita. Nelson. 1993. "Prostitution: Where Racism and Sexism Intersect." *Michigan Journal of Gender & Law* 1: 81–89.

Veseley, Rebecca. 2002. "U.N. Women's Treaty Molds San Francisco Government." *Women's e-News*, July 25. http://www.womensenews.org/article.cfm/dyn/aid/983/context/archive, accessed November 11, 2010.

Vogel, David. 2005. *The Market for Virtue: The Potential and Limits of Corporate Social Responsibility.* Washington, D.C.: Brooking Institution.

Walker, Samuel, Cassia Spohn, and Miriam DeLone. 2004. *The Color of Justice: Race, Ethnicity, and Crime in America.* Belmont, Calif.: Wadsworth.

Wallace, Michael and David Brady. 2001. "The Next Long Swing: Spatialization, Technocratic Control, and the Restructuring of Work at the Turn of the Century." In *Sourcebook of Labor Markets*, ed. Ivar Berg and Arne L. Kalleberg, 101–33. New York: Kluwer Academic.

Warren, Bob. 2010. "FEMA Sending More Money to St. Bernard Parish for Hurricane Katrina Recovery." *Times-Picayune*, September 29. http://www.nola.com/katrina/index.ssf/2010/09/fema_sending_more_money_to_st.html, accessed October 22.

War Resisters League. 2009. "Where Your Income Tax Money Really Goes." FY 2009. http://www.warresisters.org/pages/piechart.htm, accessed April 23.

Wells, Don. 2007. "Too Weak for the Job: Corporate Codes of Conduct, Non-Governmental Organizations and the Regulation of International Labor Standards." Global Social Policy 7, 51: 51–73.

Western, Bruce. 2007. *Punishment and Inequality in America*. New York: Russell Sage.

Wijers, Marjan and Lin Lap-Chew. 1997. *Trafficking in Women: Forced Labor and Slavery-Like Practices in Marriage, Domestic Labor and Prostitution*. Utrecht: STV.

WILD for Human Rights. 1998. "San Francisco Board of Supervisors Passes Historic Legislation Implementing International Women's Convention Within City." Press Release, April 13.

——. 2006. *Making Rights Real: A Workbook on the Local Implementation of Human Rights*. San Francisco: WILD for Human Rights.

Willett, Cynthia, ed. 1998. *Theorizing Multiculturalism: A Guide to the Current Debates*. London: Blackwell.

Williams, David R. 1999. "Race, Socioeconomic Status, and Health: The Added Effects of Racism and Discrimination." *Annals of New York Academy of Sciences* 896: 173–88.

Williams, David R. and Pamela Braboy Jackson. 2005. "Social Sources of Racial Disparities in Health." *Health Affairs* 24: 325–34.

Williams, Richard, Reynold Nesiba, and Eileen Diaz McConnell. "The Changing Face of Inequality in Home Mortgage Lending." *Social Problems* 52 (2005): 181–208.

Wilson, Catherine. 1998. "20 Women Forced into Prostitution." *Associated Press*, April 24.

Wilson, Richard and Jon Mitchell. 2003. "Introduction: The Social Life of Rights." In *Human Rights in Global Perspective: Anthropological Studies of Rights, Claims and Entitlements*, ed. Richard Wilson and Jon Mitchell, 1–15. London: Routledge.

Wilson, William Julius. 1987. *The Truly Disadvantaged: The Inner City, the Underclass, and Public Policy*. Chicago: University of Chicago Press.

Wolf, Lisa J. 2009. "Tribal Attempt to Halt Nevada Goldmine Fails in

Court." *Environment News Service.* http://www.ens-newswire.com/ens/jan2009/2009-01-26-094.asp, accessed January 12.

Wolfensohn, James D. 2005. "Some Reflections on Human Rights and Development. In *Human Rights and Development: Towards Mutual Reinforcement,* ed. Philip Alston and Mary Robinson, 19–24. Oxford: Oxford University Press.

Wolff, Edward N. 2001. "Recent Trends in Wealth Ownership, from 1983 to 1998." In *Assets for the Poor: The Benefits of Spreading Asset Ownership,* ed. Thomas M. Shapiro and Edward N. Wolff, 34–73. New York: Russell Sage.

Womack, James P., Daniel T. Jones, and Daniel Roos. 1990. *The Machine That Changed the World: The Story of Lean Production.* New York: Harper.

Wood, Robert. 2009. "U.S. Posture Toward the Durban Review Conference and Participation in the UN Human Rights Council 2009." www.state.gov/r/pa/prs/ps/2009/02/119892.htm, accessed May 9.

Writing Group for the Consortium for Health and Human Rights. 1998. "Health and Human Rights." *Journal of the American Medical Association* 280: 462–64.

Wronka, Joseph. 1994. "Human Rights and Social Policy in the United States: An Educational Agenda for the 21st Century." *Journal of Moral Education* 23: 261–74.

Zizek, Slavoj. 2004. "Against an Ideology of Human Rights." In *Displacement, Asylum, Migration,* ed. Kate E. Tunstall, 56–85. Oxford: Oxford University Press.

CONTRIBUTORS

Katie Acosta teaches Sociology and Latin American Studies at Tulane University. She is also an affiliate of Tulane University's Gender and Sexualities Studies program and the African Diaspora Studies Program. Her areas of specialization include Latina/o sexuality, gender, Latin America, immigration, and race and ethnicity. She is currently working on a book project that explores how lesbian, bisexual, and queer Latinas negotiate families of choice and origin, using a gendered analysis of how sexually nonconforming Latinas reconcile their sexualities with family members, negotiate cultural expectations, and combat compulsory heterosexuality. In addition to several book chapters, her work can be found in *Gender & Society* and *Black Women, Gender and Family*.

Jennifer Allen is founding Executive Director of the Border Action Network, a human rights community organization that works with immigrant and border communities in Arizona to build the capacity of immigrant families to become better prepared, organized, and effective at promoting human rights and advocating for policy change in the border region, in Arizona and nationally. She has been a community organizer and advocate working for social and environmental justice for more than twenty years. She has written and contributed to dozens of reports, essays, and other publications. She has been on the boards of directors and advisory boards of many state and national projects and organizations and is a frequent speaker at national conferences.

William T. Armaline teaches and is the Undergraduate Program Coordinator in the Department of Justice Studies at San Jose State University. He is a multidisciplinary scholar activist who works primarily in the fields of sociology, education, and human rights. His areas of interest include sustainable political economic and ecological theory, critical race theory and anti-racism, critical pedagogy and transformative education, critical ethnography, inequality and youth, prison abolition, and drug policy reform.

Angie Beeman teaches at the City University of New York-Borough of Manhattan Community College. Her research interests include racism theory, media, social movements, and gender. She has published research on racism and film in Ethnic and Racial Studies, predatory lending in Critical Sociology, and domestic violence in Violence Against Women. Her dissertation, which received an award from the Society for the Study of Social Problems, examined the strategic use, limitations, and challenges of color-blind ideology in grassroots interracial social movement organizations.

Judith Blau is Professor of Sociology at the University of North Carolina, President of the U.S. chapter of Sociologists Without Borders (dedicated to the advance of human rights), on the Executive Council of the AAAS program in human rights, 2011-12 chair of the Human Rights Section of the American Sociological Association, and founder and director of the Human Rights Center of Chapel Hill & Carrboro. Her book *Race in the Schools* received the 2005 Oliver Cromwell Cox Award by ASA. She has published several books on human rights with Alberto Moncada: *Human Rights: Beyond the Liberal Vision, Justice in the United States: Human Rights and the U.S. Constitution, Freedoms and Solidarities: In Pursuit of Human Rights, Human Rights: A Primer*, and co-editor (with Mark Frezzo) of *Sociology and Human Rights*. She is coeditor with Keri Iyall Smith of *Public Sociologies Reader*.

Colleen Casey teaches in the School of Urban and Public Affairs at the University of Texas at Arlington. Her current research focuses on access to credit, specifically, the effects and implementation of policies and programs designed to stimulate reinvestment in low-income, urban communities. Her work has been published in journals such as the *Journal of Planning Education and Research* and *Critical Sociology*, and she has co-authored reports for the Brookings Institution. Most recently, she was a visiting scholar for the Federal Reserve Bank Atlanta in the Community and Economic Division, focused on research related to disparities in access to credit for low-wealth, minority entrepreneurs.

Abraham P. DeLeon teaches Foundations of Education at the University of Texas at San Antonio in the Department of Educational Leadership & Policy Studies. His research interests are interdisciplinary, spanning cultural studies, critical pedagogy, anarchist theory, critical animal studies, space and place, postcolonial theory, and autoethnography. His publications have appeared in journals such as *Educational Studies, Equity & Excellence in Education, Critical Education*, and *Theory in Action*, and he has written chapters in a wide variety of edited book collections. He was also a member of the editorial collective that published *Contemporary Anarchist Studies: An Introductory Anthology of Anarchy in the Academy* and co-edited *Critical Theories, Radical Pedagogies: Towards New Perspectives for the Social Studies* with E. Wayne Ross.

Julie Beth Elkins is Assistant Vice Chancellor for Student Life and Learning, University College at Indiana University-Purdue University. She has provided national leadership in civic engagement through her research and former role as director of academic initiatives at Campus Compact. Prior to her work at Campus Compact, she served as spokesperson for Corporate Social Responsibility at the University of Connecticut, where she provided national leadership for working with students on the Designated Supplier Program and was an elected member to the Workers Rights Consortium. The American College Personnel Association (ACPA) recognized her as a Diamond Honoree for her outstanding and sustained leadership in the field of student affairs. ACPA's Standing Committee for Lesbian, Gay, Bisexual, Transgender Awareness established the Julie Elkins Community Service Award in honor of her work on HIV/AIDS prevention, collaboration, education, and leadership in the field of higher education.

Bill Frelick, Director of the Human Rights Watch refugee program, monitors, investigates, and documents human rights abuses against refugees, asylum seekers, and internally displaced persons, and advocates for the rights and humanitarian needs of all categories of forcibly displaced persons around the world. Before joining Human Rights Watch, he directed Amnesty International USA's refugee program and the U.S. Committee for Refugees (USCR), which he served for 18 years. He was editor of USCR's annual *World Refugee Survey* and monthly *Refugee Reports*. He has traveled to refugee sites throughout the world and is widely published. He taught in the Middle East in 1979-83 and was co-coordinator of the Asian Center of Clergy and Laity Concerned in 1976-79.

Andrew S. Fullerton teaches Sociology at Oklahoma State University. His research interests include work and occupations, political sociology, social stratification, and quantitative methods. His work has been published in journals such as *Social Forces, Social Problems, Sociological Methods & Research, Public Opinion Quarterly,* and *Social Science Research*. He is currently working on several projects related to contingent employment, including a cross-national study of the relationship between flexible work practices and perceived job insecurity.

Davita Silfen Glasberg is Professor of Sociology and Associate Dean of Social Sciences in the College of Liberal Arts and Sciences at the University of Connecticut, and former Director of the University of Connecticut Human Rights Minor Program. She has taught both undergraduate and graduate courses and authored or coauthored six books and dozens of scholarly journal articles on issues of power and oppression, human rights, finance capital and the state, predatory lending, and inequality and diversity. Her article (coauthored with William T. Armaline), "What Will States Really Do for Us? The Human Rights Enterprise and Pressure from Below," appears in *Societies Without Borders*. Her latest book (coauthored with Deric Shannon), is *Political Sociology: Oppression, Resistance, and the State*.

Barbara Gurr is an advanced graduate student in Sociology at the University of Connecticut. She has been Director of the Women's Studies Program at Southern Connecticut State University and Assistant Director of the Women's Studies Program at the University of Connecticut. Her research on reproductive health care for Native American women has been published in *Journal of the Association for Research on Mothering* and *International Journal of Family Studies*.

Zoe Hammer teaches Political Studies as a member of the faculty of Cultural and Regional Studies at Prescott College, where her teaching and research focus on the intersections of culture, power, and globalization through the lenses of critical cultural studies. She is active in the human rights and immigrants rights movements in Arizona and nationally, sitting on the Board of Directors of the Border Action Network and as a member of the U.S.-Mexico Border and Immigration Task Force. She has also served on the Boards of the American Friends Service Committee Criminal Justice Steering Committee, the Progressive Communicator's Network Criminal Justice Working Group, and the Institute for Restorative Justice.

Shareen Hertel is Associate Professor of Political Science at the University of Connecticut and holds a joint appointment with the university's Human Rights Institute. She has served as a consultant to foundations, NGOs, and UN agencies in the United States, Latin America, and South Asia. She has written professionally on the UN role in economic and social development, and helped develop a standard for labor rights monitoring in global manufacturing (SA8000). She is the author of *Unexpected Power: Conflict and Change Among Transnational Activists* and co-editor of *Economic Rights: Conceptual, Measurement, and Policy Issues.* She serves on the editorial boards of *Human Rights Review, Human Rights and Human Welfare,* and the International Studies Intensives book series at Paradigm Publishers. She is an Advisory Board member for Counter-Sourcing Incorporated (a fair trade apparel sourcing company) and a member of the University of Connecticut President's Committee on Corporate Responsibility, which guides University policy on sourcing and manufacturing of logo-bearing apparel and other products.

Miho Iwata is an advanced graduate student in Sociology at the University of Connecticut with a Graduate Certificate in Women's Studies. Her research focuses on an intersectional approach to social inequalities in the U.S. and Japan. Her recent research projects include an examination of simultaneous (ethno-) racialization and racialized gendering of non-Japanese nationals/ immigrants residing in Japan, and the effects of race/ethnicity, class, gender, and immigration history/status on aging experiences among Asian Americans and Asians residents in the U.S.

Barret Katuna is an advanced graduate student in Sociology at the University of Connecticut, specializing in human rights, political sociology, and gender. Her M.A. thesis focused on the social impact of feminist network organizing. She is a UN delegate to the Economic and Social Council (ECOSOC) for Sociologists for Women in Society (SWS) and has helped guide the SWS relationship with the UN given her background knowledge from her 2005 internship at UN Headquarters for the Department of Public Information, Non-Governmental Organization Section.

Sang Hea Kil teaches in the Justice Studies Department at San Jose State University. Her work focuses on whiteness, racism, media studies, immigration, and the U.S.-Mexico border in an interdisciplinary, scholar-activist perspective. She was a member of Border Action Network beginning in 2002 and served as a board member for in 2003-6.

Shweta Majumdar Adur is an advanced graduate student in Sociology at the University of Connecticut. She received a Master's degree in International Development from the University of Pittsburgh and a Master's in Sociology from Jawaharlal Nehru University, New Delhi. Her research interests include gender, sexuality, race, ethnicity, human rights, and immigration. She is a recipient of the Taraknath Das Award (University of Pittsburgh) and has won two competitive human rights research grants from the Human Rights Institute, University of Connecticut. She has been actively involved with several development projects in India and was Program Management Intern at Management Systems International, Washington, D.C.

Stacy A. Missari is an advanced graduate student in Sociology at the University of Connecticut, specializing in gender, sexualities, health, and human rights. She uses mixed methods to explore women's agency and resistance and continues to investigate the role of human rights discourse in shaping domestic violence legislation and advocacy in the U.S. Her dissertation research explores agency at the individual level through a quantitative examination of sexual subjectivity among adolescent girls.

Kenneth J. Neubeck is Professor Emeritus at the University of Connecticut and former director of the interdisciplinary undergraduate human rights minor program. He volunteers as executive director and board vice-president of Amigos Multicultural Services Center, an immigrant rights organization in Eugene, Oregon. He is a founder and a co-coordinator of the Community Coalition for Advancement of Human Rights, an informal network of social justice groups and their allies in the Eugene area. He serves on the City of Eugene Human Rights Commission, which is engaged in exploring ways international human rights principles and standards can be implemented at the local community level (see www.humanrightscity.com). He is the author of *When Welfare Disappears: The Case for Economic Human Rights and Welfare Racism: Playing the Race Card Against America's Poor*, co-authored with Noel Cazenave. His current scholarship focuses uon efforts to implement the human rights framework at the local community level.

Tola Olu Pearce is a Medical Sociologist and Professor at the University of Missouri, Columbia, with a joint appointment in Sociology and Women's and Gender Studies. She received her Ph.D. from Brown University. Her areas of specialization are women and health, race and ethnicity, and development/globalization. She teaches courses that address human rights issues, particularly "Gender and Human Rights in Cross-Cultural Perspective" and "Women, Development, and Globalization." Recent publications include "Globalization and the Cycle of Violence in Africa," in *Race Struggles*; "Women's Rights," in *The Leading Rogue State: The U.S. and Human Rights*); "The Contextual Impact of Development and Globalization on African Women," *MU Peace Studies Review*; and "Keeping Children Healthy: The Challenge of Preventive Health Care Among Women in Southwestern Nigeria," *Jour-*

nal of Comparative Family Studies. She has worked as a consultant on several United Nations projects at UN-ECA headquarters in Addis Ababa.

Amanda Ploch is a student of the New York University School of Law and a contributing member to the school's *Journal of International Law and Politics*. Her fields of interest include international law and prisoners' rights, having interned in Ghana and South Africa and volunteered in multiple prisons. She hopes to pursue a career in public interest law.

Aheli Purkayastha received her master's degree in International Political Theory from the University of Edinburgh, Scotland, where she explored the normative and ethical implications of global human rights violations. As an undergraduate at Bryn Mawr College, USA, where she received her bachelor's degree in the History of Art and Political Science, she worked on a variety of social justices issues on campus as president of the oldest collegiate Self-Government Association. She is currently interning for the Global Policy Forum.

Bandana Purkayastha is Professor of Sociology and Asian American Studies at the University of Connecticut. She has published several books and thirty peer-reviewed journal articles and chapters on the intersections of race/gender/class, transnationalism, ethnicity, and human rights. Among her books are *The Power of Women's Informal Networks: Lessons in Social Change in South Asia and West Africa* (coedited with Mangala Subramaniam), *Negotiating Ethnicity: Second-Generation South Asian Americans Traverse a Transnational World*, and *Living Our Religions: Hindu and Muslim South Asian American women Narrate Their Experiences* (with Anjana Narayan). She has won several awards for graduate and undergraduate teaching. She serves on several international and national research committees and the Editorial Board, South Asian Diasporas, and is Deputy Editor of *Gender & Society*, the leading journal for gender scholarship in sociology.

Kathryn Strother Ratcliff is Associate Professor of Sociology at the University of Connecticut. Her areas of particular interest are health, women's health, and reproductive health. She is editor of *Healing Technology: Feminist Perspectives*, a book that emerged from a women's health conference at UConn, and author of *Women and Health: Power, Technology, Inequality and Conflict in a Gendered World*. She is currently working on a book on aging.

Ranita Ray is an advanced graduate student in Sociology at the University of Connecticut. Her research interests include human rights, urban food insecurity, qualitative methods, and crime and deviance. She has conducted both U.S.-based and international research in human rights. Her current research analyzes the processes involved in the localization of global human rights ideas through the ethnography of a state human rights commission in India.

Dwanna L. Robertson is a Graduate in Residence at the University of Massachusetts-Amherst and a citizen of the Muscogee (Creek) Nation. Her research primarily focuses on the construction and persistence of social inequality, particularly for Indigenous groups, with regard to work and occupations, race, gender, and socioeconomic parity.

Deric Shannon is an advanced graduate student in Sociology at the University of Connecticut. He is a coeditor of *Contemporary Anarchist Studies*, the first anthology of anarchist scholarly work, as well as author of numerous books, chapters, and journal articles, typically on radical political thought. He is an assistant editor of the academic journal *Theory* in *Action* and serves on the Board of Directors for the Transformative Studies Institute. He is director of Transformative Radio, a radical web radio station featuring lectures and interviews for those interested in social justice, tangible resistance, and radical change. His current research interests include culture and social change; sexualities and queer studies; and radical political traditions.

Chivy Sok, an educator, trainer, and researcher on human rights and child labor, currently serves on the Steering Committee of the Ginetta Sagan Fund of Amnesty International USA. The Fund is dedicated to supporting courageous women who risk their lives to promote and protect human rights of women and children around the world. She also provides philanthropic consulting services in a variety of areas, including human rights, women's rights, corporate accountability, environmental justice, and sustainable agriculture. She is former Program Director of Columbia University's Center for the Study of Human Rights and former Deputy Director of the University of Iowa Center for Human Rights (UICHR). She has worked on a number of human rights projects and NGOs during the last decade, including serving as Co-Director of the Women's Institute for Leadership Development for Human Rights and the National Campaign Coordinator at the Cambodian Association of Illinois.

Chandra Waring is an advanced graduate student at the University of

Connecticut. Her interests include race/ethnicity, racism, gender, qualitative research methods, and pedagogy. She won the Association of Black Sociologists (ABS) Graduate Student Paper Award in 2009 for her paper "The Racial Remix: How Black/White Biracial Americans Conceptualize and Situationally Re-Conceptualize Race." Her current research explores the complex interaction patterns of black/white biracial men and women.

Christine Zozula is an advanced graduate student in Sociology at the University of Connecticut. Her research interests include crime, law, deviance, gender, and culture.

INDEX

Abu Ghraib, 2

African Americans, xiv, 1, 29, 37–38, 43, 49, 69–70, 72, 95, 157, 176, 184, 189–94, 196, 198, 203, 265n3a

American Declaration of the Rights and Duties of Man, 110

American Civil Liberties Union (ACLU), xii, 58, 134

American exceptionalism, xiii, 74, 227

American Recovery and Reinvestment Act of 2009, 75

Amnesty International, 2, 194, 195, 197, 218, 233

anarchism (anarchist theory), 84–86

Andean Free Trade Agreement (AFTA), 148

Arendt, Hannah, 247

Asian Americans, 100, 120, 128, 135, 176, 180, 185–86, 216, 257–58n1d, 265n3a

Association of Community Organizations for Reform Now (ACORN), 44, 57–67, 75; direct confrontations and tactics, 62; Hartford chapter, 44, 58–59; history, 58–59; human rights language (lack of), 62–66; "homesteading campaign," 61; use of stories and narratives, 59–62

asylum, 126, 138–45, 156, 260n1

banking, 35, 43. *See also* Freire, Paulo

banks, 3, 8, 10, 34, 39, 41–45; racialized economic injustice, 42. *See also* predatory lending; World Bank

basic human needs (human rights), 26, 55, 64, 73, 91, 111, 213, 218, 247. *See also* cultural rights; education; food security; health rights; housing rights

Bill of Rights to U.S. Constitution, 147, 153, 242

biracial population, 185

Books Not Bars (BNB), 197–98

Border Action Network (BAN), 146–54; border patrol agents, 140, 145–46, 148–49, 153, 261n3; principles, 150–51

Bureau of Immigration and Customs Enforcement (Department of Homeland Security), 139

Bureau of Labor Statistics (BLS), 30, 256n1

Bush, George H. W., 76, 227

Bush, George W., 36, 52, 76, 87, 128, 140, 213, 217, 232

La Campesina, x

capitalism, xiv, 5, 49, 51, 53, 56, 89, 165, 202, 206–11, 246–49; feminist economists, 207; and human rights perspective, 206–10; and individualism 208–11; neoliberalism, 24, 86, 89, 203, 207, 247–49

capital punishment, 2, 92, 232, 242

Carter, Jimmy, 226

Center for Economic, Social and Cultural Rights, x

Center on Housing Rights and Evictions, x

Central American Free Trade Agreement (CAFTA), 148

children's rights (juvenile justice). 189–98; caging of kids of color, 191, 194–97; Raise the Age Campaign, Connecticut, 197; Wilkes-Barre, Pennsylvania, exploitation of children by judges, 189–90

Christianity, 103, 115, 117, 122, 158, 208, 258n5

Citizens United v. Federal Election Commission, xiv

citizenship, 126, 163; multicultural, 121, 259n15; post-national, 163–64, 166, 170–72. *See also* immigrants; sexual citizenship; women's rights

ACKNOWLEDGMENTS

This book has been a tremendous labor of love and a collective effort by many to produce an accessible and relevant resource for human rights scholarship in the U.S. We thank all the many graduate students who have worked closely with us to create wonderful scholarly pieces that fit well together and who have cheerfully subjected themselves to our exacting standards. In fact, many of the papers contributed by graduate students began in a graduate seminar on Human Rights taught by Bandana Purkayastha. Her fabulous mentoring helped to polish and refine their broad ideas into focused scholarly papers.

We also wish to thank all the activists and human rights practitioners who generously contributed their very precious time and invaluable on-the-ground experiences, without which we could not have connected our academic insights to real-world truths. We are indebted to the anonymous reviewers for their terrific and spot-on attention to detail, their stimulating challenge to us for coherence between the different voices, and their invaluable suggestions, which together guided us to a stronger, more cohesive collection.

A very special thanks is owed to Barret Katuna for her meticulous copy-editing and indexing of this manuscript. She has been tireless, independent, and extremely reliable. Without her, we are certain we would have missed countless editorial errors. We are also grateful for the first-rate editorial work and stewardship of this manuscript from Peter Agree, his editorial assistant Julia Rose Roberts, and Managing Editor Alison Anderson at the University of Pennsylvania Press. It was a great pleasure to work with all of you!

As for institutional support, we would like to formally acknowledge the Department of Justice Studies and College of Applied Arts and Sciences at San Jose State University, and the University of Connecticut Human Rights Institute. The SJSU Department of Justice Studies and broader College of Applied Arts and Sciences have been greatly supportive of this project, and continue to show their commitment to human rights scholarship with what now seems to be an emergent Human Rights Program, expected to take shape in the 2011-12 academic year under the efforts of William Armaline and a collective of progressive scholars in the Bay Area and CSU/UC systems. Furthermore, the University of Connecticut Human Rights Institute provided a great deal of support and influence in motivating us all to collaborate on such a project. This project began to some degree with a grant from the Institute to develop a Sociology course on "Human Rights in the United States." Bandana Purkayastha and Davita Silfen Glasberg have been teaching and refining that course ever since, recognizing the need to develop their own volume for such a course. In terms of theoretical origins, this project also began with William Armaline's conceptual development of the *human rights enterprise*, illustrating the need to conceptualize struggles to define and realize human rights beyond the actions and duties of states and formal Human Rights regimes (e.g., international law). We quickly realized that this concept provided a powerful theoretical framework lending substantial connective links for the various contributions of the book. Where William drafted this work in part during graduate study in the University of Connecticut Department of Sociology and the Human Rights Institute, and where many of the contributors of this volume presented their research at conferences hosted by the Institute, we would like to thank the Institute, its members, and the Department of Sociology for providing forums for the development of several works in this volume and for providing venues for meaningful graduate scholarship in the field of Human Rights.

We (editors Davita, Bandana, and William) would like to acknowledge our friendship and mutual support during this truly remarkable coediting journey. We learned from each other and look forward to growing and learning a great deal more from forthcoming collaborative efforts. We have each become better scholars from our friendship, and highly recommend other scholars take advantage of opportunities to do the same.

Davita would like to thank her children Morgan and Gillian and Gillian's partner Scott for the wonderful human beings that they are and their sublime sense of humanity, civility, fairness, and equal rights. They remind me daily of why we do what we do, and of what matters most in this life. I hope the world we leave them is one in which they can enjoy the basic rights defining what it means to be a human being. And I trust that they will continue the urge to make sure all around them enjoys those rights as well.

Bandana would like to thank her anchors-in-life Indra and Aheli, and her family across multiple countries, for living lives committed to human rights. She would also like to acknowledge some remarkable friends and colleagues—Amii Omara Otunnu, UNESCO Chair for Global Human Rights for North America, Narissa Ramdhani, CEO, Ifalethu (South Africa), Ela Gandhi (South Africa), Yakin Erutuk (former Special Rapporteur, Violence Against Women, UN), Margaret Abrahamson (Hofstra University, USA), Shanthi Rao (USA), Meena Gopal (SNDT, India) and Nandini Manjrekar (TISS, India)—for ongoing inspiration on how to "walk the talk."

Finally, William would like to thank his partner Nicole Steward and dog Chomsky for reminding him of just how lucky we are to be alive. He would like to thank his friends and comrades Deric Shannon and Abraham DeLeon for their solidarity and commitment to forging new space in academe for aggressively and unapologetically radical work—a fruitful effort thus far. He would also like to thank his father, William D. Armaline, stepmother, Kathleen Farber, and sister, Abigail Clingo for their unconditional love and support. Finally, he would like to thank his grandparents, Jim and Rosie Armaline, who taught him the importance of both love and courage in attempting to create a better world.